McGRAW-HILL PUBLICATIONS IN THE
BOTANICAL SCIENCES

EDMUND W. SINNOTT, Consulting Editor

Flowers

and Flowering Plants

SELECTED TITLES FROM

McGRAW-HILL PUBLICATIONS IN THE BOTANICAL SCIENCES

EDMUND W. SINNOTT, *Consulting Editor*

Arnold—An Introduction to Paleobotany

Avery et al.—Hormones and Horticulture

Babcock and Clausen—Genetics

Boysen Jensen and Avery and Burkholder—Growth Hormones in Plants

Braun-Blanquet and Fuller and Conard—Plant Sociology

Eames—Morphology of Vascular Plants

Eames and MacDaniels—An Introduction to Plant Anatomy

Fitzpatrick—The Lower Fungi

Gäumann and Dodge—Comparative Morphology of Fungi

Haupt—An Introduction to Botany

Haupt—Laboratory Manual of Elementary Botany

Hill—Economic Botany

Hill, Overholts, and Popp—Botany

Johansen—Plant Microtechnique

Loomis and Shull—Methods in Plant Physiology

Lutman—Microbiology

Maximov—Plant Physiology

Miller—Plant Physiology

Pool—Flowers and Flowering Plants

Sass—Elements of Botanical Microtechnique

Seifriz—Protoplasm

Sharp—Introduction to Cytology

Sharp—Fundamentals of Cytology

Sinnott—Botany: Principles and Problems

Sinnott—Laboratory Manual for Elementary Botany

Sinnott and Dunn—Principles of Genetics

Smith—Cryptogamic Botany
    Vol. I, Algae and Fungi
    Vol. II, Bryophytes and Pteridophytes

Smith—Fresh-water Algae of the U. S.

Swingle—Textbook of Systematic Botany

Weaver—Root Development of Field Crops

Weaver and Clements—Plant Ecology

Wodehouse—Pollen Grains

There are also the related series of McGraw-Hill Publications in the Zoological Sciences, of which A. Franklin Shull is Consulting Editor, and in the Agricultural Sciences, of which Leon J. Cole is Consulting Editor.

Frontispiece

CHARLES EDWIN BESSEY
1845–1915

Dr. Bessey proposed the main features of the outline of classification
that is adopted in this book.

Flowers
and Flowering Plants

An Introduction to the Nature and Work of Flowers

and the Classification of Flowering Plants

BY

RAYMOND J. POOL, Ph.D.

Professor of Botany and Chairman, Department of Botany
University of Nebraska

Second Edition
Seventh Impression

McGRAW-HILL BOOK COMPANY, Inc.
NEW YORK AND LONDON
1941

FLOWERS AND FLOWERING PLANTS

TO THE MEMORY OF MY FATHER AND MOTHER

WILLIAM HENRY POOL

AND

MARY LOUISA POOL

PIONEERS OF THE PRAIRIES WHOSE SACRIFICES
MADE MY SCHOOLING POSSIBLE

AND

TO THE MEMORY OF A GREAT TEACHER

CHARLES EDWIN BESSEY

WHO LED ME FOR A TIME
TOWARD NATURE'S EXPANDING HORIZON

PREFACE TO THE SECOND EDITION

The publication of a new edition of this book has afforded an opportunity to incorporate new material and to make certain other modifications which reflect suggestions that have been gratefully received from teachers throughout the country. The author regrets that he was unable to introduce all the proposals made by his friends in other institutions.

An entirely new chapter has been added in order to present a brief treatment of the more prominent *vegetative* features that are helpful in taxonomic work. A change that will be revealed by casual examination affects the large, folded chart. This has been simplified and illustrated so that it is not quite so much of a "puzzle" to the student who is beginning work of this kind. A new diagram has also been introduced (page 352) in order to present an interpretation of the apetalous, diclinous, and anemophilous groups that is not shown in the preceding outline. The map showing the ranges of various floras and manuals (Fig. 211) has been revised to include a few important additions to the growing literature in that phase of the subject. To the reference books noted in the first edition has been added a short list of valuable American works that have been published since 1929.

The two short chapters dealing with an outline of the history of classification have been moved to a position immediately following the treatment of the various groups of flowering plants. This change makes for more continuity in the treatment of the principal material of the book.

In response to requests from many students and from other teachers who have used the book there has been added a brief glossary which includes the more important terms used in the book.

RAYMOND J. POOL.

LINCOLN, NEBRASKA,
April, 1941.

ix

PREFACE TO THE FIRST EDITION

The field of biology involved in this book is clearly indicated by its title, *Flowers and Flowering Plants*, and its purpose and general content by its subtitle, *An Introduction to the Nature and Work of Flowers and the Classification of Flowering Plants*.

The book is largely the outcome of a vigorous and constant desire to interest college students and others in the essential nature, development, and classification of flowering plants during the past twenty-two years. The author has found attractive opportunities herein for the presentation of the essential features of the scientific mood and method in general along with our study of these plants. Certainly, few other groups of objects supply more attractive and useful materials for these purposes.

Botanical science has been bountifully fruitful in the past, but someone has said that "the productive natural scientist himself has done little to impart to the people at large the living spirit which animates his labor, the instructive philosophy which guides it, or the methods which make it effective." In so far as a comprehension of the flowering plant world is concerned I fear that this is notably true. Possibly this well-known situation is due in considerable degree to the fact that taxonomists have lost themselves so completely in *codes, congresses*, and *conservanda*. It is to be regretted that this is so largely true for that subdivision of botany that should make the vegetable kingdom a well-known realm to intelligent folks who really wish to know it.

The conception of a flowering plant as a living, working mechanism and as a more or less plastic entity leads naturally to an interest in plants as *units of life*, and, *therefore*, in the possibility of grouping them into various subdivisions which may portray something of the more or less *natural interrelationships* of various degrees. An appreciation of plant relationships should do much to excite further observation and study wherever one may go. Men have sought such relationships for centuries. My experience teaches me that college students and others are really interested in the relationships that are so conspicuous among flowers.

I am fully aware of the fact that botanists are not yet in possession of the information that would enable them to construct a phylogenetic classification of the flowering plants in which the origin and position of each group and the sequence of development can be clearly established by critical examination of all the evidence possible to secure. The evidence from anatomy, morphology, geology, geography, serum analysis, and genetics is slowly accumulating that will perhaps render such a classification possible sometime in the far-distant future. As yet we cannot say whether the flowering plants have had a polyphyletic or a monophyletic origin. Until investigations have supplied the necessary data, the complete story of the origin and development of flowering plants and the proposal of a thoroughly consistent phylogenetic classification will remain impossible. Even if the arrangement utilized in this book is found to be all wrong in future years it will, nevertheless, have served a most valuable purpose in this twentieth century if it leads groping students to obtain even a birdseye view of a more or less orderly system in the great world of flowering plants which must certainly appear as a heterogeneous conglomeration of unrelated things to the uninitiated.

The book is intended for students who have had an introduction to general botany, but it is thought that it will be thoroughly understood by anyone else who is willing to take it up studiously and in its entirety.

I have endeavored to play up the *family* as the group that may be used more effectively in classification and in an attempt to present some of the more clearly demonstrated cases of relationship. The outstanding feature of the treatment of the families is seen in the use of new types of graphic formulæ and charts to depict floral anatomy and evolution. This method is comparatively new in published form, but it has been used in our classes at Nebraska for twenty-eight years, the plan in general having been originated by Clements, in 1900. A similar plan was published in brief form by the same author in 1908, and 1912, and again in 1913; by Bergman in 1917; and by F. E. and E. S. Clements in 1927 and 1928 in, *Flower Families and Ancestors* and in *Flowers of Coast and Sierra*. The only use of this form of chart in a regular textbook to date is in *General Botany* by Holman and Robbins, 1927, where a brief reference is made to it.

The formula method of depicting prominent features of families and the grouping of the families on our chart in accordance with the general plan known here as the "Besseyan system" have been of inestimable value in the presentation of this great group of plants to students and others. The chart presented must be viewed in the light of a relatively simple production (although considerably more extensive than any yet published) but the author trusts that it is sufficient, nevertheless, to suggest almost limitless possibilities to the interested teacher and student.

The author of a book of this sort is largely dependent upon works of a more or less similar sort that have already appeared. Certain of these sources are really classic throughout the world, such for instance as the following great works: Engler, *Die Natürlichen Pflanzenfamilien;* Wettstein, *Handbuch der Systematischen Botanik* (3d Ed., 1924); LeMaout and Decaisne, *A General System of Botany*, the valuable English edition by Hooker; Baillon, *Histoire des Plantes*, with the English edition, *The Natural History of Plants*, by Hartog; Lindley, *The Vegetable Kingdom;* Bentham and Hooker, *Genera Plantarum;* and A. de Candolle, *Prodromus systematis naturalis regni vegetabilis*. Many other publications have contributed values that are deeply appreciated. Among these I would mention the following: Bentham, *Illustrated Handbook of British Flora;* Kerner, *Pflanzenleben*, and the English edition of this work, *Natural History of Plants*, published by Blackie & Son Ltd., and Henry Holt & Company; Rendle, *The Classification of Flowering Plants;* Hutchinson, *The Families of Flowering Plants;* Bailey, *Manual of Cultivated Plants;* Sargent, *Plants and their Uses;* Chase, *First Book of Grasses;* Hitchcock, *A Textbook of Grasses;* and numerous manuals, floras, and monographs that can not be enumerated here. I have drawn freely upon these and have made proper acknowledgment of the same in the usual manner.

Nearly all of the illustrations in the book have been prepared under my direction by that master botanical artist and draftsman, Mr. F. Schuyler Mathews. He has redrawn and adapted many figures for our use from numerous sources, but especially from the classic works of LeMaout and Decaisne, and Baillon. A few figures have been redrawn by special permission from Gager, *General Botany*, and Robbins, *Botany of Crop Plants*, published by P. Blakiston's Sons Co.; Warming-Potter, *A Handbook of Systematic Botany*, published by The Macmillan Company; Mathews, *Field Book of American Wild Flowers*, by G. P. Putnam's Sons, and from Kerner, *Natural History of Plants*, by Henry Holt and Blackie & Son Ltd. A few of the figures have been made from original drawings which Mr. Mathews has graciously placed at my disposal. This book would be a poor thing indeed and, I fear, utterly lacking in appeal in the absence of the hundreds of figures that have been reproduced from pen-and-ink drawings by the skillful hand of Mr. Mathews. Prof. T. J. Fitzpatrick assisted with the proof sheets.

RAYMOND J. POOL.

LINCOLN, NEBRASKA,
   October, 1929.

CONTENTS

CONTENTS

FLOWERS
AND
FLOWERING PLANTS

CHAPTER I

INTRODUCTION

The Angiosperms or flowering plants are at once the most
varied, useful, and numerous of all of the major groups into which
the vegetable kingdom is commonly divided. At least 150,000
species of flowering plants have been described. New species are
being added each year by the extended survey of the vegetation
of the earth and by a more critical examination of the older
materials. They are very evidently a rapidly expanding or
evolving group. They dominate the world of plants today.
Such facts reflect the success that has attended flowering plants
in their long struggle for existence under the manifold variations
of terrestrial and aquatic environments.

To this vast array of organisms must also be added thousands
of varieties, races, strains, etc. of flowering plants that have been
brought into being largely through the efforts of man. These
owe not only their origin but also their perpetuation largely to
man and to the care he has bestowed upon them. These are
really much-coddled forms. When man's guiding genius is
relinquished they are likely to "revert" to inferior or worthless
forms.

Form, Mode of Life, Distribution.—Flowering plants exhibit
a great variety of form and mode of life. Some of them are
minute disks of very simple construction floating on the water.
Others are gigantic trees, 300 feet or more tall and with a body
structure and life history rivaling those of higher animals in
complexity. Some of them live for a few brief weeks, but
centuries are spanned by the activities of others. They are seen
at the seashore, on the very tops of high mountains, and in the

withering heat of vast deserts. They are conspicuous in the tangled luxuriance of equatorial forests, and others are scattered over the frozen soil and among the glaciers and snow fields in the Arctic and Antarctic regions. They are typically supplied with chlorophyll, so they are independent organisms, but numerous species have become degenerate parasites or saprophytes living the life of a mildew or toadstool in so far as nutrition is concerned. Some of them have even developed structures by which they may entrap and partially devour insects and other small creatures. This is indeed a curious and interesting feature of certain flowering plants, but the carnivorous habit in plants is probably more interesting than significant.

Value of Flowering Plants.—Flowering plants are very largely responsible for the maintenance of all other living things on earth, and yet hundreds of them are of the nature of worthless weeds or for other reasons are undesirable. They contribute foods in enormous quantities and of great variety for the millions of creatures comprising the animal kingdom, including man. They produce hiding places for the animals of the wilds and they contribute a multitude of materials that seem to be necessary for the happy homes of men.

THE FLOWER

The outstanding structure in the life history of flowering plants is the flower (Fig. 1). The flower and the structures that are developed because of its presence are the features that stamp these organisms as unique and as quite different from all other plants known. They all produce flowers of some sort, although these might not be recognized as flowers in every case by the man in the street. And some of them produce structures that are strikingly flower-like to the uninitiated but that are not flowers at all in the point of view of the botanist or in the economy of the plant. Thus some of the first things to be learned in the study of flowering plants have to do with the flower as the most distinctive element of their structure and behavior.

Definition of the Flower.—It is quite impossible to define a flower briefly and tersely. Flowers are too complex and too variable in structure and behavior to permit of strict definition or even of very brief description. The chief physiological significance of the flower is seen in the fact that it is the principal seat of reproduction in flowering plants. It is effectively constructed to insure fertilization of the eggs which it produces, and so it may be stated that the flower is the organ or combination of organs (Fig. 1) of the plant that makes sexual reproduction possible. The flower is, in a very definite sense, a sex organ or a collection of sex organs placed in relationships that are distinctive of flowering plants.

The reproductive significance of flowers must be clearly sensed if one is to comprehend the many varieties of form, color, odor, size, etc. of flowers, that are among the striking characteristics of this group of plants, because these details are usually intimately associated with the phenomenon of sexual reproduction as it occurs within the flower. These plants have developed a great many different kinds or types of flowers which differ much in detail, but they all agree in that their primary rôle is to produce

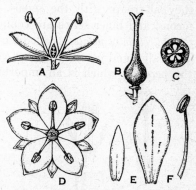

Fig. 1.—The gross anatomy of a typical flower. *A*, vertical section of a flower showing sepals, petals, stamens, and pistil grouped symmetrically upon the axis; *B*, the pistil with all other parts removed, showing ovary, style, and stigma; *C*, transverse section of five united carpels (pistils); *D*, a symmetrical flower viewed from the front; *E*, one sepal (to the left) and one petal (to the right); *F*, a single stamen showing filament and anther.

fruits and seeds. Their success in caring for this great work has been the astounding contribution of the group, as can be demonstrated by a few observations in almost any community.

ANATOMY OF THE FLOWER

The flower is, anatomically, a highly modified and specialized stem or branch of a stem bearing appendages (Fig. 1). This is readily noted if a very young flower is examined before the various parts have opened. The pedicel or flower stalk is very evidently a branch of the main body or stem system of the plant. At the distal end of the pedicel is a structure closely resembling a common bud. The outer leaves or scales are commonly green, but they may be of almost any color. Like the scales of an ordinary bud, these leaves protect the delicate structure within the flower. These outermost leaves or scales of the flower are known collectively as the "calyx" (Fig. 1, *A*,

D and *E*). Each scale is called a "sepal," *i.e.* the *calyx* is composed of *sepals*. Another set of leaves (Fig. 1, *A* and *D*) is disclosed when the flower (or bud) opens, and these are particularly noticeable because they are commonly *white* or *brightly* colored. These lie just within the calyx (Fig. 1, *A* and *D*) as a rule and they alternate with the sepals. The modified leaves of this second and inner series are commonly known as "petals," and the *collection* of *petals*, is called the "corolla" (Fig. 1, *A*, *D* and *E*). The calyx and corolla together constitute the *floral envelope* or the *perianth* which is an important part of the flower because

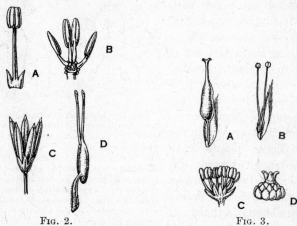

Fig. 2.   Fig. 3.

Fig. 2.—Stamens and staminate flowers. *A*, a single stamen of onion, *Allium; B*, stamens of wallflower, *Erysimum; C*, staminate or male flower of boxelder, *Acer negundo; D*, a single stamen of blueberry, *Vaccinium (after Le M. and Dec.)*.

Fig. 3.—Incomplete flowers. *A*, the pistillate or female flower of willow, *Salix; B*, the staminate or male flower of willow; *C*, the staminate flower of oak, *Quercus; D*, the pistillate flower of oak *(after Le M. and Dec.)*.

of the protection it affords to the delicate sex organs that lie in the interior. The perianth is usually the showy part of the flower also, either on account of its color or shape, or both. It plays a very important rôle in connection with pollination, fertilization, and seed production as will be noted in greater detail in a later chapter. The sepals and petals may be referred to as the *accessory organs* of the flower (Fig 1).

The Essential Organs.—As the dissection of the flower is continued another set of very different appendages is found attached to the pedicel inside the corolla. These are the *stamens* (Figs. 1, *F*; 2 and 3) and they are essentially the *male sex organs*. The stamens may be very numerous or in some flowers there may be

FRUITS AND SEEDS

Relation of Flowers to Fruits and Seeds.—Pistillate or female flowers are as a rule necessary in every individual flowering plant that produces seeds. Thus, care should always be exercised in selecting plants if certain desirable features involve the presence of pistillate flowers and the products of their behavior. A friend once complained of the failure of the bittersweet plants which he had moved from the woods to his back lawn to produce the beautiful, well-known scarlet berries in the autumn. Examination disclosed the fact that the plants in question were exclusively staminate or male and so could not be expected to fruit. The experience taught the friend a simple lesson in the biology of flowering plants.

Pollination.—The transfer of pollen grains produced by the stamens of flowers to the stigmas of the pistils is known as "pollination." The pollen (Fig. 13) is ripe and ready to be scattered about the time the flower buds open, but the movement is not greatly affected by any power which the plant possesses. Whether the transfer is through short distances, as it usually is not, or through comparatively long intervals, as it usually is, the two most prominent external agencies in pollination are *wind* and *insects*. Only in a few cases is the stigma of a given flower pollinated by the pollen from that same flower. As a matter of fact, such self-pollination is usually prevented because the pollen is distributed before or after the stigma is ready to receive it, and in other ways self-pollination and self-fertilization are prevented. There are many other types of flower behavior that serve to render self-pollination relatively impossible. A comparatively few cases are known of perfect flowers in which the stigma and stamens lie in contact with each other so that self-pollination may occur before the flower opens.

Fertilization in Flowers.—The union of a male sex cell or sperm produced by a pollen grain with the female sex cell or egg produced inside an ovule within the ovary is commonly called "fertilization" (Figs. 25 and 26). This is usually made possible in flowering plants by the growth of a long, slender protuberance, known as the "pollen tube" and produced by the individual pollen grain, which grows through the soft, juicy tissue of the stigma and style, by which the sperm cells are carried into the ovule and discharged near the egg. Fertilization is the crowning achievement of the flower since in this act a potentially new

but few of them. Each stamen is composed of a slender stalk or *filament* at the top of which is a lobed, bag-like *anther* which produces the *pollen grains* (Fig. 13) in which the male *germ cells* eventually arise. Pollen grains collectively are commonly known as *pollen*. The anthers are commonly yellow and each anther may produce a great many *pollen grains* which are liberated when slits or pores are formed in the anthers. Each pollen grain usually produces two *male gametes* or *sex cells*, the generative cells. Thousands and even millions of pollen grains are produced in the flowers of certain plants.

The Pistil.—The fourth floral organ is the *pistil* or *carpel* (Fig. 1, *B* and *C*), which usually stands in the very center of the flower and is, therefore, surrounded by the stamens, petals, and

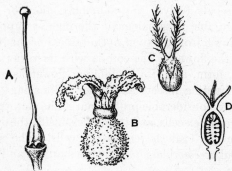

Fig. 4.—Forms of pistils. *A*, The pistil of tobacco, *Nicotiana*; *B*, of walnut, *Juglans*; *C*, of wheat, *Triticum* (after Le M. and Dec.); *D*. of a pink, *Spergularia* (after Mathews).

sepals. The pistil is usually distinctly different from any of the other parts of the flower. It is more or less flask-shaped or pitcher-shaped, with a bulbous base (Fig. 4, *A* and *D*) and a more or less elongated stalk leading upward. The enlarged base is called the "ovary" (Fig. 1, *B*; Fig. 4) and the stalk leading from the ovary is called the "style." The tip of the style is often glandular and it is called the "stigma." The stigma is frequently more or less expanded into a bulb or disk, or cut into two, three, or more slender segments. There is a well-developed cavity in the ovary of the pistil and in this cavity one to many *ovules* are produced. The ovules are usually attached to the central axis of the ovary (Fig. 1, *C*) or to the inner wall. Each ovule usually contains an *egg*, the *female gamete* or *sex cell*.

Ovary, Fruit and Seed.—The ovary may be *simple* or *compound*. A *simple* ovary is composed of a single carpel or pistil. A *compound* ovary is composed of two or more carpels (Fig. 1, *C*) or pistils grown together more or less firmly. In compound pistils the styles are usually united also, sometimes even to the very tip of the stigma. A simple pistil or each cell (carpel) of a compound pistil (Fig. 4, *D*) may contain a single ovule or many ovules. The *pistil* (ovary) normally develops into a *fruit* and each *ovule* develops into a *seed*.

The Flower as a Working Unit.—So much for the four regular parts of a complete flower, *sepals, petals, stamens, pistils.* The interplay of these parts in connection with the work of the flower as a whole may now be summarized briefly. A fine illustration of the biological principle known as the *division of labor* is found herein. The sepals (calyx) are commonly more or less green and so they are able to supplement the regular supply of food coming to the flower from the stem, at the same time that they afford protection for the flower. The corolla with its variety of colors, color patterns, form, and size in different flowers is particularly valuable in attracting insects and other pollinating animals as well as affording considerable protection. The stamens produce the sperms or male sex cells, and the ovules, inside the ovary of the pistil, produce the eggs or female sex cells. The sepals and petals are useful *accessory organs*, but the stamens and pistils are *essential organs*.

VARIATIONS OF FLOWERS

Complete Flowers.—The flowers of most species of flowering plants possess both stamens and pistils, and also petals and sepals. Such flowers may be termed "complete" flowers (Fig. 5) since they have all four of the regular appendages that are characteristic of flowers. Violets, geraniums, primroses, heathers, bluebells, snapdragons, roses, honeysuckles, lilies, irises, and orchids are representative of groups in which complete flowers are very common.

Incomplete Flowers.—Many different species of flowering plants produce flowers that lack one or more of the four regular parts. For instance, certain flowering plants are known which do not have *petals* or *sepals*, as is shown by some buttercups, buckwheats, willows, cottonwoods, hickories, grasses, cattails

(Fig. 3). In a goodly number of groups there are species in which sepals and petals are lacking but the stamens and pistils are present. These flowers may be called "incomplete" but "perfect," since they still possess the essential organs, the stamens and pistils. In others the stamens and pistils are produced in totally separate flowers upon the same individual plant (Fig. 3). This is the case in some members of the buckwheat family, in certain grasses (as maize, wild rice, etc.), cattails, arrowheads, grapes, hickories, walnuts, chestnuts, oaks, etc. There are still other flowering plants in which the staminate and pistillate flowers are formed on totally separate individuals of the species, as in the poplars (cottonwoods, aspens, etc.), willow, ash, hemp,

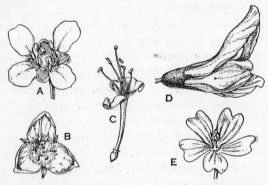

Fig. 5.—Different kinds of flowers. *A*, a regular flower with four sepals and petals and six stamens as in a mustard, *Cochlearia; B*, spiderwort, *Tradescantia; C*, honeysuckle, *Lonicera; D*, clover, *Trifolium; E.* rose mallow, *Hibiscus* (after Le M. and Dec.).

mulberry, certain maples, *Ailanthus*, etc. (Figs. 2*C*; 3*A* and *C*). The situation in these latter cases is much like that in the higher animals in which the individuals are strictly differentiated on a sexual basis, *i.e.*, they are males or females. Thus in cottonwoods some trees are staminate or male only, and others are pistillate or female only. This condition is more common among flowering plants than is popularly known, and it explains why every individual plant in certain species does not produce fruits and seeds. Obviously, an individual plant which develops stamens only, and is therefore exclusively male, is quite incapable of producing fruits and seeds. Some flowering plants produce both perfect and imperfect flowers and various other combinations all on the same individual.

individual arises, which under normal conditions may develop into a mature plant of the same kind that produced it.

Formation of Fruits and Seeds.—Soon after fertilization has been accomplished, the flower parts surrounding the ovary tend to collapse, wither, dry out, and fall away. The stamens, petals, and sepals disappear rather soon, and the style and stigma of the pistil are either shed or become more or less completely lost in the transformation of the pistil into the fruit (Figs. 6 and 7). The ovules, inside which the eggs have been fertilized, are promptly transformed into seeds (Figs. 35 and 36) as the fruit ripens. The fruit at maturity is essentially a trans-

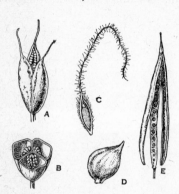

Fig. 6.   Fig. 7.

Fig. 6.—Types of dry fruits. *A*, capsule of autumnal lily, *Colchicum; B*, transverse section of the same; *C*, tailed achene of anemone, *Anemone; D*, simple achene of buttercup, *Ranunculus; E*, silique of mustard, *Brassica* (*after Le M. and Dec.*).

Fig. 7.—Fleshy fruits. *A*, cluster of berries of currant, *Ribes; B*, two drupes of cherry, *Prunus* (*after Mathews*).

formed ovary, inside of which there are one or more seeds each of which contains a miniature plant or embryo of the next generation. This embryo is commonly surrounded by or filled with an abundance of food which greatly enhances its chances for later development or germination. The seed as it is shed from the plant in this stage has much in common with the fertilized avian egg as it is discharged from the body of the mother bird. Each has a more or less firm covering composed of one or two layers of resistent tissues or material, and inside of each is a living embryo with an abundant supply of food. This essential similarity is further reflected in the fact that the two structures are among the most common objects that supply food for man and beast.

The End of the Cycle.—The production of fruit and seed terminates the cycle in so far as the individual flower or crop of flowers are concerned. The plant may continue to produce succeeding generations of flowers and seeds just as long as environmental conditions outside the plant make such activities possible or until disease due to any one or a combination of causes so weakens the plant that it no longer can supply the material and the energy necessarily required for such vitally important processes.   Degeneration then overtakes the plant and it is likely either to succumb rather rapidly or to linger for years as a pitiable, crippled, worthless, and more or less unrecognizable image of its former beauty.

CHAPTER II

STRUCTURE OF THE FLOWER

It has been noted that a flower is a more or less highly differentiated and specialized branch of the stem system in the flowering plants. This modified branch becomes transformed into hundreds of different types of flowers. The distal end or apex of the floral branch upon which the regular organs that constitute the important features of the flower are developed is termed the "receptacle" or "torus." Ordinarily this is merely a more or less thickened, expanded or hollowed-out tip of the branch. There is often a more or less leaf-like appendage at the base of the pedicel of the flower known as the "floral bract."

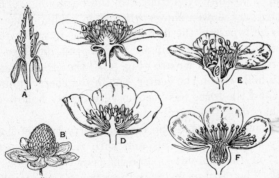

FIG. 8.—Flowers to show various types of axis and placement of perianth. *A*, vertical section of a flower of mousetail, *Myosurus minimus*, showing a slender, spire-like axis and many separate carpels (*after Baillon*); *B*, a flower of buttercup, *Ranunculus*, with the spirally arranged carpels on a cone-like axis (*after Baillon*); *C*, vertical section of a flower of raspberry, *Rubus*, with its dome-like central axis and spreading disk-like axis, and many separate stamens and carpels (*after Le M. and Dec.*); *D*, vertical section of a buttercup flower (*after Le M. and Dec.*); *E*, vertical section of bridal wreath, *Spiraea*, flower showing deepening of the axis and reduction in number of carpels (*after Baillon*); *F*, vertical section of flower of rose, *Rosa*, showing further deepening of the axis until it has become urn-like (*after Baillon*).

Form of the Receptacle.—In the buttercup, magnolia, and the tulip tree the receptacle is more or less dome-shaped, conical or spire-like (Fig. 8). The stamens, petals, and sepals are attached near the base of this receptacle, and the carpels are arranged

11

spirally over the upper portions of the same receptacle. This
type of flower is called a "hypogynous" flower. The central
part of the receptacle of the strawberry flower is of this nature
(Fig. 8) and after fertilization it becomes greatly enlarged, very
juicy, usually bright red, and, in short, is transformed into the
"fruit" or edible part (Fig. 32, *C*) of that plant. The blackberry
and the raspberry (Figs. 8 and 32, *B*) produce the same type
of torus but it is not excessively developed in either. The torus
becomes a portion of the edible structure in the blackberry,
dewberry, and the loganberry; but in most varieties of raspberries it remains on the stem as the "berries" are picked. In
the roses (Fig. 8, *E* and *F*) and their kin and in the evening
primroses and various other types the receptacle or torus becomes
disk-like, cup-shaped, pitcher-shaped, or even tubular (Fig. 136)
and it bears the sepals, petals, and stamens arranged cyclically
on the upper or outer rim. This type of torus or axis has been
developed by a deepening and hollowing of an axis which was
disk-like or possibly even conical in the beginning. The axis of
the strawberry flower shows what is in reality a combination
of the cone type and the disk type of torus in which the former
becomes impressively dominant as the fruit develops. In the
closely related bridal wreath (Fig. 8, *E*) the disk-like axis is per-
ceptably hollowed in the center, but in the cherry, plum, peach,
and almond the torus has become very deeply hollowed until it
is urn-shaped or almost tubular.

Perigynous Flowers.—The rose or cherry type of flower with
a deeply hollowed-out torus and with the sepals, petals, and
stamens on the summit is known as a "perigynous" flower
(Fig. 8). The pistil or pistils in these flowers are attached to the
bottom of the cup-shaped torus (Fig. 8 and 9), but this is in reality
the morphological apex or tip of the general floral axis, so that in
reality the sepals, petals, and stamens are inserted at a point
morphologically below the pistil and, hence, the pistil is really
superior, as in the buttercup. Nevertheless, the distinction is
fairly easy to note in mature flowers and it constitutes a useful
feature of such types which has long been used in practical
classification.

Hypogynous and Epigynous Flowers.—Most flowers are
hypogynous, *i.e.*, the ovary is *superior* or it is inserted on the tip
of the torus (Figs. 8, 102, 112, 113 and 121), but there are many
flowering plant species in which the ovary is *inferior*, *i.e.*, the

flower is *epigynous* (Figs. 9, 153, 156, 159, 174, 175, and 177). Good examples of the latter situation are found in the carrot, coffee, honeysuckle, bluebell, sunflower, evening primrose, iris, and the orchids. This striking difference has followed the deepening of the cup-shaped torus as in the rose (Figs. 8 and 9), and the subsequent union of this structure with the ovary so that the ovary and the lower portion of the torus appear to be a unit structure. Other flower parts may also become united with the ovary so that the inferior ovary is not necessarily exclusively receptacular in every case. In *Fuchsia* (Fig. 156) and many other flowers the union between torus and ovary has not only

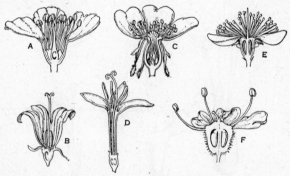

Fig. 9.—Examples of perigynous and epigynous flowers as shown by vertical sections. *A*, almond, *Amygdalus (after Le M. and Dec.); B*, bluebell, *Campanula (after Baillon); C*, rose, *Rosa (after Le M. and Dec.); D*, coffee, *Coffea (after Baillon); E*, myrtle, *Myrtus (after Le M. and Dec.); F*, carrot, *Daucus (after Baillon).*

been so complete as to produce an *inferior* type of ovary, but the axis has also been prolonged into a slender tubular structure extending well beyond the upper limit of the ovary which bears stamens, petals, and sepals on the rim. These differences in the nature and form of the torus coupled with differences in the attachment of the other parts of the flower are very helpful earmarks in the placement of the species of flowering plants in their proper groups.

The cone-shaped receptacle with superior ovary in hypogynous flowers is regarded as a more primitive or "lower" type than the cup-shaped receptacle in perigynous flowers. The inferior ovary of epigynous flowers is regarded a still higher type in most modern systems of classification which pretend to take account of possible phylogeny.

THE FOUR REGULAR ELEMENTS OF THE FLOWER

Sepals, Petals, Stamens, Pistils.—The four regular parts of a complete flower, sepals, petals, stamens, and pistils are related to the torus of the flower and to each other in a very definite fashion (Fig. 1). The outermost parts are the *sepals* and these taken together constitute the *calyx*. The next series, going toward the center of the flower, is composed of the *petals*, known collectively as the *corolla*. Calyx and corolla together constitute the *perianth* and they are commonly more or less leaf-like units that differ greatly in size, color, shape, number, and duration. The calyx is usually composed of as many sepals as there are

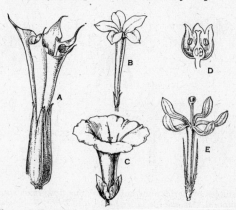

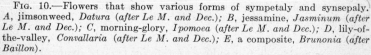

Fig. 10.—Flowers that show various forms of sympetaly and synsepaly. *A*, jimsonweed, *Datura* (*after Le M. and Dec.*); *B*, jessamine, *Jasminum* (*after Le M. and Dec.*); *C*, morning-glory, *Ipomoea* (*after Le M. and Dec.*); *D*, lily-of-the-valley, *Convallaria* (*after Le M. and Dec.*); *E*, a composite, *Brunonia* (*after Baillon*).

petals in the corolla, but in some groups (purslanes, poppies, etc.) there are commonly fewer sepals than petals. The sepals are usually green or inconspicuously colored, however in some families (buttercups) they are sometimes colored like petals and they take the place of petals, but in still others (tulip, Easter lily, onion) sepals and petals are colored alike and are scarcely distinguishable except by position. The showiness of most flowers is usually due to the presence of brightly colored petals, but in a number (Clematis, Pasque flower) this quality may be due solely to brightly colored sepals that have taken the place of the petals.

Size of Flowers.—The size of flowers as represented by the spread of the open perianth varies from almost microscopic in certain grasses and water plants to an enormous structure 4 or 5 feet in diameter and weighing 15 pounds in certain species of *Rafflesia* parasitic on the roots of grapes in the tropical forests of the Malay archipelago.

Union of Floral Elements.—The individual members of both calyx and corolla are separate from each other in many flowers. Such flowers are said to be "polysepalous" and "polypetalous," respectively (Figs. 8 and 9). In many other flowers the sepals appear to be more or less united to produce a continuous girdle (Figs. 9 and 10) about the flower. Such a calyx is termed "gamosepalous" or "synsepalous." The petals appear united also to form a more or less tubular or rotate corolla in many flowers to produce what is called a "gamopetalous" or "sympetalous" corolla. The united part is the *tube* and the spreading parts or the lobed border is the *limb* (Fig. 10). The perianth with united parts is commonly regarded as derived or "higher" (or later) than the perianth with separate parts.

Regular and Irregular Flowers.—Most flowers are beautifully symmetrical, *i.e. regular* or *actinomorphic*, because of the radial symmetry of their development (Figs. 1, 8, 10 and 113). But many flowers are more or less unsymmetrical, irregular, or *zygomorphic, i.e.*, lopsided, because some of the petals on one side of the gamopetalous or polypetalous corolla are larger or they have a different shape from the other portion of the flower (Figs. 11, 141, 144 and 146).

The Flowers of Beans.—In the beans and their kin (Figs. 11 and 146) may be seen one of the most familiar types of floral irregularity or zygomorphy. The bean (or sweet pea) flower is composed of five petals in three distinct sets or groups. The large petal in the back or upper part of the flower is the *standard* or *banner;* in front and usually below is the *keel* made up of two petals; and to the right and left of the keel are the other two petals, the *wings* (Figs. 11, A and 146). The broadly expanded standard, the narrow, elongated keel, and the wings beneath the standard and more or less clasping the keel, serve to produce a very distinctive type of irregular corolla called the "papilionaceous" corolla.

The Flowers of Mints.—In the mints, the tube of the corolla is commonly deeply split into two irregular lobes (Figs. 11 and 144). The upper lobe is usually erect and is composed of two petals, and the lower lobe, composed of three petals, is more or less spreading. This is known as a *bilabiate, i.e.* a two-lipped corolla.

Many other natural families of flowering plants show zygomorphic flowers of great variety of form and color pattern. The orchids (Fig. 203) and snapdragons (Figs. 11 and 141) are notable groups in this connection in which form and color serve to produce hundreds of curious and complicated types. The calyx is sometimes involved in zygomorphy also (Fig. 115), but as a rule not to such an extreme degree as in the case of the corolla.

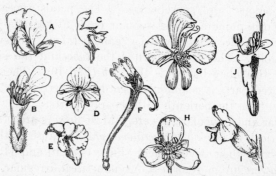

Fig. 11.—Flowers that show various types of zygomorphy, sympetaly, and position of the ovary. *A*, pea, *Pisum* (*after Baillon*); *B*, bugle, *Ajuga* (*after Le M. and Dec.*); *C*, a mint, *Lamium* (*after Le M. and Dec.*); *D*, speedwell, *Veronica* (*after Le M. and Dec.*); *E*, sesame, *Sesamum* (*after Le M. and Dec.*); *F*, honeysuckle, *Lonicera* (*after Baillon*); *G*, monkshood, *Aconitum*, partially dissected (*after Baillon*); *H*, water plantain, *Alisma*, an actinomorphic flower with which to compare the others (*after Le M. and Dec.*); *I*, snapdragon, *Antirrhinum* (*after Le M. and Dec.*); *J*, valerian, *Valeriana* (*after Le M. and Dec.*).

Zygomorphy and Pollination.—The interest in zygomorphic flowers is increased by the brilliant and bizarre differentiations introduced by the color patterns of many species. The whole problem of zygomorphy is locked up with the outstanding fact that such flowers are almost without exception *entomophilous* (Fig. 21, *A* and *B*). Some of the better known and more striking features of this relationship to insects are treated in the chapter on the work of flowers.

The Stamens.—The next regular flower parts seen as we go into a flower from the outside are the stamens (Fig. 12). These are attached to the torus in one or more series inside the corolla (Fig. 8), or, in the gamopetalous corolla, they are usually attached to the inner surface (Figs. 10 and 11) of the corolla tube. The group of stamens is sometimes called the "andrœcium." The number of stamens per flower varies greatly in different species. The flowers of cattail (Fig. 185), willow (Figs. 3 and 127) and ash often have but a single stamen. The flower of the olive (Fig. 134) has two, and most grass flowers (Figs. 193, 194 and 196) have three stamens. Many flowers have four or five and some have many stamens. A single flower of the saguaro or great cactus, *Carnegiea*, had 3,482 stamens by actual count.

Structure of Stamens.—Each stamen usually consists of a more or less elongated and narrow, slender stalk or *filament*, bearing an oblong, inflated, two-lobed, bag-like *anther* at the top (Fig. 12). The filament is very short or even entirely lacking in some flowers so that the anther is brought down very close to the torus or corolla tube, as the case may be, but in others the filament is greatly elongated, very thin, slender and thread-like in comparison with the rather bulky anther. The attachment of the anther to the filament is either at the lower end of the anther, *i.e.*, *basal*, or laterally near the

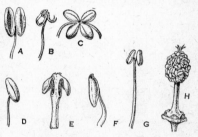

Fig. 12.—Various types of stamens showing various forms of dehiscence. *A*, *Calandrinia; B*, bearberry, *Arctostaphylos; C*, balm, *Melissa; D*, globe-daisy, *Globularia; E*, barberry, *Berberis; F*, wintergreen, *Pyrola; (after Kerner) G*, linden, *Tilia; H*, mallow, *Malva.*

central axis of the anther, *i.e.*, *versatile* (Fig. 12). The stamens of a given flower are usually free or separate from each other, but in a few groups they become united either by their filaments or by their anthers (Fig. 12, *H*). Thus in the androecium of the mallows the filaments of the many stamens are united well up toward the anthers so that a complete sheath is formed that envelops the ovary (Fig. 12, *H*). The many stamens of the orange flower are united into several groups by the union of the filaments. In the pea (Fig. 146, *D*) there are two sets of stamens, nine in one set in which the filaments are united, and one separate stamen. In the thistles and their kin (Fig. 177, *D*) the filaments are free but the anthers are joined together forming a tube through which the style pushes.

The Anther.—The anther when young contains from one to four elongated cavities (called "cells") in which the *pollen grains* (Fig. 13) arise. When the anther is mature it usually contains two pollen cavities or cells in each of which quantities of powdery or waxy pollen are produced. The two cells are often separated by the upper portion of the filament, the *connective*, which is prolonged from base to tip of the anther. The anther cells usually open when the pollen is mature by the formation of an apical pore in each sac, or more commonly by a longitudinal slit (Fig. 12, *A*, *B* and *F*), through which the pollen grains sift out.

Pollen and Pollen Grains.—The pollen grains are usually so small as to appear as very tiny specks to the unaided eye, but they may be produced in such numbers as to form clouds of pollen at the time of maximum discharge and they sometimes cover the ground underneath plants with a layer of

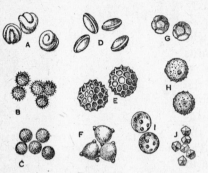

Fig. 13.　　　　　　　Fig. 14.

Fig. 13.—Pollen grains from various species. *A*, monkeyflower, *Mimulus; B*, a mallow, *Hibiscus; C*, mallow, *Malva; D*, gentian, *Gentiana; E*, climbing bells, *Cobaea; F*, nightshade, *Circaea; G*, pink, *Dianthus; H*, pumpkin, *Cucurbita; I*, bindweed, *Convolvulus; J*, dandelion, *Taraxacum (after Kerner).*

Fig. 14.—A single pollen grain germinating. The exine and intine show plainly *(redrawn).*

impalpable greenish or yellowish powder. The enormous number of pollen grains produced by higher plants is one of their most astounding characteristics. This has been judged as a very wasteful habit because of the fact that much more pollen is produced than appears to be needed.

Structure of Pollen Grains.—The individual pollen grains are usually unicellular and their form (Fig. 13) varies considerably for different flowering plants but they are usually more or less spherical, ovoid, or disk-like. The cell wall is in two layers, the one a delicate inner layer, known as the "intine," and the other a heavier and more resistant outer layer, the "exine" (Fig. 14). The thick exine is often thrown into striking folds, bands, ridges, or low protuberances and spines. Germ pores (Fig. 14) are located in the exine among the other markings that appear on the surface. The pollen tube (Fig. 14) emerges from one of these pores when the pollen grain germinates. The germ pores of the pollen grains in some squashes are covered by a lid which pops off when the pollen tube is ready to emerge during the early period of germination. The number and location of the germ pores are usually constant for a given species. These features give a surface configuration to pollen grains which is so nearly characteristic of the different species that it may be used for purposes of identification.

The Pistil.—The fourth and innermost part of the complete flower is the pistil (Figs. 1, 3, 4 and 15) or group of pistils which lie in the center of the flower upon the top of the torus (superior) or are embedded within it (inferior) and are surrounded by the stamens, petals, and sepals. The three common relationships

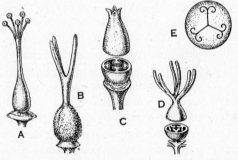

Fig. 15.—Certain forms of pistils and ovaries. *A*, rose mallow, *Hibiscus* (*after Baillon*); *B*, tea, *Thea* (*after Baillon*); *C*, grass of Parnassus, *Parnassia* (*after Mathews*); *D*, sundew, *Drosera*; *E*, diagram of the transverse section of a tricarpellary ovary.

between the pistil and the receptacle or torus have already been discussed. We will confine our study in this place to the finer structure and variations of the pistil itself. The number of pistils in each flower differs greatly for different species. The flowers of some plants produce a single, simple pistil as in the cherry and peach, while others produce two, three, four, five or more separate or united carpels per flower (Fig. 15). The pistil or group of pistils in a flower is known as the "gynœceum."

Nature of the Pistil.—The pistil is normally flask-shaped or bottle-shaped and is made up of three parts or subdivisions. The enlarged, more or less bulbous, hollow, basal portion is termed the "ovary." The ovary is commonly drawn out into an elongated neck, the "style." The tip or expanded or divided extremity of the style is commonly roughened and glandular and is termed the "stigma" (Figs. 1 and 15). The style is very short and even lacking in some flowers so that the stigma is *sessile*, *i.e.* brought down very close to or directly upon the ovary.

The Ovary and Ovules.—The ovary is the part of the pistil which bears the *ovules*. This is a hollow structure in which the ovules are borne in definite positions along the inner wall of the ovary (Fig. 15, *D*) or upon the central axis or floor (Fig. 1, *C*) of that important structure. Some flowers produce but a single ovule in the pistil, but most flowers produce several (Fig. 15, *C* and *D*) and a few species produce several hundred or even thousands. A single flower of the giant cactus, *Carnegiea*, showed (by actual count) 1,980 ovules.

Simple Pistils and Compound Pistils.—So far we have had in mind a single or simple pistil. This simple pistil or *carpel* in the very young flower is a flattish structure which gradually becomes hollowed out and folded so that the margins unite to form a closed, pouch-like organ bearing the ovule or ovules along the suture (placenta) formed by the union of the two margins (Fig. 15, *D*). In some species there are several or even many simple pistils of this sort in each flower, and they remain distinct, *i.e.*, not united, and later they ripen into individual, separate fruits. But in most flowering plants having flowers with several or many carpels per flower the carpels become united to form a *compound pistil* (Fig. 15). The sutures of the individual carpels in a compound ovary are axially placed and the midribs are external so that a compound ovary often contains as many cavities or "cells" as there are carpels represented. A compound ovary becomes "one-celled" in some flowers (primrose, violet) by the disappearance of the septa between the different carpels.

Degree of Union of Carpels.—The union of the carpels in a compound ovary is sometimes so complete as to affect the style and even the stigma (Fig. 15) where little hint as to the actual condition may be seen. In flowers where there are two or more separate styles or stigmas it is often safe to assume that the ovary is compound. The number of subdivisions in the style or stigma (Fig. 15) in such cases may indicate the number of carpels in the ovary, but this relation is not always conclusive. The number of carpels in a compound ovary is often indicated also by conspicuous longitudinal ridges or creases on the outer surface of the ovary, but this relationship may also be misleading. The *locules — a small cavity or chamber* [handwritten annotation]

number of carpels represented in an ovary can usually be determined in most plants only by making thin sections (Fig. 15) across the median part of the structure and noting the number of locules or cells. In such sections of one-celled, compound ovaries the number of parietal placentae may be indicative of the number of carpels present.

Importance of the Ovules.—The most important part of the pistil is the ovule because that is the structure in which the egg is formed and in which fertilization occurs. After fertilization the *embryo plant* develops within the ovule to a certain degree when the whole structure becomes transformed into a *seed*, and as such it usually separates from the body of the parent plant. The ovules are in reality the forerunners of seeds.

Number and Nature of Ovules.—The number of ovules per pistil or carpel varies greatly for different species, but as a rule there are two or more ovules per simple pistil or per carpel in polycarpellate pistils. In some of the species of the buckwheat family, and typically in the grasses, there is a single ovule in each ovary. There are many flowers with one or more carpels represented in the ovary in which but a single seed matures, all of the other ovules having aborted and disappeared. Even in such regularly single-seeded fruits as cherries, plums, and almonds, a fruit with two seeds is occasionally found. The game of our childhood as we looked expectantly to find a "filopena" when we were cracking almonds or peach pits recalls this fact. The simple pistil of these plants always has two ovules, but usually one of them is aborted. Certain other species, such as primroses, tobacco, snapdragons, cactuses, and orchids with compound ovaries, produce scores or even hundreds of ovules per ovary, but all of these may not develop into seeds in every case. The ovules in a single flower of the giant cactus, *Carnegiea*, were counted and it was found that there were 1,980 of them, but as a rule the juicy fruits of that species produce but a few mature seeds.

Position of Ovules in the Ovary.—Each ovule is an oval or egg-shaped body attached by a stalk, the *funiculus*, to its axis or placenta inside the ovary (Fig. 24). The part of the ovary to which the ovules are attached is called the "placenta." The placentae are commonly located along the sutures formed by the union of the edges of the carpel as it closes in its very early growth. The number of placentae in an ovary usually is the same as the number of carpels represented in the ovary. The

placentae are said to be "parietal" (Fig. 15, *C* and *D*) if they are
on the outer ovary wall as in the willow and currant; if they are
borne by the central axis of the ovary (the common axis of the
carpels) they are said to be "axillary," (Figs. 106, 107, 186 and
201) as in lilies, irises, etc.   In the primroses (Fig. 128) the partitions between the five carpels of the ovary disappear very early,
thus leaving a mass of tissue in the basal portion of the ovary,
the remnant of the axis, upon which the ovules are attached.
This type of ovule insertion is called "free central placentation."

INCOMPLETE FLOWERS

Flowers Lacking Perianth.—The regulation features of complete flowers have been considered here, but it will be recalled
that it was pointed out in the introduction that not all flowers

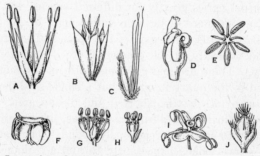

Fig. 16.—Incomplete flowers.   *A*, male flower of amaranth, *Amaranthus;*
B, female flower of *Amaranthus* (*both after Le M. and Dec.*); *C*, female flowers of
hazel, *Corylus* (*after Baillon*); *D* and *E*, female and male flowers respectively
of pistachio, *Pistacia* (*after Le M. and Dec.*); *F*, male flower of walnut, *Juglans*,
(*after Le M. and Dec.*); *G* and *H*, apetalous flowers of elm, *Ulmus* (*after Le M.
and Dec.*); *I* and *J*, male and female flowers respectively of nettle, *Urtica* (*after
Le M. and Dec.*).

are complete.   The flowers of many species of flowering plants
lack one or more of the regular parts (Fig. 16).   The petals are
lacking in some cases, as in certain buttercups, buckwheats, and
nettles, and in still others the sepals are also lacking so that
there is no perianth present at all as in willows, duckweeds,
pepper, *Trachodendron.*   The flowers of many other species
produce a very inconspicuous calyx or only the merest vestiges
of a perianth, as in figs, valerian, and composites.   Many
flowers are known in which the perianth is lacking wholly or
in part, but these flowers contain stamens and pistils (Fig. 16).
Such flowers are *incomplete*, in that they lack the perianth, the
accessory parts of a flower, but they are, nevertheless, *perfect,*

because they possess *stamens* and *pistils*, the *essential organs* of a flower.   These are *monoclinous*, or perfect flowers.

Diclinous Flowers.—There are other flowering plants in which the whole perianth is present or absent, or the calyx alone may be present, and in which there are only stamens or pistils but not both (Figs. 2, 3, 4 and 16).   This is the situation in willow, cotton-wood, hickory, oak, walnut, spurge, green ash, boxelder, maize, wild rice, cattail, arrowhead, grape, chestnut, bittersweet, and some members of the buckwheat family.   This phenomenon is included under the term "dicliny," or the condition known as "diclinism."   Two common conditions prevail among such spe- cies.   In one group the pistillate (female) and staminate (male) flowers are borne by the *same individual* but upon *different parts*, *i.e.*, not in the *same flower*.   Such plants are said to be "*monœcious*."   The hickory, oak, chestnut, walnut, cattail, maize, arrowhead, cucumber, and spurge represent this condition (Figs. 167, 168 and 182).   In the other group, the stamens and pistils are not only borne by *different flowers* but these flowers are *also* produced by *totally different individual plants*.   Such species are said to be "*diœcious*."   The willow, cottonwood, green ash, papaya, boxelder, hemp, datepalm, hop, mulberry, osage orange, tree-of-Heaven, etc., represent this type (Figs. 3, 16, 127).

Comparisons with Animals.—It will be seen at once that diœcious flowering plants are sexually differentiated much as are the higher animals, that is, the individuals of this nature are male or female but not both male and female, as is true of the individuals that are monœcious and that produce perfect flowers.   Obviously, if one wishes to produce fruits and seeds in diclinous species he must have both pistillate and staminate individuals in close enough proximity to insure pollination.   It is interesting to note, in passing, that sexual differentiation has not gone so far, that is, it has not affected nearly so large a proportion of flowering plants, the highest plants known, as it has in the mammals, the highest animals.

Polygamous Species.—A few species of flowering plants that produce their stamens and pistils in different flowers also produce perfect flowers.   Such plants are said to be "polygamous."   Certain species of maple, ash, and buckwheat are of this nature. These combine various degrees of monocliny and dicliny.

Flower-like Structures.—Reference should be made to certain interesting flower-like structures commonly regarded as flowers

(Figs. 17 and 18) that in reality are not flowers, or perhaps more than flowers. The *Poinsettia*, a popular Christmas house plant in America, will serve to illustrate one of these peculiar features. The large, beautiful, and showy group of bright scarlet structures at the top of the branches, sometimes 6 or 8 inches in diameter is usually considered a flower, popularly. However, the true morphology of that structure is quite different from what is commonly supposed. The large, scarlet, leaf-like parts are in reality *leaves* that develop a red pigment in place of the usual chlorophyll. Taken together these constitute a radial fringe known as an "involucre," which really performs the function of the regular perianth, but which is a distinct affair and wholly separate from the inconspicuous true

FIG. 17.　　　　　　　　　　　FIG. 18.

FIG. 17.—The showy involucre of dogwood, *Cornus florida*, with the group of small flowers in the center. The whole structure passes as a single flower, popularly, (*after Baillon*).

FIG. 18.—Unopened and mature heads of marigold, *Calendula officinalis*, showing the closed involucre in the young heads and the ray and disk flowers in the opened head (*after Baillon*).

flowers that are clustered near the center of the whorl of brightly colored bracts. Similar features are associated with the flowers or flower clusters in certain dogwoods, *Cornus florida* (Fig. 17), clematis, and Japanese paper plant.

The Flowers of Composites.—The *Compositae*, to which belong sunflowers, asters, daisies, dandelions, goldenrods, calendulas, thistles, chrysanthemums, and their kin, are unique in that the structure that is commonly called a "flower" is in truth a cluster of many flowers (Fig. 18). A single "flower" in a dandelion

(Fig. 178) often contains as many as 100 to 200 tiny, separate, very closely grouped flowers on a common receptacle. This flower cluster is known to botanists as a "head." The heads in the big Russian sunflower usually contain several hundred individual flowers which become transformed into a corresponding number of dry fruits (achenes) or "seeds" arranged in a beautifully symmetrical pattern over the greatly enlarged receptacle. The composites, the dogwood and *Poinsettia* and their kin furnish fine material for the discussion of the question of "when is a flower not a flower" or "when is a flower more than a flower."

Pathological Growths.—Travelers in the tropics sometimes note curious saucer-like, woody growths on the roots of certain trees that grow in that part of the world. These are sometimes several inches broad and they exhibit a beautiful radiate symmetry, with fringed or lacerated border, but evidently formed from wood. These "wooden flowers" are not flowers at all, of course, but abnormal or pathological growths produced as the result of the action of some mistletoe parasite that infects the trees.

Summary of the Organization of Flowers

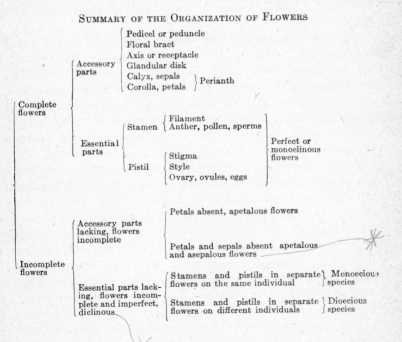

CHAPTER III

THE WORK OF THE FLOWER

The preceding chapters have largely dealt with the flower from the anatomical and morphological standpoints, although reference to processes and functions were not altogether lacking. A study of the flower as a living, working unit will now be presented. Flowers are understood in their true value and significance only if the dynamic rôle that they perform in the life history of flowering plants is appreciated.

Significance of Reproduction.—A very large proportion of the energy of plants is devoted toward the preparation of new individuals for succeeding generations. Reproduction, in a word, is the most significant of all of the vitally active processes common to flowering plants because herein lie most of the potentialities for the future.

The flower has already been characterized as the unit of sexual reproduction, *par excellence*, in flowering plants. The association of flowers with seed production is common knowledge, but comparatively few students are familiar with the sequence of details associated with the phenomenon. Flower structure will be examined in somewhat greater detail than has already been done in order that the outline of this important and dynamic process in the life of flowering plants may be sketched.

The General Nature of Sex.—Sexual reproduction normally occurs only when two *sex cells*, one a *sperm*, the *male* cell, and the other an *egg*, the *female* cell, or their equivalent, each carrying certain inheritances of the parent organism, come into intimate contact so that their contents become inseparably united with each other to produce a *zygote*, which is at once the first cell of the new individual. The sperm *alone* never develops a new individual, and it is *very rarely* that the egg is capable of further development until it is *fertilized* by a sperm. The development of an embryo from an unfertilized egg is known in a very few species of flowering plants, and in some such the phenomenon by no means takes the place of the regular behavior. The process is known as "par-

26

thenogenesis," and it has been reported in the dandelion, meadow
rue, everlasting (*Antennaria*), *Alchemilla*, and possibly others.

Sexuality in Flowers.—Fertilization in flowers is involved in a
series of more or less complex structures and activities, but these
may be reduced to about five, all of which are preliminary and
subsidiary to the last which is the most important and crowning
event. The plant must provide male cells, *sperms*, and female
cells, *eggs*. This it does, as has already been noted, in the pollen
grains of stamens (Figs. 12, 13, 14 and 25), and in the ovules of
the ovaries (Figs. 1, 4, 15, 23 and 26). Then the pollen grains
must be carried from the anthers to the stigma of the pistil
(pollination). Then the pollen tube must be developed in order
that the sperms may be carried through the tissues of stigma and
style to the ovules in the ovary within which the eggs are located.
When the pollen tube enters the ovule and discharges the sperms
in the immediate vicinity of the egg, *fertilization* (Fig. 25), or the
fusion of the sex cells, is readily accomplished.

POLLINATION

Pollination, by which is meant the transfer of pollen grains
from anther to stigma in flowers, as a forerunner of fertilization,
is one of the most varied, important, and interesting phases of
the work of flowers. And yet the plant in itself may have little
to do with this process directly, because pollination is often
brought about by some external agency such as wind or water,
or even by a totally separate and different organism such as a
bee, moth, or bird.

Self-pollination versus Cross-pollination.—One might naturally suppose that the pollen produced by a given flower would
pollinate that flower and that the sperms produced by certain
of those pollen grains would fertilize the eggs in the ovules
of the same flower. This would be self-pollination and self-
fertilization. This actually happens in certain species, but it is
not by any means the rule among flowering plants. The vast
majority of flowering plants appear to have worked out the
details of their development so that self-fertilization is prevented.
The fact is that cross-pollination and, therefore, usually also
cross-fertilization is the rule among flowering plants. Indeed,
cross-fertilization is also the rule in the groups below the Angiosperms. It would appear that some great biological significance
is associated with this fact. Many experiments since the time of

Darwin support the contention of that great investigator that cross-pollination (cross-fertilization) generally results in the development of stronger individual plants and a stronger race.

Effect of Inbreeding.—Plants or animals that are produced by self-fertilization are said to be "inbred." The effects of inbreeding are strikingly illustrated in the first generation of corn (maize) produced by this method. The individual plants are very noticeably dwarfed as a whole and the ears that they form are greatly reduced in size and often distorted or otherwise abnormal and poorly filled. When individuals of this sort are cross-bred again the vigor may be at once restored in much the original form and degree.

Types of Pollination.—Students of pollination phenomena refer to self-pollination as "autogamy," and to cross-pollination as "allogamy." Cross-pollination (allogamy) between flowers

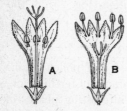

Fig. 19.—Dimorphism in partridge berry, *Mitchella*. *A.* flower with long style and short stamens; *B*, flower with short style and long stamens.

of a given individual is termed "geitonogamy," and between flowers of totally separate individual plants "xenogamy." Geitonogamy occurs in those plants that have monoclinous flowers, *i.e.*, those with perfect flowers, and also in those that are monœcious, *i.e.*, those species with staminate and pistillate flowers separated upon different parts of the individual. Xenogamy alone is possible in plants with imperfect flowers and in diœcious species, *i.e.*, those with staminate and pistillate flowers borne by totally different individuals of the species.

How Flowers Prevent Self-pollination.—The advantages associated with cross-pollination and cross-fertilization are reflected in the great variety of flower behavior and in the bizarre floral structures that have been developed through the ages that tend to prevent self-fertilization. The flowers of diclinous species must of course be cross-pollinated. The stamens and stigmas in monoclinic species usually mature at different times. This naturally prevents self-fertilization, and at the same time renders cross-fertilization imperative. Flowers of this sort are said to be "dichogamous," and the phenomenon is termed "dichogamy." Such flowers are said to be "protandrous" if the pollen is mature before the stigma is receptive, and "protogynous" if the stigma is ready before the pollen is mature. Certain monoclinous flowers (primrose, partridge berry, etc., Fig. 19) prevent self-pollination to a considerable degree by an interesting type of dimorphism. Some of the flowers of this plant bear their stamens high upon the corolla tube, near the open throat of the corolla, but the stigma is much lower down in the tube and never approaches the anther. In other flowers the stamens are inserted low down on the inner surface of the corolla tube, and the stigma occupies the position about level with the throat of the corolla (Fig. 19). Now the eggs in the ovules of the flower with low stigma may be fertilized only by sperms produced in the pollen grains of the stamens that are placed low, and the eggs in the flower with the stigma in the throat may be fertilized by the sperms of pollen grains borne by the stamens in the throat. This floral pattern renders cross-pollination imperative. There are still other flowering plants that produce flowers that are sterile to their own pollen, and, because of this, pollen from another source is necessitated. The iris prevents self-pollination by placing its stamens in a close-fitting groove underneath the petal-like lobes (Fig. 201) of the style in which the stigmatic surfaces are on the upper surface. The anthers are held very closely pressed against the under surface by the tensed filaments. The pollinating bee strikes the stigma only as he enters the flower so that foreign pollen alone is deposited. After working the flower the bee leaves without touching the stigma so that the pollen of a given flower is rarely deposited upon its own stigma.

External Factors in Cross-pollination.—The most effective agents that bring about cross-pollination are water, wind, and animals including insects, and a few other types. Not many flowering plants are pollinated by water. Some of these, *Ceratophyllum, Zostera,* are totally submerged and are pollinated under the water. In other cases, *Ruppia, Callitriche,* the pollen floats on the surface of the water where it comes into contact with the stigma. One of the most interesting and best known cases of pollination by means of water is in the eelgrass, *Vallisneria spiralis,* a submerged plant with grass-like leaves, which is more or less common in lakes and ponds. This is a diœcious species in which the pistillate flowers are borne upon a slender thread-like scape that stretches upward until the flowers are brought to the surface of the water. The staminate flowers are borne beneath the water but when about mature they break off and rise to the surface where they expand as floating flowers and discharge their pollen.   After the stigmas of the pistillate flowers receive the pollen from the floating staminate flowers the scapes contract spirally and the fruits are ripened beneath the surface.   A somewhat similar case has been described for the waterweed, *Elodea canadensis.*   Other aquatic species in which the plant is wholly submerged raise their flowers well above the surface of the water and the pollen may then be carried by wind or insects, as in the laceleaf, *Aponogeton fenestralis,* and the water buttercup, *Batrachium trichophyllum.*   The flowers of some submerged aquatic species, as in the latter, may not open because of abnormally high water and so self-pollination becomes the rule under such conditions.

Cross-pollination by Wind.—Many flowering plants and practically all Gymnosperms are usually pollinated by wind.   The

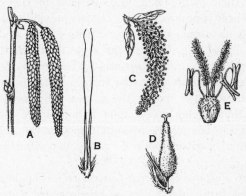

Fig. 20.—Wind-pollinated flowers.   *A*, male catkins of birch, *Betula; B*, female flowers of hazel, *Corylus; C*, male catkin of willow, *Salix; D*, female flower of *Salix; E*, perfect flower of wheat, *Triticum (after Baillon).*

influence of other pollinating agents is negligible among the latter. Perhaps the most conspicuous wind-pollinated, or *anemophilous*, flowering plants are the members of the group "amentiferae" including the willows, *Salix*, poplars, *Populus*, oaks, *Quercus*, hickories, *Hicoria*, chestnuts, *Castanea*, beeches, *Fagus*, birches, *Betula*, hazels, *Corylus*, alders, *Alnus*, hornbeam, *Ostrya*, etc. (Figs. 20, 167, 168 and 169), and the grasses, including the cereals (*Gramineae*) (Figs. 193 to 199), sedges (*Cyperaceae*) (Fig. 192), and certain species of other groups such as the elms, *Ulmus*, nettles, *Urtica, Urticastrum*, hops, *Humulus*, etc. (Figs. 108 and 110).

Nature of Wind-pollinated Flowers.—Wind-pollinated flowering plants are commonly characterized by flowers that are inconspicuous because of their size or lack of nectar or odor and brilliant colors, and by the production of a great abundance of dry or oily powdery pollen. The stigmas of such flowers are often much branched or plume-like, feathery, or hairy. These details doubtless assist in the catchment of greater numbers of pollen grains than would otherwise be possible. The minute size and lightness of pollen grains contribute to the ease with which they are carried by the wind, but doubtless a very small number, compared with the enormous numbers liberated, ever reach the stigmas. Uncountable numbers of wind-carried pollen grains never reach the flowers and so are lost without performing their function. It would seem that many anemophilous species could greatly reduce the amount of pollen produced and still take little chance of becoming weakened or threatened by extinction.

Amount of Pollen Produced.—The quantity of pollen produced in anemophilous flowering plants has been investigated for a number of species. Thus Hassall, about a hundred years ago, found nearly 250,000 pollen grains in a single blossom of dandelion, *Taraxacum* (Fig. 179). A peony, *Paeonia*, flower with 175 stamens produced 21,000 pollen grains per stamen or a total of 3,675,000 for the flower. A rhododendron plant produced 72,600,000 pollen grains. The amount of pollen in Indian corn is usually impressive as one walks through a field at the time of blooming. The ground is often covered by a dusty layer of pollen at such time and the plants themselves are enveloped in a powdery mantle of pollen. One investigator reports that a single plant of maize produced as many as 50,000,000 pollen grains.

Pollination in the Grasses.—Not all grasses are pollen-producers like maize. The low-growing species, especially, produce less; but perhaps the low stature and the density of the population in such species more than compensate for the relatively small pollen crop. Another advantage in such species is seen in the fact that the pollen sifts through and is blown thoroughly about among the individuals of the denser grassy associations before it is carried away. It should also be noted that the flowers of many wind-pollinated species are reduced or incomplete in that they lack petals or even both petals and sepals, so that the material and energy that go into the formation of the perianth may be available for stamen and pollen formation.

Distances Involved in Pollination.—The distance to which pollen grains are ordinarily carried by the wind is probably not as great as might be supposed. The data on this question are rather few and somewhat uncertain. Finely divided dust has been carried by the wind from Africa to Switzerland, and the pollen grains of pine have been blown 400 miles or more from where they were produced. Pollen has been gathered on ships at sea 20 to 40 miles from shore. The tiny seeds of a certain pitcher plant, *Nepenthes ampullaria*, are reported to have been carried by the wind for 1,500 miles. So that it is possible that the pollen grains of many anemophilous species are occasionally carried for great distances by the wind, but the biological importance of this fact is doubtless more interesting than significant. The relatively short period of viability and the vicissitudes imposed by meteorological conditions tend to support this conclusion.

Animals as Pollinating Agents.—There are many more species of flowering plants pollinated by animals than by all other agencies combined. The insects are by far the most important animals concerned here, but a few flowering plants, *Abutilon*, *Fuchsia* (Fig. 156), *Fritillaria*, *Bignonia*, *Lonicera*, *Oenothera* (Fig. 156), and *Impatiens*, are pollinated by birds, especially humming birds. Certain tropical species are pollinated by bats, and a few, *Arisaema*, *Calla*, *Aspidistra*, by snails and slugs. The interrelations between flowers and insects have attracted biologists for many decades. There are numerous publications on this subject in many languages from all parts of the world.

Pollination by Insects.—Insect-pollinated flowers produce less pollen than do anemophilous species, but this reduction is amply compensated for in the numerous, extremely varied, and often bizarre floral modifications that render insect-pollination certain (Fig. 21). The perianth is of the utmost value in such flowers. It seems probable that the color, odor, size, and form of flowers are largely to be interpreted in terms of the attractiveness afforded for the insect visitors. The intimacy of the dependence of certain flowers upon certain insects for pollination is often impressive. Thus F. Darwin writes that:

"The coordination between a flower and the particular insect which fertilizes it may be as delicate as that between a clock and its key." The son of the great Darwin meant *pollination* by "fertilization" in the statement quoted, of course, because insects do not *fertilize* flowers at all. We should expand the figure and understand that insects may apply the *key* (pollen) to the *socket* (stigma) but unless the *spring* (egg) is *wound* (fertilized) the *clock* (new generation) is *impotent.*

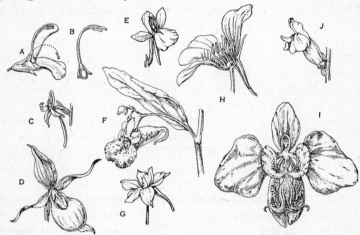

Fig. 21.—Insect-pollinated flowers. *A*, mechanism in sage, *Salvia glutinosa; B*, the stamens of *Salvia* showing the long curved filaments and the connective; *C*, orchid, *Orchis; D*, lady's slipper, *Cypripedium (after Le M. and Dec.); E. Orchis (after Le M. and Dec.); F*, balsam, *Impatiens (after Le M. and Dec.); G*, larkspur, *Delphinium (after Le M. and Dec.); H*, nasturtium, *Tropaeolum (after Le M. and Dec.); I*, a tropical orchid, *Phalaenopsis (after Kerner); J*, snapdragon, *Antirrhinum (after Le M. and Dec.).*

Danger of Exaggeration.—This is a field of biology with so much that is impressive that one may become so enthusiastic as to slip very easily (almost unconsciously) in the pitfall of teleological reasoning. Many rather uncertain statements have been made concerning the constancy of insect attention and the close degree of correlation between shape of flower and insect, weight of insects and floral mechanisms, color and odor and insect species, etc. Recent extensive experimentation would indicate that the commonly supposed delicacy and intimacy of such correlations may be considerably exaggerated. Further investigations may remove some of the "romance" from this alluring field, but they will probably endow it with even a greater wealth of definitely established scientific truth than is at present available.

Why and How Flowers Attract Insects.—Insects visit flowers because they have found that flowers have something important to contribute to their material welfare. They do not *enjoy* flowers simply for their *color* or *odor*, but for the *food* that they secure, prosaic as this may seem. The visitors are attracted by brilliantly colored and openly displayed banners and more or less sweet-smelling perfumes, but they go to flowers to get a sustaining volume of *food* in the form of pollen and nectar. The poetized busy bee improves each "shining hour" in calling upon its floral neighbors, primarily, in order that it and its associates will have *something to eat* when darkness surrounds its visits with uncertainty and when winter comes to lay waste to its store of fresh food. The colors and odors that attract the insects are mostly pleasant or agreeable to us also, and we utilize the colors for decorative purposes and extract many of the pleasant odors for the preparation of perfumes, but, of course, these are not features of concern on the part of the flowers or insects. The olfactory preference of some animal pollinators must vary considerably from ours because we find them visiting certain flowers, as in carrion-flower, *Smilax herbacea*, skunk cabbage, *Spathyema*, and fetid milkweed, *Stapelia*, etc., in which the odor is exceedingly unpleasant and nauseating.

Quantity of Pollen Gathered.—Many insects consume quantities of pollen as food which they get from inconspicuous and scentless flowers as well as from flowers of the more popular nature. Brilliant flowers are sometimes scentless (at least to man) but they are visited by insects for the pollen that they produce. The amount of pollen consumed by insects is probably inconsequential since there is still an abundance for fertilization, but the masses of pollen that certain insects (bumblebees) eat and collect is rather impressive. Clements and Long report that the honeybee, *Apis mellifica*, sometimes carries a load of pollen (of *Rubus deliciosus*) that is more than half the weight of the bee, but the load was usually less than that. In another bee, *Andrena crataegi*, the pollen load varied from 5 to 17 per cent, and in a bumblebee, *Bombus juxtus*, from 1 to 61 per cent of the insect's weight in twenty-three determinations. Sometimes the load of pollen was pure, *i.e.*, from a single plant, but in other cases the load represented a mixture of the pollens from two or more plants. Flowers have developed many different structural devices to assist in sprinkling or dusting the insect with pollen and to insure the loading of the insect in a manner which will best suit cross-pollination demands.

The Nectar of Flowers.—The flowers of many species are attractive to insects or other pollinating animals because of the presence of *nectar* which is also a valuable food. Nectar is gathered from flowers and stored for future use in enormous quantities as *honey*. The nectar is a saccharine exudation produced by areas of glandular tissue in various parts of flowers. The nectar-forming structure is commonly called a "nectary" (Fig. 22). Nectaries are usually so placed in a flower that the insect cannot reach them without becoming dusted with pollen and at the same time dusting pollen which he carries from other flowers upon the stigma. The nectaries in many flowers are cushion-like or cup-shaped (Fig. 22), and are placed at the bottom of the sepals (*Castanea*) or at the base of the petals as in lilies

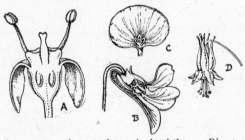

FIG. 22.—Various types of nectaries. *A*, buckthorn, *Rhamnus; B*, violet, *Viola; C*, buttercup, *Ranunculus; D*, columbine, *Aquilegia* (redrawn).

and buttercups or they may surround the basal part of the pistil. Flowers with slender corolla tubes usually have the nectaries toward the base of the tube so that the insect must actually crawl into the flower, or it must have a long tongue in order to get the nectar. In many other species the nectary has become a part of some specially formed portion of the flower as in the well-known spurs of the petals in the columbine, *Aquilegia*, and in certain distinctive petals in violet, *Viola*, in many orchids, *Orchis, Platanthera, Diura*, and in *Tropaeolum* (Fig. 21). A certain orchid, *Angraecum sesquipedale*, of Madagascar, produces a nectary that is of the form of a slender whiplash hanging from the under surface of the lip of the flower. The nectary reaches a length of $11\frac{1}{2}$ inches, and it bears 1 inch or more of nectar in the base. This flower is pollinated by a moth with a long tongue or proboscis.

Zygomorphy and Pollination.—Plants with zygomorphic or irregular flowers (Fig. 21) are of special interest in connection with a study of cross-pollination by insects. The corolla in such species is often of a size and form as to admit only certain types of insects on their way to secure pollen or nectar or both. Sometimes in these cases as in other tubular corollas an insect will cut a hole in the base of the corolla tube opposite the nectary and will feed in that manner instead of crawling into the flower. The insect cheats the flower in this degree, but fortunately there are not many insects that make this manner of feeding their regular practice.

Pollination in the Mints.—Members of the mint family, *Labiatae* (Fig. 144), snapdragon family, *Scrophulariaceae* (Fig. 141), bean family, *Leguminosae* (Fig. 146), and the orchid family, *Orchidaceae* (Fig. 203), furnish a great many varieties of zygomorphic flowers and related types of insect behavior. The glutinous sage, *Salvia glutinosa*, will serve to illustrate one of the floral mechanisms of mint flowers that assists in securing cross-pollination (Fig. 21, *A* and *B*). The corolla of the flower in this species is very deeply two-lipped, with the upper lip narrow, erect and developed in the form of a hood with the two stamens hidden underneath. The lower lip (composed of three petals) is broadened, flattish, and spreading, so as to form a natural landing board for the pollinating bee. The nectar is placed in the bottom of the slender corolla tube. Each of the two stamens has a short, upright filament which is prolonged above into a slender, curved connective bearing the anther at the upper end and below the point of connection with the filament it is extended into an enlarged bulbous or flattened base (Fig. 21, *B*). The form of the entire structure is such that it lies snugly within the narrow upper lip of the corolla, with the anther underneath near the hood-like top of the lip. The stamen is hinged to the corolla tube lightly at the point of the union between filament and connective, with the basal or short, rather heavy and blunt segment of the connective projecting into the cavity of the corolla tube, and the upper portion or much longer and slender segment of the connective closely following the curved form of the upper lip. The stamen is free to swing down and up on the hinge as indicated, but the lower, blunt portion of the connective is usually heavier than the upper portion of the connective and anther so that it serves as a bulb to hold the curved connective and anther in the position indicated unless the bulb is depressed by some outside force. (Fig. 21). When a bee lights upon the expanded lower lip and crawls into the corolla tube in search of nectar his forehead strikes the bulb or the lower end of the connective which is forced downward and backward as he moves farther into the corolla. This movement swings the long slender part of the connective and the anther from its position underneath the hooded upper lip and causes the anther to strike the back of the insect's body dusting it with pollen. The slender style is also usually placed underneath the upper lip of the corolla, but it is usually immature and short at the time the pollen of a given flower is ripe. The style matures later and hangs down between the two lips of the corolla so that when the bee enters an older flower in which the stigma is receptive the slender style is so curved that the stigmas strike the back of the bee at the same spot at which it was touched by the anthers of the younger flower.

Pollination in the Orchids.—The orchids show many interesting and curious adaptations to insure cross-pollination by insects (Fig. 21, *C, D, E,* and *I*). The case of the Madagascar orchid referred to with the long slender nectaries in which pollination is accomplished by a moth with a proboscis nearly 12 inches in length is one that illustrates to what extremes these relationships may go. The flower of the lady's slipper orchid, *Cypripedium,* is also adapted to pollination by insects of a particular kind (Fig. 21, *D*). One of the petals in this flower is formed like an inflated bag (the "slipper") with a relatively small aperture in the upper surface. The aperture is guarded or partly closed by a flap of membranous tissue which permits the entrance of many different kinds of insects in search of food. The pollen and stigma are so placed as to touch certain insects as they enter and leave these bag-like flowers. Certain bees enter the bag-like lip of the corolla through the opening in the upper surface. Most such insects that enter the sack find difficulty in crawling out at the point of entry and so they die and their bodies decompose within the sack. Bees with sufficient strength are able to escape by pushing their way through the opening between the flap and the edge of the aperture. Now, the stigma is on the underside of the flap (Fig. 21, *D*), and near it are two masses of gelatinous pollen (pollinia) so placed that the bee gathers them up as he crowds his way out of the trap, only to deposit some of them on the stigma of another flower when he enters it.

Sterile Pollen.—A curious feature of cross-pollination of flowers by insects is seen in the fact that intricately complete modifica-

tions for this purpose have frequently resulted in the development
of flowers that are absolutely sterile to their own pollen.   And
on the other hand, dozens of supposedly entomophilous species
have been found to be habitually self-pollinated.   Kirchner
has reported that this is true in fifteen species of European
orchids, and about 150 extra-European orchids are known to be
of the same nature.   These facts seem paradoxical in the light of
the common interpretations of floral behavior that have been
presented.   Why certain plants should go to all the trouble of
evolving flowers with striking colors and odors that certainly
attract insects, and with forms so intricately constructed as
to fit them for the visits of certain insects, and then remain
self-pollinated and self-fertilized without any evident loss of
vitality or vigor is indeed a puzzle.   The phenomenon should
at least teach the student that so-called "laws" in the biological
world are not to be trusted with the constancy of the laws of the
mathematical and astronomical world.

Germination of the Pollen Grains.—We have learned that the
principal function of the anther of the stamen is to produce the

pollen grains.   Each pollen grain is one of four
cells which are developed in a series of pollen
mother-cells that are deeply embedded in the
anther.   When the pollen sacs open to permit
the discharge of the pollen grains (or soon thereafter) each grain normally contains two or three
cells (nuclei) one of which is called the "tube
nucleus" and the other one or two are the
"generative nucleus" or the male cells or sperms.
The pollen grains germinate on the glandular
surface of the stigma and the principal structure
formed is a slender, very delicate, thin-walled
tubular structure known as the "pollen tube," in
the protoplasm of which are embedded the two

Fig. 23.—Ger-
minating pollen
grain showing the
two sperms and
the tube nucleus
(*redrawn*).

sperms or gamete nuclei and the tube nucleus (Fig. 23).   The
pollen tube emerges from the pollen grain through one of the germ
pores which are characteristic spots in the exine or outer wall of
the pollen grain.   The pollen tube, with the tube nucleus near
the tip, continues its growth through the style, however long or
short it may be, until it enters the cavity of the ovary.   The
tube is then directed toward the open end of an ovule which it
enters.   It is reported that the older portion of the pollen tube

withers as the apex advances farther and farther on its course toward the ovary.

Form and Position of Ovules.—The ovules are the most significant parts of the pistil for it is within them that the *eggs* are developed. A normal ovule is a tiny, very delicate, oval or egg-shaped structure attached to the placenta by means of a firm stalk or *funiculus* (Figs. 24, 25 and 26). In some flowers the funiculus is straight and the ovule then stands out straight into the cavity of the ovary. This type of ovule is called an "orthotropous" ovule. The funiculus in other cases is elongated and grown to the rest of the ovule which is curved about nearly at right angles to the stalk, and thus produces a "campylotropous" ovule. In a third type the funiculus of the mature ovule becomes

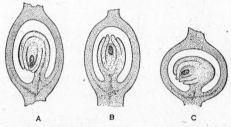

Fig. 24.—Sectional diagrams of ovaries to show types of ovules and their attachment. *A*, anatropous ovule; *B*, orthotropous ovule; *C*, campylotropous ovule.

curved at the apex to such a degree that the body of the ovule lies against it, and completely reversed so that the opening is directed toward the placenta. This is the "anatropous" type of ovule. The orthotropous ovule is regarded as the most primitive type, but the anatropous type is the most common among the modern flowering plants (Fig. 24).

Detailed Structure of the Ovule.—Each ovule proper is composed of one or two coats or *integuments* enclosing a rounded mass of very soft, juicy tissue called the "nucellus" (Fig. 24). The integuments grow outward from the funiculus and almost completely surround the nucellus, though there is always left an opening, called the "micropyle," at the outer end of the ovule. Embedded in the nucellar tissue is a relatively large cavity or *embryo sac*, within which there is at first a single large nucleus (Figs. 24 and 25). The term is prophetic of the fact that the embryo plant of the new generation is to be formed within this cavity. The primary embryo-sac nucleus grows and divides a number of times to produce eight nuclei which are arranged in two groups of four each, one group at the micropylar end and the other group at the opposite end of the embryo sac. Then one nucleus from each of these groups moves to the center of the sac and the two fuse in that position. The group of three nuclei at the outer end of the sac is called the "egg apparatus." One of these is the *egg*, and the other two the *synergids* (Fig. 25).

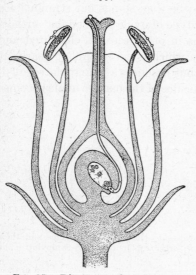

The three nuclei at the opposite pole are called the "antipodals." Normally only one of the three nuclei in the egg apparatus is an egg, but the others may possibly serve as eggs also under certain unknown conditions. The antipodals have also been known to produce embryos, as have some of the cells of the nucellus immediately surrounding the embryo sac (Fig. 25).

FERTILIZATION OF THE EGG

When the normal cells within the embryo sac have completed the above cycle of development, and have become grouped as indicated,

Fig. 25.—Diagram to show the general anatomy of a complete flower and the process of fertilization.

the embryo sac is mature and the egg is ready to be fertilized. If the sperms from a bursting pollen tube are discharged into the embryo sac at this time, one of the sperms *unites* with the *egg* and *fertilization* is thereby accomplished (Figs. 25 and 26). The other sperm often passes on deeper into the sac to fuse with the *equatorial nucleus*. This phenomenon has been called "double fertilization."

Development of the Embryo.—The fertilized egg or zygote absorbs food and begins to grow and divide to form the embryo which gradually pushes back into the cavity. Concurrently with this development the equatorial nucleus (primary endosperm nucleus) with which the second sperm fused also begins to divide and to form a tissue which comes to surround the embryo more or less completely in many flowering plants. This tissue, which is usually very richly supplied with accumulated foods, is known as the "endosperm" (Fig. 26).

Maturation of the Seed.—Embryo and endosperm (when present) continue to develop rather rapidly and with these activities come very profound changes in the ovule and the surrounding ovary. These changes culminate in the transformation of the *ovules* into *seeds* and of the *ovary* into the *fruit* (Fig. 26). The micropyle is sealed by a plug of cork and the coats or integuments of the ovule harden, dry out, and in many cases

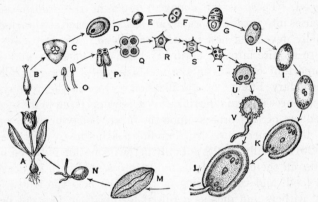

FIG. 26.—Diagrams to illustrate the sexual cycle in flowers. *A*, mature plant with flower; *B* to *K*, inclusive, structure of the ovary and stages in the development of the embryo sac and egg to the time of fertilization; *O* to *V*, inclusive, structure of the anther and development of the pollen grains to the formation of the pollen tube and sperms; *L*, pollen tube entering the micropyle of the ovule; *M*, embryo that develops in the embryo sac by the growth of the fertilized egg, and seed developed by the transformation of the ovule; *N*, germination of the seed.

develop a very characteristic color, to remain as the seed coats. After a series of well-defined early growth stages the embryo becomes a clearly established structure with its root, stem, and leaves outlined and it comes to fill the cavity of the old embryo sac. In some cases the embryo uses the food furnished by the endosperm and surrounding nucellus to such a degree that little or no food remains so that the embryo practically fills the cavity inside the integuments.

With the above significant activities completed the subsequent changes in the flower merely involve the maturation of seeds and fruit which introduces so many striking features that they may be treated more appropriately in a separate chapter.

CHAPTER IV

FRUITS AND SEEDS

One series of floral activities comes to a close when the eggs in flowers are fertilized and another chain of important processes is initiated. These latter changes result in the *transformation* of ovaries into *fruits* and *ovules* into *seeds,* and each seed includes a partially developed new plantlet or *embryo.* We may now proceed to inquire into the nature and behavior of fruits and seeds as important elements in the life histories of flowering plants.

Secondary Effects of Fertilization.—One of the remarkable consequences of sexual fertilization in flowers is seen in the secondary effects of this process upon the future behavior of the ovary and its immediately surrounding structures. Fertilization (Fig. 26) normally results not only in the formation of the embryo, but also in the change of the ovule into a seed with its accumulated food, and the ripening of the ovary into the fruit. The ovary withers and dies as a rule if fertilization does not occur. It may be pointed out that the embryo would be quite helpless in most cases to develop a new individual in the absence of the secondary developments involved in the seed and fruit. These furnish the embryo with food and afford significant protection until environmental conditions render further development possible.

FRUITS

Definition of Fruits.—The term "fruit" has a very much broader and more significant meaning in plants than is reflected in the popular use of the term in daily life. The botanist endeavors to base his concepts in this connection, as in the case of all other structures, on the point of view of the plant, so to speak. The development and structure of fruits may be understood best from a study of the flower parts from which they develop. The regular features of the ovary may be recognized in many mature fruits, even in such enormous ones as the coconut and watermelon. Among flowering plants, fruits are *fundamentally* the transformed and *ripened ovaries* of the flowers containing *seeds.* No other parts of the flower are associated with the fruit in the great majority of species, but in certain species some other portion of the flower, such as the receptacle (as in strawberry and apple) also feels the stimulus of fertilization to such a degree that it becomes greatly modified and may be inseparably associated with the mature fruit (Figs. 32 and 34).

Popular Conceptions Are Misleading.—Such a conception of fruits will at once include many structures not popularly known as fruits and exclude certain well-known structures commonly thought of as fruits. Botanically, a kernel of wheat or oats (Fig. 31, *E*), an acorn (Fig. 168), a sunflower "seed" (Fig. 27, *E*), a flaxseed pod, a tomato, and a peanut pod are true fruits, but

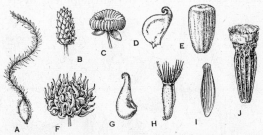

Fig. 27.—Dry fruits. *A*, a tailed achene of Pasque flower, *Pulsatilla* (*after Le M. and Dec.*); *B*, cluster of achenes of Adonis, *Adonis* (*after Le M. and Dec.*); *C*, achenes of water plantain, *Alisma* (*after Le M. and Dec.*); *D*, single achene of buttercup, *Ranunculus* (*after Le M. and Dec.*); *E*, achene of sunflower, *Helianthus* (*after Baillon*); *F*, cluster of achenes of Clematis, *Clematis* (*after Baillon*); *G*, single achene of Adonis, *Adonis* (*after Le M. and Dec.*); *H*, achene of cornflower, *Centaurea*, with pappus (*after Le M. and Dec.*); *I*, ribbed seed of *Escallonia* (*after Le M. and Dec.*); *J*, achene of teasel, *Dipsacus* (*after Baillon*).

such is not the popular conception. Popularly, a navel orange, a banana, and even a potato are known as fruits, but they certainly lack some of the regular features of fruits from the botanical point of view. The age-old attempt to distinguish between "fruits and vegetables" merely reflects the common fact that popular conceptions and definitions frequently cut across well-defined scientific knowledge and usage.

Variations in Fruits.—Fruits exhibit almost as great variety in size, color, shape, texture, number, duration, etc. as do flowers (Figs. 27, 28, 29, 30, 31, 32, 33 and 34). Some fruits are so small as to be scarcely visible to the unaided eye, but others are enormous things, perhaps more than a foot in diameter and weighing several pounds as in the coconut and the Jack fruit of tropical forests.

Types of Fruits.—The two broadest groups or types of fruits
are *fleshy fruits* and *dry fruits*.   Most fruits may be included in
one or the other of these two types.   Fleshy fruits (Figs. 32, 33
and 34) are commonly very watery or juicy and more or less
brightly colored.   The colors of fleshy fruits usually contrast
with their background, a feature which is significant with reference to dissemination by animals.   Dry fruits (Figs. 27, 28, 29,
30 and 31), on the other hand, are usually gray, brown, or some
other dull color and they do not contrast with their surroundings
except in a few cases.   Many shapes are seen in the fruits of
flowering plants, but the form of the mature fruit is frequently
that of the ovary.   They often become greatly distorted, however, by later growth and by the development of features that

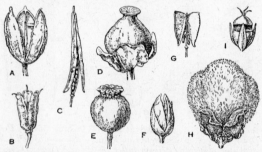

Fig. 28.—Dry fruits.   *A*, capsule of iris, *Iris* (*after Le M. and Dec.*); *B*,
follicles of monkshood, *Aconitum* (*after Le M. and Dec.*); *C*, silique of a mustard,
Cheirinia (*after Le M. and Dec.*); *D*, capsule of waterlily, *Nymphaea*; *E*, capsule
of poppy, *Papaver* (*after Baillon*); *F*, capsule of tobacco, *Nicotiana* (*after Le M.
and Dec.*); *G*, silicle of shepherd's purse, *Bursa* (*after Le M. and Dec.*); *H*, opened
capsule with cottony seeds of cotton, *Gossypium* (*after Baillon*); *I*, utricle
of amaranth, *Amaranthus* (*after Le M. and Dec.*).

are not prominent in their youth.   The many forms of crook-
necked and scalloped squashes and the great variety of seed
capsules are scarcely anticipated in the structure of the ovary
at the time of fertilization.   The ovary wall becomes very thin
and dry in most dry fruits.   In one-seeded dry fruits the ovary
wall is so thin and it envelops the dry seed so tightly and conforms
so closely with the shape of the seed that the whole passes as a
"seed," as in sunflower, dandelion, buttercup, clematis, etc.
(Fig. 27).   The kernels of wheat, corn, and many other grasses
are in reality dry, one-seeded fruits in which the ovary walls and
seed coats are extremely thin, dry, and practically inseparable.

The food in dry fruits is largely confined to the seeds.   In
fleshy fruits the ovary wall, or some part of it, as well as the

internal tissues in many, become thickened but remain soft, fleshy, juicy, palatable, nutritious, and attractive. The food in fleshy fruits is largely accumulated in the thickened walls or partitions of the fruit, and the food within the seeds is commonly discarded or is in such small quantity as to be negligible from the standpoint of animal nutrition. The number of fruits produced varies greatly for different species but is likely to be determined in any given species by the age of the individual and environmental conditions. Likewise the duration of fruits is extremely variable, probably being longer in dry fruits as a class than in fleshy fruits. The very fleshiness of fleshy fruits contributes (through more rapid decay) to their earlier disintegration.

Number of Seeds in Fruits.—Many fruits, especially dry fruits, and some fleshy fruits, produce a single seed, but many other dry fruits and fleshy fruits contain scores, hundreds, or even thousands of seeds. Dry fruits with a single seed are usually separated from the plant as a whole, the fruit functioning much as a single seed. But dry fruits with many seeds usually open at maturity to permit the escape of the seeds, and the empty fruits may remain on the plant indefinitely. Fleshy fruits normally remain closed at maturity whether they contain one or more seeds. The seeds of dry fruits are released from the fruit by propulsion or by the decay of the surrounding fleshy tissues, or by the digestion of those tissues within the bodies of animals that have eaten the fruits.

Since fruits are very helpful in the classification of plants and in the delimitation of many of the families of flowering plants we should examine somewhat more closely the common varieties of dry and fleshy fruits.

TYPES OF DRY FRUITS

Dry fruits may be subdivided into two general groups depending upon the number of seeds produced and whether the fruit opens naturally at maturity (dehiscent) or remains closed (indehiscent).

The Achene.—The commonest type of one-seeded, indehiscent, dry fruit is the *achene* (Fig. 27), produced by the buttercup, strawberry, arrowhead, and the sunflowers and their kin. Functionally achenes are little more than seeds, although the thin, dry ovary wall which covers the single seed very closely may serve some useful purpose in certain cases. The fruit of clematis

(Figs. 27, *F*, and 39, *C*) is essentially an achene in which the style persists and becomes greatly elongated and plumose. In many composites the vestigial calyx known as the *pappus* remains at the top of the achene as a whorl of papery scales, barbed bristles, or a tuft of long, silky hairs (Figs. 27, *H* and 178, *C* and *D*). In these forms, as in the clematis, these additional details are of great significance in connection with dissemination.

The Samara.—A *samara* is a dry, one-seeded, indehiscent fruit (Figs. 29, 38 and 166) in which portions of the outer wall of the ovary become extended to produce more or less prominent wings as in the elm, maple, and

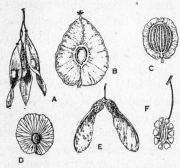

FIG. 29.—Dry fruits. *A*, winged fruits of tree-of-Heaven, *Ailanthus*; *B*, samara of elm, *Ulmus* (*after Baillon*); *C*, wing-margined mericarp of *Lomatium* (*after Baillon*); *D*, samara of *Hiraea* (*after Le M. and Dec.*); *E*, winged fruit of maple, *Acer*; *F*, lobed samara of *Artedia* (*after Kerner*).

ash. Certain plants (*Dipterocarpus, Rumex*) produce a winged calyx which surrounds the fruit and serves much the same rôle as the wings formed from the ovary wall.

Nuts and Nut-like Fruits.— *Nuts* are rather complicated dry fruits, commonly with a single seed usually formed from an ovary with more than one carpel, and supplied with a variety of coverings (Figs. 30, 33, 167 and 168). The shell is usually quite hard and is more or less completely overlaid with a covering which is hairy, scaly, fibrous, or almost as hard and resistant as the ovary wall (shell) itself. The *acorn* (Fig. 168) of an oak is a nut which is partially enveloped by a cup formed at the base. The acorns of certain oaks and the nuts of hazel, beech, and chestnut are more nearly completely covered by a leafy or very rough or spiny coat corresponding to the acorn cup of the oak. The hull or husk of the walnut (Fig. 167), butternut, and hickory nut represent another type of covering in which flower parts other than the pistil take part. The husk of the coconut (Fig. 30, *A*) is very thick and contains valuable fibers. The betel nut is the fruit of another palm resembling the coconut except that the husk is much more loose and open. The smooth, three-sided pili nut has an extremely thick and hard shell. Brazil nuts (Fig. 36, *A*) are the seeds of a large Amazonian tree in which the fruit is a spherical or pear-shaped capsule 2 to 3 inches in diameter with a very hard woody wall. Each bears from 12 to 30 "nuts" or seeds.

Mericarp or Schizocarp.—The characteristic paired fruit of the carrot and its relatives is known as a "mericarp" or "schizocarp" (Figs. 29, *C*, and 172). This is developed from a bicarpellary ovary in which the two opposite carpels develop into independent fruits, each bearing a single seed. Each of the one-seeded halves pulls away from the common axis between them.

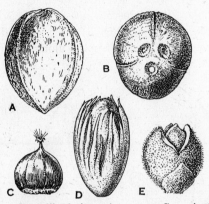

Fig. 30.—Nuts and nut-like fruits. *A*, coconut, *Cocos*, in the husk (*after Le M. and Dec.*); *B*, end view of coconut with husk removed (*after Le M. and Dec.*); *C*, nut of chesnut, *Castanea* (*after Le M. and Dec.*); *D*, fruit of nutmeg, *Myristica*, showing aril (*after Baillon*); *E*, female flower of *Myristica* with fruit developing (*after Baillon*).

The Caryopsis or Grain.—The fruit of most grasses including the cereals is peculiar and quite unique. This one-seeded fruit is known as a "grain or caryopsis," and it is characterized by such an intimate relationship and union between the inclosed seed and the enveloping ovary that the two are separated with difficulty, even with the aid of the microscope in following the development of the fruit from the ovary (Figs. 31, *E*, and 199). The caryopsis is little more than a seed for all practical purposes, though from the strictly botanical viewpoint it must be classified as a fruit.

The Capsule.—A *capsule* (Figs. 28, 31, 39, *B*, and 113) is a dry, dehiscent fruit developed from a compound ovary in which each carpel opens longitudinally along the carpellary septa (*Azalea*) or in the middle of the carpels (lily) or by pores toward the top of each carpel (poppy). Each ripening carpel in the capsule produces several or many seeds, and as they ripen, the carpels tend to pull away from each other especially at the apex of the fruit.

The Silique.—The *silique* (Figs. 28, *C* and 121) is a several-seeded fruit developed in a bicarpellary ovary in which the two carpels pull away from the central partition or septum at maturity. This is the common type of fruit in the *Cruciferae*, or mustard family (Fig. 121). The common radish, *Raphanus*, is a familiar mustard in which this does not occur. The capsule or silique of this plant is indehiscent.

The Legume.—A *legume* (Fig. 31, *C*) is formed from a simple pistil and at maturity the fruit splits along two opposite longi-

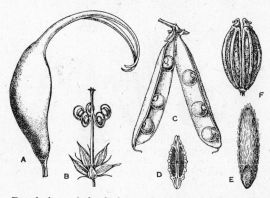

Fig. 31.—Dry fruits. *A*, hooked capsule of unicorn plant, *Martynia* (*after Le M. and Dec.*); *B*, tailed fruits of geranium, *Geranium* (*after Baillon*); *C*, legume of pea, *Pisum* (*after Le M. and Dec.*); *D*, sectional view of mericarp of *Lomatium* (*after Baillon*); *E*, grain of oat, *Avena* (*after Baillon*); *F*, mericarp of caraway, *Carum* (*after Baillon*).

tudinal sutures. This type of fruit is very common among the members of the bean and pea family which fact has led to the common name "legumes" being applied to that family. The legume in some species is curiously coiled, as in alfalfa or lucern, in some species of which the pod is so tightly coiled and so spiny as to resemble a bur. The legumes of certain tropical plants are very large and leathery or woody.

The Loment.—A *loment* is in reality a legume, but it is peculiar because it is usually very flat and tends to break up into several one-seeded segments. The surface of the segments in the

oments of some ot our native American legumes (*Meibomia*) is
covered by many low hooked hairs which make them very tena-
ciously adherent to one's clothing if one brushes against the
fruits in our prairies or woodlands. The relation of this feature
to dissemination is obvious.

The Follicle.—A *follicle* (Fig. 28, *B*) is a dry, several-seeded
fruit formed from a single carpel which splits along one side only.
There may be two or more follicles produced from a single flower
as in the milkweed, dogbane, larkspur, columbine, peony. The
two follicles produced by each flower in the milkweed and dogbane are formed from each of the two carpels in the bicarpellary
ovary.

TYPES OF FLESHY FRUITS

Fleshy fruits (Figs. 32, 33 and 34) are all indehiscent. There
are three general groups of fleshy fruits on the basis of the number
of pistils or carpels represented, and the number of seeds pro-

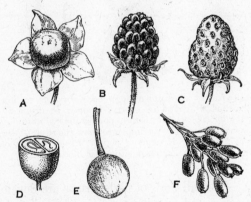

Fig. 32.—Fleshy fruits. *A*, berry of belladonna, *Atropa* (*after Le M. and
Dec.*); *B*, aggregate fruit, "berry," of raspberry, *Rubus* (*after Baillon*); *C*, similar
fruit of strawberry, *Fragaria* (*after Baillon*); *D*, section of berry of coffee, *Coffea*
(*after Baillon*); *E*, berry of *Smilax* (*after Le M. and Dec.*); *F*, cluster of berries of
barberry, *Berberis* (*after Baillon*).

duced. They all agree in the development of considerable
fleshy tissue as the ovary or axis is changed into the fruit.

The Drupe.—A *drupe* (Fig. 33, *B* and *C*) or "stone fruit"
is formed from a simple pistil as a rule, or at least the fruit is
typically single-celled, and it normally produces a single seed,
though now and then a second seed is formed. The other com-

mon features of a drupe include an exterior layer or *pericarp* of fleshy tissue, beneath which is a heavy stony layer or *endocarp* the "stone," with the seed proper lying inside the stone or "pit." The morphology of the layers varies somewhat for different drupes. The fruits of peaches, plums, cherries, olives, and apricots are the most familiar examples of drupes. The almond may perhaps be considered to be a drupe also, since it is fleshy like a peach until it is well grown, but it becomes dry as the seed matures and finally the covering (pericarp) splits open and the nut or "pit" is uncovered (Fig. 33, *F*). The part that is eaten in the almond is, of course, the seed. A coconut (Fig. 30, *A* and *B*) and a walnut (Fig. 167) have characteristics of a drupe, but in both of these the pericarp eventually becomes dry and fibrous.

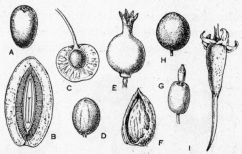

FIG. 33.—Fleshy fruits. *A*, drupe of dogwood, *Cornus; B*, section of drupe of olive, *Olea; C*, section of drupe of cherry, *Prunus; D*, drupe of buckthorn, *Rhamnus* (*after Baillon*); *E*, leathery fruit of pomegranate, *Punica* (*after Baillon*); *F*, endocarp of peach, *Amygdalus*, laid open to show the seed; *G*, drupe-like fruit of Russian olive, *Elaeagnus; H*, fruit of pepper, *Piper; I*, fruit of mangrove, *Rhizophora*, with seedling developing in situ (*after Baillon*).

The Berry.—Several kinds of fleshy fruits are developed from flowers with compound or polycarpellate pistils. A *berry* (Fig. 32, *A*) is a fleshy, many-seeded fruit that is usually developed from a compound ovary in such a manner that the whole structure has a very thin covering and is internally very fleshy and juicy and the seeds are imbedded in the common flesh of a single ovary. Illustrations of berries are seen in currants, gooseberries, cranberries, blueberries, guava, and tomatoes.

The Pepo.—A *pepo* is a berry-like fruit of considerable size in which the outer wall of the fruit is developed from the receptacle and this becomes toughish or very firm and hard. The internal structure of a pepo is commonly much like that of a berry. Common examples of the pepo are seen in the water-melon, cucumber, gourd, cantaloupe, pumpkin, and squash.

Citrocarp or Hesperidium.—The fruit of the orange, lemon, lime, and grapefruit (Fig. 34, *C*) is more or less berry-like inter-nally, but this type is usually given the separate designation "hesperidium." The term "citrocarp" would be a good expres-sion for this type of fruit since *hesperidium* has a purely fanciful mythological origin. The thick, leathery rind beset with numer-ous oil glands, and the interior mass composed of several wedge-shaped locules, with or without seeds, are characteristic of this kind of fruit.

The Pome.—A *pome* is a fruit that is mostly fleshy throughout but it is developed largely from the cup-shaped receptacle which more or less completely surrounds the several carpels in the flower. Well-known examples of the pome are found in the fruits of apples, pears, and quinces. The flesh of the ripe apple consists very largely of the greatly thickened cortex of the floral axis or recep-tacle ("calyx cup") and the pith of the receptacle. The five carpels with their smooth, parchment-like compartments occupy the central position and make up, with certain other structures, what is known as the "core" of the apple. That is, the "core" really contains the ripened pistils, but in this case they are not included in the popular conception of a fruit, at least they are not eaten, unless perchance one is very hungry.

Aggregate and Accessory Fruits.—A third general class of fleshy fruits are very peculiar in their morphological composition because of the interrelationship between the receptacle and ovary and the excessive development of the receptacle. As a rule many ovaries and many seeds are involved in the development of these fruits and in some of them several to many distinct flowers are represented in the finished fruits.

An *aggregate* fruit is a fleshy structure developed by the single receptacle of a single flower, but the receptacle becomes more or less enlarged and bears many simple, true fruits of the nature of achenes or drupes. This fruit is derived from a single flower with many separate pistils, as in the custard apple (*Anona*), strawberry, blackberry, loganberry, and dewberry (Figs. 32 and 34). The fruit of a strawberry (Fig. 32, *C*) is composed of an enormously enlarged receptacle, more or less uniformly dotted with numerous widely separated *achenes*. The true fruits here are the achenes, but the edible portion is the axis, the true fruits being eaten as a rule as "seeds" because it is a nuisance to remove them. Some writers have made the strawberry the type of another class of fruits called "accessory fruits," because of the dominant part played by the axis in the ripe structure. In the blackberry (Fig. 32, *B*), dewberry, and loganberry the receptacle does not develop to such a degree as in the strawberry, but the many individual carpels enlarge and are transformed into "drupelets" exactly like so many diminutive cherries clinging to the receptacle. Here we have an *aggregate* of fruits which together make up the major volume of edible material in these fruits. These drupelets are directly comparable to the achenes (or "seeds") of the strawberry. The raspberry presents another

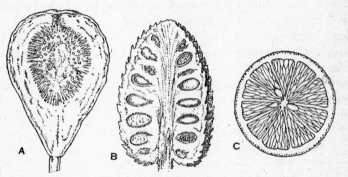

Fig. 34.—*A*, vertical section of the fruit of fig, *Ficus (after Baillon); B*, vertical section of the fruit of custard apple, *Anona (after Baillon); C*, transverse section of fruit of orange, *Citrus (after Le M. and Dec.)*.

difference in that the cluster of drupelets separate from the receptacle when mature, so that the ripe "berry," consisting of a cup-shaped cluster of drupelets may be lifted off from the dome-like receptacle. In the strawberry it is the large fleshy axis or receptacle that contributes the food, and the true fruits or achenes ("seeds") are eaten because they cannot be readily avoided; in the blackberry, dewberry, and loganberry the important edible part is the cluster of drupelets or true fruits, the axis being relatively small and unimportant; in the raspberry only the aggregation of drupelets or true fruits are eaten, since the receptacle remains on the bush when the berries are picked. Thus we see that these so-called "berries" are structures really very different from true berries in the botanical sense.

Multiple Fruits.—*Multiple fruits* in contrast to aggregate fruits are formed from the ovaries of many separate closely clustered flowers, or, in other words, these fruits are derived from a cluster of flowers instead of from a single flower. Examples of multiple fruits are seen in the mulberry and pineapple. In the mulberry the clusters of pistillate flowers are separate from the staminate flowers, and they are crowded very closely together. Each of these flowers has a single, one-celled ovary enclosed by a thick, fleshy calyx of four sepals. After fertilization the sepals close over the ovaries, each unit becomes increasingly fleshy and enlarged and more or less united to its neighbors to form the "berry." The ripe pineapple is also a cluster of fruits formed by single separate flowers densely clustered on a central axis. The floral bracts and other flower parts become fleshy and greatly enlarged and consolidated into what appears to be a single unit structure at maturity, quite misleading as to its proper morphological interpretation.

The Fruit of the Fig.—The fig (Fig. 34, *A*) produces another peculiar type of fruit in which many flowers are involved. The fig is in reality a hollowed-out receptacle with a lining of numerous, tiny, separate flowers. Pistillate and staminate flowers may be mingled together within the same receptacle or, in some species, they are produced by different receptacles. Each pistillate flower has a simple pistil and little or no perianth. After fertilization this ovary develops into a nutlet with a single seed and the whole structure becomes more or less imbedded in the wall of the enlarged and very fleshy or gelatinous receptacle. This curious thing has been called a "syconium." The ripe fig consists of the enlarged, fleshy receptacle which encloses many nutlets ("seeds") produced by the pistillate flowers which line the cavity of the receptacle (Fig. 34, *A*). Here again is a fruit in which the receptacle constitutes the major portion of the fruit.

The various types of fruits considered in this chapter may be brought together in tabular form as follows:

			Achene
		One-seeded, indehiscent	Samara
			Nut
			Schizocarp
			Caryopsis
Dry Fruits			
		Many-seeded, dehiscent	Capsule
			Silique
			Legume
			Loment
			Follicle
		Pistil mostly simple and one-seeded	Drupe
			Berry
Fleshy Fruits		Pistil compound, but single flower. Seeds many	Pepo
			Pome
			Hesperidium
			Aggregate
		Pistils many from one or many flowers. Seeds many	Accessory
			Multiple
			Syconium

Tabular Summary of Fruits

SEEDS

Some additional features of seeds as developed by flowering plants will now be considered.

The great variation in detail that the seeds of different flowering plants reveal is perhaps surprising when it is recalled that they are formed within the ovary under conditions that appear to be quite uniform. So characteristic are seeds that they are very useful agents in the classification of plants. Indeed, many species of flowering plants produce seeds that are so strikingly characteristic as in themselves to furnish an absolutely infallible clue to the identity of the species or variety. Plants that are, superficially, very similar often produce seeds that are strikingly different. And, on the other hand, seeds that are closely similar may be produced by plants that are very different, as in the dodder and alfalfa. Federal and state seed experts utilize such facts in the detection and measurement of impurities (foreign seeds) in commercial seeds.

The Origin and Nature of Seeds.—A seed is produced as a result of the fertilization of an egg within the embryo sac of an ovule (Figs. 25 and 26), which, in turn, is attached at some point inside the ovary of the flower. There may be as many seeds matured as there are ovules, but that probably seldom happens. The difficulties surrounding pollination and fertilization interfere to prevent the development of so large a proportion of the ovules into seeds. There are scores of ovules in the common commercial banana ovary and there are hundreds or even thousands of them in the ovary of flowers of many orchids but none of these ovules may develop seeds at all. A certain orchid, *Maxillaria*, produces as many as 1,750,000 seeds in the ovary of a single flower. In the cherry and almond there are usually two ovules in the ovary. Only one of them, however, regularly develops into a seed, though now and then both form seeds.

Seeds are usually relatively small structures when they are mature and become separated from the parent plant. Nevertheless, they may carry a living embryo for great distances and under proper conditions they may give rise to a new individual far from the plant that produced them. Man finds in seeds a very convenient form in which to transport plants from one area of the world to another.

Physical Features of Seeds.—The size, shape, texture, color and longevity of seeds are as variable as flowers (Figs. 35, 36, and 37). Certain tropical orchids produce seeds that are as fine as dust, whereas in the coconut the seed may be several inches in diameter. Although we have a generalized conception of the shape of seeds few of us are aware of the multitude of variations in form and surface features that are to be seen in seeds.

Typically more or less globular or oval, they range in form to extremely thin and flat, or greatly elongated, smooth, wrinkled, pitted, angled, furrowed, twisted, coiled, or irregularly distorted, and often more or less covered with hairs as in cotton, *Gossypium*, milkweed, *Asclepias*, or supplied with broad and extremely delicate, membranous wings as in *Pithecoctenium* (Figs. 35, 36, and 37). Seeds are typically very firm and hard when ripe,

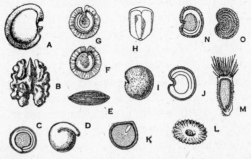

Fig. 35.—Seeds. *A*, flat seed of moonwort, *Lunaria* (*after Le M. and Dec.*); *B*, walnut, *Juglans; C*, lamb's quarters, *Chenopodium; D*, beet, *Beta; E*, Russian olive *Elaeagnus; F* and *G*, winged seed of *Spergularia* (*after Le M. and Dec.*); *H*, fleshy seed of pomegranate, *Punica; I*, bouncing bet, *Saponaria; J*, section of same; *K*, iris, *Iris; L*, spiderwort, *Tradescantia* (*after Le M. and Dec.*); *M*, section of achene of cornflower, *Centaurea*, showing the single seed within; *N* and *O*, baby's, breath, *Gypsophila*.

but they may become very soft during the germination period. The seeds of a tropical South American palm, *Phytelephas*, furnish the "vegetable ivory" of commerce, and are used in making buttons.

Significance of Colors in Seeds.—The variety of coloring and color patterns are perhaps the most conspicuous external differentiation that seeds show. Nearly every color known can be matched in seeds from shining jet black to less somber brown and gray to peculiarly striking bright blue, yellow, red, scarlet, etc. The mingling or mottling of colors and tints is also a noteworthy feature of many seeds. As in fruits the gay colors are to be associated with very different possibilities of dissemination than is true for the more somber or dull-colored seeds. Seeds and fruits that are scattered by wind or water are usually inconspicuously colored, but the bright and showy seeds and fruits more commonly appeal to animal agents of migration.

Seeds and Fruits Often Confused.—Seeds and some of the smaller fruits are not always readily distinguished. This is particularly true for the dry one-seeded fruits such as achenes (Fig. 27), which for all practical purposes are in reality seeds. The possible confusion in this regard with reference to the morphology of the grains of corn, wheat, and other grasses has already been pointed out. The use of the term "seed" by the practical grower of plants carries with it the thought that an essential item of the most common and useful methods of plant propagation involve the presence of true seeds, whatever may be the nature of associated structures. Onion seed and turnip seed in the everyday sense are also seed in the botanical sense. Seed corn and seed wheat as used in ordinary agricultural parlance are in reality true fruits (caryopses) of a highly specialized type. Seed oats and seed barley frequently are even more than seeds and fruits, for in many varieties of these common crops the old dry scales (flowering glumes and palets) of the flowers have persisted and completely surround the grain as the "husk." Potato "seed" is almost invariably composed of tubers or subdivisions of tubers that are planted in the soil. Few people have ever seen the true fruits and seeds of the Irish potato. The fruits ("fruit balls") are much like diminutive tomatoes (berries) produced by potato flowers in the usual way and bearing many seeds. These are not used at all in the regular production of our great crops of potatoes. The "seed" so-called of sweet potato is composed of roots or sections of the roots of this plant. The true seeds of the sweet potato are produced in a capsule much like that of an ordinary morning-glory. The sweet potato is, indeed, a species of true morning-glory.

There are also numerous true seeds that are not popularly regarded as seeds. Thus the *kernels* of nuts such as walnuts, pecans, almonds (Figs. 35, *B* and 36, *A*), etc., are true seeds, as are "peanuts," beans, and peas (Fig. 31, *C*), although these are not commonly regarded as such.

Distinguishing Features of Seeds.—Botanically, true seeds possess certain regular features which become their distinguishing characteristics. The embryo plant inside is the most important constituent of a seed.   This is merely a new living plant whose growth has been suspended for a time by conditions attendant to the ripening of fruit and seed.   This embryo always has a central axis or stem called the "hypocotyl," bearing at one end the embryonic root or *radicle,* and at the other end the rudiments of a *bud.*   The seeds of some plants produce embryos so large that this bud becomes so well developed as to produce a distinctly leaf-like structure called the "plumule."   The *cotyledons* or "seed leaves" are attached to the stem at some distance below the terminal bud or plumule.   Most flowering plants (Dicotyledons) produce two opposite cotyledons, and in some of these the cotyledons are more or less distinctly leaf-like, but in most species they are decidedly lacking in the typical features of

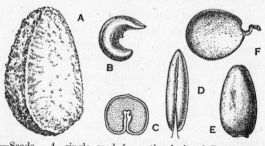

Fig. 36.—Seeds.   *A,* single seed from the fruit of Brazilnut, *Bertholettia; B,* moonseed, *Menispermum; C,* transverse section of horny seed of date, *Phoenix; D,* surface view of seed of *Phoenix; E,* chocolate, *Theobroma; F,* Kentucky coffetree, *Gymnocladus.*

leaves.   The cotyledons are frequently crowded out of the seed along with radicle, hypocotyl, and plumule, at the time of germination and actually reach above the surface of the ground where they develop chlorophyll and function as true leaves. In many other flowering plants especially in the grasses (Monocotyledons) the situation with reference to the cotyledons is quite different.   The seeds of corn or wheat, for instance, show an embryo with hypocotyl, radicle, and plumule, but there is a single lateral cotyledon.   This cotyledon is scarcely at all leaf-like, never being pushed outside the seed during germination and developing chlorophyll, but remaining within the seed and functioning as a digestive organ for the embryo.   Such a cotyledon is known as the scutellum.

Seeds with Several Embryos.—Seeds normally contain but a single embryo.   A number of flowering plants, however, produce seeds with more than one embryo. Thus certain members of the citrus or orange group, particularly the grapefruit, *Citrus grandis*, frequently show this condition. One sometimes finds several seeds with more than one embryo in a single grapefruit. If all of the seeds of a series of grapefruits are germinated (very easily accomplished) one will almost invariably secure a larger number of seedlings from the fruits than there were seeds in the respective fruits. The extra embryos in seeds have diverse origin, from nucellar buds, and possibly from multiple embryo sacs within a given nucellus. The phenomenon of polyembryony is doubtless more interesting than significant, because it is too rare to be of any great value as a supplement to normal reproduction.

Foods and Other Materials in Seeds.—Another important item in the makeup of seeds is the *food* which was accumulated in the seed before it was cut off from the parent plant. The three classes of foods: *carbohydrates*, including sugars, starches, and celluloses; *proteins;* and *fats,* including rather heavy nitrogenous foods as well as heavy and lighter oils, are included in greater or less quantities in practically all seeds. The seeds of certain species, such as beans, buckwheat, and cereals, such as maize, wheat, rice, are rich in starch; in others, such as peanuts, walnuts, Brazil nuts, castor beans, flax, coconut, and cotton there is a relatively high proportion of fats; and in others, such as beans and peas, there is a considerable quantity of protein. The seeds of certain species, notably asparagus, coffee, datepalm, and vegetable ivory, contain massive tissues in which the cell walls become enormously thickened by the accumulation of secondary cellulose (hemicellulose) which also serves as food for the embryo during the period of germination (Fig. 36, *C*). The seeds of the vegetable ivorypalm produce large masses of an exceedingly hard, bony tissue of this sort that is used commercially in the manufacture of "pearl" buttons, knife handles, etc.

Value of Foods in Seeds.—The presence of quantities of food is of inestimable value not only to the plant, for which they are produced, but also to man, who long ago learned to use such objects as sources of essential food supplies for his own maintenance. Amazing quantities of seeds are used as food for man and beast each year.

Localization of the Food in Seeds.—The foods accumulated within seeds are mostly collected in one or the other of two differ-

ent portions of the seeds.   In one case the food is largely confined
to the cells of the embryo itself, and the embryo practically *fills*
the *cavity* of the seed (Fig. 35, *I*).   This type of food accumulation is illustrated by the seeds of peanut, bean, pea, clover, alfalfa,
apple, oak, hickory, and almond.   Many other species use the
persistent endosperm as a storehouse for the food, as in corn,
wheat, and other cereals, castorbean, and morning-glory.   The
endosperm, more or less heavily packed with the food, closely
envelops the *embryo* (Fig. 35, *K*) and fills in the space between
the latter and the covering of the seed.   The origin of the
endosperm from the fusion of the second sperm with the equatorial nucleus of the embryo sac at the time of fertilization has
been described.   Seeds with endosperm supplied with foods have
been called "albuminous" seeds, and seeds with little or no
endosperm, but with the foods contained by the embryo have
been termed "exalbuminous" seeds.   The tissue with such striking features as noted for the ivorypalm, date, asparagus, etc. is
really endosperm, and the hemicellulose accumulated therein
surrounds the embryo very closely.   Nevertheless, the embryo
of such plants is equipped to digest the food represented in those
thickened cell walls and so to utilize it during germination, in
much the same manner in which the more common foods of other
seeds are transformed and assimilated by the growing embryo.

Covering of Seeds.—The *seed coats* constitute the covering
of the seed.   These are usually the transformed integument or
integuments (Figs. 23 and 25) of the ovule.   As the ovule
gradually changes into the seed the integuments become thickened, and hardened, sometimes becoming exceedingly tough,
hard, and woody, so that the living embryo is enclosed by a
very resistant, protective covering.   The value of such a condition, so common among seed plants, must be obvious when we
recall the fact that the embryo is a very delicate, living thing
and that it is finally separated completely from the body of the
parent.   Not only that, it may also be placed in very unfavorable
and dangerous conditions so that it would surely perish if it were
not for the effective protection afforded by the seed coats.

The Inner Coat.—Besides the thick outer seed coat or *testa* of
major importance, certain seeds also have an inner, membranous
coat which immediately invests the embryo or the endosperm
and embryo.   The seeds of a few species, as waterlily and certain
sedges produce an *aril*, or a loose and more or less baggy, air-

containing, membranous modification of the outer coat which aids in dispersal.

Further Details of Seeds.—Mature seeds exhibit a great variety of surface markings (Figs. 35 and 36) and configurations as has already been mentioned, but they all agree in showing a minute pore or pit that marks the position of the micropyle of the ovule which became sealed as the seed matured The *hilum* is the scar left on the spot where the seed separated from its attachment in the ovary. Seeds that have been formed from inverted ovules (Fig. 23), as in the pansy, sometimes show the ridge along one side extending nearly from one end to the other formed by the ovulary stalk (funiculus) which becomes grown to the side of the ovule. This ridge is called the "raphe."

Behavior of Ripe Seeds.—Vital activity in seeds is at a very low ebb at the time the seeds are ripe or when they are freed from the parent plant. This is of great value since the embryo is very delicate and is quite likely to be severely injured if it were to continue growth under the varied conditions into which seeds go. A noteworthy exception to this general rule is in the mangrove, *Rhizophora*, (Fig. 33, *I*), in which the embryo continues its development without cessation until a good-sized seedling is developed in position upon the axis of the flower. The new plant is often a foot or more long before it drops from the parent plant. This is a phenomenon that closely compares with vivipary in mammals.

Delayed Germination of Seeds.—Suppression of activities inside the seed during dissemination and for long periods thereafter in many cases appears to be related to the *dryness* of the tissues of the ripe seed. The phenomenon of *delayed germination* is also of tremendous value to the plant in meeting the vicissitudes of an environment that is likely to be very uncongenial to flowering plant activities for considerable periods of time. Seeds that show these characteristics, and seeds that are capable of retaining their vitality for long periods, even under conditions of stress, are likely to be the most successful as organs of maintenance for the species concerned.

CHAPTER V

HOW FLOWERING PLANTS TRAVEL

One of the noticeable tendencies of flowering plant species is to move about from place to place over the earth. A given species may disappear from an area for a time and then reappear at some later date, and a strange species may suddenly become more or less prominent in a region where it had previously been unknown. The phenomenon of the movement or *migration* of plants through narrow or extensive limits is an observation common to almost everyone. Herein lies one of the most dynamic of all of the processes that together constitute the active phases of the life cycle of flowering plants.

NATURE OF PLANT MIGRATION

Migration is commonly understood to include all types and degrees of movement that tend to carry plants away from a parent individual or outward from an established center. Ordinarily we may and should distinguish between *migration*, as the *movement* of plants, and *establishment*, which may or may not follow the movement. Migration and establishment are obviously two very different biological processes.

Freedom of Movement.—The relative freedom of movement or locomotion of individual animals as compared with individual plants is one of the few significant differences between animals and plants. And yet many species of plants are capable of quickly spreading their individuals over wide areas. Plants in general are compelled to equip themselves for moving about in order to reduce the population pressure, an environmental relation that is also conspicuous among animals. So we must conclude that migration is a biological necessity for plants as well as for animals.

Capacity for Migration.—An important factor affecting plant migration is the *capacity* of the plant to migrate. This capacity is expressed in plant ecology by the term "mobility." The degree of mobility is largely determined by the efficiency of structural modifications as acted upon by the various factors of the environment. We say that the mobility of flowering plants with large, heavy fruits or seeds is *low*, but in species with tiny, light fruits or seeds equipped with *wings* or *tufts* of *hairs* that catch the *wind*, mobility is *high*.

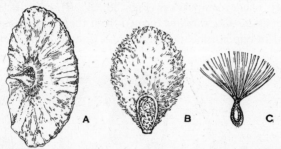

Fig. 37.—Seeds.—*A*, the seed of *Pithecoctenium* with a very broad membranous wing; *B*, seed of cotton, *Gossypium*; *C*, seed of milkweed, *Asclepias*.

Aids to Migration.—The structural modifications in flowering plants related to migration are very numerous and varied. Most of such modifications affect only the fruits or seeds, but other parts of the plant are occasionally utilized for these purposes. The numerous anatomical details of flowering plants that are of value to the species through their relation to dispersal or migration may now be roughly classified and described. This discussion will deal first with fruits and seeds as related to migration. Our classification is based primarily on the agent, factor, or force concerned with or operating upon the disseminules.

FACTORS IN MIGRATION

Wind.—Wind is one of the most impressive and effective factors in the migration of flowering plants. The modifications of the fruit or seed that favor dispersal by the utilization of wind or air currents are numerous. Certain of these are provided with *wings* that are more or less membranous. Here we have maple, ash, elm, birch, certain members of the carrot and grass family, etc. in which the wings are a portion of the *fruit* (Figs. 28, *G*, and 29), and *Catalpa*, *Bignonia*, trumpet vine, etc., in which the wing is a part of the *seed*. Other fruits or seeds are supplied with long *silky* or *woolly* hairs. Examples of this type are seen in anemone and *Clematis*, in certain species of which the *fruits* (achenes) are more or less covered by the hairs, and in willow, cottonwood, aspen, cotton, milkweed, willowherb, in which the *seed* is the part modified for dispersal by wind (Figs. 37, *A, B, C*). Fruits with long *plumose style*, with high degree of mobility, are seen in *Clematis* (Fig. 39, *C*), Pasque flower, alpine *Sieversia*, and others.   Fruits with *parachute-like tufts of hairs*, with exceedingly high mobility, are illustrated by dandelion, lettuce, salsify, and many other composites (Fig. 38, *A, B*).   Fruits with a membranous *sac-like envelope* formed from the ovary or calyx are developed in hop hornbeam, bladdernut, ground cherry, etc.

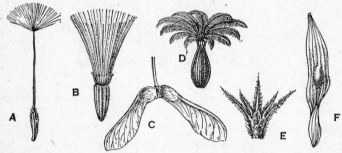

Fig. 38.—Types of disseminules.   *A*, in dandelion, *Taraxacum; B*, in ironweed, *Vernonia; C*, in maple, *Acer; D*, in valerian, *Valeriana; E*, in *Brunonia; F*, in tree-of-Heaven, *Ailanthus*.

Animals.—Animals of great variety also assist in many ways to distribute plants.   The more common modifications of fruits or seeds may be noted in this connection.   Fruits with *hooks* or *barbs* that attach the parts to passing animals are numerous. (Figs. 38, *E* and 39, *A* and *D*.)   The degree of mobility in these cases is very high as a rule.   Illustrations are afforded by cocklebur, bedstraw, Spanish needles, wild liquorice, agrimony, avens, *Lespedeza*, unicorn plant (Fig. 31, *A*), etc.   The burdock may be included here also, but in this plant the hooks are at the tips of the involucral bracts that surround the head of flowers.   Fruits with *awns* or *beards* that are needle-like or very rough or hairy so that they cling to the fur or feathers of passing animals are developed in many species.   Many grasses are included in this group, notably porcupine or needle grass (Fig. 199, *F*), triple-awned grass, wild barley, June grass (*Bromus*), etc., other fruits are provided with *spines* developed on the surface, as in sandbur, and puncture weed (*Tribulus*).   Still other fruits or seeds are *fleshy* and are eaten by birds and other animals and may be carried in large numbers for great distances (Figs. 32 and 33). Here we have many species with various types of fleshy fruits such as drupes in the cherries, berries in great numbers, pomes in haws, etc. The seeds in such fruits are usually protected by a stony envelope ("pit") or seed coat so that they resist the destructive action of the animal's digestive system and they are usually regurgitated or discharged with the excrement unharmed (Fig. 33, *C*). Fruits or seeds of other species are covered with adherent *glandular hairs* or *viscid secretions*, as in the chickweeds, sages, catchflies. Nuts and nut-like fruits and seeds are also carried away by certain animals, especially rodents, and in this way such plants as hickory, walnut, and beech are scattered.

Plants are also scattered far and wide by man, often without relation to the natural mobility of the plant. Thus a person may carry large, heavy seeds or fruits half-way around the world and grow the plants in a place where the species might never have occurred without man's help. Man may also carry plants unintentionally as is often done. Man may affect great movements of plants through distances and in a very short time in a manner that is wholly impossible with any other agent of migration. Many undesirable weeds and other plants have been brought into a country by travelers from foreign lands.

Water.—Certain plants are able to migrate by means of water in the form of tides, ocean currents, streams or surface flow in lakes or on the land. There are two principal types of structures that make this kind of migration possible, the best known example of which is the case of the coconut. The thick, fibrous husk of the coconut (Fig. 30, *A*) coupled with the very hard shell of the "nut" (Fig. 30, *B*) render the structure practically impervious to water so that these fruits have been known to drift for long distances in the sea. The impervious or air-containing fruits of certain sedges and waterlilies adapt these to flotation on the water also. Surface run-off also affects considerable movement of seeds and fruits that lie upon the ground, but there is no particular morphological feature of the propagules related to this type of water influence, although many seeds and fruits that are scattered in this manner are buoyant.

Gravity and Glaciers.—The force of gravity and glacier movement are of some importance in migration in mountainous areas and in the Arctic and Antarctic regions. The significance of glacial action as related to plant migration in the past can hardly be overemphasized, but glaciers play only a local and relatively insignificant rôle in migration today.

MODIFICATIONS OF THE PLANT

Explosive Fruits.—The fruits of some plants are more or less *explosive* when ripe and this phenomenon serves to scatter the seeds. The distance to which the seeds are propelled may not be very great in any one season, but the effect becomes of importance when continued through the years. Several different mechanisms are involved in explosive fruits, but they mostly agree in the sudden release of pressure of sufficient magnitude to disrupt the fruit and send the seeds flying. Some of these fruits are said to burst with a report like a pistol shot, as in the "sand-box tree" of the West Indies. In some cases the sudden and forcible collapse of the fruit with the discharge of the seeds

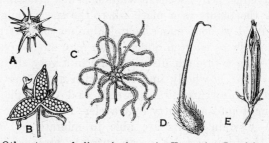

Fig. 39.—Other types of disseminules. *A*, *Krameria*; *B*, violet, *Viola*; *C*, clematis, *Clematis*; *D*, avens, *Geum*; *E*, sorrel, *Oxalis*.

is due to a drying out of different layers of the ovary wall at different rates thus developing counter strains in the tissues to such a degree that certain layers are suddenly overcome. Some such conditions as these obtain in the fruits of the violet (Fig. 39, *B*), certain vetches, *Oxalis* (Fig. 39, *E*), castor bean and witchhazel (Fig. 150, *C* and *D*), resulting in the sudden ejection of the seeds. The seeds of the witchhazel may be fired as far as 10 feet away from the capsules in which they are formed. The origin of the tension differences in other fruits is found in the osmotic pressure of the ripening tissues in the walls of the fruits or seeds, as in the common "touch-me-not" (Fig. 115) of our woodlands, and the so-called squirting cucumber, *Ecballium*, of the Mediterranean basin. The fruit in the latter plant is like a small fleshy cucumber with a bristly surface. The stalk of the fruit is hooked and it projects for some distance into the end of the fruit. As the fruit ripens the interior mass containing the seeds becomes gelatinous and the tissues adjacent to the base of the stopper-like stalk become weakened. The tissues in the wall of the fruit develop great tensions and become distended. The principal focus of this pressure is directed toward the gradually weakening tissues about the base of the stalk. At a certain point in the ripening process the pressure overcomes the resistance of the tissues in an annular zone about the stalk, resulting in the sudden forcing of the stalk outward; the distended walls contract and much of the juicy, mucilaginous contents of the cucumber, including the seeds, are squirted out through the hole.

Vegetative Modifications.—The fruit and seed are the most common, varied, and useful features of the plant as related to migration, but certain plants utilize certain vegetative peculiarities to an effective degree in this connection.

Tumbleweeds.—The form of the entire aerial portion of the plant in certain species contributes in a very important degree to the mobility of the species. This is the case in those plants that are commonly known as "tumbleweeds" as represented by Russian thistle (*Salsola*), *Cycloloma*, etc. in which the bushy plant breaks off at or near the surface of the ground and may be rolled along for long distances in open windy regions. As a rule such plants carry many fruits and seeds that are sown as the bushy structure tumbles along. The finely branched panicles of many grasses and fragments of other species may be distributed in this same manner. Large portions or fragments such as winter buds of paludose or submerged plants bearing seeds or otherwise capable of establishing themselves are distributed by means of water as in the frogbit, pondweeds, etc.

Offshoots.—The most common vegetative structures for migration are of the nature of *offshoots* of considerable variety of form and effectiveness. These are usually modifications of some regular organ of the body such as a stem, root, or leaf which stretches away from the parent body and "strikes root" in such a manner as to establish a potentially new individual. The connection with the parent may be completely broken later. Many species that propagate in this manner may show many series of these offsets or "new generations" still linked with the original individual.

The most numerous modifications of this sort are stems, morphologically, although because of their common subterranean position they are popularly regarded as roots. Such structures are even sometimes much more like roots than stems in their superficial characteristics, but they are ordinarily easily classed with stems upon the basis of their finer structure and morphology. There are also numerous species which produce aerial vegetative stems that are admirably adapted to migration and asexual propagation.

The Rhizome.—Rhizomes are usually slender, greatly elongated, more or less horizontal underground stems with scattered scales or scale-like leaves at the nodes, and lateral and terminal buds (Figs. 40, 41 and 42). Erect branches which emerge and develop

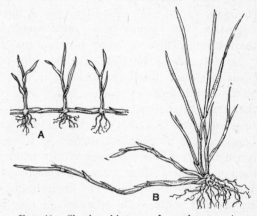

Fig. 40.—Thick rhizome of iris, *Iris (after Mathews).*

Fig. 41.—Slender rhizomes of quack grass, *Agropyron.* A, young growth with new shoots; B, older plant (*after Mathews*).

the aerial portions of the plant are formed from lateral buds, but many such branches die back each year in numerous temperate climate species. Rhizomes remain alive in the soil and they form new lateral and terminal buds from year to year as well as lateral branches and thus serve to carry each new generation farther and farther away from the parent with which they may maintain an indefinite continuity. In this manner, the soil in the general level at which this rhizome complex develops may be so permeated with rhizomes and roots arising therefrom as to resist vigorous wind or wave action.

Many species of flowering plants develop rhizomes, among them being *Iris* (Fig. 40), cattail, pondweed, banana, Canada thistle, bindweed, morning-glory, Solomon's seal, peppermint (Fig. 42), and many grasses such as sugar cane, Johnson grass, quackgrass (Fig. 41, *B*) and marrowgrass. This method of migration and propagation is the outstanding feature of the behavior of the sand-binding grasses and other plants of sand dunes and other shifting soils. Rhizomes are sometimes called rootstocks, the two terms being essentially synonymous.

Tubers.—Tubers are shortened, greatly thickened, more or less fleshy segments of underground stems in which the usual stem characteristics are even more completely suppressed or masked than is the case in rhizomes. Many species produce tubers, among which may be mentioned Irish potato, wild pea (*Apios*), sunflower or Jerusalem artichoke, *Begonia*, and elephant's ears (*Colocasia*). The tuber may form at the end of a slender rhizome-like stem, as in the Irish potato, or there may be a series of bead-like tubers arranged at intervals along the

stem as in *Apios*. There is usually a terminal bud or cluster of buds at the outer end of a terminal tuber, and there are also many buds scattered over the surface or imbedded beneath the surface of

FIG. 42.—Rhizomes of peppermint, *Mentha piperita (after Mathews)*.

the tuber. The "eyes" of a potato are in reality buds with reduced scales and little external evidence of their true nature. Since the eyes are buds that represent the outer tips of potential lateral branches one can readily understand the necessity of having at least one "eye" on each seed piece when potatoes are planted. The true structure and morphology of these strikingly modified stems may be determined only by tracing their development or by means of a careful anatomical examination of the mature tubers. The practical value of tubers and rhizomes to mankind in plant culture cannot be overestimated.

Corms.—Corms (Fig. 43, *E* and *G*) are also underground stems but they are typically vertical or erect, greatly shortened or flattened, solid axes that are often broader than long, bearing a tuft of roots at the lower surface, and a few dry, scale-like leaves scattered over the curved surface of the body. The leaves are reduced in some cases to inconspicuous dry scales. The nodes and buds are scarcely discernible in most corms. The corms are thus tremendously broadened and flattened leafless underground stems, of great value in propagation because of the accumulated food that they contain. Their rôle in migration is a minor one because of the slowness with which new corms are formed adjacent to the old ones and because of the relatively slight distance gained by each new crop. Examples of corms are furnished by *Crocus, Gladiolus, Cyclamen,* and Jack-in-the pulpit, *Arisaema,* (Fig. 43, *E* and *G*).

Bulbs.—Bulbs (Fig. 43, *A, B, C* and *D*) as a rule are also congested underground stems in which the stem is greatly reduced and the leaves take the form of thick and more or less succulent scales that completely cover the stem. A fringe of roots is developed at the base of the stem on the lower surface of the bulb. In contrast to a corm which is almost exclusively

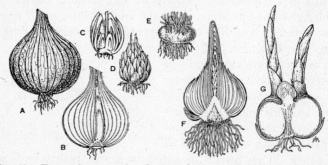

FIG. 43.—Types of congested underground stems. *A,* bulb of onion, *Allium; B,* vertical section of same*; C* and *D,* bulb of lily, *Lilium;'\E,* corm of cyclamen, *Cyclamen; F,* bulb of hyacinth, *Hyacinthus,* showing internal structure; *G,* vertical section of the corm of crocus, *Crocus* (*after Mathews*).

stem with only vestigial leaves, a bulb has an inconspicuous stem covered by prominent leaves which constitute the dominant feature of bulbs as in the onion, lily, hyacinth, tulip, etc. (Fig. 43, *A, B, C* and *D*). The bulb usually produces a terminal bud and a few lateral buds in the axils of some of the scales. The new bulbs are usually developed from these axillary buds (Fig. 43, *B* and *C*) and after they reach a certain stage they become detached from the parent bulb and in this way serve to spread the plants slowly from year to year.

Runners and Stolons.—A runner (Fig. 44) is a slender, trailing or descending, aerial stem which is practically leafless or upon which the leaves are conspicuously reduced. Runners arise as axillary growths of the parent plant and they are commonly very different in appearance from the ordinary stems. When the tip of such a stem touches the ground it may take root and develop a new shoot at that point. The strawberry (Fig. 44) and buffalo grass are plants that develop runners to a very fine degree and in such a manner as to assist considerably in the gradual dispersal of those plants. The thickening of the strawberry bed by this method of migration is a tendency very familiar to all strawberry growers. The competition brought about by this tendency must be constantly prevented if satisfactory crops of strawberries are to be grown. One who knows the vegetation of the Great Plains is aware of the same method of migration in connection with the behavior of buffalo grass. A study of the habits of buffalo grass revealed some runners that had formed as many as 25, 31, and 49 distinct and growing contacts with the

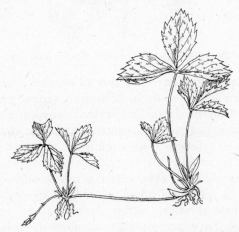

Fig. 44.—Runners of the strawberry, *Fragaria* (*after Mathews*).

earth. These runners were respectively 5, 8, and 23 feet long and they were still connected with the parent plant.

Stolons.—The attempt is sometimes made to distinguish runners from "stolons," and raspberry, currant, etc. are cited as plants that migrate by the utilization of stolons. The only conspicuous differences between the stolon of the raspberry and the runner of a strawberry are seen in the fact that the raspberry structure is higher above the ground as the cane arches over to bring its tip down to the surface of the ground, and it has more leaves in evidence.

Offsets.—Another type of aerial stem of value in migration is the offset (Fig. 45). This is of the nature of a very short, thick and comparatively leafy runner that produces a new shoot with a rosette of leaves when it comes into contact with the ground or before, and it may establish a permanent soil connection by developing roots on the under surface.   Such offshoots are usually associated with a plant of rather compact growth in the form of rosettes as in the houseleek (Fig. 45).   This method of migration in such plants commonly results in the development of a dense bundle or mat of very closely set individuals.

FIG. 45.—Offsets developing in houseleek, *Sempervivum* (*after Mathews*).

Velocity of Migration.—The rate of migration of species by means of fruits and seeds is, of course, typically much more rapid than by any one or another of the above vegetative methods. And yet these methods are effective and sure (even if slow) because of the extended connection with the parent plant which enables the potentially new individuals to maintain themselves until well established, even under severe conditions of stress that arise.   A surprisingly large number of species of flowering plants produce rhizomes, corms, bulbs, tubers, runners, and offsets which have become very significantly combined with fruits and seeds in propagation and migration.

CHAPTER VI

FORMS AND RELATIONSHIPS IN FLOWERS

Comparatively little observation is sufficient to impress one with the fact that there are many kinds of flowers, based upon the number and arrangement of the common morphological elements, *i.e.* sepals, petals, stamens, pistils, and axis that enter into the constitution of the flower. Further study demonstrates that these elements also vary greatly as to *form*, *position* and *degree of union* in different flowers. The outstanding anatomical feature of flowers, is, in short, that the *floral design* or *plan* of the flower shows great variety. This plan serves as the most important guide to the segregation of flowering plants into their major groups. The pattern or design of flowers as reflecting relationships is of great value in the natural classification of flowering plants. This is one of the most interesting phases of systematic botany, and one for which even the amateur or novice may become very enthusiastic.

Some Common Flowers.—The everyday conception of roses, mints, legumes, geraniums, buttercups, irises, lilies, orchids, etc. may not exactly convey a sense of fundamental relationships but it is certainly suggestive. The ability to read some of the secrets of floral affiliations in the flower design of unknown species adds a pleasure and a zest to one's travel akin to the same reactions that come to students of birds or butterflies. Such an interest will not only lead one into a finer and more intimate touch with the natural history of plants, but it will also help the intelligent to formulate a much more adequate conception of the nature and meaning of the natural world as a whole.

We may now proceed to the examination of a number of representative flowers to illustrate some of the many variations of flowers that have been mentioned and that are more or less distinctive of the various orders and families. These features will enable us to build a foundation for the classification of flowering plants.

Primitive Flowers and Derived Flowers.—There is much evidence to support the conclusion that the flowering plants with their flowers developed after a *spiral* plan or design, *i.e.*, flowers in which the carpels or stamens or both, and even the petals and sepals are arranged in a series of *spirals* (Figs. 8, *A* and *B*; 46, 98, 99, 102, and 103) over the axis, are more primitive than those with flowers with parts arranged on the whorled or *cyclic* plan, *i.e.*, flowers in which the parts are arranged on the axis in a series of *whorls, circles* (Figs. 10, 47, 48, 49, 50, 131, 186, and 201), or *cycles*. This appears to be true even though the vast majority of the species of flowering plants represented in modern floras show flowers constructed according to the latter design. Botanists now agree almost unanimously that the flowering plants with spiral flowers are *primitive* or "low" and that those with cyclic flowers are *derived* or "high," and that the latter have developed from the former through long eons of time. Agreement is also fairly unanimous that the first or most primitive flowering plants were of the nature commonly known as "woody" plants. It is furthermore seen that the *spiral type* of flower is correlated with those groups, *i.e.*, the lowest groups, and that the *cyclic flower plan* is adopted by the vast array of *higher, herbaceous* species. This relationship apparently goes so far in a few groups such as the legumes, which include both woody and herbaceous forms, that the herbaceous species have produced a more advanced type of flower than is shown by the woody species. This condition may be demonstrated by a comparative examination of such representatives of the group cited (Figs. 5, *D*; 11, *A*; and 146) as clover, *Trifolium*, or scarlet runner, *Phaseolus*, with the honey locust, *Gleditsia*, or thorn, *Acacia*.

Some Spiral Flowers.—Many species in the families of the buttercup order, *Ranales*, may be cited to illustrate some of the features of spiral flowers and variations of this type. The mousetail, *Myosurus*, and the common buttercup, *Ranunculus*, produce flowers (Figs. 8, *A* and *B*; 46, *A* and *D*; and 102) in which the many separate carpels are arranged over a more or less spire-like or dome-shaped axis in a series of beautifully symmetrical spirals, and the numerous stamens are also disposed upon the axis in a series of spirals immediately below the carpels. The arrangement of the carpels in these plants is emphatically reflected as the axis enlarges after fertilization and the individual carpels develop into a globular or elongated group of achenes. The successive spirals are also nicely shown by the scars left on the axis when the fruits have fallen. The carpels and stamens are attached in this manner also in the woody magnolias, *Magnolia* (Fig. 46, *B*, and 98), tulip tree, *Liriodendron*, and in many herbaceous members of this large group such as windflower, *Anemone*, Virgin's bower, *Clematis*, mousetail, *Myosurus*, marsh marigold, *Caltha* (Fig. 102, *B*), etc. The white waterlily, *Nymphaea alba*, produces flowers in which the petals and stamens are also arranged spirally.

Cyclic Flowers.—The cyclic flower plan may be illustrated by a few of the great number of forms that are well known. Cyclic flowers appear to have developed from spiral flowers by a progressive shortening or condensation of the axis, thus bringing the parts together in closer or more compact spirals, until the whorled

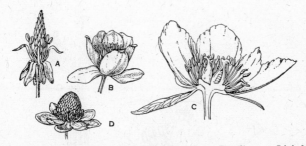

Fig. 46.—Flowers of: *A*, mousetail, *Myosurus minimus; B*, tulip tree, *Liriodendron; C*, peony, *Paeonia; D*, buttercup, *Ranunculus (after Le M. and Dec.).*

or cyclic arrangement is accomplished and a cycle is developed for each of the four floral elements (Figs. 47, *A* and *B*; 48, 49, 123 and 125). The cyclic flower often shows a broadened receptacle upon which the succession of flower parts are disposed in cycles. Along with the evolution of the cyclic flower has gone the introduction of a much more definite number in all of the floral elements, in contrast with the degree of uncertainty in this regard that is characteristic of the lowest types of the spiral forms.

Common Cyclic Flowers.—The flowers of the strawberry, *Fragaria*, (Fig. 47, *A* and *B*) a member of the *Rosales*, are interesting for the reason that the many separate carpels are *spirally* arranged over a typically cone-shaped, ranalian axis, but the many stamens are arranged in *cycles* near the edge of the *disk-like flange* (Fig. 47, *B*) attached to and encircling the base of the conical portion of the axis. The five petals and five sepals are also arranged in successive cycles farther out on the edge of this disk. The flower is evidently more or less intermediate between the typically spiral type and the typically cyclic type, the carpels being spiral, and the three other elements being cyclic. In the flower of the mountain mahogany (Fig. 47, *C*) pear or apple, *Pyrus, Malus* (Fig. 145, *D*), the conical axis is gone, the numerous carpels are reduced to five, and these have become embedded in a *depression* of the fleshy axis, surrounded by the stamens, petals, and sepals in cyclic order. The geranium, *Geranium* (Fig. 48, *B*), has five sepals, five petals, ten stamens, and five carpels, all grouped in a very perfect cyclic manner. The flower of flax, *Linum* (Fig. 113), is composed of five sepals, five petals, five stamens, and five carpels arranged in the same way. The

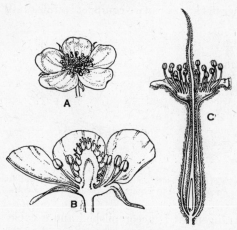

Fig. 47.—Flowers of: *A*, strawberry, *Fragaria; B*, vertical section of a flower of *Fragaria; C*, vertical section of a flower of mountain mahogany, *Cercocarpus* (*after Le M. and Dec.*).

cyclic flower of a lily, *Lilium, Scilla, Tulipa, Hyacinthus* (Figs. 48, *A* and *C*; 186 and 187), etc. is composed of three sepals, three petals six stamens, and three *united* carpels.

Tubular Flowers.—The arrangement of the four floral elements is essentially cyclic also in those flowers in which the calyx and corolla are tubular, *i.e.* those in which the sepals are "grown together" to form a gamosepalous calyx and in which the petals are "grown together" to form a gamopetalous corolla (Figs. 50, 134, 138, 164, 174, and 175). Examples of these floral plans are seen in the primrose, *Primula* (Fig. 128), with its five "united" sepals, five "united" petals, five stamens (on the corolla tube) and its one pistil; in the sweet william, *Phlox*, with its five sepals, petals, stamens, and three united carpels (Fig. 137); and in the snapdragon, *Antirrhinum*, with its five sepals. five irregular petals formed into a two-lipped corolla, its four stamens, and its two united carpels (Fig. 151). The axis of the flower in these cases has been reduced to a slightly expanded platform at the top of the pedicel upon which the parts are disposed.

Epigynous and Cyclic Flowers.—Flowers with inferior ovaries are usually cyclic also as is seen in such forms as the carrot, *Daucus*, with its four or five sepals and petals, four or five stamens, and two-celled inferior ovary (Fig. 49, *C*), and in the honeysuckle, *Lonicera*, *Diervilla*, etc., with its five vestigial sepals, five petals "united" to form an irregular and often two-lipped corolla, five stamens, and its compound, inferior ovary (Figs. 49, *A*, and 174).

Some Uncertainties.—The student must not understand that it is readily possible to classify all flowers as either spiral or cyclic. These conditions merely represent a general tendency among flowering plants. There are many exceptions to the rule in this case as there are in many other principles or tendencies that are illustrated by living things. Thus we find that the perianth may be cyclic in *Magnolia* (Fig. 98), a member of the group in which spiral flowers are most clearly and typically developed. And, on the other hand, the floral elements are arranged more or less spirally in the cactus flower and in the flowers of certain other forms, in which other floral characteristics would indicate that these species are in reality of a much higher type than is accorded to the groups with spiral flowers. The cactuses even have the indefinite number of perianth parts and stamens that are commonly associated with more primitive groups. The cactus group represents one of the numerous puzzles that confronts the person who attempts to arrange the many subdivisions of the flowering plant world in an orderly and systematic natural classification. The tendency seems to be to relate these plants to the spiral-flowered forms, *Ranales* (Fig. 102), through certain intermediary groups such as the roses, *Rosales* (Fig. 145), and myrtles, *Myrtales* (Fig. 153).

There are many major fundamentals of floral design besides the spiral and cyclic plans. Some of these have been involved in statements regarding different kinds of spiral and cyclic flowers and others have been noted briefly in an earlier chapter on flower structure.

The Number of Floral Parts.—The number of subdivisions or parts in each of the four elements of the flower presents an additional useful aid in classification and enables us also to establish another "law" or principle of evolution as it is applied to flowering plants. The floral elements of primitive flowering plants are, in general, more or less numerous and indefinite in number. But in derived and higher flowers the tendency is toward reduction in number, and especially toward the development of a definite number of parts in each of the four series of elements. These tendencies are noted in the stamens and carpels more strikingly and in a larger number of species than in connection with sepals and petals. Perianth parts appear to become established on a definite numerical basis

Fig. 48.—Flowers of: *A*, squill, *Scilla; B*, geranium, *Geranium; C*, tulip, *Tulipa* (*after Le M. and Dec.*).

before stamens and pistils. As development proceeds the number of stamens tends to become the same as the number of petals, but the number of carpels is frequently reduced to fewer than the petals. The greater reduction of carpels is probably more than counterbalanced, however, in many cases by the multiplication of ovules. In many of the highest types the reduction also affects the ovules, but in those (*Compositae*, Figs. 176 to 180) the extreme reduction has been accompanied by other significant changes that have more than made up for the potential loss.

Tendency toward Constancy.—The tendency toward the differentiation of flowers with a fairly constant number of sepals and petals culminates rather early in the production of two distinctive patterns or floral designs that are correlated with other features to segregate flowering plants into the two major subdivisions, Monocotyledons and Dicotyledons. The latter group, commonly regarded as the more primitive, produces flowers that have the perianth typically composed of four or

five each of sepals and petals. The Monocotyledons, commonly
regarded as having been derived from the lower Dicotyledons,
produce flowers in which the perianth is typically composed of
three sepals and three petals. The rule is that flowers produce a
calyx and a corolla that are distinguished from each other.
The tendency of this distinction to be uncertain is seen mostly
in certain types such as lilies, *Lilium, Tulipa, Erythronium,*
magnolias, *Magnolia,* and other buttercups, *Ranales,* which are
regarded as relatively primitive.

The Union of Flower Parts.—The tendency for the subdivisions of the four regular parts of the flower to become "united,"
and the degree of the union affected is another variable factor in
connection with the development of floral designs. This tend-

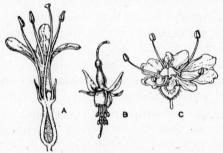

Fig. 49.—Flowers of: *A,* honeysuckle, *Lonicera; B,* fuchsia, *Fuchsia; C,* carrot
Daucus (after Le M. and Dec.).

ency affects the carpels first of all. Certain lower species,
as of *Geranium, Linum,* etc. with indefinite or separate perianth
segments have united carpels, but the many carpels in the most
primitive groups are separate, *i.e.,* the flowers are *apocarpous.*
Separate carpels, *i.e., apocarpy,* is regarded as a primitive
character, as are separate sepals, petals, and stamens. Practically all of the flowering plants above the few groups that constitute the lower plexus of the branch have united carpels, *i.e.,* the
flowers are *syncarpous,* and the number of carpels reduced below
that of stamens and perianth segments.

Syncarpy: the Union of Carpels.—The union between the
carpels of compound ovaries may be slight in certain flowers as
geranium, *Geranium,* hollyhock, *Althaea,* and flax, *Linum,* or it
may be so complete as to affect even the style and stigma as in
primroses, *Primula,* and mustards, *Bursa.* Many flowering
plants, as legumes, *Leguminosae* (Fig. 146), and barberries,

Berberidaceae (Fig. 101), produce flowers with a simple pistil or single carpel.

Union of Sepals and Petals.—The sepals and petals of many flowers appear to have grown together to form a more or less bell-shaped, tubular, or funnel-form calyx, a *gamosepalous* (or synsepalous) calyx, and corolla, a *gamopetalous* (or sympetalous) corolla (Figs. 50, 131, 133, 134, 138, 174, and 175). This is the situation in practically all of the species of primroses, *Primulaceae* (Fig. 128), heathers, *Ericaceae* (Fig. 131), gentians, *Gentianaceae* (Fig. 133), nightshades, *Solanaceae* (Fig. 139), mints, *Labiatae* (Fig. 144), snapdragons, *Scrophulariaceae* (Fig. 141), forget-me-nots, *Boraginaceae* (Fig. 140), bluebells, *Campanulaceae* (Fig. 175), and composites, *Compositae* (Figs. 176 to 180). The expressions that are commonly used to refer to these conditions are misleading, because they depict merely the superficial nature of the perianth whorls; whereas the actual history of their development is quite different. The so-called "united" sepals and petals are really not united to form the "synsepalous" calyx and the "sympetalous" corolla because they have not, as a matter of fact, ever been separate. We must examine the very young, meristematic flower in order to understand this situation. Such a flower will show the four floral elements merely as four series of zonal primordia at the end of the pedicel or axis and these develop later into sepals, petals, stamens, and pistils. A flower that has five sepals and five petals at maturity will show five tiny humps or points of meristem that represent the beginnings of the sepals, and five similar points mark the beginnings of the petals. If these two separate and distinct sets of meristematic primordia continue to grow and elongate separately, and if they remain separate until the flower is mature the flower will, of course, have five separate sepals and five separate petals. But in many cases such a circular zone or whorl of sepal or petal primordia becomes elevated on the edge of a continuous, hollow and more or less cylindrical band of meristem which continues to grow upward in more or less telescopic fashion so that the primordia of the sepals, or petals as the case may be, merely represent somewhat isolated points on a cylindrical ridge of tissue common to all of the primordia of a given cycle. When this type of growth is completed in the mature flower it results in the formation of the well-known tubular calyx or corolla. Thus we see that the four or five points on the outer rim of the corolla or calyx of a gentian flower, *Gentiana* (Fig. 133), or the flower of a madder, *Cinchona* (Fig. 173), or coffee, *Coffea* (Fig. 173), are not to be explained (as they sometimes are) by stating that the tendency of the sepals or petals to "unite" or "grow together" was terminated before the tips were reached.

Indications of Relationships.—Synsepalous and sympetalous flowers are commonly regarded as higher than aposepalous (separate sepals) and apopetalous (separate petals) flowers, and as having been derived from the latter types. It seems that "united" sepals occur in many more forms than "united"

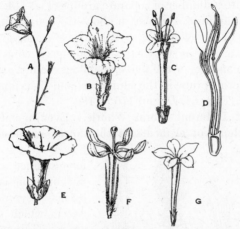

Fig. 50.—Flowers of: *A*, bluebell, *Campanula; B*, trumpetflower, *Tecoma; C*, teasel, *Dipsacus; D*, vertical section of a flower of cornflower, *Centaurea; E*, morning-glory, *Ipomoea; F, Brunonia; G*, jessamine, *Jasminum* (*after Le M. and Dec.*).

petals, but many species are found among primitive families, *Ranunculaceae* (Fig. 102), *Papaveraceae* (Fig. 119), *Violaceae* (Fig. 118), etc., that are aposepalous. Comparatively few Monocotyledons show synsepaly and sympetaly, but among the Dicotyledons we find an enormous group (*Sympetalae*) in which these conditions are very common and represented by a great many variations in detail.

The degree of "union" between the sepals and petals is also very variable. In some flowers the sepals (as in legumes) or petals (as in flaxes) are united very slightly at the base, but in others, such as nightshades, *Solanum*, morning-glories *Ipomoea* (Fig. 138), *Convolvulus*, and blueberry, *Vaccinium* (Fig. 131), they are so completely "united" that the tips scarcely show in the flowers of some species.

Union of Stamens.—The stamens are also united in the flowers of many species in a number of different families.   In the mallow or cotton family, *Malvaceae* (Fig. 105), the filaments of the many stamens are united to form a continuous sheath that completely surrounds the base of the carpels.   The anthers are free and they usually appear as a fringing collar underneath the spreading stigmas that push out beyond the sheath.   This feature constitutes one of the useful earmarks of that family.   The numerous stamens in the flowers of the citrus group, *Rutaceae* (Fig. 114), especially in the oranges and their kin, *Citrus*, are united by their filaments into a number of separate groups (Fig. 114, *E*) but they do not form an unbroken sheath about the pistil.   In the lobelia group, *Lobeliaceae* (Fig. 175, *C*), the five stamens are united by their anthers, and in some cases the filaments cohere to form a tube.   The anthers of the five epipetalous stamens are regularly united to form a tube in the sunflowers and their immediate kin, *Compositae* (Figs. 51, *D*, and 176 to 180).

Union of Different Floral Whorls.—Even members of two different whorls or elements of the flower are united in some flower types. The commonest illustration of this phenomenon is illustrated by many sympetalous species in which the stamens are raised upon the corolla tube and are attached by their filaments to the inner face of the petals.   This is the condition found in nearly all sympetalous species. Such stamens are

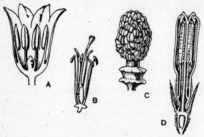

Fig. 51.—Flowers of: *A*, asparagus, *Asparagus*; *B*, lily, *Lilium*; *C*, rose mallow, *Hibiscus*; *D*, *Helenium* (after Le M. and Dec.).

said to be "epipetalous." Specific cases may be cited in primroses, *Primulaceae* (Fig. 128), morning-glories, *Convolvulaceae* (Fig. 138), sweet williams, *Polemoniaceae* (Fig. 137), verbenas, *Verbenaceae*, mints, *Labiatae* (Fig. 144), snapdragons, *Scrophulariaceae* (Fig. 141), honeysuckles, *Caprifoliaceae* (Fig. 174), and coffees, *Rubiaceae* (Fig. 173).

Unusual Conditions.—The orchids, *Orchidaceae* (Fig. 203), present a curious case of the union of stamens and carpels, in which a special structure, the *column*, is formed by the fusion of greatly modified and simplified stamens and style.   A more or less similar arrangement is exhibited in the flower of the Dutchman's pipe, *Aristolochia*, but this case is simpler than that typical of orchids.

Actinomorphy and Zygomorphy.—Other fundamental contrasts among the general schemes of floral design appear in the form or symmetry of the flower. Most flowers are *actinomorphic* or radially symmetrical, *i.e.* they are regular in form in all directions from the center (Figs. 8, 9 and 10). This condition is reflected in the more or less distinctly star-shaped or rosette nature that is so popularly associated with flowers. This effect is given by flowers in which the parts in each of the four floral whorls are exactly alike (or very nearly so) in form. The calyx, and particularly the corolla are the parts most commonly of major importance in this matter, but nevertheless the stamens and pistils also develop with perfect radial symmetry in many flowers. There are, however, many species of flowering plants in which the flowers are not so regular in form because certain members of one or more of the floral whorls are different in shape from the other members of the same series. This condition results in the production of lopsided flowers. These irregularities may become surprisingly extreme and peculiar. Such flowers are said to show *bilateral* symmetry instead of *radial* symmetry and they are known among biologists as "zygomorphic" flowers (Fig. 11). The bizarre forms and intricate mechanisms developed in zygomorphic flowers are among the most interesting features of flowering plants (Fig. 52). Such forms are found in many different families but they are particularly common in only a few such as the legumes, *Leguminosae* (Fig. 146), the mints, *Labiatae* (Fig. 144), the foxgloves or snapdragons, *Scrophulariaceae* (Fig. 141), the violets, *Violaceae* (Fig. 118), the composites, *Compositae* (Figs. 176 to 180), and the orchids, *Orchidaceae* (Fig. 203).

Zygomorphy in the Corolla.—The corolla is the most strikingly modified part in zygomorphic flowers. Thus in the legumes the flower commonly has five petals, but these are of three quite different shapes and sizes and they come to occupy three different positions in the plane of the flower. One of the petals is usually much wider or larger than any of the others and this one lies in the upper portion of the flower as its most conspicuous part, as in sweet peas, *Lathyrus*, and has been called the *banner* or *standard* (Fig. 52, *F* and *G*). The *wings* (Fig. 52, *F* and *G*) are two smaller and usually narrower petals which lie on either side and

commonly, more or less, underneath the banner. The other two
petals are usually quite narrow and smaller than the wing petals
and are sometimes more or less united along their lower edges to
form the *keel* (Fig. 52, *F* and *G*) of the flower. The petals in
the three parts of the flower are often differently colored, and this
serves to intensify the irregular nature of the flower. The
stamens and pistils are closely enclosed by the keel.

The Mint Flower.—The tubular corolla of the mint flower
(Fig. 144), as in catnip, *Nepeta*, is deeply cleft longitudinally
into two lips of dif-
ferent shape, size,
color, and position.
The upper, more or
less narrow, arching
or erect lip is usually
composed of two
"united" petals,
underneath which
the stamens and
style are usually
placed, and the
lower lip, commonly
broad and conspic-
uous, more or less
lobed and differ-
ently colored from
the upper lip, is

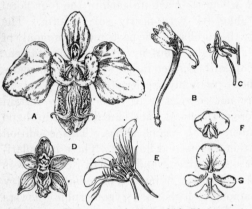

Fig. 52.—Flowers of: *A*, an orchid, *Phalaenopsis*
(*after Kerner*); *B*, honeysuckle, *Lonicera* (*after Baillon*);
C, orchid, *Orchis* (*after Le M. and Dec.*); *D*, orchid,
Epipactis (*after Kerner*); *E*, *Tropaeolum* (*after Le M.
and Dec.*); *F*, pea, *Pisum*; *G*, same with corolla dissected
(*after Baillon*).

composed of three "united" petals. The lower lip serves as a landing platform for bees that come in search of food (Fig. 11, *C*).

The Flower of the Violet.—The five spreading petals of the
violet (Fig. 118) are very diverse in form. A larger, lower petal
usually forms a bag-like appendage or spur at its base, which
tends to break up the symmetry of the flower. The zygomorphic
nature of the violet is still further intensified by the irregularity
of the stamens, two of which are inferior and have nectaries
seated in spur-like appendages.

Zygomorphy in Tubular Flowers.—The zygomorphic features
of the tubular flowers in the figwort or snapdragon group (Figs.
11, *I*, and 141) are extremely diversified, ranging from flowers
that are only slightly bilobed to those that are very strikingly
lopsided, with upper and lower lips of very different form, with

the throat of the corolla closed by elastic lips, as in the true snapdragon, *Antirrhinum* (Fig. 141), or the lower lip developed in the form of a great inflated and gaudily colored sac as in the slipperwort, *Calceolaria*, etc. The stamens are also very frequently of two different types in this family.

Zygomorphy in the Orchids.—The most numerous, varied and interestingly complicated types of zygomorphy are doubtless found in the orchid family, *Orchidaceae* (Figs. 52, *A*, *C* and *D*, 203). The orchid flower usually has three separate sepals and three separate petals, a tricarpellary inferior ovary, and one or two greatly modified stamens (Fig. 21, *C*, *D*, *E* and *I*). The three sepals are similar or nearly so, and are mostly different in color from the petals. The petals are usually in two sets. Two lateral petals are usually alike and constitute one of the sets. The third petal, called the *lip*, is very dissimilar and usually larger, often broad and spurred as in *Orchis* (Fig. 21, *C*), or saccate as in *Cypripedium* (Fig. 21, *D*), and *Cattleya*, or lobed as in *Orchis*, *Diuris*, or fringed as in *Blephariglottis*, or variously cut (Fig. 21, *I*), and commonly very differently colored. Sometimes the two lateral petals are also enlarged and distinctively fringed and marked by striking color combinations. The stamens of orchids are reduced to one or two, two-celled anthers with the pollen borne in two to eight pear-shaped, stalked, waxy or powdery masses or *pollinia*, which are united by elastic threads, and these are intimately connected to and more or less hidden in a specialized structure representing the style and stigma. There are certain orchids, *Catasetum*, that have developed two strikingly different types of zygomorphic flowers one of which is male and the other female.

Zygomorphy and Relationship.—The greatest expression of zygomorphy occurs in groups of flowering plants that are clearly of advanced types on the basis of other characteristics, and cases of the phenomenon are relatively scarce among the groups that are more primitive on other grounds. The principle or "law" here is that the earlier or more primitive flowering plants are those that produce radially symmetrical or actinomorphic flowers, and that those with zygomorphic flowers are the higher and derived forms. The principle significance of zygomorphy is seen in its relation to cross-fertilization through the agency of insect visitors, as has already been stated in the section dealing with pollination.

The Number and Kinds of Carpels and Ovaries.—The number of carpels ("cells") in the compound ovary and the position of the ovary in the flower are other details that are included in the design of flowers. It has already been pointed out that some flowers have many separate carpels, and that many others have relatively few carpels that are united to form a compound ovary. Ovaries of the latter type are most frequently *bicarpellary* (composed of two united carpels or "cells"), *tricarpellary* (three carpels), *tetracarpellary* (four carpels), or *pentacarpellary* (five carpels). Some flowers have ovaries that are *polycarpellary*. Each carpel in the compound ovary of lower groups commonly produces several ovules, so that each flower, whether with many or few carpels produces numerous ovules, but in higher groups the number of ovules per carpel tends to become reduced, and in many of the highest plants (as in *Compositae*) each flower produces but a single ovule in what is morphologically a bicarpellary ovary. Species of flowering plants in the more primitive groups tend to produce numerous ovules per flower, either in many, one-celled, separate pistils or in a single two- to-many-celled ovary, but species in the more advanced and derived groups tend to produce few ovules per flower.

Hypogyny and Epigyny.—The two commonest floral plans in so far as the position of the ovary is concerned are the *hypogynous* flower (Figs. 8 and 46) and the *epigynous* flower (Figs. 9, 49 and 51). Hypogynous flowers are those in which the receptacle is more or less dome-shaped or conical, upon which the floral elements are arranged more or less horizontally or one above the other with the sepals outermost or lowermost, followed in order by petals and stamens with the carpels or ovary innermost or topmost. In such flowers the *pistil* is said to be "superior," and the *perianth* is said to be "inferior." This is the more primitive plan and it is illustrated by the flowers of magnolia, *Magnolia*, buttercup, *Ranunculus*, wind flower, *Anemone*, flax, *Linum*, radish, *Raphanus*, primrose, *Primula*, and a host of others. Epigynous flowers are those in which the ovary has become deeply imbedded in a more or less cup-shaped receptacle with which it becomes inseparably fused so as to constitute a unified structure. The other flower parts, *i.e.*, sepals, petals, and stamens, appear to rise from the top of the ovary, or at least they are borne on a rim near the upper extremity of the fused ovary and axis. In this case the *ovary* or pistil is said to be "inferior," and the *perianth* is said to be "superior." This is the more advanced flower plan and it is illustrated by many species in groups that are placed relatively high in our modern natural schemes for the classification of flowering plants, such as honeysuckle, *Lonicera* (Figs. 49 and 52), coffee, *Coffea* (Fig. 173), madder, *Rubia* (Fig. 173), dandelion, *Taraxacum* (Fig. 178), thistle, *Carduus*, and the orchids, *Orchis, Cypripedium*, etc.

Perigynous Flowers.—A floral plan more or less intermediate between the hypogynous and epigynous types is represented by the rose or cherry (Figs. 9 and 47). The receptacle in these flowers is deeply concave or cup-shaped, and the pistils are attached more or less loosely to the bottom and in the center of this hollow axis, but the axis and the pistils are not grown together as in epigynous flowers. The sepals, petals, and stamens are attached in the usual order to the *summit* or *rim* of the *axis*, so that these floral elements *appear to surround* the *pistils*, instead of being attached below or above the pistils. This type of flower is commonly said to be "perigynous" (Figs. 9 and 47). It is evidently a transitional form between the hypogynous plan and the epigynous plan of floral design, a relation which is shown in some systems of classification.

Incomplete and Imperfect Flowers.—Incomplete and imperfect (monœcious or diœcious) flowers (Figs. 2, 3, 16 and 20) reflect in modified form many of the designs that have been treated in the preceding paragraphs. The plans of such flowers are different from the more usual types simply because the petals or the sepals and petals, or the stamens or the pistils may be lacking in the individual flower. The common interpretation has been that these are indicative of primitive relationships, that the species with such flowers have not yet developed the high degree of perfection that is mirrored in those species with complete and perfect flowers. But the alternative and more or less opposite conclusion has grown and spread rapidly among botanists during the past few years. This interpretation teaches that species with incomplete and imperfect (monœcious or diœcious) flowers are not primitive forms but in reality higher forms in which the flowers have become "reduced" or "simplified," that is to say they have *lost* certain floral elements. Considerable evidence to contradict the former conclusion and to support the latter contention is now available. This doctrine also teaches that diœcious species are to be regarded as more advanced than monœcious species.

CHAPTER VII

FLORAL DIAGRAMS AND FORMULAE

A very brief introduction to the problems of flower forms or designs that are revealed by the flowering plants of the world has been presented in the foregoing chapter. But these hints, few and briefly put though they really are, may perhaps bewilder the student because of a seeming multiplicity of details. The great wealth and variety of flower plan is indeed not lacking in puzzles to many who have spent years in a study of flowering plants. It will be profitable, therefore, to consider the nature and use of pictorial, empirical, and diagrammatic methods or other formal means of representation to portray the design of flowers at a glance.

Skillfully made *photographs* and *sketches* prepared with great care for floral details have been very useful aids to the earnest student as he begins to study flowers. But the assistance that such materials give is rather limited and at times uncertain.

THE METHOD OF FLORAL DIAGRAMS

Floral *diagrams* that depict the nature of the flower and many of the details of its structure have served a very useful purpose in graphically portraying much that has been considered in the preceding chapter. The different floral elements are shown in such diagrams by more or less diagrammatic symbols, and these indicate perfectly and in proper relation many important features of the flower so that one with a good power of visualization has little difficulty in picturing the actual flower. The student will profit greatly by the preparation of these diagrams, especially during his earlier contacts with flowering plants when he has little knowledge of floral design. We may illustrate the method and the valuable possibilities of this aid by means of a few examples which are shown in the accompanying diagrams of the flowers of a number of families.

Diagram of the Buttercup Flower.—The diagram of the *Ranunculus* flower, *Ranunculaceae*, shows the five separate sepals as five slender crescents with their edges more or less overlapping on the outer rim of the figure as they would appear in a transverse section of the flower (Fig. 53, *A*). The five separate petals are indicated by a second whorl of arcs alternating with the symbols for the sepals. Next note the symbols of the many separate stamens arranged in the space between the petals and the carpels at the center of the diagram. Finally, in the very

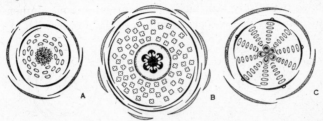

Fig. 53.—Floral diagrams. *A*, buttercup, *Ranunculus*; *B*, cactus, *Opuntia*; *C*, columbine, *Aquilegia* (after *Le M*. and *Dec.*).

center, is shown the group of many, separate carpels that are characteristic of the plants in this group. Thus it is seen that certain features are clearly shown that are characteristic of the great group to which this plant belongs. An important point that the diagram does not bring out is the fact that the flower is a hypogynous flower. The spiral type is also difficult to portray

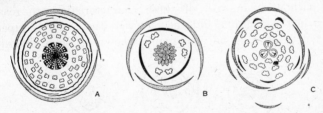

Fig. 54.—Floral diagrams. *A*, poppy, *Papaver*; *B*, water plantain, *Alisma*; *C*, monkshood, *Aconitum* (after *Le M*. and *Dec.*).

by the diagram. The diagram as it stands might indicate that the flower of *Ranunculus* is perfectly cyclic throughout.

Details shown by Diagrams.—The columbine, *Aquilegia*, is a member of the *Ranunculaceae* also, but the flowers of this plant have only five separate carpels as compared to the many in *Ranunculus*, and each of the five petals is spurred (Fig. 53, *C*). These features are clearly reflected in the diagram. The numerous stamens and the normal sepals are shown about as they are in *Ranunculus*. A flower type with many stamens and many united carpels is shown by the poppy, *Papaver rhoeas* (Fig. 54, *A*). The flower of aconite or monkshood, *Aconitum* (Fig. 54, *C*), another member of the *Ranunculaceae*, is strikingly zygomorphic. This feature is contributed by one of the five dark blue petals which is helmet-shaped and protects two of the additional petals which serve as long-stalked, tubular, two-lipped nectaries. The remaining petals are narrow and inconspicuous or they are entirely wanting. There are numerous stamens and three, many-ovuled carpels to complete the flower. All of these

Fig. 55.—Floral diagrams. *A*, mallow, *Malva*; *B*, orange, *Citrus*; *C*, milkweed, *Asclepias (after Le M. and Dec.)*.

features are shown in the diagram. The cactus flower (Fig. 53, *B*) has many separate stamens and several united carpels.

The flower of the common *Oxalis, Oxalidaceae*, has five separate sepals, five separate petals, ten more or less united stamens, five of which are glandular, and five carpels grown together in a compound ovary (Fig. 56, *A*). The flower is perfectly cyclic and actinomorphic. All of these characteristics are readily shown in the diagram, but the fact that the ovary is superior and not inferior is not commonly shown in such diagrams.

Fig. 56.—Floral diagrams. *A*, sorrel, *Oxalis*; *B*, a mustard, *Erysimum*; *C*, sweet pea, *Lathyrus (after Le M. and Dec.)*.

Zygomorphy Shown by Diagrams.—The type of zygomorphy peculiar to the beans and their kin, *Leguminosae*, can also be nicely illustrated by the diagram method (Fig. 56, *C*). The flower of sweet pea, *Lathyrus odoratus*, shows the typical structure and arrangement of flower parts with the corolla composed of banner, wings, and keel, the five symmetrical sepals, the ten stamens, nine grown together and one separate, and the simple pistil (Fig. 56, *C*).

Other Floral Types Shown by Diagrams.—The mustard family, *Cruciferae*, is another group in which the typical floral plan can be shown very well by means of a diagram. The flowers of the common shepherd's purse, *Bursa*, or wallflower, *Erysimum*, have four separate sepals, four separate petals, six stamens, and a bicarpellary ovary (Fig. 56, *B*). The flower is actinomorphic, cyclic, and hypogynous. All of these features except the position of the ovary are shown in a diagram as for rocket, *Erysimum* sp. (Fig. 56, *B*).

FIG. 57.—Floral diagrams. *A*, asparagus, *Asparagus*; *B*, spiderwort, *Tradescantia*; *C*, fritillary, *Fritillaria* (after *Le M. and Dec.*).

The Lilies.—The flower structure of lilies and their kin, is nicely illustrated by the floral diagram method (Fig. 57). These flowers, as shown in *Asparagus* (Fig. 57, *A*), *Tradescantia* (Fig. 57, *B*), *Fritillaria* (Fig. 57, *C*), usually have three separate sepals, three separate petals, six stamens, and a tricarpellary ovary. The flower is actinomorphic and hypogynous. The closely related irises, *Iridaceae*, differ from lilies in having only three stamens and an inferior ovary. The difference in stamens is readily shown by the diagram of *Iris*, but the epigynous flower

FIG. 58.—Floral diagrams. *A*, orchid, *Orchis*; *B*, iris, *Iris*; *C*, lily-of-the-valley, *Convallaria* (after *Le M. and Dec.*).

is not contrasted with the hypogynous flower of the lily by means of the diagram (Fig. 58, *B*).

The Orchids.—The extreme zygomorphy and reduction of stamens in the orchids, *Orchidaceae*, may be indicated in floral diagrams for members of that family (Fig. 58, *A*). Thus in the showy orchid, *Orchis*, the greatly enlarged and inflated petal known as the "lip" is shown as a distortion on one side of the diagram, and the union of stamens and style and stigma into a

single mass is clearly indicated, as is the tricarpellary ovary.   The
epigynous nature of the flower is not shown by the diagram
(Fig. 58, *A*).

Sympetaly Shown Also.—Additional details of floral design
such as the tubular corolla and epipetalous stamens are readily
depicted by the diagram method.   Both of these features are
represented in hosts of Dicotyledons and they are shown in the
floral diagram of the common potato, *Solanum tuberosum* (Fig.
59, *A*).   The flower is actinomorphic, and hypogynous and it

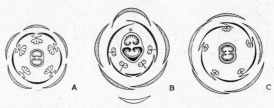

Fig. 59.—Floral diagrams.   *A*, potato, *Solanum; B*, snapdragon, *Antirrhinum;
C*, tobacco, *Nicotiana (after Le M. and Dec.).*

has five separate sepals, five "united" petals to form a rotate
corolla, five stamens attached to the shallow corolla tube on the
lines between the petals, and a bicarpellary ovary with many
ovules in each carpel (Fig. 59, *A*).   The fact that the petals are
united is shown by the connective between them, and the epipetalous stamens are shown by a connection with the petals.
A similar diagram is shown for tobacco, *Nicotiana* (Fig. 59, *C*).

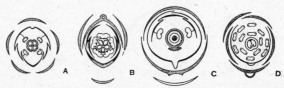

Fig. 60.—Floral diagrams.   *A*, of a mint, *Lamium; B*, balsam, *Impatiens; C*,
bladderwort, *Utricularia; D*, larkspur, *Delphinium (after Le M. and Dec.).*

The flowers of the foxglove family, *Scrophulariaceae*, are
sympetalous, zygomorphic, and bicarpellary.   The diagram for
the flower of the snapdragon, *Antirrhinum*, reflects these features
(Fig. 59, *B*).   The five sepals are "united" to form a gamosepalous calyx, and the five petals are "united" to form a tubular
or gamopetalous corolla which is two-lobed.   The four stamens
are attached to the inside of the corolla tube (Fig. 59, *B*).   Other
zygomorphic types are shown by the mints as in *Lamium*

(Fig. 60, *A*), balsam (Fig. 60, *B*); bladderwort (Fig. 60, *C*), larkspur (Fig. 60, *D*).

Union of Stamens Indicated in the Diagram.—Flowers in which the stamens are united by their filaments are represented by the mallows, *Malvaceae* (Fig. 85), and the citrus group, *Rutaceae* (Fig. 94). The floral diagram of a mallow, *Malva sylvestris*, illustrates the five free sepals, five free petals, and the ring formed by the union of the filaments of many stamens that completely surrounds the cluster of many united carpels at the

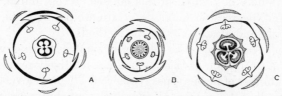

FIG. 61.—Floral diagrams. *A*, phacelia, *Phacelia; B*, primrose, *Primula; C*, bluebell, *Campanula (after Le M. and Dec.).*

center of the flower (Fig. 55, *A*). The flower of the orange group, *Citrus aurantium*, has five separate sepals and petals, many stamens grown together by their filaments into several separate groups but not forming a continuous ring about the ovary with several united carpels (Fig. 55, *B*).

Other forms of floral diagrams are shown by phacelia (Fig. 61, *A*); primrose (Fig. 61, *B*); bluebell (Fig. 61, *C*); flax (Fig. 62, *A*); lilac (Fig. 62, *B*); cucumber (Fig. 62, *C* and *D*).

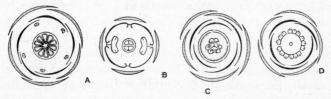

FIG. 62.—Floral diagrams. *A*, flax, *Linum; B*, lilac, *Syringa; C*, cucumber, *Cucumis*, female; *D*, cucumber, *Cucumis*, male *(after Le M. and Dec.).*

THE METHOD OF FLORAL FORMULAE

The *formula method* of various types has also been used for many years to express flower structure or floral design and relationships. The kinds of formulae developed differ considerably. They are designed to show graphically many features of flower structure and relationships and their values in classification.

Floral "Elements" and Floral "Compounds."—The formulae presented herewith appear at first to resemble the well-known formulae that constitute such an important item in the equipment of chemical language. But the resemblance is naturally very superficial. If similar to chemical formulae at all, it is only in the use of symbols for the floral "elements" and in the attempt to reflect something of the structural relationships of different flowers by writing the symbols together so as to show the flower "compound" as a whole. A surprisingly large number of flowers may be treated in this manner so that different floral types and degrees of phyletic relationships may be shown graphically and at a glance by the method.

Symbols Necessary.—The number of symbols necessary for the successful utilization of this method are relatively few, even for a large number of flower types (page 159). This is a very important feature of the system and one which contributes greatly to its outstanding success. The multiplication of symbols becomes necessary, of course, if great numbers of plants are involved, but the greatest values of the method lie in the delineation and separation of the common orders and families in graphic contrast. The scheme may now be illustrated by some representative examples, including the forms that have already been used to outline the possibilities of the floral diagram method.

Structure of the Formula.—The formula of the *Ranunculus* flower shows (Fig. 63, *A*) the use of the method to illustrate the primitive type of flowering plant. The calyx (number of sepals) appears in the formula as Ca and the corolla (number of petals) as Co, stamens as S and pistils as P. The number of parts in each of the four floral whorls, *i.e.*, the number of times each "floral element" is represented in the "floral compound" is indicated by an exponent. Thus in this particular plant there are usually five sepals and five petals so these facts are indicated in the formula by writing the appropriate figures as exponents, and the many or indefinite number of stamens and pistils are shown by using the infinity sign to convey the thought of an indefinite or irregular number of stamens and pistils. The whole formula may then be written as in Fig. 63, *A*, with all elements on a single plane to represent the hypogynous nature of the flower. The fact that the stamens and carpels are represented as numerous and as being present in an indefinite number, and that they are separate, is understood to convey the fact that the flower, in so far as the essential organs are concerned, conforms to the *spiral type*, and the plant, therefore, belongs to a relatively "low" or primitive group.

Examples of Formulae.—The formula for *Ranunculus* may be very readily generalized so that it may reflect a broader series of floral "compounds," the family *Ranunculaceae*, for example. Such a formula would be written as is shown in Fig. 63, *B*. This portrays at a glance that the members of this family produce flowers that have many sepals and petals or they may be as few as three or none at all, with stamens typically always numerous, and pistils numerous to comparatively few, the latter condition being represented by x in the exponent. That is, this formula means that one might expect to find flowers produced by some members of this family with sepals anywhere between, say fifteen and three, petals anywhere from an indefinite number to none whatever, but the stamens numerous in all, and the carpels numerous in some flowers, but with a tendency to reduction to a smaller, more definite number in others. The typically hypogynous nature of the flower throughout the family is reflected in the horizontal one-storied nature of the formula. The closely related magnolia family, *Magnoliaceae*, differs from this family mainly in the woody nature of its species and in an even greater tendency toward indefiniteness in the number of the parts in the flower. These characteristics are shown in the formula (Fig. 63, *C*) and the uniformity of the exponents reflecting plasticity for all four of the floral elements. The formula for the *Malvaceae* shows certain features in common with the above families (Fig. 63, *D*).

$$\frac{C\overset{5}{a}\,Co^5\,S^\infty\,P^\infty}{A_{CH}} \quad A$$

$$\frac{C\overset{3\text{-}\infty}{a}\,Co^\infty\,S^\infty\,P^{x\text{-}\infty}}{A_{CH}\,F_{OL}\,B_{AC}} \quad B$$

$$\frac{C\overset{x}{a}\,Co^x\,S^\infty\,P^\infty}{S_{AM}\,F_{OL}} \quad C$$

$$\frac{C\overset{5}{a}\,Co^5\,S^\infty\,P^{5\text{-}\infty}}{B_{AC}\,C_{APSULAR}} \quad D$$

F1G. 63.—Floral formulae. *A*, buttercup, *Ranunculus;* *B*, buttercup family, *Ranunculaceae;* *C*, magnolia family, *Magnoliaceae;* *D*, mallow family, *Malvaceae.* See page 159 for symbols.

A weakness of all such methods as a detailed portrayal of the nature of plant groups should be noted at this point. Diagrams and formulae, when broadly generalized, are likely to convey misleading conceptions unless the student understands that they are not intended to exhibit the nature of the flowers of all of the genera and species that are commonly included under the various orders and families in standard manuals and other works on classification. They are meant to show only the broad general nature of the various groups involved, and the student must expect to discover exceptions and inconsistencies that cannot be overcome by the method unless it is presented in much greater detail in order to treat a much larger list of forms. But such a plan would largely defeat the values of the scheme for all but the extreme specialist who really does not need the method anyhow. Such details must be of necessity treated in the usual descriptive manner. Thus in the magnolia family, whose general nature has been shown in the formula, we have the tulip tree, *Liriodendron,* the flowers of which have only three sepals, but six petals, a degree of regularity not implied in the family formula. But even in this species the nature of the stamens and pistils clearly indicates that the plant is a comparatively low form, and it is inferentially close to the other group discussed, so that the value of the formula is by no means completely destroyed.

Additional Possibilities.—The further possibilities of the formula method may be illustrated by an examination of the formulae of some other well-known groups of flowering plants. Many other features of the scheme, as well as the practical value of the same will be included in the sections dealing with classification. Let us consider next a type that is markedly different from the types that have been illustrated by use of the *Ranunculaceae* and *Magnoliaceae.* The phlox or sweet william family, *Polemoniaceae,* is very strikingly different from the buttercup family in the structure of its flowers. Many features of this difference may be shown in the family formula as in Fig. 64, *B.* The first thing that catches our eye in this formula in contrast with the floral "compound" of the buttercups is that the stamens have been placed above the line occupied by the three other floral elements. Next note that the number of sepals, petals, and pistils is not nearly so varied, in fact being represented by a single figure and thus allowing for no common variation, and that the respective exponents are circled. The

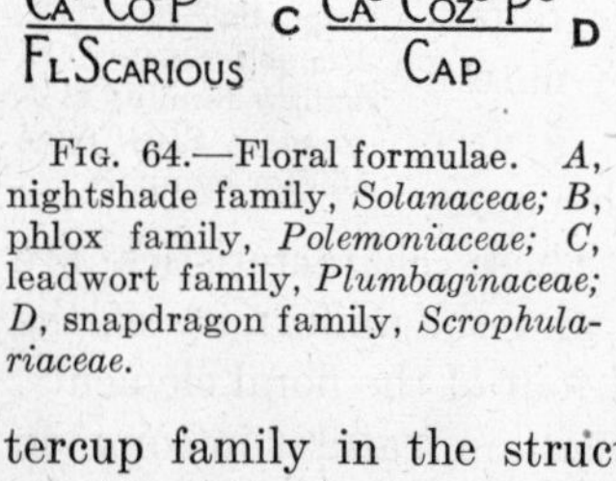

FIG. 64.—Floral formulae. *A,* nightshade family, *Solanaceae; B,* phlox family, *Polemoniaceae; C,* leadwort family, *Plumbaginaceae; D,* snapdragon family, *Scrophulariaceae.*

circle about the exponent of any floral element means that the elements are united. In other words, it is found that the flowers in this family have five sepals that are "united" to form a campanulate or tubular calyx, that the five petals are "united" to produce a tubular corolla, and that the carpels are reduced to three, and, furthermore, that these are united to form a tricarpellary ovary or pistil. This observation now helps to visualize the situation with reference to the stamens, for it is learned that sympetalous flowers usually have epipetalous stamens. The most natural manner to represent this feature of the flower is to write the symbol for the stamens above (upon) the symbol for the corolla with its united petals. The fact that the five stamens are attached to the corolla tube and opposite the lobes (opposite the petals)may be shown in the formula by a vertical bar at the end of the stamen line. The definite number of parts and the prevalence of united parts will indicate that the flower is cyclic instead of spiral and, consequently, representative of a high group. The formation of a capsule as the usual type of fruit is indicated by a self-explanatory symbol below the plane of the hypogynous flower (Fig. 64, *B*).

Formulae Contrast Essential Differences.—The readiness with which the formulae serve to contrast essential differences between families may again be illustrated here. The potato family, *Solanaceae*, is commonly thought to be closely related to the phlox family, and these two families are usually placed near each other in books on classification. But there must be differences between the families or there would be no value served in separating them in the manuals. The essential similarities and the outstanding differences are reflected in the two formulae (Figs. 64, *A* and *B*). The resemblances first appear at a glance. It will be noticed that the calyx, corolla, and stamens are shown exactly as in the *Polemoniaceae*, or phloxes. But later it is discovered that the pistil is *bicarpellary* instead of *tricarpellary*, and one of the most useful points of differentiation among the two families is thus found. Certainly these contrasts, as well as the similarities, are presented more quickly by this means than in a lengthy description or even in floral diagrams. They also portray at a glance the fact that these two families are representative of very much higher forms of flowering plants than are the buttercups and magnolias, according to the criteria for primitive or "low" groups and derived or "high" groups that have been stated.

Formulae Also Show Zygomorphic Nature.—Flowering plant families in which zygomorphy is an outstanding feature present many interesting possibilities to one enthusiastic to show flower design by means of empirical formulae. The figwort or snapdragon family, *Scrophulariaceae*, will furnish some excellent examples (Fig. 64, *D*). The flowers in this family are typically irregular or very zygomorphic. The perianth is composed of four or five "united" sepals, and the corolla of five petals of diverse form united to form a tubular, two-lipped corolla, with two petals in one lip and three in the other. Upon the limb of the corolla are borne the two, four, or five stamens. The ovary or pistil is composed of two united carpels. The fruit is usually a many-seeded capsule. The formula may be constructed to show all of these features, as in Fig. 64, *D*. The representation of the gamopetalous, zygomorphic corolla is accomplished by making the symbol for the corolla *Coz* instead of simply *Co*. The variable number of stamens and the nature of the ovary are represented in the usual manner. The formula indicates with a brief study the similarities which exist between this family and the *Solanaceae* and *Polemoniaceae* and at the same time the basis (zygomorphy) upon which it is readily distinguished from those families. The formula may be less generalized and more specialized in such a manner as to represent the essential design of many of the genera within the family, but as has been indicated that is not the purpose of the present work.

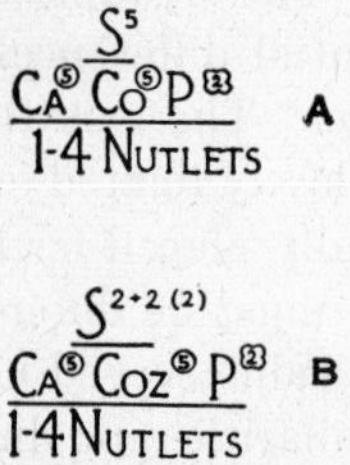

$$\overset{S^5}{\underset{\text{1-4 Nutlets}}{Ca^{\circledS}\,Co^{\circledS}\,P^{\circledR}}} \quad A$$

$$\overset{S^{2+2\,(2)}}{\underset{\text{1-4 Nutlets}}{Ca^{\circledS}\,Coz^{\circledS}\,P^{\circledR}}} \quad B$$

Fig. 65.—Floral formulae. *A*, forget-me-not family, *Boraginaceae*; *B*, mint family, *Labiatae*.

Formula for the Mints.—The mint family, *Labiatae*, also represents many interesting features of zygomorphic flowers (Fig. 65, *B*). This family is similar to the snapdragons in so far as zygomorphy is concerned, but there are certain differences in the floral design of the two families that may be pictured graphically by means of the formulae. The formula for this family clearly brings out these features, as shown by Fig. 65, *B*. The calyx and corolla symbols are the same as in the snapdragon family, and the stamens do not show any significant points of difference. On the other hand, the pistil in the mints is represented as being composed, as in the snapdragons, of two united carpels, but the symbol clearly indicates that each of these is deeply two-lobed.

This condition of the pistil is furthermore reflected in the fruits, as indicated below the line, which are of the nature of four "bony nutlets." The ovary is bicarpellary, and each carpel is deeply lobed or grooved. A single seed develops in each of the two lobes of each carpel, and the four segments separate at maturity as characteristic nut-like fruits that often belie their true morphology. Thus it is readily seen that one of the greatest contrasts between mints and snapdragons is in the nature of their pistils.

Further Values in Formulae.—It may be instructive at this point to introduce another family with actinomorphic flowers but which has a pistil very much like the mints. This is the puccoon or forget-me-not family, *Boraginaceae*, in which the formula indicates striking differences as compared with mints, but it also shows the essentially similar ovary, as shown in Fig. 65, *A*. The fact that the perianth is radially symmetrical is shown by the formula, and this is the most evident difference between the flowers of the two groups.

A student may sometimes be puzzled by a flower from which the corolla has fallen, but which still shows the four ripening nutlets in the bottom of the calyx. If there are no flowers with corollas to be found on the specimen the question as to whether the plant is a mint or a puccoon may have to be settled by an examination of the vegetative characteristics which are frequently decisive.

Formulae to Show Hypogyny and Epigyny.—A further principle of floral design that may be nicely shown by means of formulae is the position of the ovary in the flower, *i.e.*, whether it is superior (flower hypogynous) or inferior (flower epigynous). All of the floral patterns so far illustrated by a formula have a superior ovary and they may serve as examples of that type of formula.

Formula for the Umbellifers.—Epigynous flowers are of various kinds depending upon the relation of other floral elements besides the pistil. Two or three types may be chosen to represent these. The celery or parsley group, *Umbelliferae*, produces flowers (Fig. 68, *D*) with a bicarpellary pistil which has become completely merged with the cup-shaped receptacle so as to form an inferior ovary with a flange or rim about the upper portion upon which the perianth and stamens are disposed. The five separate and regular sepals, the five separate and symmetrical petals, and the five stamens are all inserted on the edge of the receptacle or disk at the top of the ovary.   These characteristics are all indicated in the family formula for this group as is shown at a glance in Fig. 68, *D*.   This may be termed a "two-storied" flower in which the pistil constitutes the lower story and the perianth and stamens the upper story.   It will be recalled that the flowers of phloxes, mints, snapdragons, nightshades, forget-me-nots are also two-storied, but in all these the stamens being upon the corolla constitute the upper story, and the lower story includes the perianth and pistils, as in all hypogynous flowers. It is noted that the calyx and corolla are composed of separate parts and that the stamens are not attached to the perianth in any manner.   As usual, certain vegetative features and fruit characteristics may be shown below the base line of the formula.

The Formula for the Madders.—The madders or coffee family, *Rubiaceae*, also produce flowers with an inferior ovary, but the

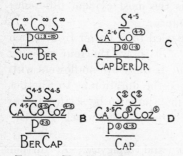

FIG. 66.—Floral formulae.   *A*, cactus family, *Cactaceae*; *B*, honeysuckle family *Caprifoliaceae*; *C*, madder family, *Rubiaceae*; *D*, bluebell family, *Campanulaceae*.

two to six sepals and four or five petals are commonly "united" to form a "limb" and tubular corolla respectively, and the stamens are "inserted" on the throat or tube of the corolla (Fig. 66, *C*).   The pistil is composed of one to eight carpels, usually two, united to form a compound ovary. This floral design when expressed in formula manner reveals at once the three-storied nature of the flower as well as a considerable degree of variation in the composition or number of floral elements of the flowers of the plants usually included in this family, as in Fig. 66, *C*.   The pattern of the flower clearly indicates that these plants are higher than the umbellifers.

Epipetalous Stamens Easily Represented.—A three-storied flower with zygomorphic corolla is found in a number of the highest families.   Thus in many honeysuckles, *Lonicera*, the tubular corolla is slashed into two irregular lips, a condition that may be shown in the formula by the device already described (Fig. 66, *B*).   In the bluebell or harebell, *Campanula*, which belongs to the family, *Campanulaceae*, the flowers are beautifully actinomorphic or radially symmetrical and the ovary composed of three to five carpels, as in Fig. 66, *D*. The stamens are more normal in structure but are sometimes free from the corolla.

The Cactus Type.—The cactus type, *Cactaceae*, introduces another interesting floral pattern that is strikingly contrasted with the foregoing types by means of the formula, as in Fig. 66, *A*. There are many separate sepals and petals borne on the upper surface of the rim of the urn-shaped axis and an indefinite number of stamens also on the axis surrounding the style. The ovary is inferior and is one-celled, but composed of 3 to many carpels. This condition is represented by the usual exponent to indicate the number of carpels present in the pistil, in this case one, followed by a colon and 3 and the infinity sign, so that the symbols to show the structure of the pistil are written as shown in the formula (Fig. 66, *A*).

Formulae for Monocotyledons.—All of the examples used to illustrate the principles and the possible values of the floral formula so far have been selected from the Dicotyledons, but the same schemes are readily adapted to show the features of floral design among the Monocotyledons. For examples, the arrowheads, *Alismaceae*, is a group of Monocotyledons closely related to the buttercups in the Dicotyledon series. This relationship may be shown in the formula along with the differences that really make these plants Monocotyledons, as in Fig. 67, *A*. The calyx and corolla are composed of three separate parts, or sepals and petals may be lacking (in some species); there are usually many stamens although there may be as few as six, and there are many separate carpels. The symbols for stamens and pistils indicate that the flowers are spiral in so far as those organs are concerned. The three-parted perianth is a monocotyledonous tendency. The hypogynous nature of the flower is represented in the usual manner. Symbols below the base line show that the members of the group are monœcious or diœcious and that the fruit is usually an achene. The usual mass of information of a family is here condensed into relatively small space (Fig. 67, *A*).

$$\frac{C_A{}^3 C_O{}^3 S^{6 \cdot \infty} P^{6 \cdot \infty}}{P_F M_O D_I A_{CH}} \quad A$$

$$\frac{C_A{}^3 C_O{}^3 S^{6(3)} P^\circledS}{C_{AP} B_{ER}} \quad B$$

$$\frac{C_A{}^3 C_O S^{3 \cdot 6} P^{\circledcirc\circledcirc\circledcirc}}{C_{HAFFY} F_L C_{AP}} \quad C$$

Fig. 67.—Floral formulae. *A*, water plantain family, *Alismaceae*; *B*, lily family, *Liliaceae*; *C*, rush family, *Juncaceae*.

The Lily Type in Formula.—The best known type of Monocotyledon is probably the lily or some of its close variants. The

floral design of the lilies, *Liliaceae*, is shown by means of a
formula (Fig. 67, *B*), and this may be readily varied to show the
greater details necessary to delimit subordinate groups or even
genera.   The tripartite nature of the flowers of lilies is strikingly
reflected in the formula.   The definite number of parts, and
especially the three pistils united to form a tricarpellary ovary
clearly indicate a much higher type than is shown by the arrowhead formula.

The Amaryllis Contrasts with the Lily.—Amaryllises are also
well known Monocotyledons, and they are not commonly dissocia-
ted from the true lilies in the popular conception.   The formula
for an amaryllis shows that the members
of that group, *Amaryllidaceae*, are in
reality very different from the lilies.
The group includes also such familiar

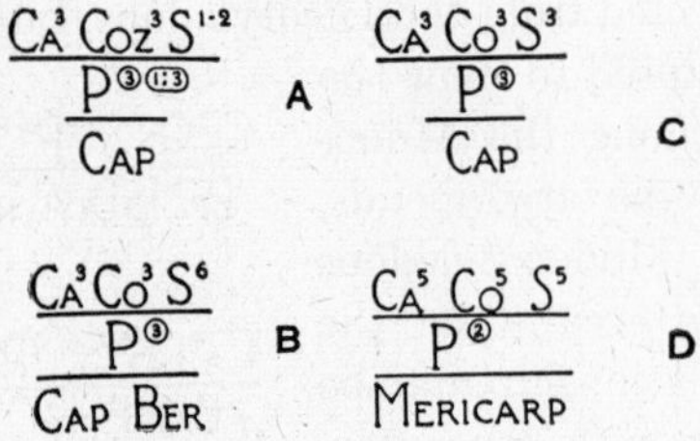

FIG. 68.—Floral formulae.   *A*, orchid family, *Orchidaceae; B*, amaryllis family,
Amaryllidaceae; C, iris family, *Iridaceae; D*, parsley family, *Umbelliferae*.

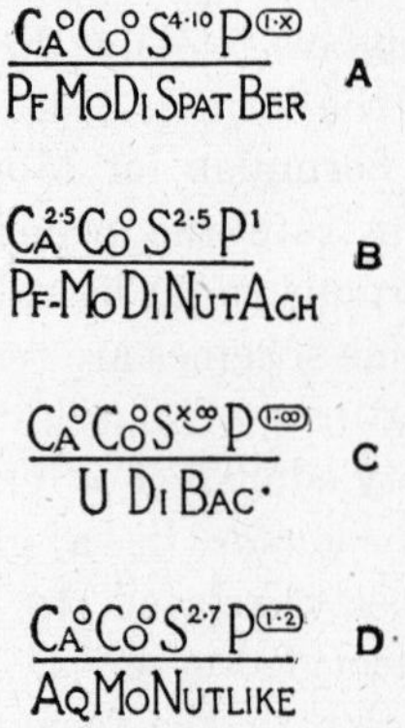

FIG. 69.—Floral formulae.   *A*. arum family, *Araceae; B*, goosefoot family,
Chenopodiaceae; C, screw-pine family, *Pandanaceae; D*, cattail family, *Typhaceae*.

plants as the various species of *Narcissus*, often called lilies but
which differ from true lilies in having inferior ovaries (Fig. 68, *B*).

The Iris Type.—The flags, *Iris*, and blue-eyed grasses, *Sisyrin-
chium*, belonging to the iris family, *Iridaceae*, reflect the lily and
amaryllis pattern with still another variation.   These flowers
have three sepals, three petals, three stamens, and a tricarpellary,
inferior ovary, the reduction of stamens to three distinguishing
them from the amaryllids, all of which is shown in Fig. 68, *C*.

The Orchid Formula.—The orchids introduce numerous and
extremely varied zygomorphic types as a culmination of the
monocotyledonous series.   More than 15,000 species are known.
The details of orchid flowers may be found to present more
puzzles for the formula maker to solve than any other group,

and yet the generalized formula (Fig. 68, *A*) for the family is not difficult to construct. The three sepals are normal or symmetrical, but the corolla is extremely zygomorphic on account of one of the three petals that is modified in a long series of odd forms, from broadly expanded and lobed or fringed lips to curious inflated bags or pitchers. The reduction in number and specialization of the stamens are also features of this family (Fig. 68, *A*). The intimate connection of the stamens with the pistil, at least with the style or stigma may be shown in the formula by a connective between the two symbols concerned.

Various types of apetalous families are reflected in formula form in Fig. 69. Numerous additional features of floral formulae and their use as aids in depicting flower structure, and in the classification and determination of natural relationships and possible lines of descent in flowering plants, will be included under sections dealing with the various groups. The many possibilities in these directions are as fascinating as they are exhaustless.

CHAPTER VIII

FLOWER CLUSTERS

It has been seen that the *plan* of the flowers is quite distinctive in flowering plants. It is also true that the *arrangement* of flowers or their aggregation into clusters upon the plant are more or less constant for the different species.

Single Flowers and Clusters of Flowers.—The individual flowers of many species of flowering plants are borne singly at the end of a more or less greatly elongated stalk or branch of the main axis of the plant. This is the case in such familiar

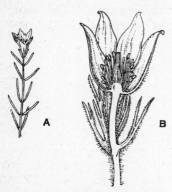

plants as bluebell, *Campanula*, (Fig. 70, *A*), tulips, *Tulipa*, magnolia, *Magnolia* (Fig. 98), wake robin, *Trillium*, poppies, *Papaver* (Fig. 119), Pasque flower, *Pulsatilla* (Fig. 70, *B*), waterlily, *Nelumbium* (Fig. 103), and windflower, *Anemone*. The stalk which bears the flower at the top is called the "peduncle." Such flowers are usually conspicuous because of their relatively large size and brilliant coloration. On the other hand, the flowers of most species are gathered more or less closely together in simple or branched

FIG. 70.—Inflorescences. *A*, single flower of bluebell, *Campanula*; *B*, single flower of Pasque flower, *Pulsatilla*.

groups or clusters in such a manner as to increase their conspicuousness, whether the individual flowers are large or small, brilliantly colored or less conspicuously marked. The stems or stalks of the individual flowers are called "pedicels," the *main* axis or stem in such cases being called the peduncle (Fig. 70, *B*).

The great Swedish botanist, Linnaeus, suggested the term *inflorescence* to express the mode of flower arrangement and the term has been adopted throughout the world.

Inflorescences and Relationship.—Single flowers and loosely branched inflorescences are regarded as "low" or primitive, and the more finely branched and densely compacted inflorescences are regarded as "high" or derived. The degree of branching and the density of aggregation vary within extremely wide limits. These relationships appear to be correlated with many other criteria that have been set up as evidences of the relative degree of specialization or advancement that different groups of flowering plants exhibit.

The Kinds of Inflorescences.—The two broadest types of inflorescences or flower clusters are determined by fundamentally different methods of growth in the floral branches of the stem of the plant. In one case the continuously growing axis of the inflorescence has the flowers borne as usual in the axes of the reduced leaves or bracts, with the oldest flowers at the base and the progressively younger ones toward the tip. The tip of the inflorescence continues its upward growth and the whole thing becomes more and more elongated (Fig. 71, *C*). As long as this growth continues new flower buds are opening at a short distance below the very tip upon which the youngest buds are often aggregated into a very dense cluster. It frequently happens that the fruits may be nearly mature at the base of such an inflorescence when there are many unopened and still very young flower buds at the tip of the same inflorescence. The opening of the flowers and the progressive maturation of the fruits and seeds in such flower clusters proceed from the base toward the tip, or in reality from the circumference toward the center when we think of the cluster in its morphological unity. This sequence is *centripetal*, and it is produced by the indefinite or *indeterminate* growth of the floral axis. This kind of inflorescence is *racemose*, and it is by far the more common of the two general types among flowering plants (Fig. 71 and 72).

THE RACEMOSE TYPE

The Raceme.—There are several different forms or varieties of the racemose type of inflorescence. One of the commonest of these is the *raceme*, illustrated by such plants as currant, *Ribes aureum* (Fig. 71, *A*), dagger weed, *Yucca gloriosa* (Fig. 71, *D*), Solomon's seal, *Vagnera stellata*, lily-of-the-valley, *Convallaria*, hyacinth, *Hyacinthus* (Fig. 186, *B*), agrimony, *Agrimonia*, fireweed, *Chamaenerion*, and pine sap, *Hypopitys*. The pedicels of the various flowers in a simple raceme are distinct and of about the same length at maturity so that a simple or unbranched raceme (Fig. 71, *A*) tends to become more or less cylindrical in form with a rather abruptly or broadly tapering tip as the flowers on the lower pedicels reach maturity.

The Spike.—The *spike* (Fig. 72, *B*, *C* and *D*) is a typically racemose inflorescence with an elongating axis that bears scattered single flowers without stalks or pedicels, *i.e.*, the flowers are *sessile*. Plants that produce this type of inflorescence are mullein, *Verbascum*, plantain, *Plantago* (Figs. 72, *B* and 129, *A*), pondweed, *Potamogeton*, orchids, *Orchis rotundifolia*, glasswort, *Salicornia*, and prairie clover, *Kuhnistera*. The various flowers usually fall away from the axis of the spike separately or indi-

Fig. 71.—Inflorescences. *A*, raceme of currant, *Ribes;* *B*, axillary flowers of partridge berry, *Mitchella;* *C*, panicle of bluebell, *Campanula;* *D*, compound panicle of yucca, *Yucca gloriosa.*

vidually. The axis may be persistent after all, or nearly all, of the flowers have fallen. Certain other peculiar spike-like flower aggregates may be included here as variations of the typical spike.

The Catkin.—A *catkin* (Fig. 72, *A*) is of the nature of a spike, but it commonly produces only staminate or pistillate flowers, and at maturity the whole structure falls away as a unit, as in the staminate inflorescence of birch, *Betula* (Fig. 72, *A*), walnut, *Juglans*, hickory, *Hicoria*, hazel, *Corylus*, chestnut, *Castanea*, oak, *Quercus*, and in both the staminate and pistillate inflorescences of willow, *Salix* (Fig. 127, *A*, *B*, *D* and *E*), and cottonwood, *Populus* (Fig. 127, *C*). The distinction between a catkin and a spike is sometimes difficult to make, but the endeavor is probably of value. The catkin-like spikes of pistillate flowers in the mulberry, *Morus*, become the ripe "fruits" or mulberries in the popular sense.

The Spadix.—The *spadix* in the calla lily, *Calla, Richardia,* Jack-in-the-pulpit, *Arisaema* (Fig. 190, *B*), skunk cabbage, *Spathyema,* calamus, *Acorus,* the arrowarum, *Peltandra,* dasheen, *Colocasia,* and other members of the arum family, *Araceae,* is a more or less elongated, congested, and thickened, fleshy axis bearing the sessile, commonly fleshy flowers which are perfect, pistillate, or staminate. The spadix is commonly surrounded and partly enclosed by the *spathe* (Fig. 190) which is often believed to be a flower because of its brilliant coloration. In the Jack-in-the-pulpit the spadix is "Jack" and the spathe is the "pulpit" within which he stands.

The "spike" or "head" in many wild grasses and cereals such as in timothy, *Phleum* (Fig. 198, *A*), *Hordeum,* and in cultivated rye, *Secale,* wheat, *Triticum,* and barley, *Hordeum,* is in reality a compound, spike-like inflorescence. There is a sessile cluster of flowers (a spikelet or group of spikelets) at each node in this floral axis instead of a single flower as in the typical spike.

The Corymb.—The *corymb* is a racemose inflorescence in which the pedicels of the lower or older flowers are much longer than those of the upper or younger flowers. This condition tends to bring

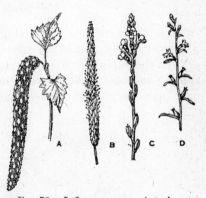

Fig. 72.—Inflorescences. *A*, male catkin of birch, *Betula; B*, spike of plantain, *Plantago; C*, spike of vervain, *Verbena; D*, bracted spike of lobelia, *Lobelia.*

all of the flowers of the entire cluster to lie in a single plane, and so the inflorescence is more or less convex or flat topped. Examples of this type of inflorescence are afforded by candytuft, *Iberis,* and certain cherries, *Prunus cerasus.*

The Umbel.—The *umbel* is an inflorescence in which the axis is very short and more or less knob-like, upon the top of which the numerous pedicels appear to arise (Fig. 73, *A* and *B*) from about the same point, and, spreading radially, raise their flowers to form a convex or flat-topped cluster. The pedicels are sometimes called the *rays* of the *umbel.* The floral bracts at the bases of the pedicels are brought close together at the axis of the umbel. In many cases this cluster of bracts is rather

conspicuous and they form the *involucre*. This type of flower
cluster is very common in the group of plants known as the
"umbellifers," *Umbelliferae* (Fig. 172), to which belong the
carrot, *Daucus*, dill, *Anethum*, celery, *Apium*, parsnip, *Pastinaca*,
myrrh, *Myrrhis*, and caraway, *Carum*, as well as in the onion,

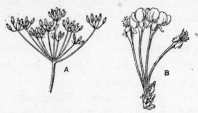

Fig. 73.—Inflorescences. *A*, compound umbel of *Lomatium; B*, simple umbel
of cherry, *Prunus.*

Allium, milkweed, *Asclepias* (Fig. 136), and ginseng, *Panax*.
The order of blooming in the corymb and the umbel is centripetal
or from the outer (lower) edge toward the center (upper), as in a
typical raceme. The flowers on the border of the umbel
may open very much earlier than those in the center of the

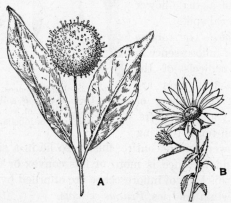

Fig. 74.—Inflorescences. *A*, head of buttonbush, *Cephalanthus: B*, head o*
rosinweed, *Grindelia.*

inflorescence. After the fruits have started to form on the
pedicels in the umbels of certain species (carrot) the clusters
become tightly infolded to form a rather compact ball with most
of the fruits in the center of the tangled mass of pedicels.

The Head.—A *head* is an inflorescence of the racemose type in
which the numerous flowers are sessile; *i.e.*, it is much like an

umbel in which the flowers lack pedicels or is of the nature of a shortened, globular spike (Fig. 74). This type of flower cluster is also often globular or almost spherical as in the buttonball tree or sycamore, *Platanus*, buttonbush, *Cephalanthus* (Fig. 74, *A*), alsike clover, *Trifolium hybridum*, and in the pistillate inflorescence of osage orange, *Toxylon*. The head is the characteristic inflorescence in the composites, *Compositae* (Fig. 74, *B*), or the group to which sunflower, *Helianthus*, dandelion, *Taraxacum*, lettuce, *Lactuca*, goldenrod, *Solidago*, etc., belong. The flower in a popular sense in this family is in reality an *inflorescence* which contains many or even hundreds of separate true flowers.

THE CYMOSE TYPE

The second general type of flower cluster or the *cymose* inflorescence (Fig. 75) differs markedly from the racemose type because the upward growth of the floral axis is early brought to a close by a

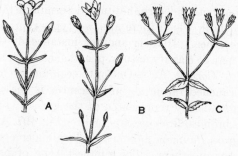

FIG. 75.—Inflorescences. *A*, simple cyme; *B* and *C*, other forms of the cyme.

terminal flower. The first or oldest flower to open is at the tip and the later or younger flowers appear progressively lower down on the axis; in other words, the tendency for the floral axis to elongate is definitely terminated by the presence of the flower at the tip. The growth of the floral axis in this case is *determinate*. The opening of the flower buds proceeds from tip to base or from center to circumference in such flower clusters, which are therefore of the *centrifugal* type (Fig. 75). The cyme is thus seen to be the exact opposite of the raceme in the position of the youngest and oldest flowers and in the sequence of blooming. Cymose flower clusters are not nearly so common as the racemose type.

The Solitary Flower.—The simplest type of cymose or determinate inflorescence is seen in those plants in which a solitary, terminal flower is produced on the peduncle, as in the poppy, tulip, etc.   But in those plants which produce a cluster of flowers on the peduncle the simplest unbranched forms are represented by the crab apple, *Pyrus*.

The Fascicle.—A *fascicle* is a cyme with the flowers very closely crowded as in campion, *Lychnis*, and sweet william, *Phlox*.

The Glomerule.—A *glomerule* is a cyme which is still more condensed or compacted, much like a head.   This inflorescence may usually be distinguished from a head by the order of opening of the flower buds, *i.e.*, they open from the center to the circumference as in all types of determinate inflorescence.   Certain species of dogwood, *Cornus*, box, *Buxus*, and nettle, *Urtica*, illustrate this type of flower cluster.

COMPOUND INFLORESCENCES

There are also many kinds of branched or "compound" flower clusters among both indeterminate and determinate inflorescences, and still others in which there are two types represented in the same inflorescence.   Here is another instance of the practical inability of man to classify natural phenomena to his satisfaction.

The Panicle, Corymb, Etc.—One of the commonest forms of compound or branched racemose inflorescences is the *panicle* (Fig. 71, *C*), so abundantly represented in the grasses (Figs. 197 and 199) such as bromes, *Bromus*, oats, *Avena* (Fig. 197, *A*), bluegrass, *Poa*, panic grass, *Panicum*, as well as in Virginia creeper, *Parthenocissus*, and many others.   The simplest type of panicle is like that of the Virginia creeper in which the group of flowers is much like an ordinary raceme, but with a simple raceme produced where there would be a single flower in the ordinary raceme.   This type of branching is seen in its extreme form in the "compound panicle" in which the branching runs into several branch orders. The compact inflorescence of certain other grasses such as wheat, *Triticum*, and Italian rye, *Lolium*, is also compound in the sense that the main axis, the *rachis*, is branched to form the *rachilla* of the *spikelets*, upon which the sessile flowers are borne.   Certain species of hydrangea, *H. cinerea*, produce compound corymbs. Compound cymes are seen in the common elder, *Sambucus*, mountain ash, *Sorbus*, black haw, *Viburnum*, and in many hydrangeas.   Many of the umbellifers, *Umbelliferae* (Fig. 172), produce compound umbels, in which there are two (possibly more) series of branches formed. The secondary umbels are then called "umbellets," and the secondary clusters of bracts about the bases of the secondary pedicels in the umbellets are termed "involucels."

Mixed Clusters.—Inflorescences in which some of the above types are mixed are shown by the horse-chestnut, *Aesculus hippocastanum*, lilac, *Syringa*, and privet, *Ligustrum*, in which the primary branching order is of the indeterminate order, but the secondary or ultimate branching order is partly or wholly determinate. Such an inflorescence may be elongated or contracted and it is called a "thyrsus." The elongated, loose, panicle-like inflorescence of this type is seen in meadow rue, *Thalictrum*, and the contracted, pyramidal form is seen in lilac, horse-chestnut, and privet.

OBLIQUE INFLORESCENCES

Spikes, racemes, and cymes are produced in certain families, *Boraginaceae*, *Hydrophyllaceae*, which become strikingly lopsided because the flowers fail to develop on one side of the axis. This condition is commonly intensified by the continued elongation of the floral axis by the development of lateral branches formed in the axils of leaves on one side of the stem only. Such clusters are known as "scorpoid" spikes, racemes, or cymes.

STERILE FLOWERS, BRACTS, ETC.

Sterility of Certain Flowers in the Inflorescence.—The flowers in some of the higher types of inflorescence are functionally differentiated into those that are inconspicuous but which perform the normal function of reproduction, and those that are very conspicuous and as such serve to attract pollinators. The conspicuous flowers in many such species have become sterile so that they serve only for attracting the insects to the inflorescence. These conditions are seen in a great variety of forms in the composites, *Compositae* (Figs. 176 to 180), where in many species of the sunflower type the outer row of flowers in the head become brilliantly colored and they form a gay band or ring of radiating flowers, hence *ray* flowers. These surround a dense cluster of less showy, but nevertheless very important flowers that occupy the central part of the head, the *disk*, and are therefore called *disk* flowers. The prominent ray flowers contribute an essential showiness to the inflorescence, but they often suffer the loss of their stamens, and frequently their pistils also. The sacrifice certainly rebounds to the great advantage of the species so constituted because a single visit from a bumblebee, coming as to a single flower, may supply sufficient pollen to fertilize the eggs in scores or even hundreds of flowers. The possession of this nature as a regular feature of the life history is largely responsible for the common opinion that the composites are the highest of all flowering plants.

Floral Bracts, Involucres, Etc.—The same sort of attractiveness in the inflorescence of many other species is secured through the coloration and placement of a perianth-like cluster of vegetative bracts. Thus in the callas, *Calla*, Jack-in-the-pulpit, *Arisaema*, and many of their kin, *Araceae* (Fig. 190), the colored *spathe* that surrounds the spadix (the real inflorescence) serves the function of attractiveness much as would be supplied by a gaily colored corolla. The flowers themselves are very small, inconspicuous, and often are not seen from the outside because of the sheathing spathe. But the spathe, although not a part of the flower, is the banner that lures the pollinators and so makes fertilization possible. The beautiful, white, petal-like bracts that surround the inconspicuous clusters of flowers in the flowering dogwood of the south, *Cornus florida* (Fig. 171, *A*), and of the northwest, *Cornus nuttallii*, serve the same purpose. The three beautiful magenta or purple bracts enveloping the true flowers of Japanese paper plant, *Bougainvillea*, are of the same nature and perform the same function. A similar situation is illustrated by the brilliant scarlet or purple bracts that constitute the attractive whorl or rosette surrounding the cluster of unattractive flowers at the top of the stem in the magnificent Central American Poinsettia, *Euphorbia pulcherrima*, so popular at Christmas time, and the white or white-margined bracts in a similar position about the flowers of the common snow-on-the-mountain, *Euphorbia marginata* (Fig. 116, *E*), of the prairies and plains of North America.

The Biological Meaning of Flower Clusters.—There is doubtless considerable biological significance attached to the different kinds of flower clusters. It is impossible for us as yet to interpret the meaning of many of the finer details associated with the higher types of inflorescences, as is true for many of the other structural features of plants, but, nevertheless, we are able to see important values associated with the broader aspects of flower groupings. For instance, many of the advantages of the prominent conspicuousness of large, brilliantly colored, single flowers are doubtless secured in those species with many very much smaller flowers by arranging them in more or less closely aggregated clusters. In this way the inflorescence composed even of very tiny flowers, each with most attractive color combinations but which would be scarcely seen alone, becomes a very conspicuous affair. The cluster resembles a single large flower. This, naturally, is greatly to be desired for the showiness of a *single large flower* here becomes the property of a *cluster of flowers* for the attraction of pollinating insects. Insects visit and pollinate the *cluster* of *flowers* as readily as they visit and pollinate the single flower. This condition may normally result in the production of a comparatively greater crop of offspring, much to the advantage of the species with the multiple-flowered inflorescence.

CHAPTER IX

VEGETATIVE CHARACTERISTICS OF FLOWERING PLANTS

Considerable emphasis has been given to the fact that the *flower* is really the most distinctive feature of the flowering plants. The various groups that the biologist recognizes in the classification of those plants are largely and more or less easily differentiated because of the great variety of detail exhibited by flowers. A given natural group of flowering plants owes its principal biological distinction to the presence of a certain type or kind of flower. This type of flower is different from the flowers that characterize other groups. Thus we find that the most reliable, practical, and scientific basis for the recognition of the various natural groups of flowering plants is revealed by the nature of the flowers that they produce. Much attention must be given, therefore, to the careful study of the comparative morphology of flowers as the primary and most dependable basis of classification.

The flowers of a given group of flowering plants show much less tendency to vary widely than do the other structures of the plants, and it is for this reason that the characteristics of flowers are the most dependable features for use in any scheme of classification. Nevertheless, the vegetative or somatic structures of flowering plants are also of great value in a simple classification or in extensive scientific taxonomy. These characteristics include all the organs of the plant other than those immediately involved in the structure of the flower. They include the great variety of form and structure of roots, stems, and leaves that are associated with flowering plants. Such characters are extremely varied and numerous, since they often reflect the influence of more or less local or transient conditions of the environment, as well as being present to a characteristic degree for the various species under all conditions.

In spite of their greater variability the vegetative organs of flowering plants are exceedingly useful, along with flowers, in working out the usual diagnostic characteristics of different plants. The vegetative characteristics that are so useful in classification are reflected by a technical terminology that is quite distinct from that used in the description of flowers. To give the principal vegetative structures of flowering plants, together with some of their more or less common variations, and a sampling of the vocabulary utilized in their description is the object of this chapter. Further details in the matter of the special terminology and use of the terms involved in systematic description are to be mastered only by extended use of the standard manuals and floras in the laboratory and field.

ROOTS

The roots of a plant normally grow downward into the soil and more or less firmly anchor the plant in place. Roots are, therefore, typically subterranean. There are numerous species of flowering plants, however, that produce roots that are wholly or in part *aerial* (Fig. 78). The roots of certain orchids are truly aerial, many of them never reaching the ground, and the so-called "prop roots" of maize and screw pine are also partly aerial. On the other hand the main *stems* of certain species are subterranean, and so there is considerable popular confusion because of the common assumption that all underground parts are *roots*. The distinction between roots and stems must include other features (external and internal anatomy, development) besides their position.

FIG. 76.—The fleshy root of a carrot; an enlarged taproot of a biennial (*from Pool, Basic Course in Botany, Ginn and Company*).

Roots differ from stems in their development and internal anatomy, in the absence of more or less regular nodes and internodes, and in the absence of leaves. The roots of certain plants, under certain conditions, develop adventitious buds from which leafy shoots or "root sprouts" arise, as in the poplar, apple, and black locust. Roots are often formed on the leaves of certain plants, also, and they are produced in abundance on the aerial stems of various species (Fig. 78). Roots usually branch very irregularly, although the form of the root (Fig. 76) and the root system (Fig. 77) are quite characteristic of different species and under different conditions of the environment.

Kinds of Roots.—Roots that are fine, thread-like, and often provided with long, slender, and numerous branches of about the same diameter are called *fibrous roots*. Such roots are revealed especially by the grasses (Fig. 77) and sedges. The outer branches of the root systems of trees and shrubs, the fine branches of many fleshy roots (Fig. 76), and the roots that arise from underground stems are also fibrous.

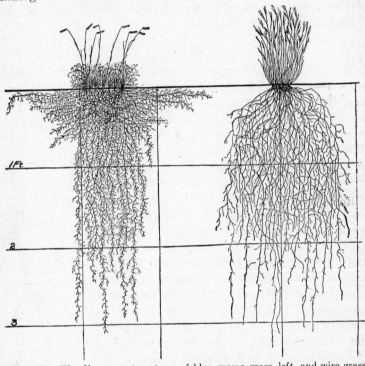

Fig. 77.—The fibrous root systems of blue grama grass, left, and wire grass, right (*from Weaver and Clements, Plant Ecology, Fig. 159, page 316, McGraw-Hill Book Company, Inc.*).

Roots that are notably enlarged by the formation of tissues that are stored with water and food are termed *fleshy roots*. Good examples of fleshy roots are seen in the carrot (Fig. 76), turnip, radish, and beet.

The main root and its numerous branches in most trees and shrubs become greatly thickened and dominated by hardened, woody tissues and so may be called *woody roots*. The woody root is usually covered with much the same cortical tissues and bark that are characteristic of the stems of such plants. The woody roots of tne Dicotyledons grow in diameter by the formation of annual rings as do the stems of such plants. The progressive development and increasing woodiness of the root system of such plants keep pace, more or less, with the development and age of the aerial portions of the plant.

The more or less spreading cluster of large fleshy or tuberous roots of the dahlia are called *fascicled roots*. Other descriptive terms for roots are used in books on classification, such as *fusiform*, for fleshy roots like those of the dahlia and sweet potato, and *napiform*, for those of the turnip and certain beets.

Root Systems.—The fully developed root or *root system*, as to origin and duration, is either *primary* or *secondary* (or adventitious). The primary root and root system arise from the hypocotyl of the embryo. The primary root is the first root that appears as the seed germinates, and it usually grows directly downward. The *main* axis of the root system developed from this is the *primary* root; if it persists, it is called the *tap root*, as in the carrot, sweet clover, and dandelion. The branches of the primary root or tap root are often fibrous and are called *secondary* roots. The primary root is very short-lived in many plants, and it is succeeded by a secondary root system which arises from the epicotylary region of the seedling or from almost any vegetative shoot. The secondary roots and root system of this type become the permanent roots that are so characteristic of the grasses (Fig. 77) and many other Monocotyledons. The roots that arise on such modified, underground stems as bulbs (Fig. 43), corms (Fig. 43), tubers, rhizomes (Fig. 68), on such aerial stems as stolons, runners, and on cuttings or slips and leaves are also secondary roots. Secondary roots are often called *adventitious* roots, irrespective as to where or how they are formed.

Duration of the Root.—The length of life of the normal individual plant depends upon the duration and effectiveness of its root system. In relation to this fact the taxonomist recognizes three types of flowering plants, namely, *annuals*, *biennials*, *perennials*. Annual species are those in which the individuals live but one year (or growing season). Biennials live for two years, perennials for more than two years.

Annuals arise from seeds, produce their regular vegetative characteristics, flower, fruit, and die in a single year. Such plants are generally herbaceous or even fleshy. But the individuals of certain annual species under certain environmental conditions may become very large and develop much woody tissue; in fact, they may *tend* to become biennial or even perennial. Certain plants are known as *winter annuals*. These are normally annuals in which the seeds if planted in the autumn will germinate and a certain aerial growth will be produced in the fall and will live through the winter. Growth is greatly retarded during the winter but it is resumed again the following spring, with the production of flowers and a new crop of seed, after which the plants die as in winter wheat. A notable feature of the life history of winter annuals is the development of a rather extensive root system in the autumn. The aerial development

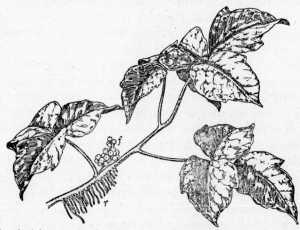

Fig. 78.—Aerial roots of poison ivy, at *r*; fruits at *f* (*from Pool, Basic Course in Botany, Ginn and Company*).

at that time is commonly in the form of a dense cluster of leaves on a short shoot (a rosette).

Biennials require two full years (growing seasons) for the completion of their individual life cycle from seed to seed. The seeds germinate the first year, and the young plants develop a good root system and an aerial rosette of leaves or a well-developed leafy shoot. The root and shoot are usually supplied with a rich store of food by the end of the first vegetative year, but no flowers are produced. During the second year the individual plants form their flowers and seeds and, with the exhaustion of their root systems, die. The stems of biennial species are also usually herbaceous, but various species may produce large individuals with an abundance of woody tissues.

Perennials are plants that live and continue to grow for two or more years. Numerous perennials produce herbaceous aerial shoots that die at the close of the first year and each succeeding year, but the root system (and underground stem system) may persist for many years and continue to produce the usual aerial, annual shoots, as in many grasses, sedges, rhubarb, and asparagus. Numerous other perennial species produce aerial shoots from perennial root systems that are also perennial and that continue to live and grow (more or less) from year to year, as do the roots, as in our common trees and shrubs.

STEMS

The stem or shoot of the plant, with its few or many branches, usually grows upward into the light. It is an effective system whose primary value to the plant as a whole is to display the leaves in such a manner as to favor their food-making activities. Exceptions to the generally erect or ascending habit of stems are seen in numerous species that produce stems so short and inconspicuous that such plants are said to be *acaulescent* or stemless. The slender stems of certain species crawl along the surface of the ground or climb upward by means of the coiling habit or by the use of tendrils or aerial roots that anchor the weak stems to the support. Still other species produce some or all of their stems underground. The habit and structure of stems are so variable among different species that such vegetative features are of great value in classification. These characteristics are reflected by an extensive and more or less technical vocabulary, a representative sampling of which we may introduce at this point.

Typical Stems.—All stems have *nodes* (joints) and *internodes* (intervals between the nodes), in contrast with roots, and the leafy shoots and their branches originate in *buds* at the nodes or at the tip of the shoot and its branches (Figs. 79, 80).

Buds are embryonic or immature shoots in a dormant state and are commonly covered, especially in the *winter buds* of trees and shrubs, by *bud scales*, which in themselves are modified leaves. A *terminal bud* may occur at or near the tip of the shoot and its branches, and from such buds the longitudinal growth of the shoots is produced. The lower buds are called *lateral buds*, and these are *axillary buds* (Figs. 80, 84) if they arise in the *axils* of the *leaves* (as they usually do).   When more than one lateral bud occurs in an axil. either at the right and left of the central bud or above the latter, such extra buds are called *supernumerary buds*, as in the honeylocust.   Buds that have no bud scales are called *naked buds,* as in *Geranium* and *Kalmia.*   Injuries to the inter-nodes may result in the formation of *adventitious* buds almost anywhere between the nodes; such buds often form on the leaves of *Bryophyllum.*

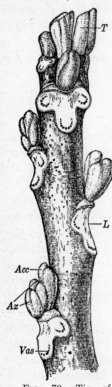

FIG. 79.—Tip of butternut twig show-ing terminal bud at *T,* leaf scar at *L,* acces-sory bud at *Acc,* axillary bud at *Ax,* bundle scars at *Vas* (*from Pool, Basic Course in Botany, Ginn and Company*).

If a bud gives rise to a leafy shoot, it is termed a *leaf bud;* if to a flower or inflores-cence, it is called a *flower bud.*   When a bud gives rise to a leafy shoot and flowers, it is called a *mixed bud.*   Transitions from bud scales to typical l e a v e s are shown in *Pittosporum.*

When the scales of a bud fall, they leave more or less distinctive bud-scale scars (Fig. 80) that mark the former position of the bud scales at the nodes.   A series of such bud-scale scars left by terminal buds some-times marks several years' growth in elon-gation of the branches.   But such scars become obscure or even eliminated com-pletely as woody stems become older and thicker.   Buds vary greatly in arrangement, numbers, size, shape, color, and nature of the surface and in the number, arrangement, color, size, shape, and surface nature of the bud scales.   The characteristics of buds are of especial value in distinguishing different species of trees and shrubs in winter.

Kinds of Stems.—As to *age,* stems are *annual, biennial,* or *perennial,* much as has been noted for roots, since the length of life of the root determines the duration of the stem.   It has been pointed out that many perennials produce shoots that live for a single year, even though the root system is truly perennial, whereas, in many species, the shoot system is also perennial and the latter may become massively or exten-sively developed.   Many perennials form highly modified underground stems from which arise the "new plants" or aerial shoots each year.

As to position, stems are *aerial* or *subterranean* (submersed). The *aerial* shoot system is more or less erect in most species, but in many species the stem is more or less *prostrate, decumbent, creeping, crawling,* or *climbing.* Climbing stems are usually slender and weak, and they are able to cling to a support by means of the *twining habit* or by the formation of *tendrils* or *aerial roots.* Numerous terms are employed to describe these features. Certain species with aerial stems often form special branches that are helpful as propagative structures. Among such modified aerial shoots may be mentioned *stolons, runners,* and offsets (see Chapter VIII). Stolons are slender branches of the shoot that creep over the surface or near the surface of the ground, often rooting and forming new shoots at the nodes. Runners are much like stolons (Fig. 44), but they form a single node between rather long internodes. The bud at the tip of the outer node of a runner often takes root and so may develop a new plant in that position which may eventually separate from the parent shoot system by the breaking of the long internode. Offsets are relatively short and often more or less fleshy stolon-like branches of a short stem (Fig. 45) forming a cluster of leaves at the

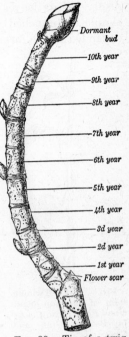

Fig. 80.—Tip of a twig from the horse-chestnut showing a terminal dormant bud, numerous leaf scars with their bundle scars, and transverse bands of bud-scale scars marking terminal growth for 10 years (*from Pool, Basic Course in Botany, Ginn and Company*).

tip. Such modified branches as offsets are usually associated with plants of rather compact growth in the form of rosettes, as in the houseleek (Fig. 45). The primary value of all of these and similar types of aerial stems is in relation to natural vegetative propagation. Man utilizes such natural tendencies to propagate certain economic species for his own advantage.

Special reference should be made to *tendrils, thorns,* and *cladophylls* as modifications of the aerial stem (Fig. 82). Tendrils are usually slender, leafless branches of the shoot that are very sensitive to contact stimuli; they are thus especially useful in attaching the stem to a support, and in that way they enable the weak short plant to climb into an advantageous position for the display of its leaves to light. The tip of the tendril may be simple or branched into fine hair-like segments, or it may be expanded in the form of an adhesive disk, as in the Boston ivy.

It should be noted in passing that the tendrils of certain plants (Fig. 146*A*) are modifications of leaves or leaflets.

Branches are sometimes modified to form thorns. These are simple or unbranched, as in the osage orange, or they are branched as in the honeylocust. The stems of desert shrubs and trees often grow slowly, and many of their branches become dwarfed and more or less thorn-like.

Cladophylls (phylloclades) are more or less flattened, leaf-like stems, that may quite readily be mistaken for true leaves, the functions of which they do perform. Certain species of asparagus, *A. asparagoides*, and the Scotch broom, *Ruscus aculeatus*, produce typical cladophylls.

Fig. 81.—Twining stem of the hop plant (*from Pool, Basic Course in Botany, Ginn and Company*).

The cactuses with strongly flattened, green internodes, and those with more or less cylindrical, columnar, and ribbed green stems, in which the nodes and internodes may or may not be prominent, may also be mentioned among the peculiar or special types of aerial shoots.

The *subterranean shoot system* is usually so highly modified and specialized for vegetative propagation as to be confused with the root system. So effective are the various types of subterranean stems in multiplication that many economic species are regularly propagated in this manner by growers. The essential features of the more common modifications of this sort are presented in Chapter V, with special emphasis upon migration and ecesis. All these structures (Figs. 40 to 45), with their various intergradations and other details, are utilized to a considerable degree by taxonomists in drawing the descriptions for use in classification. The behavior of the subterranean stem system and of certain of the highly specialized aerial shoots as well has received special and prominent consideration and application in connection with the recent emphasis upon the value of vegetation in the practical problems of soil conservation.

Special Features of Stems.—Reference has already been made to the presence of bud-scale scars on the surface of shoots, especially of the branches of woody stems. We may also refer

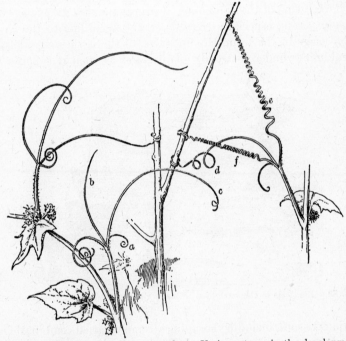

Fig. 82.—Tendrils of the bur cucumber. Various stages in the development of tendrils are shown at *a, b, c, d, e,* and *f* (*from Pool, Basic Course in Botany, Ginn and Company*).

here to the *leaf scars* that are left on the surface of the shoot when the leaves fall. The latter are so distinctive of different species (Figs. 79, 80) and are so readily described as to be of considerable value for purposes of identification. It should be remembered that a new leaf is never formed in the exact position of a former leaf.

Lenticels.—The surface of the internodes of many woody shoots also reveals the presence of prominent *lenticels*. These are raised, sunken, or otherwise circumscribed spots of such distinctive color, form, and size in the outer bark that they are readily differentiated from the adjacent surface of the bark (Fig. 83). They commonly appear as rounded, oval, or horizontally elongated spots or streaks that are characteristic of various species and ages of twigs. They are composed of tissues that aid in the aeration of the underlying and deeper portions of the twigs. Lenticels are especially prominent in the birch, elder, and cottonwood.

Bark.—One of the commonest features that we associate with woody plants, especially trees, is *bark*. According to the common usage of the term, this includes all the tissues outside the cambium cylinder in woody plants, and as such it consists of

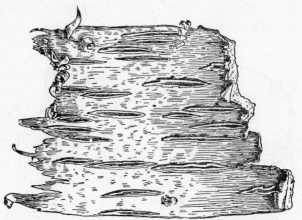

Fig. 83.—Lenticels in the bark of wild black cherry (*from Pool, Basic Course in Botany, Ginn and Company*).

various tissues, including cork, in extremely varied combinations. The bark of many species is quite distinctive; hence, it is of value in classification. Large trees and even saw logs are readily identified by the experienced woodsman and forester by the bark alone. In spite of the extreme value of bark from the standpoint of taxonomy, we find that satisfactory and dependable terms have not yet been put into use for its reliable description. Such expressions as "smooth bark," "rough bark," "scaly bark," "shag bark" are so general as to be of little value for accurate taxonomic work. The situation is also complicated by the fact that the bark on the older branches and the main trunk of old trees is very different from that on the younger branches of the current twigs and young trees. The bark of young twigs often shows certain details that are helpful for diagnostic purposes but that are entirely lacking on the older twigs of the same individual tree or shrub. The variations in the bark that characterize the shoot from youth to old age must be available if bark is to to be of major value to the taxonomist.

Other Surface Features of Stems.—The surface of herbaceous species and the young shoots of woody plants is often more or less covered with hairs or scales of various types or coated with granular, sticky, or resinous substances that are helpful for descriptive purposes. These characteristics are likely to vary with the age of the shoots, too, and even to show puzzling differences as among different portions of the same individual or different individuals of apparently the same species under different environmental conditions.

Various technical terms are in common taxonomic use to include these features in the preparation of the diagnoses one finds in the various floras and manuals. Since the same, or nearly the same, features are also found in the surface markings of leaves, where they are more often utilized in detail, they will be presented in our treatment of the vegetative characteristics of leaves to follow immediately.

LEAVES

The green color of vegetation is usually due to the presence of an abundance of green leaves which are in turn colored by the presence of the well-known but complex pigment chlorophyll. The most significant primary function common to all green leaves is manufacture of carbohydrate foods. Leaves are the most variable, anatomically, of all of the regular parts of the plant, notwithstanding their uniform primary functions. There are several well-known species of flowering plants (the orchid, *Corallorrhiza*) that are not even green and that, because of the absence of chlorophyll, are saprophytes. The gross and the minute morphology of mature leaves varies widely among different species, among different individuals of the same species, and even among different parts of the same individual. Many flowering plants may, nevertheless, be readily recognized by their leaves alone. The value of leaves (as well as of other vegetative structures) in taxonomic work is distinctly limited unless extensive observations and comparisons are made under various conditions. Even then due consideration must be given to the extreme variability of leaves.

Typical Leaves.—Leaves are typically characterized by their green, expanded, very thin *blade* or *lamina*, which is attached to the aerial stem at a node by the leaf stalk or *petiole* (Fig. 84). We must point out, however, that *all* true leaves are not green, nor are they all broad and thin, nor are they confined to aerial shoots. The petiole is often lacking, and then the leaf is said to be *sessile* (Fig. 87, *C*). The petiole itself is extremely variable as to length, thickness, and form of base and cross-section. And then *stipules* are present in many species. Stipules are lateral, more or less leaf-like, outgrowths (usually two) at the base of the petiole (Fig. 84). They are sometimes large and distinctly leaf-like, permanent, and so characteristic as to be very useful for purposes of classification, as in the willow, poplar, and rose. Stipules are absent in many species (as mustards), whereas in others they have fallen by the time the leaf is mature. They develop as a "leaf sheath" (ocrea) that more or less completely surrounds the stem in the buckwheat and smartweed. In certain plants (*Galium*) the stipules are so much like the blades of the sessile leaves as to be indistinguishable from them.

Fig. 84.—Representative leaf. *A*, blade; *B*, petiole; *C*, stipules; *D*, axillary bud.

Arrangement of Leaves.—The leaves of flowering plants are arranged on the stem in a definite and regular manner. In many species they are *opposite; i.e.*, there is a leaf on opposite sides of each node. In other species the leaves are *whorled* or *verticillate; i.e.*, there are more than two (three or more) at each node. In many species only one leaf occurs at a node; the leaves are then arranged in a definite *spiral* order at the successive nodes and are said to be *alternate*. When the two leaves occur on opposite sides of each node, each pair is usually placed at right angles to the pair immediately above or below, thus forming four vertical rows of leaves. Certain plants, notably the grasses (including maize), in which the leaves are alternate form two vertical rows (ranks) of leaves, whereas in other alternate-leaved species there are three-to-many rows. In some species both opposite and alternate leaves occur upon the same individual.

Vernation.—Young leaves are usually folded or rolled in the bud in a definite manner. The manner of folding or rolling, which may be determined from transverse sections of the buds, is termed *vernation*. When not folded or rolled at all, they are said to be *straight*.

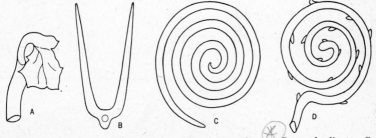

Fig. 85.—Types of vernation. *A*, inflexed or reclinate; *B*, conduplicate; *C*, convolute; *D*, circinate.

The principal types of vernation are: *inflexed* or *reclinate* (Fig. 85, *A*), in which the blade or upper part of the leaf is bent back over the lower part; *conduplicate* (Fig. 85, *B*), in which the blade is folded lengthwise along the midrib (as leaves in a book) the two halves being thus brought face to face, usually with the lower faces outermost, as in oak and cherry; *convolute* (Fig. 85, *C*), in which the blade is rolled lengthwise, from side to side, like a scroll, as in rose and plum; *circinate* (Fig. 85, *D*), in which the blade is rolled from the tip toward the base, with lower surface outermost, as in sundew (and ferns); *involute* (Fig. 86, *A*), in which both edges of the blade are inrolled lengthwise over the *upper* surface toward the midrib, as in violet; *revolute* (Fig. 86, *B*,) in which both edges of the blade are inrolled lengthwise over the lower surface toward the midrib, as in dock; *plicate* (pleated), in which the blade is creased and folded back and forth (accordion-like) along the main veins like a pan (Fig. 86, *C*), as in the palmately veined leaves of mallows and geraniums.

Venation.—The visible veins (vascular bundles) of the blade are so distributed as to be helpful for diagnostic purposes. These common vegetative characteristics are referred to by the term *venation*. In respect to venation, leaves are *pinnately veined* (feather-veined) when the prominent subdivisions of about equal size diverge from the prominent midrib toward the margin of the blade and are approximately parallel (Figs. 87, *B*; 91, *A*). When the more prominent veins radiate from a common point at or near the base of the blade, the venation is said to be *palmate* or *digitate* (Fig. 87, *A*). In *parallel* venation the principal veins (of about equal size) extend from the base to the tip of the blade and are more or less parallel, and the branches of these veins are

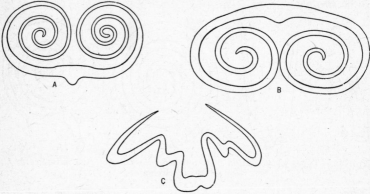

Fig. 86.—Types of vernation. *A*, involute; *B*, revolute; *C*, plicate.

inconspicuous (Fig. 87, *C*). When the veins appear as a more or less irregular network of gradually diminishing size, the term *net* venation is used.

Simple and Compound Leaves.—With reference to the configuration of the blade, leaves are either *simple* (Figs. 84, 87, 90) or *compound* (Fig. 88, *A* and *B*). The blade may be regular in outline with no marginal indentations whatsoever, or it may be indented, lobed, or deeply cut on the margin; but as long as it is in a single unit or piece, it is *simple*. The leaves of many plants are completely divided and the two or more pieces separated into individual parts called *leaflets* (Fig. 88, *A* and *B*); such leaves are then designated *compound leaves*.

The leaflets of compound leaves show all the common characteristics of simple leaves except that all the leaflets of a given compound leaf lie in a single plane, do not have stipules, and do not bear buds in their axils. The continuation of the axis (petiole) of a compound leaf is called the *rachis*. There are two kinds

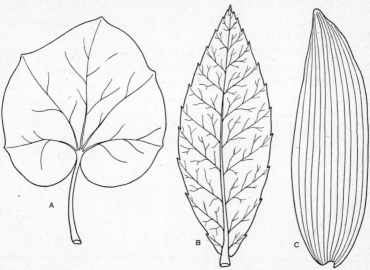

FIG. 87.—Types of venation. *A*, palmate; *B*, pinnate; *C*, parallel. All these leaves are simple. *A* is petiolate; *C* is sessile.

of compound leaves, *palmately compound*, in which the leaflets diverge from a common point at the tip of the petiole, as in the

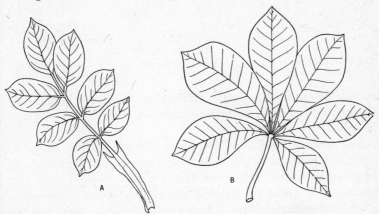

FIG. 88.—Compound leaves. *A*, pinnate; *B*, digitate or palmate.

horse-chestnut (Fig. 88, *B*), and *pinnately compound*, in which the leaflets are distributed along two sides of the common rachis (Fig. 88, *A*). The rachis of such a leaf is, in fact, homologous

with the midrib of a simple pinnately veined leaf. The leaflets of a pinnately compound leaf may *themselves* be compound
one or two times, as in the honeylocust and certain acacias. Such
leaves are said to be *twice* or *doubly compound*, or *bipinnate*, or
twice pinnate, or *thrice pinnate*.

The Outline of the Leaf.—The outline of simple leaves and of
the leaflets of compound leaves is among the most variable of all
leaf characteristics. Because of such extreme variation, these
features are often puzzling, and the terms for them in our tax-

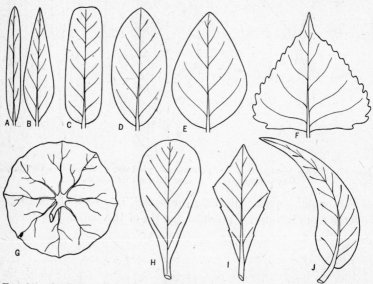

Fig. 89.—Outlines of leaves. *A*, linear; *B*. lanceolate; *C*, oblong; *D*, elliptical;
E, ovate; *F*, deltoid; *G*, orbicular (peltate); *H*, spatulate; *I*, cuneate; *J*. seculate.

onomic descriptions are often difficult to use concretely and consistently. They are, nevertheless, among the commonest terms
of systematic botany.

The General Outline.—The outline of the leaf or leaflet is
described as *linear* when it is very narrow and usually much
longer than broad, with more or less nearly straight sides and
ending in a blunt or tapering apex (Fig. 89, *A*); *lanceolate*,
when lance-shaped, broadest below the middle, and usually
tapering gradually to a pointed apex (Fig. 89, *B*); *oblong*, when
rectangular, with nearly straight sides and with rounded base
and tip (Fig. 89, *C*); *elliptical*, like an ellipse, broadest at the
middle, tapering broadly and evenly to the rounded base and

tip (Fig. 89, *D*); *ovate*, when egg-shaped, much broader below the middle, with base rounded and apex blunt or rounded (Fig. 89, *E*); *orbicular*, more or less nearly circular (Fig. 89, *G*); *deltoid*, like a delta or triangular (Fig. 89, *F*); *seculate*, sickle-shaped, more or less like a curved and oblique lanceolate leaf (Fig. 89, *J*); *spatulate*, spoon-shaped, broad and rounded above the middle, tapering gradually to a narrow base (Fig. 89, *H*); *palmate*, like the leaf of a fan palm; *cuneate*, wedge-shaped, usually narrow but broader above the middle, then tapering toward the base, with sides usually straight (Fig. 89, *I*). *Oblanceolate* and *obovate* leaves are inversely lanceolate and ovate, respectively.

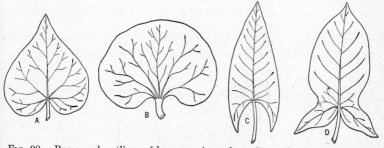

Fig. 90.—Bases and outlines of leaves. *A*, cordate; *B*, reniform; *C*, saggitate; *D*, hastate.

The Base of the Leaf.—With particular reference to the base of the blade, simple leaves may be: *cordate*, heart-shaped, rounded and indented at the base (with a sinus) and tapering broadly to the apex (Fig. 90, *A*); *reniform*, kidney-shaped, broader than long, with a sinus at the base (Fig. 90, *B*); *saggitate*, arrow-shaped, with a deep sinus at the base and the projecting sides of the base of the blade (auricles) turned inward (Fig. 90, *C*); *hastate*, halberd- or spear-shaped, with auricles turned outward (Fig. 90, *D*); *peltate*, shield-shaped, with the petiole inserted at or near the center of the blade (Fig. 89, *G*); *auriculate*, with auricles or "ears" formed by the projection of the two sides of the base of the blade, as in saggitate and hastate leaves; *oblique*, with the two sides of the blade unequal, especially at the base (Fig. 91, *A*); *decurrent*, in which the blade appears to "run down" the sides of the stem (Fig. 92, *A*); *connate*, in which the bases of two opposite leaves appear to have fused about the stem (Fig. 91, *B*); *perfoliate*, in which the stem appears to pass through the base of the blade (Fig. 91, C); *sheathing*, in which the expanded base of the petiole more

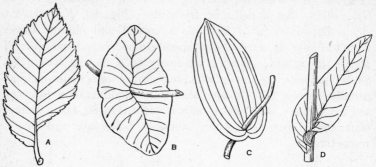

FIG. 91.—Bases of leaves.   A, oblique; B, connate; C, perfoliate; D, clasping.

or less completely invests the stem (Fig. 92, B); *clasping*, in which the blade of the sessile leaf partly invests the stem (Fig. 91, D).

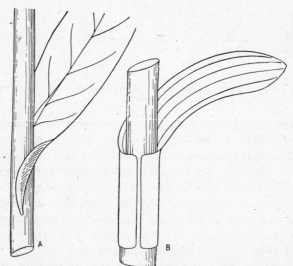

FIG. 92.—Bases of leaves.   A, decurrent, B, sheathing.

The Tip of the Leaf.—With reference to the apex or tip of the blade, leaves are *acuminate* when narrowly tapering to a sharp point (Fig. 93, A); *acute*, when tapering more broadly to a sharp point (Fig. 93, B); *obtuse*, when tapering abruptly to a point (Fig. 93, C); *aristate*, when ending in a bristle or awn (Fig. 93, E);

cuspidate, when ending with a sharp, rigid point (Fig. 93, *D*); *truncate,* when the tip seemingly is cut off square or nearly so (Fig. 93, *F*); *retuse,* when the tip is rounded or slightly notched (Fig. 93, *G*); *emarginate,* when decidedly notched (Fig. 93, *H*).

The Edges of the Leaf.—The edges or margins of the blade of leaves and leaflets exhibit a wide variety of modifications in the nature of indentations. Terms in use to describe the common types of these include, for the shallower indentations, the following: *entire,* said of leaves the margins of which are smooth, *i.e.,* not cut or toothed in any manner (Fig. 94, *A*); *repand* or undulate, having the margin wavy (Fig. 94, *B*); *sinuate,* with deeper, wavy indentations (Fig. 94, *C*); *serrate,* with marginal teeth like

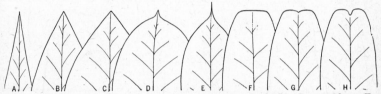

Fig. 93.—Tips of leaves. *A*, acuminate; *B*, acute; *C*, obtuse; *D*, cuspidate; *E*, aristate; *F*, truncate; *G*, retuse; *H*, emarginate.

a saw, especially with teeth pointing forward (Fig. 94, *E*); *serrulate,* with very small or fine teeth (Fig. 94, *D*); *dentate,* having the margin cut with teeth (fine or coarse) that point straight outward (Fig. 94, *F*); *crenate,* scalloped, or having broad rounded teeth (Fig. 94, *G*). Terms used for more deeply cut edges are: *incised,* having the margin deeply cut into irregular or jagged teeth (Fig. 95, *A*); *lobed,* cut more deeply into curved or angular lobes (Fig. 95, *B*) or cleft, cut, or lobed so that the sinuses extend about halfway to the midrib; *parted,* cut so that the sinuses between the lobes extend nearly to the midrib (Fig. 95, *C*); *divided,* cut entirely to the midrib, as in compound leaves (Figs. 88; 95, *D*). When the leaf is of the pinnate form of venation, the forms of lobing or dividing are described as pinnately lobed, cleft, incised, parted, divided (Fig. 88, *A*). When the venation is palmate, the terms are, of course, palmately lobed, cleft, incised, parted (Fig. 95, *C*), divided. The number of lobes or divisions of such leaves vary and are indicated by such terms as pinnately or palmately three-lobed, -cleft, -incised, -parted, or -divided. When the divisions are numerous and more or less fine and narrow, we use such expressions as *dissected*, *multifid*, or pinnatifid, or pinnately dissected.

Variations in the Surface of Leaves.—The upper and lower surfaces of the leaves of numerous species are smooth and slightly modified; but, in many others, the lower, the upper, or both surfaces are marked by the presence of hairs, scales, or resinous or waxy coatings of various kinds. Some of the more common details of such modifications are revealed by the following selected terms which one often sees in taxonomic descriptions.

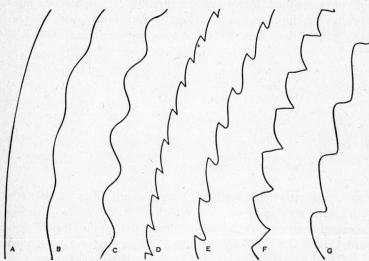

Fig. 94.—Edges of leaves. *A*, entire; *B*, repand (undulate); *C*, sinuate; *D*, serrulate; *E*, serrate; *F*, dentate; *G*, crenate.

The *glabrous* leaf is devoid of pubescence or hairs; the *glabrate* leaf is almost lacking in hairy covering, or the leaf becomes glabrous at maturity. Various types or degrees of hairiness are implied in such technical terms as *canescent*, coated with fine white or hoary hairs; *hirsute*, with stiff hairs; *hispid*, with bristly hairs; *pilose*, with soft, slender hairs; *puberulent*, with very fine, down-like hairs; *scabrous*, rough to the touch; *sericeous*, with silky pubescence; *strigose*, with rigid hairs or bristles; *villous*, with long, shaggy hairs; *floccose*, with tufts of soft, silky hairs. Of a different (not hairy) sort of epidermal modification we find the *squarrose* (squarrate) type, with minute scales, and the *verrucose*, with minute warts or blunt projections; *glutinous*, sticky or mucilaginous; *glandular*, with glands in the surface or gland-

tipped hairs; *glandular-punctate*, dotted with resinous glands; ✗
glaucous, covered with a whitish, bluish, or greenish waxy mate- ✗
rial or "bloom"; *pulverulent*, covered with a finely powdery sub- ✗
stance; *pruinose*, covered with a coarse granular material.   There ✗

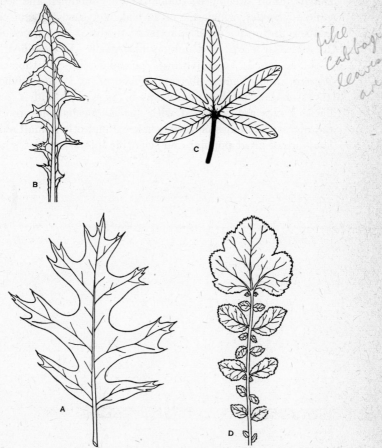

Fig. 95.—Edges of leaves.   *A*, incised; *B*, sinuately lobed or incised; *C*, palmately
parted; *D*, pinnately divided.

are various additional terms that one notes in the descriptions of
leaves (many of which also apply to stems) in taxonomic works.

Special Kinds of Leaves.—Certain species of flowering plants
produce vegetative structures that are properly known as leaves,
but these may be so modified as to appear quite different from
typical leaves.   Among these structures may be mentioned the

bracts and *bracteoles* or greatly reduced leaves that often accompany the individual flowers in an inflorescence; *scales* or storage leaves and the dry scales of bulbs, corms, tubers, and rhizomes (Figs. 40 to 45) and the regular components of scaly buds; certain *tendrils* (as in sweet pea) that are highly modified and sensitive leaflets; *stipules*, which are often leaf-like; the *spines* of certain cactuses and other desert plants are modified leaves, petioles, or the rachis of a leaf.   Of unique interest are the modified leaves of the so-called "insectivorous" plants as those of the sundew, *Drosera*, and Venus' flytrap, *Dionaea*, and the pitcher-like leaves of the "pitcher plants" as in *Sarracenia* and *Nepenthes*. These leaves are equipped with special mechanisms to entrap and digest the bodies of various insects and other small animals. They are of great popular and scientific interest.

CHAPTER X

THE CLASSIFICATION OF PLANTS

The primary object of this book is to assist students in their endeavor to master the knowledge requisite for the proper understanding and interpretation of flowers and for the classification of flowering plants. Classification, in general, is a convenience and a necessity of all phases of modern life. The necessity and the great convenience of classification must be apparent in the daily life of each of us. We are all enabled to do much more, to accomplish more because the facts, the customs, and the work of past ages and of our time have become fairly well classified and systematized. So human life, in its complexity and variety of interests, profits greatly from the age-old endeavor to classify.

Science attempts to systematize knowledge. It is therefore readily understood that classification is one of the first requirements of systematized knowledge. Civilization has progressed, in fact very largely, with the slow growth of the ability of people to classify and to systematize the materials, the thoughts, and the ideals with which the human race is associated.

TAXONOMY

Principles of Classification.—The endeavor to arrange plants into groups and subdivisions is commonly spoken of as "classification." Certain practices, rules, or principles of classification have gradually developed during the centuries, and, today, we have the subdivision of biology known as "taxonomy" which deals primarily with the principles of classification. The word, *taxonomy*, comes from two Greek words meaning "arrangement" (or classification) and "law." So taxonomy treats of the laws governing the arrangement or classification of plants. Taxonomy naturally contributes greatly to the orderly study of plants and to the *systematization* of our knowledge of plants, so that phase of botany in which taxonomy is the principal interest is called "systematic" botany.

The Basis of Classification for Plants.—We may base our classification of flowering plants upon a great variety of characteristics possessed by the members of this largest and most varied group of the vegetable kingdom. We may use such features as environmental conditions, methods of obtaining food, anatomy, life history, size of body, color of flowers, uses in daily life, geographic distribution, etc., as the bases of classification. Thus we may distinguish such groups as *land* plants and *water* plants; *shade* plants and *sun* plants; *parasitic* plants and *saprophytic* plants; *simple* plants and *complex* plants, *alpine* plants and *lacustrine* plants, etc. And, of course, we should understand that various less comprehensive subdivisions may be made of the primary groups or subdivisions. All of the above and many other types of classification may be found in the books dealing with the varied interests that man takes in plants.

The difficulties involved in a classification which shall include all flowering plants known may be appreciated when we understand that this branch of the vegetable kingdom contains at least 150,000 different kinds of plants that are now known to botanists. A recent estimate by a British botanist places the number at 230,000 species. But this condition should not be staggering because some other groups of natural objects contain many more types or different kinds than that.

Evolution of Plants.—Botanists now understand that the plants of the vegetable kingdom in all parts of the world are related through time as well as space. In other words, when traced back far enough, all plants are found to have had common ancestors. This means that we regard the plant world as a vast assemblage of organisms in many diverse groups, but all linked more or less closely together by similarity of structure and development. Such similarity may be close or distant, or, in other words, the relationship may be near or remote. Some plants may be close to certain ancestral types, but others may be quite distantly related to those same ancestors. This is what we mean by relationship among plants. It is a conception somewhat similar to relationship among groups of animals and among the families of human beings. It is in reality a sort of "blood" relationship, but we must not understand that plants possess a body fluid like the blood of higher animals. We might perhaps question the conclusion that relationships among the higher animals are determined largely by the blood which flows through their bodies. That fluid is of chief importance from the standpoint of nutrition, rather than of primary significance in heredity, which is of great value in really determining relationship. Indeed, inheritance is well known among plants and among many animals in which there is no blood.

Natural and Artificial Systems.—So in botany as in zoology we commonly endeavor to group or to classify organisms in accordance with what is understood about their original relationship. Relationship, "blood relationship," is the basis for our commonly used classifications of the organisms constituting the vegetable kingdom. This is known as "phylogenetic" or natural classification, in contrast with "artificial" classification which may be based upon any other characteristics of the plants, even to the point of ignoring the fact of descent. In using this conception as a basis for the systematic classification of flowering plants we should keep in mind the fact that close similarity usually indicates relatively close relationships while dissimilarity indicates relatively distant relationships.

The Names of Plants.—As we look about us we readily notice that plants exist as many different and variable kinds. It has become the practice among botanists to designate the different kinds of plants as "species," and to give each species a *particular* name. We easily recognize several different kinds or *species* of oaks, maples, grasses, ferns, seaweeds, toadstools, etc., and we find that botanists have given *names* to these in order that they may refer to them intelligently. The naming of plants and the principles involved in giving names to plants are included in that phase of systematic botany known as "nomenclature."

The Number of Plants.—The study of the plant life of the world has revealed the fact that the vegetation of the earth is composed of a great many different kinds or species. Botanists have described probably more than 250,000 different species of plants, some of which are found in great numbers in many places and over a very wide territory, while others are sparingly represented and restricted to a relatively small area. Doubtless there are others that have not yet been discovered. The most noticeable differences in the vegetation of diverse regions of the world are due to the fact that different species of plants are represented there or have become dominant in the different places.

Necessity of Classification.—It is quite impossible for any one person to know all of the 250,000 species of plants that have been described from all parts of the earth. If it were not for the fact that plants exhibit the principle of relationship as conceived by botanists, and that they may be classified into various groups on this basis, the vegetable kingdom would, indeed, appear as a chaotic assemblage of very diverse types. Few people appreciate the fact that the plant world is not such a heterogeneous association of unlike forms. The main purpose of this section of our study is to learn that flowering plants may be very readily regarded in a much more systematic light, simply by mastering a few of the principles of plant classification which are now well known to botanists. The main subdivisions or groups, and the terms selected for these that are now in common use in such a classification will next be examined.

THE COMMON GROUPS

The Species Concept.—The 150,000 or more different kinds or species of flowering plants are each represented by many individuals, no two of which are exactly alike, but they vary within narrow limits. A *species* is regarded as a *group* containing all of the individuals of a particular kind of plant that exist now or that existed in the past, no matter where they were or where they may now be found. The great French botanist, de Jussieu, long ago defined a species as: *the perennial succession of similar individuals perpetuated by generation.* The conception of "similar individuals" is difficult to define, and it varies greatly with different workers, but it is ordinarily based upon a study of the significant and common characters shown by large numbers of the individuals. Mere differences in size, shape, color of body, etc., may not mean different species. Naturally some species are represented by very many individuals, as, for example, the western yellow pine, *Pinus ponderosa*, but in other cases there may be comparatively few individuals in a species as it is known today, as in the Monterey cypress, *Cupressus macrocarpa*. The number of individuals now or in the past is not necessarily an important consideration in the conception of a species or of any other group in our classification.

The specific name is an *adjective*, a *noun in apposition*, a *noun* in the *genitive* case, or a *common noun* in the *genitive plural*. If the specific name is an adjective, it must agree with the generic name in gender. Such a name is often selected to indicate some outstanding or distinguishing characteristic of the species, as *rubra,* "red," or *sericeus,* "silky." In actual practice, specific names sometimes suggest a locality, a habitat, or even a person, as *canadensis,* "in Canada," *aquatica,* "in water," *smithii,* "after Smith." Adjectives used as specific names are sometimes formed by adding the Greek termination, *-oides, -oideus, -ides,* or *-odes,* which means "resembling" or "like," to some common noun or generic name. Examples of the use of these kinds of specific names are, *Populus deltoides,* the "poplar with leaves that are delta-like or delta-shaped," and *Elymus triticoides,* "the *Elymus,* or wild rye, that resembles *Triticum.*"

If the specific name is a noun in apposition, it is in the same case, nominative singular, as the noun with which it is in apposition, but it does not necessarily agree with it (the genus) in gender. Examples of this type of binomials are: *Allium cepa,* the onion, *Prunus cerasus,* the sour cherry, and *Nicotiana tabacum,* the early name for tobacco.

When the specific name is a noun in the genitive, as it is when it is formed from the name of a person, it is usually formed by adding *i* or *ii* to the name of the person connected with the plant, as *Prunus besseyi,* Bessey's cherry, or *Plantago purshii,* Pursh's plantain.

Examples of specific names that are genitive plurals are *Colocasia antiquorum,* the colocasia of the ancients, and *Convolvulus sepium,* the bindweed of the hedges.

It would seem that it is preferable, in the preparation of specific names, to avoid the formulation of specific names that do not tend (at least) to portray some feature of the plants named. There are too many meaningless names of plants that are merely the Latinized forms of person's names, given as a supposed honor. There is a strong growing tendency to decapitalize all specific names, even those derived from the names of persons and geographical areas.

The Genus Concept.—Individual plants within certain close limits of variation are all grouped together to constitute a species. Likewise, different species may also be grouped together to form a series or group of higher rank and with wider limits of variation in our scheme of classification. These next higher groups are called "genera" (singular, "genus"). A genus is a group or a series of species just as a species is a collection of individuals but the differences between the units (species) are greater than within a species or between the units (individuals) of a species.

The genus includes those broader characteristics that are common to all of the species. Thus, all of the *species* (or kinds) of *oaks* belong to a *single* genus, *Quercus*, all of the species of *maples* to a *single* genus, *Acer*, all of the species of *elms* to a *single* genus, *Ulmus*, as illustrative of the practice of grouping *species* into *genera*.

The generic name is a noun in the singular and is always written with a capital when used technically, or the word may be decapitalized when used as a common name, as *Crocus*, crocus, *Rhododendron*, rhododendron. The capital letter is an essential feature of the name when used in the generic sense. Many generic names have been chosen to indicate some characteristic feature or features of the species included in the genus, as *Mirabilis*, the four-o'clock, from the Latin *mirabilis*, "wonderful," and *Spiranthes*, the ladies' tresses, from the Greek *speira*, "spiral," and *anthos*, "flower," from the arrangement of the flowers in the cluster. Numerous generic names are also given to honor persons, as *Claytonia*, the spring beauty, after Clayton, an early American botanist, and *Linnaea*, the twin-flower, after Linnaeus, the great Swedish botanist.

Generic names are derived from almost any language; but in form either they are the original Greek or Latin names, such as *Carum*, the caraway, or *Rosa*, the rose, or if from some other language, they must be *Latinized*. When Latinized, they are used as Latin words, as *Vernonia*, after Vernon, an early English botanist.

It would seem that scientific considerations should dictate that the practice of naming genera after persons should be discontinued since such names do not reflect the taxonomic characteristics of the plants so designated. Sometimes these "personal-honor" genera are very odd or even ridiculous, as indeed are the names of many persons.

Families, Orders, Classes.—Following these conceptions and this general plan of grouping we find it convenient to gather *all genera* into appropriate *families*, families into *orders*, orders into *classes*, and classes into *divisions*, involving progressively higher and higher (or broader) groupings. It will be observed that this whole matter may be compared to several series of compartments or pigeonholes within progressively larger compartments with the respective limits of each series more or less clearly marked. The *species* are the *smallest* pigeonholes, and there are subdivisions of the *next larger* pigeonholes, that is, *genera*, and genera, in turn, are but subdivisions of *still larger* compartments, that is, *families*, and so on, ending with *divisions* which represent the *broadest of all* of the subdivisions and contain all of the other pigeonholes of all grades. The *divisions* or "branches" may therefore be regarded as the primary or major groups or subdivisions in plant classification.

The Complete Classification.—With such a conception before us we readily see that each and every plant must occupy a certain series of such groups or pigeonholes, and that all such plants taken together constitute the vegetable kingdom. Each plant may be found in a certain definite position in this classification, just as a given pamphlet may be located in a certain building (library), in a certain room in that building, in a certain alcove, on a certain shelf, and in a certain portfolio, etc., if the library is well classified.

We may now conveniently summarize our discussion of classification and the commonly used groups or subdivisions in the classification of flowering plants as follows:

Species consist of individual plants
  Genera are composed of species
    Families are collections of genera
      Orders are collections of families
        Classes are collections of orders
          Divisions or branches are collections of classes
            The Vegetable Kingdom is a collection of plant divisions.

From this it follows that:

Every plant belongs to some *species*
  Every species to some *genus*
    Every genus to some *family*
      Every family to some *order*
        Every order to some *class*
          Every class to some *division*, and
            All plant divisions to the *Vegetable Kingdom.*

So the Vegetable Kingdom is looked upon by botanists as being readily subdivided into

Divisions (or Branches), as *Spermatophyta*, seed plants
  Classes (also subclasses), as *Dicotyledoneae*, dicotyledons
    Orders (also suborders), as *Myrtales*, the myrtles
      Families (also subfamilies), as *Myrtaceae*, myrtle family
        Genera, as *Eucalyptus*
          Species, as *globulus*, beginning with the largest or most broadly differentiated group, the *division*, and recording in order the regular sub-

divisions to the smallest or most narrowly differentiated group, the *species*. This is the outline or framework which will be used in the classification of flowering plants in this book.

PLANT RELATIONSHIP AND NOMENCLATURE

Further Ideas Concerning Relationships.—Now that we have an outline of classification before us we can point out some additional practices dealing with the relationship and classification of flowering plants. The plants belonging to any one of the above subdivisions are regarded as being more closely related among themselves than they are to the plants of the next higher group. For example, the plants of a series of families within a given order are more closely related to each other than they are to the plants in a series of families in a different order. This means that the relationships between orders are more distant than between families, and that, in general, the degree of *remoteness* of relationship *increases* as we go up the scale of subdivisions, and that the degree of *closeness* of relationship *increases* as we go down the scale.

Value of Names.—The necessity of having names for the thousands of objects with which people are concerned is so obvious that it needs no argument. Stop for a moment to observe how universal and how early in life is the recognition of such necessity characteristic of human beings. Extended refinement in the tendencies to classify things are indeed attributes which are important elements in distinguishing man from all other animals. Nomenclature (naming) and taxonomy (classification) are in fact prominent factors in the superior intelligence of the human race in general and are outstanding incidents of the daily life of mankind.

Nomenclature and Taxonomy.—The naming (nomenclature) and the classifying (taxonomy) of the objects known to man are prominent phases of science in general, but nomenclature and classification must be done systematically or else great confusion would result. Can you picture the confusion in a great department store in the absence of a carefully named, classified, and systematically arranged collection of goods? If you will follow out such thoughts in other directions you will become impressed with the necessity and the great practical advantages of systematic nomenclature and classification in daily life. But when scientists attempt to apply these principles and these methods to rocks, to birds, to insects, to bones, to medicines, and to animals and plants many folks throw up their hands in consternation with some such expression as: "O, that is too much for me," or "That is technical," or "That is *science* and I do not want anything to do with it." Such an attitude is usually a confession of a *lack of desire* to learn truth in an *orderly* manner. Science and our knowledge of science, as well as knowledge in general, can grow and improve only by giving due regard to these things.

We should not understand because the botanist must have names for plants and because plants and plant phenomena must be classified, that that is all there is to botany, and that all that a botanist knows is merely the names of plants and the terminology that is necessary to find the names. This is too often the opinion of educated folks as well as of the ignorant, due perhaps to the fact that the names of plants are quite different from the names of other objects.

Origin and Nature of Names of Plants.—Many people dislike the names of plants because they appear to be "long and difficult to pronounce," or because they are "Latin or Greek" and such languages are "dead." These can scarcely be admitted as excuses for an aversion to botanical nomenclature because many plants have very short, terse names. And, in reality, much of the so-called English or "common" language, as well as the language of science, is merely Latin or Greek transformed to a greater or lesser degree. Science is rapidly making over the world and systematizing the knowledge about the world so we should not be afraid of scientific matters, but should endeavor to learn as much as possible about the facts and principles of science.

Common Names Are Often Confusing.—Most people demand a "common" name for each plant, meaning by that that we should have a name for each plant in the language of the region in question. This is done in many places and for many plants, but, of course, the "common" name for a certain plant in English would not be a common name in French, Italian, Russian, or German for the same plant. And, furthermore, a given plant often has many different common names in the same locality of a given country, a condition that tends toward the development of a decidedly narrow view of plant life, if no better means of cataloging were at hand.

Stability of Nomenclature Is Desired.—For many years the botanists of the world have endeavored to work out a scheme whereby the names of plants would be the same in all countries and districts, irrespective of the languages or dialects spoken in those places. Such a plan is now widely adopted, and it has been agreed, furthermore, that the names of all plants shall be in Latin or Greek, and that the finished names shall be the same for all languages. This has actually been the practice among botanists for many years. We have herein the nearest approach to the acceptance of a universal language that has yet been obtained. This agreement accounts for the fact that the real name or scientific name for that plant which we call the white oak of the United States is the same no matter whether we see it in our own science magazines or books or in the scientific publications of any other nation on earth. Such names very frequently indicate some peculiarity of the plant as well as serving the function of a mere name. Ideally, this should be more nearly uniformly the case. The practical convenience of this whole scheme is obvious.

The Form of Scientific or Botanical Names.—Another point which had to be settled in the manner of plant names was just what was to constitute the name. Very different methods were adopted in bygone centuries to meet the necessity of having some means by which different plants might be designated. In ancient times, in the absence of a name in the usual modern sense, we find that a rather complete description of the plant was necessary. Later, shortened but still clumsy and unwieldy expressions were used. As more and more plants from distant parts of the world became known it became necessary to reduce or shorten the matter used in the designations of particular plants. It was finally decided that the *genus name* written with the *species name* should constitute the real name or scientific name of a plant. The tendency to write the generic name (genus) first, with a capital letter, followed immediately by the species name, usually with a small initial letter, has now become the world-wide custom. So we say that the scientific name of a plant consists of the *generic* name and the *specific* name written together as a *binomial*, the generic being the *first* name, and the specific name being the *last* name. Thus we have *Quercus alba*, the white oak, *Quercus borealis*, the red oak, *Pinus strobus*, the white pine, *Pinus resinosa*, the red pine, *Pinus rigida*, the pitch pine, etc.

Nomenclatorial Practices.—Certain similarities and differences in the use of names for plants and for human beings may be noted. There is now a tendency among Americans to drop the custom of giving "middle" names to children. This is in notable contrast to the practice of olden times of giving a series of names to children at time of christening, a tendency which is still represented in the modern world in some countries. The practice persists in the names of the royalty of certain nations. The fact that our country looks upon this as an outgrown practice is seen in the dropping of all but three of the names in common use, and a decided tendency to reduce them still further to two only, that is, a first name and a last name. Our practice is to write the names of persons with the *specific* name *first* and the *generic* name *last*, as George Brown, Mary Brown, Henry Brown, etc. But these are really not specific names and generic names, as they are used in the broad biological sense—they are merely names for *individual* human beings. The fact is that George Brown, Mary Brown, Henry Brown, and all the other Browns, as well as everyone else in the human race belong to the *same identical genus* and *species*, in the broad biological sense. The above names, like other names used in human society, are for the *individuals* of a *given species*, of the *same species*, which is *Homo sapiens*. The necessity of having different names for each individual of the human species is obvious. It is readily seen that this custom is the same as would be practiced by the farmer if he were to have a different name for each individual wheat plant in his field, or for each sugar beet in the beet field. We do not need to have names for each individual tree in our great forests or for each individual grass plant in the great prairie-plains region of North America, but the complexities of human society and government demand that we attempt to do that for the human species as the most important and troublesome member of the animal kingdom.

Linnaeus and Nomenclature.—Botanical history indicates that Linnaeus, the great Swedish naturalist, was the first biologist to use binomial names extensively and consistently for plants. He used this as the regular manner in which to designate the plants which he described in great numbers and about which he wrote so extensively. Binomials, in fact, had been sporadically suggested and used to some degree long before his time, but his monumental work of 1753, the "Species Plantarum," marks the clear establishment of this practice on a wide basis.

Scientific Names Most Definite and Reliable.—In concluding this discussion of plant names, we would urge students and others to learn the *real* names, *i.e.*, the technical names for plants, since they constitute a much more reliable clue to the identity of plants than do common or "vulgar" names. These names appear complex and difficult to learn only because they are new or uncommon in the language of the street. Surely we should not be startled by such names as *Prunus, Abies, Larix, Populus, Lithospermum, Primula, Taxodium, Poa, Crepis, Munroa* and *Pseudotsuga*, or even *Lepargyraea*, etc., when we use very commonly such names as *Rosa, Clematis, Syringa, Cyclamen, Geranium, Delphinium, Ageratum, Calendula, Rhododendron*, and *Chrysanthemum*. The fact that all such names are current, scientifically, in all lands and districts for the respective plants in question should constitute a powerful argument in favor of abandoning all so-called common names, and adopting and using only the scientific names for plants.

CHAPTER XI

PRINCIPLES OF CLASSIFICATION OF FLOWERING PLANTS

Reference has been made at various places in the preceding chapters to the features of flowers that are regarded as indicating the primitive nature and the more advanced nature of flowering plants. We may now bring these principles of classification together and consider them along with those other somatic features of flowering plants which are regarded as indicating relationships among these plants and which, therefore, are of guiding value in the arrangement of the groups in a natural or phylogenetic system of classification.

Lack of Sufficient Information.—The student must understand that the information relative to the life history and morphological details of flowering plants that we now possess is still very incomplete and that it is insufficient to establish clearly many of the detailed relationships that are necessary for the formulation of an accurate and complete natural system of classification. Many years must come and go bringing great volumes of data before botanists can propose a system of classification of flowering plants that will be truly natural and phylogenetic in all its details. Such a perfect system may perhaps never be possible because of obstacles which need not be noted here.

THE QUESTION OF ORIGIN

Origin of Flowering Plants.—The question of the origin and descent of living groups appears to be no more deeply hidden in the complex world of organisms than for flowering plants. The gap between ferns and seed plants was one of the last to be bridged by students of plant evolution. The immediate group of higher plants from which seed plants and flowering plants have probably developed is still very much of an enigma. Solutions to this problem, which has puzzled botanists for many decades, have frequently been offered during the past 50 years, but no convincing proof is at hand for any of the contentions.

The Bennettitales.—The opinion that the more nearly immediate ancestors of flowering plants were woody forms has been widely held for several years. But when investigators set out to determine if there are woody plants to be found among the wealth of fossil remains that might throw some light upon the problem much uncertainty arises. Certain studies culminated in the announcement that members of the fossil group *Bennettitales* were fern-like, pine-like, woody plants and that they produced seeds in structures that meet very well our hypothetical conceptions even of primitive flowers. These plants are evidently also closely related to the ancestors of our modern cycads and conifers. The staminate and pistillate structures were borne in cone-like groups more or less like the flowers of one of our modern magnolias, but there were also a number of details in the anatomy of the "flowers" of these early flowering-plant relatives, especially of their stamens, that were more nearly fern-like than anything else. Some of these "flowers" show a well-developed perianth also. Clearly these plants appear to be more or less intermediate between ferns and seed plants in general and flowering plants in our modern conception.

Since the announcement of these very important discoveries, botanists rather generally have accepted the idea that flowering plants have sprung from Gymnosperms that were more or less like the *Bennettitales*. These, and the immediate ancestors of the flowering plants whatever they were, disappeared from the earth long ago; but the latter were probably much like these *Bennettitales* now represented only in fossil form.

Evidence from Serum Analysis.—The ingenious and note-worthy methods of serum analysis of flowers developed by C. Mez in Germany have yielded many suggestive findings in regard to the origin and probable development of flowering plants from ancestors similar to our modern conifers, *Coniferales*, and they tend to support numerous features of the Besseyan System that were worked out by the use of other criteria.

Woody and Herbaceous Types.—Agreement is becoming general that the woody members, *Magnoliaceae*, of the buttercup group, *Ranales*, most nearly resemble the ancient types and they are, therefore, to be considered the most primitive of all modern flowering plants. The Besseyan system of classification reflects this point of view and it treats the flowering plants as a single series in so far as their origin is concerned. This system, even in its last form, is in reality a modification of the Bentham and Hooker arrangement after which it is patterned.

Relation between Dicotyledons and Monocotyledons.—Investigations of more recent years tend to substantiate the thesis that the Dicotyledons were the first types to appear and that these gave rise to the Monocotyledons at a somewhat later period. The woody buttercups, *Ranales*, are the earliest or most primitive group from which the Monocotyledons and the two branches of Dicotyledons have diverged. An abundance of evidence from the study of the vegetative as well as of the floral morphology and serum analysis of flowering plants by many investigators in America, Germany, England, and Italy, during the past 20 years would seem to establish these features as a very plausible hypothesis.

Bessey's Principles.—Bessey restated and expanded a series of "dicta" as a means of giving concrete expression to the guiding principles that have been derived from a survey of the investigations upon the ancestry and descent of flowering plants.

A more recent (1926) publication by Hutchinson, of Kew Garden, England, adopts essentially the same ideas and principles of classification as those included in the older (1915) Besseyan system. But Hutchinson separates the Dicotyledons into two main series, one of which is woody and diverges from *Magnoliales*, the other is herbaceous and diverges from *Ranales*.

The dicta or principles may be conveniently treated under two subdivisions, namely, those that pertain to the general anatomy of the vegetative body of flowering plants, and those that pertain to the flower and its work. The following treatment is somewhat modified and extended from the proposals of Bessey, Hutchinson, and others.

VEGETATIVE ANATOMY

The Vascular Bundles.—Plants with the collateral fibrovascular bundles of the stem arranged in the form of a hollow cylinder, with pith on the inside and cortex on the outside of the cylinder, as in magnolias and oaks, are more primitive than plants with fibrovascular bundles scattered through the stem with no clearly set out pith and cortex as in palms and lilies. The latter are Monocotyledons, and they are probably derived from the former type which are Dicotyledons.

Woody versus Herbaceous Species.—The woody stem, developed by the formation of much fibrous tissue in the fibrovascular bundles is more primitive than the herbaceous stem with a minimum of fibrous tissue. Woody plants, shrubs and trees are primitive. Herbaceous plants are derived from woody ancestors. Trees, in the usual sense, are primitive, and herbs have developed or descended from trees.

Climbers (lianas) are younger than erect shrubs and trees from which they appear to have been developed in response to environmental relations.

Simple and Branched Stems.—Simple or unbranched stems are primitive, and branched stems are a later development from these.

Leaf Features.—Simple leaves are primitive; compound leaves are derived and higher. Whorled or opposite leaves are derived; solitary or spirally arranged leaves are primitive. Primitive plants produced evergreen leaves, but deciduous leaves were developed later. Leaves with reticulated or netted veins appear to be primitive and leaves with parallel venation are probably a later development.

Duration of Life.—Perennials are primitive, biennials and annuals have developed later.

FLORAL ANATOMY

The Inflorescence.—Plants that produce solitary flowers are primitive and plants with many-flowered inflorescences are later and higher.

Spiral and Cyclic Flowers.—The spiral type of flower, as in *Magnolia*, is primitive, and the cyclic type, as in lilies, *Lilium*, and mints, *Mentha*, is later and derived from the former.

Number of Parts.—Plants with flowers with many or an indefinite number of floral parts or elements, as in buttercups, *Ranunculus*, and magnolias, *Magnolia*, are primitive, and plants with few parts or a definite number of parts, as in gentians, *Gentiana*, and bluebells, *Campanula*, are higher. These changes are brought about through increasing parental care and the resultant sterilization of many essential organs of the flower.

Petaly and Apetaly.—Flowers with petals, as in geranium, *Geranium*, are primitive and normal, and flowers without petals, as in oaks, *Quercus*, and birches, *Betula*, are derived from the former by loss or reduction of the parts.

Polypetaly and Sympetaly.—Flowers with the perianth parts (sepals and petals) separate, *i.e.* not "united" or "grown together," as in buttercups, as has been explained in an earlier chapter, are earlier types, and flowers with perianth parts "united," as in primroses, *Primula*, blueberries, *Vaccinium*, honeysuckles, *Lonicera*, etc. are later or higher.

Actinomorphy and Zygomorphy.—Flowers that are radially symmetrical or *actinomorphic*, as in arrowheads, *Sagittaria*, lilies, *Tulipa*, irids, *Iris*, flaxes, *Linum*, potato, *Solanum*, etc. are primitive or early in the developmental sense, and flowers that are bilaterally symmetrical or otherwise unsymmetrical or *zygomorphic*, as in orchids, *Orchis*, beans, *Phaseolus*, mints, *Nepeta*, violets, *Viola*, and snapdragons, *Antirrhinum*, are regarded as much later forms.

Hypogyny and Epigyny.—Flowers with a superior ovary (hypogyny) as in buttercups, *Ranunculus*, etc. onions, *Allium*, grasses, *Poa*, mustards, *Brassica*, primroses, *Primula*, and morning-glories, *Ipomoea*, etc. are more primitive than flowers with an inferior ovary (epigyny) as irids, *Iris*, banana, *Musa*, honey-suckle, *Lonicera*, and composites, *Helianthus*, *Aster*, etc.

Apocarpy and Syncarpy.—Flowers with separate pistils and carpels (apocarpy) as in buttercups, *Ranunculus*, etc., are more primitive, and flowers with united carpels (syncarpy) as in lilies, *Lilium*, nightshades, *Solanum*, phloxes, *Phlox*, etc. are higher and have been derived from the former. The polycarpous flower (*i.e.* a flower with many carpels) is the earlier condition and the oligocarpous flower (*i.e.* a flower with a few carpels that are usually united) is derived from it.

Concerning Stamens.—Primitive flowers have many separate stamens, *i.e.* they are polystemonous and apostemonous, and later flowers have fewer stamens, *i.e.* they are oligostemonous, and these show a tendency to become united, synstemonous. Primitive flowers typically produce more or less powdery pollen, and higher flowers tend to produce waxy or coherent pollen.

Perfect and Imperfect Flowers.—Perfect. or *monoclinous* flowers, *i.e.* flowers that have both stamens and pistils, as in buttercups, *Ranunculus*, roses, *Rosa*, cotton, *Gossypium*, etc. are more primitive than those that are imperfect or *diclinous*, *i.e.* have their stamens and pistils produced in different flowers, as in oaks, *Quercus*, wild rice, *Zizania*, ashes, *Fraxinus*, and cottonwoods, *Populus*.

Monœcious and Diœcious Plants.—There are two types among diclinous plants, *i.e.* plants with imperfect flowers. One of these is the *monœcious* type, in which stamens and pistils are produced in different flowers upon the same individual plant, as in oaks, *Quercus*, wild rice, *Zizania*, birches, *Betula*, etc. The other is the *diœcious* type, in which the stamens and pistils are produced in different flowers and these are borne by entirely different and separate plants, as in the ashes, *Fraxinus*, cottonwoods, *Populus*, willows, *Salix*, boxelder, *Acer*, etc. The monœcious condition is regarded as the more primitive, and the diœcious condition is considered to be a later development.

The Question of Seeds.—Plants that produce many seeds per flower are regarded as relatively primitive, and those that produce few seeds per flower are derived. Many higher plants have come to produce a single seed per flower, as in the composites. The seed with endosperm is regarded as indicating a lower relationship than is indicated by a seed without endosperm. The seed with a small, straight embryo imbedded in endosperm is more primitive than the seed with a large curved or coiled embryo and with little or no endosperm.

Monophylesis versus Polyphylesis.—The above principles when applied to the classification of flowering plants result in the arrangement of the groups in a manner very different from that of the Englerian plan, the most widely accepted and used system for many years. The system of Engler teaches that the Monocotyledons are more primitive than the Dicotyledons and that both groups have had a polyphyletic origin. That system also regards the flowers without petals as primitive types from which the petaliferous types have developed later. The latter is a point of view also recently expressed by Wettstein. The de Candollean, Bentham and Hooker, and Besseyan systems are exactly contradictory in regard to both of these points. Bessey regarded petaly as the original and normal condition, and apetaly was derived from this at a later date. The evidence that has been accumulating for a quarter of a century would seem to indicate that the conception of de Candolle and Bessey is the more nearly proper one and that Engler is doubtless in error when he places the *Apetalae* and *Amentiferae* at the beginning of his system instead of associating the plants of those groups with the higher groups to which they appear to be related. However, this problem is still far from being settled.

Position of Apetalous Species.—Certain investigators have made a strong case for the treatment of *Apetalae* and *Amentiferae* as derived rather than primitive on the basis of pollination and insect visitation. Entomophilous or insect-pollinated flowering plants are primitive, and anemophilous or wind-pollinated plants are derived from the former by a process of reduction. Evidence is at hand that would support the contention that such plants as grasses, sedges, and ragweeds, which are apetalous, and oaks, birches, cottonwoods, and willows, which are amentiferous as well as apetalous, and mostly anemophilous, are, indeed, to be regarded as the very highest of all flowering plants, outranking the orchids, *Orchidaceae*, and composites, *Compositae*, that for years have been regarded as the most diversified and highest of Angiosperms. It would appear that reduction of the perianth, with the consequent loss of attractiveness for pollinators has gone so far as to result in the development of a totally different method of pollination, namely anemophily. The fact that the *Amentiferae* produce ovaries with two or more *united* carpels is an additional argument against the primitive nature of these plants, and in favor of their reduced and derived nature. Primitive flowering plants produced flowers with many *separate* carpels, according to present evidence.

Engler and Bessey on Epigyny.—The Englerian system gives little weight to epigyny in the arrangement of the groups, the epigynous species being more or less distributed among hypogynous species in the same groups. The system of Bentham and Hooker and the Besseyan system make much of epigyny in the arrangement of the orders and families. The major groups *Epigynae*, *Inferae*, etc. have been conspicuous subdivisions of the latter schemes of classification for many years. The arrangement (of Dicotyledons) proposed by Hutchinson also gives considerable weight to epigyny as opposed to hypogyny in the grouping of the different series.

The Findings of Morphology.—The systems of classification for flowering plants proposed by Bessey and Clements in America and by Hallier and Hutchinson in Europe have the great merit of support from much comparatively recent work in morphological botany as well as from an examination of the evidence afforded by fossil remains and serum analysis. The Besseyan system, when it is portrayed in graphic form by means of the floral formulae already described, becomes extremely useful for the presentation of an introduction to many of the most significant features in the structure, morphology, general biology, and classification of flowering plants when arranged and expanded in the form of the chart first devised by Clements.

THE OUTLINE SHOWN BY THE CHART

The flower chart is in reality a condensed and graphic key to the families represented, depicting many of the significant characteristics of the several families that, treated in the usual manner of a manual, would cover many pages of descriptive matter in fine print. The chart also presents a much more evident and impressive idea of relationships than is possible to show in the descriptive manual. The beginning student rarely if ever senses the fact that the arrangement of the groups in a manual is meant to reflect a notion of relationship. Even when that fact is presented to him he has difficulty in forming much of a knowledge as to the nature of the groups and relationships involved because they are so completely hidden among the pages of the book.

The Three Lines of Development.—The chart is prepared in three units one of which, 1 on the left, represents the Monocotyledons, the central and right hand units, 2 and 3 representing the two main series of Dicotyledons of the Besseyan system. Lines of development are used to represent certain ideas of origin of the whole series and their divergence from the *Ranales*, as well as relationships among the subdivisions of each of the three main series. The Monocotyledons are represented as originating from the Ranalian plexus standing at the axis of the whole series. The main line of Monocotyledons begins with the arrowheads, *Alismales*, lying next to *Ranales*, and in turn higher up we see the lilies, *Liliales*, irids, *Iridales*, and the line terminates in the orchids, *Orchidales*. The important side branches of the monocotyledonous series include the arums, *Arales*, palms, *Palmales*, water weeds, *Hydrales*, and the grasses and their kin, *Graminales*. This is a fairly well standardized treatment of the Monocotyledons, although the order names and the inclusions of the various orders are not exactly the same in the Besseyan system as in other arrangements. After all, such details as the latter are of no interest or value to the beginner who has a rather big task anyhow to become familiar with the orders and families that are best known and about whose systematic position there is least disagreement among botanists.

The Dicotyledon Series.—The series of Dicotyledons on the right, 3, begins with the *Ranales* and leads into three groups of orders including the mallows, *Malvales*, geraniums, *Geraniales*, violets, *Theales*, (*Guttiferales*), mustards, *Papaverales*, (*Rhoeadales*), and the pinks, *Caryophyllales*, in the first group, followed by the primroses, *Primulales*, ebonies, *Ebenales*, and heathers, *Ericales*, and terminating in the third group of orders including phloxes, *Polemoniales*, gentians, *Gentianales*, mints, *Lamiales*, and snapdragons, *Scrophulariales*.

The other series of Dicotyledons, 2, constitutes the main axis of the whole assemblage of flowering plants and is represented on the central chart. This series begins also with the *Ranales* and continues through the roses, *Rosales*, bittersweets, *Celastrales*, parsleys, *Umbellales*, madders, *Rubiales*, and terminates in the composites, *Asterales*. Lateral branches of this line include the myrtles, *Myrtales*, cactuses, *Cactales*, and the loasas, *Loasales*, from the roses, the maples, *Sapindales*, from the bittersweets, and the harebells, *Campanulales*, from the madders.

Extent of the Chart.—The chart as we have commonly used it contains about 100 families arranged in about 30 orders. A knowledge of 100 families of flowering plants is a fine start for anyone in the field of systematic botany. There are probably many botanists who work in other branches of our subject that are not able to recognize at sight anywhere near this number of flowering-plant families. The great advantage of the system and of our methods of using it is in the short cut it affords to the family, and especially to the mastery of the floral earmarks of families by means of the graphic formulae.

Cross-lines on the Chart.—When the chart with its three branches is completed with the orders and families neatly printed and with their formulae carefully sketched opposite them, then lines are drawn across the chart that divide the families into smaller groups bounded by the various lines. For example one cross-line is so drawn as to separate the hypogynous (below the line) and the epigynous (above the line) families, another one separates the polypetalous from the sympetalous groups, still another cross-line separates the actinomorphic groups from the zygomorphic groups, and a fourth line marks the dividing line between apocarpous and syncarpous families. The three main

lines of flowering plants including Monocotyledons and the two
lines of Dicotyledons are charted side by side so that the four
cross-lines are continuous as they cut across the whole chart
from side to side.   Here and there some of the lines cross each
other vertically and this serves to differentiate still further
certain groups of families among which the desired one may be
located by the inspection of a very few formulae.   The value of
the cross-lines lies in the fact that they serve much the same
function as the subdivisions in an ordinary printed key in leading
one to an increasingly smaller group of forms among which the
family containing the flower in question may be found.   The
location of a family on the chart with a formula to which the
structure of a given flower conforms, thus becomes a very interesting quest that is rapidly perfected as one's knowledge of the
families increases until by and by it becomes possible to discard
the chart altogether, or to refer to it only occasionally when new
families are encountered.

Care in Using the Chart.—The successful use of the chart in
locating the family to which an unknown plant belongs depends
largely upon the thoroughness with which the structure of the
flower is worked out.   Naturally this determines the proper
formula to look for and if a misleading or incomplete formula
has been worked out one cannot expect to find the proper family
as readily as would be possible with greater care in flower analysis.
These facts tend to impress the essential morphology of family
types (as indicated by flower structure) upon the mind of the
worker in a lasting manner.

When the formula derived from the analysis of the flower has
been matched with that of a certain family on the chart then
one must go to the manual where the genus and species may be
found for the further classification of the plant.

Extension of the Chart Method.—The chart method here used
goes only as far as the family, but it has been found that the
method is tremendously helpful to that point as compared to
the usual laborious route through keys and through the inspection
of long family diagnoses in the books.   The scheme might possibly be extended to include the genera of various families, but
the plan might become so complicated if expanded to that degree
as to defeat its purpose except for more advanced interests.

Explanation of Symbols Used on the Chart.—The most of the
relatively few symbols that are necessary to write the formulae

CA Calyx, sepals

CA^O Sepals none

CA^X Sepals several, not a definite number

$CA^{3-\infty}$ Sepals 3 to many

CA^{4-5} Sepals 4 or 5

CA^4 Sepals 4

$CA\underset{\smile}{5}$ Sepals 5, more or less united

$CA^{\circledS}$ Sepals 5, united

CA^P Calyx a pappus

CAz^{3-5} Calyx zygomorphic

Co Corolla, petal

Co^O Petals none

Co^X Petals several, not a definite number

$Co\underset{\smile}{5}$ Petals 5, more or less united

$Co^{\circledS}$ Petals 5, united

$Coz^{\circledS}$ Corolla zygomorphic

S Stamens

S^{∞} Stamens many

S^{∞} Stamens many, united by the filaments

$S\underset{\smile}{2-4}$ Stamens 2 to 4, united by the filaments

$S\widehat{5}$ Stamens 5, united by the anthers

S^{2+4} Stamens 6, in two sets

$S^{2+2(2)}$ Stamens 4, in two sets, or 2

P Pistils or carpels

P^1 Pistil or carpel 1

P^{∞} Pistils many

$P^{\circled３}$ Ovary or pistil tricarpellary

$P^{\overline{(3\cdot\infty)}}$ Carpels 3 to many, united

$P^{\overline{(1:2)}}$ Pistil bicarpellary but one-celled

$P^{\circled２}$ Pistil bicarpellary, deeply four-lobed

$P^{\circled３}\,^{\overline{(1:3)}}$ Pistil of 3 carpels, rarely tricarpellary but one-celled

$P^{\overline{(1:3\cdot5)}}$ Pistil of 3 to 5 carpels but one-celled

$P\underset{\smile}{2-\infty}$ Carpels 2 to many, more or less united

ACH Achene

BER Berry

DI Diœcious

EVG Evergreen

MO Monœcious

PG Polygamous

SC Scales

SUC Succulent

UT Utricle

BAC Baccate

CAP Capsule

DR Drupe or drupaceous

FOL Follicle

PF Flowers perfect

SAM Samara

$SPAT$ Spathaceous

U Flowers unisexual

$$\frac{S^{4-5}\!\!\downarrow}{CA^{2-6}Co^{\overline{(4-5)}}}\Big/ P^{\circled２}$$

Ovary inferior, bicarpellary; Stamens epipetalous, opposite the lobes of Co

$$\frac{CA^3Co^3S^6}{P^{\circled３}}$$

Ovary inferior, tricarpellary; stamens on the axis

$$\frac{S^5\!\!\downarrow}{CA^{\circled５}Co^{\circled５}P^{\circled２}}$$

Stamens epipetalous, opposite the lobes of Co

$$\frac{S^5}{CA\underset{\smile}{5}Co^{\circled５}P^{\circled２}}$$

Stamens epipetalous, alternate with lobes of the Corolla

Common Symbols Used in the Chart (Fig. 96) and Following Pages of the families are self-explanatory. A list of the more common symbols employed, however, together with their explanation or interpretation, is presented on the preceding page in order that any uncertainties that are encountered in the formulae may be readily interpreted. The list includes those symbols and combinations that pertain to the structure of the flower, the formula proper, and also those used to indicate certain vegetative features, sexual peculiarities, and fruit characteristics. The latter symbols are written beneath the structural formula, and they have been found valuable as contributing further practical aid in family differentiation.

THE NATURE AND USE OF ANALYTICAL KEYS

It has been stated that the chart of flowering plants previously described is a "condensed and graphic key" to the families represented. This means that the structure of the flowers as depicted by the various formulae constitutes a guide to the identification of the groups concerned. The relationships among the various groups are also indicated by the distribution of the orders (according to formulae) on the chart. A more familiar and traditional approach to these same objectives is by means of descriptive "keys" and "synopses" which may or may not be illustrated. Some guides to the flora of certain areas consist almost entirely of such keys, and all the great manuals and floras literally bristle with keys and synopses. Such instruments are encountered in every important and valuable work of the taxonomist. It is well, therefore, that we inquire briefly into the nature and use of these significant aids to the student of systematic botany.

Keys and Synopses.—A *key*, in the above sense, has been defined by Hitchcock[1] as "an orderly arrangement of a series of contrasting or directly comparable statements, by means of which groups of the same category may be distinguished and indicated or identified." The statements involved in keys concern an almost limitless variety of floral and vegetative characteristics of the plants classified. The same authority[1] defines a *synopsis* as "a segregation of groups of the same category into successively smaller divisions according to characters common to the members. A key is primarily a mechanical device by

[1] Reprinted by permission from *Descriptive Systematic Botany* by A. S. Hitchcock, published by John Wiley & Sons, Inc.

which one may arrive at the name of the ultimate member of the group. A synopsis is primarily a taxonomic summary of characters by which the members are classified. A key is concerned chiefly with quick identification; a synopsis is concerned chiefly with showing relationships." Referring again to the floral formulae and flowering-plant chart, it may be observed that keys are more or less comparable to the formulae, synopses to the chart.

Types of Keys.—There are various kinds and combinations of keys and synopses. A key may be so constructed as to indicate *natural* relationships or affinities, or it may be drawn on a purely *artificial* basis, *i.e.*, may disregard natural or phylogenetic relationships. Keys may be plain or illustrated, simple or complex; they may be based upon flowers alone or upon vegetative characteristics alone; or they may combine various characteristics shown by the plants classified. A key may consider only the color of the flowers or the number of parts in the flowers, or it may be based upon fruits and seeds. A vegetative key may include only buds, or leaves, or stems, or all sorts of combinations of these. Even different environmental requirements are frequently included in keys.

In constructing a key, one selects the most prominent or contrasting characteristics to distinguish the broadest or primary divisions, and then the subdivisions of various degree may be identified likewise by lesser contrasting features or by characteristics of lower rank or of more detailed and restricted nature. The simplest key includes a single pair of contrasting statements, for example:

Leaves opposite...................... Genus *Acer*, maples
Leaves alternate..................... Genus *Quercus*, oaks

Or if the relatively simple key is to differentiate a larger number of groups or categories, say *species,* as well as *genera,* then additional statements must be entered in order to distinguish the plants of the smaller or more subordinate groups, for example:

Leaves opposite............ Genus *Acer*, maples
Leaves simple............ Species *saccharum*, sugar maple
Leaves compound........ Species *negundo*, box elder
Leaves alternate............ Genus *Quercus*, oaks
Leaves with rounded lobes. Species *alba*, white oak
Leaves with pointed lobes.. Species *velutina*, black oak

In the practical construction of such keys as the above, the words "genus" and "species" would be omitted. They are included here only to emphasize the primary and secondary groups or categories used. A key that embraces many genera or species must, of course, include many more contrasting or comparative statements and necessarily becomes more and more complex as the details increase.

The Bracket Key.—On the basis of fundamental structure, there are two types of keys, the *bracket key* and the *indented key*. Both of these are very useful. The mechanical structure of the bracket key may be illustrated by the following "diagrammatic" example to include seven hypothetical species:

```
1. Flowers white........................... 2
1. Flowers red............................. 5
2. Leaves opposite......................... 3
2. Leaves alternate........................ 4
3. Flowers 3-parted........................ Species 1
3. Flowers 5-parted........................ Species 2
4. Leaves simple.......................... Species 3
4. Leaves compound........................ Species 4
5. Flowers in spikes...................... Species 5
5. Flowers in racemes..................... 6
6. Fruit white............................ Species 6
6. Fruit red.............................. Species 7
```

The Indented Key.—The indented key, in a great variety of forms, is the key most widely used and seen in floras and manuals throughout the world. The mechanical contrasts between the bracket key and the indented key may be illustrated in a simple manner by "keying out" the seven species used in the foregoing illustration of the bracket key, as follows:

```
Flowers white
  Leaves opposite
    Flowers 3-parted...................... Species 1
    Flowers 5-parted...................... Species 2
  Leaves alternate
    Leaves simple........................ Species 3
    Leaves compound...................... Species 4
Flowers red
  Flowers in spikes...................... Species 5
  Flowers in racemes
    Fruit white.......................... Species 6
    Fruit red............................ Species 7
```

It will be readily noted from the foregoing examples that the indented key leads more *directly* to the various subdivisions and is more easily "followed through." This is because the interconnections between the various subdivisions of the indented key are so grouped or spaced as to be more easily and accurately read—they lead more directly to the several species involved.

When the successive divisions of a key are always in pairs, the key is said to be *dichotomous.* Both indented and bracket keys are often constructed in this manner.

Longer Keys.—In keying out a great many plants, the key may become very long and complicated and thus may be more or less difficult to follow, because the contrasting subdivisions may be separated widely, sometimes even by several pages. The difficulties incurred because of this situation are relieved somewhat by using certain letters, numbers, signs, or other symbols to mark the corresponding subdivisions in the keys. An example of this useful device, applied to the foregoing simple bracket key, may be shown as follows:

   I*a*. Flowers white
      2*a*. Leaves opposite
         3*a*. Flowers 3-parted...................... Species 1
         3*b*. Flowers 5-parted................... Species 2
      2*b*. Leaves alternate
         3*a*. Leaves simple...................... Species 3
         3*b*. Leaves compound.................. Species 4
   I*b*. Flowers red
      2*a*. Flowers in spikes...................... Species 5
      2*b*. Flowers in racemes
         3*a*. Fruit white........................ Species 6
         3*b*. Fruit red......................... Species 7

An example of an actual indented key, long in use, is the following key[1] to the genera of the pink family, *Caryophyllaceae*, of the Rocky Mountains.

Sepals united, forming a tubular or ovoid calyx.
   Ribs or nerves of calyx 10 or more.
      Calyx-teeth foliaceous........................... 1. *Agrostemma.*
      Calyx-teeth short.
         Styles 3....................................... 2. *Silene.*
         Styles 5....................................... 3. *Lychnis.*
   Ribs or nerves of calyx 5........................... 4. *Saponaria.*

[1] Coulter, J. M. and A. Nelson, *New Manual of Botany of the Central Rocky Mountains*, p. 180. American Book Company, 1909.

Sepals distinct or nearly so.
 Petals deeply emarginate or bifid.
  Capsule dehiscent to the base; styles mostly 3 . . . . . . 5. *Stellaria.*
  Capsule opening at summit only, by teeth, styles
   mostly 5. . . . . 6. *Cerastium.*
 Petals entire or barely emarginate.
  Stipules wanting.
   Styles 5. . . . . 7. *Sagina.*
   Styles 3.
    Seeds not appendaged at the hilum. . . . . 8. *Arenaria.*
    Seeds with an appendage (strophiole). . . . . 9. *Moehringia.*
  Stipules present, usually scarious and conspicuous.
   Capsule opening by 3 valves to the base. . . . . 10. *Spergularia.*
   Capsule indehiscent, or essentially an achene. . . . . 11. *Paronychia.*

Coulter and Nelson's key[1] to the species of *Populus*, poplars, aspens, cottonwoods, in the Rocky Mountains illustrates a relatively simple key of the indented type that is based on the characteristics of the leaves alone, as follows:

Petioles flattened laterally.
 Leaves suborbicular. . . . . 1. *P. tremuloides.*
 Leaves broad, more or less deltoid.
  Abruptly acuminate, crenately serrate. . . . . 2. *P. occidentalis.*
  Gradually acuminate, deeply sinuate-dentate. . . . . . 3. *P. Wislizenii.*
Petioles round or furrowed.
 Leaves pale beneath. . . . . 4. *P. balsamifera.*
 Leaves green, scarcely lighter beneath.
  Oblong-lanceolate. . . . . 5. *P. angustifolia.*
  Ovate, abruptly long-acuminate. . . . . 6. *P. acuminata.*

The student must understand that keys, even at their best, are but selected assortments of only a few of the characteristics of the group of plants involved. He should know that he is likely to find exceptions to the statements contained in them, but these should not discourage him or lead him to doubt the value of the work in question. Variation is one of the greatest laws of biology. Keys and taxonomic diagnoses can attempt to record only the outstanding or the usual and most distinctive features of plants. It would not be at all practical or useful to state all the possible exceptions that may be encountered. The larger the group represented in the particular classification, the greater the number of details that must be considered and the more likely it will be that allowance will have to be made for the possible exceptions to the statements in the key. Only by the

[1] *Ibid.*, p. 127.

gradual mastery of a knowledge of the "typical characteristics" that delimit the natural groups of flowering plants, and with careful consideration of the possibility of variations and exceptions to be noted in all diagnoses, can one build up a growing familiarity with the limitations of the natural groups that constitute the flora of the world.

MANUALS AND FLORAS

The only reliable scientific guide to the flora of a given area, whether small or large, is likely to be so technical as to discourage all but the most enthusiastic and serious student of nature. Taxonomy must utilize a critical and technical terminology to accomplish its complicated objectives. There are always many more species of plants in an area than is apparent to the uninitiated; and when all these are systematically treated in the usual scientific manner, with the necessary terminology to differentiate them and the technical names to designate them, the popular-minded person becomes lost in the "maze of scientific jargon" and is likely to think that it is all useless.

A manual or flora is an analytical and descriptive presentation of the nature and the names of the plants of the area in question. The most common use of such a work is to find the names of plants in order that they may be referred to in a definite and intelligible manner. Manuals are supplied with keys to the major groups as well as to the subordinate categories, down to the species. Sometimes the keys and the descriptions of the species are accompanied by illustrations. A manual usually covers a relatively large territory or section of a country, as is illustrated by Britton's *Manual of the Flora of the Northern States and Canada* and Gray's *New Manual of Botany*, covering northeastern United States. A local flora deals in the same way with a more limited area, as a state, county, or even a single valley; Rydberg's *Flora of Montana* and *Flora of the Black Hills of South Dakota* and Mackenzie and Bush's *Manual of the Flora of Jackson County, Missouri* are examples of local floras.

Besides keys and synopses to the families, genera, and species, many manuals also include descriptions of all these groups, as well as notes on the range or geographical distribution, habitat characteristics, and other features that aid in the identification of the plants. The student must understand that all these helps are the product of the wide experience and knowledge of the authors. He must learn to allow some leeway in regard to the descriptive material and to understand the situation if he finds individual plants that do not exactly "fit into" the keys and descriptions of his manual or flora. Keys and diagnoses are so constructed as to illustrate the average of many individuals, the *species*, in other words. This means that it is seldom safe to rest one's identification upon a single specimen, unless one's knowledge already goes far beyond that particular individual. In short, variations in size, range, habitat, and morphological characteristics of the vegetative body, and even of the flowers and fruits, are likely to be found among the individuals of all species of flowering plants. Only the wide experience and seasoned judgment that come with years of taxonomic work can produce competence in this line of technical work or in any other branch of science.

Study of Selected Families.—We may now consider the general nature of a number of families of flowering plants selected to illustrate the foregoing principles of classification and arrangement of orders and families. Most of these orders may be found on the chart. The illustrations used in connection with practically all of the groups included are selected with the idea of portraying a few of the details of the foliar, floral, and fruiting habits of the respective families.

CHAPTER XII

SELECTED ORDERS AND FAMILIES OF DICOTYLEDONS

The Dicotyledons are the most varied and numerous of modern Angiosperms. They are represented in the flora of the world by a great many more types and species than are their close relatives and differentiates, the Monocotyledons. The proportion of Dicotyledons to Monocotyledons now described is about four to one, there being approximately 120,000 species of the former and about 30,000 species of the latter.

Vegetative Nature of Dicotyledons.—The stems of Dicotyledons are typically characterized by the presence of fibrovascular bundles arranged more or less in the form of a hollow truncated cone with pith in the center and with cortex enveloping the outer surface, all of which regions diverge downward from a mass of meristematic tissue at the tip of the stem. The lateral branches of the stem are developed after the same plan and they have essentially the same structure. A short section of such a stem or branch may be more or less cylindrical in form because of slight taper and in such cases the layers of tissues that make up the stem are somewhat of the nature of overlapping organically connected cylinders (Fig. 77, *B*).

Growth and Length of Life.—All of the meristem becomes differentiated into permanent tissues in many Dicotyledons so that the life of the individual plant is terminated at the close of a single growing period, and the plant is therefore called an "annual." In many other Dicotyledons a zone of meristem persists or remains undifferentiated between the xylem and phloem of the fibrovascular cylinder as the individual passes into and through the resting period. Such plants are capable of continued growth with each successive active period and are, therefore, called "perennials." The xylem portions of the central cylinder in many such plants is built up by the annual formation of a new layer of wood over the preceding layer, and in this way the stem increases in diameter as well as in height.

These so-called "annual rings" of perennial Dicotyledons are in reality annual *layers* of wood that are not *rings* at all, but they take the form of the *entire individual* composed of its main stem and all the living branches. They appear as a series of more or less perfectly concentric rings only in a cross-section of the stem (Fig. 97, *B*).

The first or primary leaves (cotyledons) on the stems of Dicotyledons are usually two in number, and they are opposite. The secondary or mature leaves are typically netted veined, and they are opposite, alternate, or whorled.

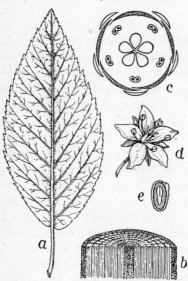

Floral Pattern in Dicotyledons.—The flowers of Dicotyledons are typically *four-parted* (tetramerous) or *five-parted* (pentamerous), that is, they have a perianth in which there are *four* or *five* parts represented in the calyx and the corolla, or in the calyx alone in those flowers which lack the corolla (Fig. 97). Certain species of the group lack petals, and others lack both petals and sepals.

Fig. 97.—The general features of the leaf, structure of the stem, flower, and seed of the Dicotyledons. *A*, leaf; *B*, section of stem; *C*, section of the flower (diagram); *D*, single flower; *E*, section of seed (*after Gager, General Botany*, published by P. Blakiston's Son and Co).

ORDER RANALES, THE BUTTERCUP ORDER

The order *Ranales* as considered here includes several families of both woody and herbaceous nature. The group contains many woody species, but there are also numerous species that are little or not at all frutescent. This situation has led certain authors to separate the woody forms from the herbaceous forms and to include the former in the order *Magnoliales* (Magnolia order), retaining the order *Ranales* for the herbaceous species alone. For our purpose we need not make this differentiation, but we may understand that the woody members are the more primitive and the herbaceous members are the later or derived types.

The typical flower of the *Ranales* is hypogynous and perfect, and commonly complete. The carpels are numerous and separate or sometimes united, and in many forms they are arranged spirally over a more or less cone-shaped axis. The stamens are also numerous and typically arranged spirally below the carpels. Petals and sepals are separate, the petals sometimes lacking. The flowers are typically actinomorphic but certain forms such as larkspur, *Delphinium*, and monkshood, *Aconitum*, produce strikingly zygomorphic flowers.

THE MAGNOLIA FAMILY

The *Magnoliaceae*, or magnolia family (Fig. 98) are a group of about 10 genera and 70 or 80 species of trees and shrubs distributed through the tropical and subtropical, but mostly temperate portions of eastern North America and Asia as far north as northeastern United States and northern Japan.

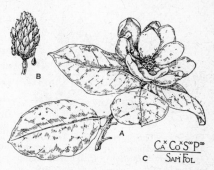

Leaves commonly large, alternate, simple, often more or less leathery, often persistent; stipules large and foliaceous, deciduous; flowers hypogynous, large, often very showy, solitary, terminal or axillary, perfect and complete; sepals and petals numerous, often similar;

Fig. 98.—The magnolia family, *Magnoliaceae*. *A*, flowering twig of *Magnolia grandiflora*; *B*, ripe fruit of same (*after Mathews*); *C*, floral formula for the family.

stamens many, free, often spirally arranged in a beautiful series; carpels many, free, arranged in close spirals over the elongated cone-like or spire-like axis, sometimes adherent in fruit; ovules 1 to 2 or more; fruit usually dry, a follicle or a samara, the group often more or less aggregated and completely covering the elongated cone-like axis; seeds large, with abundant, oily endosperm, often suspended from the cone on slender filaments.

A noteworthy genus of the family is *Magnolia*, of which there are many important ornamental species such as the American, *M. acuminata*, and the old world *M. soulangeana*. The name *Magnolia* is derived from the name of a man, Pierre Magnol, a seventeenth century French botanist. Another member of the group, *Liriodendron tulipifera*, the tulip tree of eastern United States, is an important species which furnishes an excellent commercial timber known as "white wood" or "yellow poplar." This species is also planted as an ornamental. The name, *Liriodendron*, comes from words meaning tree and lily, *i.e.*, a tree bearing lilies.

THE PAPAW FAMILY

The *Anonaceae*, commonly known as the papaw or custard apple family (Fig. 99) include woody plants of the nature of trees, shrubs or vines with aromatic wood. The family contains 50 or more genera and several hundred species that are mostly tropical in both the eastern and western hemispheres, but there are a few species that are found in temperate climates, as in the American papaw.

Leaves alternate, simple, entire, without stipules; flowers hypogynous, mostly perfect, but sometimes imperfect; sepals commonly 3, separate or somewhat united; petals usually 6, often in two series; stamens many, separate, spirally arranged at the base of an elongated or congested axis;

FIG. 99.—The papaw family, *Anonaceae*. *A*, papaw, *Anona*; *B*, floral diagram of *Anona* (*after Baillon*); *C*, floral formula for the family.

carpels usually many, separate or sometimes united in the fleshy fruit, developing into an elongated, fleshy, aggregate fruit or a large berry, or in other cases becoming transformed into dry fruits; seeds large, embryo very small; endosperm conspicuously wrinkled or *ruminate*.

The family includes the North American Papaw, *Asimina triloba*, a low tree or bushy shrub growing as far north as New York, Michigan and Nebraska, noted for the large aromatic, juicy fruits that ripen in the autumn. These fruits are sometimes known as "poor man's bananas." The better known and more widely distributed forms are the numerous tropical species such as the "soursop" or "Juanabana," *Anona muricata* (Fig. 99), the "sweetsop," *A. squamosa*, and the "custard apple," *A. reticulata*, all of which produce large edible fruits. Soursop is widely planted, and the sap of the large fruit is used as a beverage and for the preparation of jellies, and the juicy pulp is used for conserves. The fruits of these plants are sometimes 6 or 8 inches long and about as broad, and more or less heart-shaped, the dark green surface being commonly roughened by the projection of the ends of the individual carpels. The seeds are imbedded in a copious white, fleshy or tallow-like pulp.

THE NUTMEG FAMILY

The *Myristicaceae* are commonly known as the nutmeg family (Fig. 100). The members of the family are largely tropical trees grouped in 8 or more genera and about 100 species. They are mostly evergreen broadleaf trees with wide distribution in the tropics where they are frequently seen in cultivation.

Leaves alternate, simple, entire, commonly evergreen; flowers small, diœcious, actinomorphic, apetalous, in axillary clusters; calyx three-lobed, more or less globose or funnel-shaped; stamens (in separate staminate flower) 2 to 30, filaments united into a column (mona d e l p h o u s), aborted ovary commonly present; pistil 1, superior, one-celled, ovule 1, style very short or none; fruit fleshy, dehiscing by two valves; seeds with a fleshy, laciniate aril; endosperm abundant, fatty, ruminate.

Fig. 100.—The nutmeg family, *Myristicaceae. A*, leaves and fruit of nutmeg, *Myristica fragrans (after Baillon); B*, section of fruit; *C*, floral formula for the family.

The common nutmeg of commerce is *Myristica fragrans* (Fig. 100), a tall tree with striking aroma that produces berry-like fruits 1.5 to 2.0 inches long. The fruit splits into two valves showing the scarlet aril surrounding the nutmeg which is enclosed in a hard shell. The aril becomes the *mace* of commerce, and the familiar spicy nutmegs are the firm seeds surrounded by the hard shell. The mace is used as a spice and the ground seed constitutes the popular aromatic flavoring material known as grated nutmeg.

THE LAUREL FAMILY

The laurels, *Lauraceae*, are mostly trees and shrubs but there are also a few parasitic herbaceous vines included in the family.

There are about 40 genera and 1,000 species in the family and they are almost exclusively tropical in their distribution, but a few are known in subtropical and temperate climates. They are all very aromatic.

The leaves are mostly alternate (rarely opposite) simple, leathery, and evergreen in tropical species, thin and deciduous in most temperate climate forms, aromatic; flowers apetalous, inconspicuous, yellow or green, actinomorphic, perfect, diœcious or polygamous; calyx six-parted; stamens in 3 to 4 whorls of three each, anthers opening by upwardly hinged flaps; ovary superior, one-celled, one-ovuled, style filiform or short; fruit a berry or drupe, indehiscent, edible in certain species; seed large, without endosperm.

The two best known members of the family in the United States are the native Sassafras, *Sassafras*, of the east and the California laurel, *Umbellularia californica*, a spicy evergreen ornamental in that state. The spicebush, *Benzoin aestivale*, is a very aromatic native shrub of eastern United States where it is seen in woods and along streams. The bay tree of the florists, *Laurus nobilis*, has been popular for ornamental purposes because of the ease of pruning and clipping it into any desired form. The camphor tree, *Camphora officinarum*, also belongs in this family. It is an evergreen, broadleaved tree native to Japan and China, and planted in India, and is the most important natural source of camphor. Most natural camphor has been supplied by Japan, but this material is now manufactured in America. The cinnamon bark of commerce is produced by *Cinnamomum zeylanicum*, a close relative of the camphor tree, cultivated in Ceylon.

One of the most interesting genera of the *Lauraceae* is *Persea*, with 50 species native to the tropics and subtropics of both the old and new world. Some of them produce edible fruits, notably *P. gratissima*, commonly known as avocado or alligator pear. This species is grown widely in the tropics and in California for its popular edible fruits. The large, fleshy fruit (drupe) is more or less pear-shaped and contains a single, large, "stone" or "pit" imbedded in a thick layer of oily flesh.

THE BARBERRY FAMILY

The *Berberidaceae*, or barberry family (Fig. 101), includes some 10 or more genera and 200 species of shrubs and herbs (some of them climbers) mainly distributed in the temperate portions of the northern hemisphere from Central Asia to India, and also along the Andes to the Straits of Magellan. Many of the species are beautiful and popular ornamentals.

Leaves alternate, simple or compound; flowers solitary or in racemes or panicles, perfect, actinomorphic, hypogynous; sepals and petals usually 6, similar, commonly in two or more series; petals often nectariferous; stamens about as many as the petals and opposite them, sometimes sensitive, free, anthers opening by two valves hinged at the top; ovary superior, one-celled, with

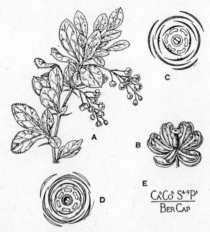

Fig. 101.—The barberry family, *Berberidaceae*. *A*, flowering branch of barberry, *Berberis* (*after Le M. and Dec.*); *B*, single flower of *Berberis* enlarged (*after Baillon*); *C*, floral diagram of *Berberis* (*after Le M. and Dec.*); *D*, floral diagram of *Berberis* (*after Baillon*); *E*, floral formula for the family.

few to many ovules; style short or none; fruit a berry or capsule; seeds with abundant endosperm.

The barberries cultivated for landscape decoration in North America are mostly species of the large genus *Berberis*, of which there are several that are popular. The common barberry, *B. vulgaris*, and the Japanese barberry, *B. thunbergii*, are prized for the coloration of the foliage in autumn. The latter species also produces attractive scarlet berries in profusion. These plants are most commonly grown as a hedge. The common barberry is at present in bad repute in the northern wheat-producing area of the United States because of its relation to the propagation of wheat rust. An extensive eradication campaign directed toward this species has been under way for several years in thirteen northern wheat-growing states in the hope of lessening the losses due to that disease.

The so-called "Oregon grape," *Mahonia aquifolium*, is a member of this family. Among herbaceous species of the family we may mention the blue cohosh, *Caulophyllum thalictroides*, and the mandrake or may apple, *Podophyllum peltatum*.

THE BUTTERCUP FAMILY

The *Ranunculaceae*, commonly known as the buttercups or crowfoots (Fig. 102), include about 30 genera and 1,200 species of herbaceous perennials, including a few annuals and aquatic

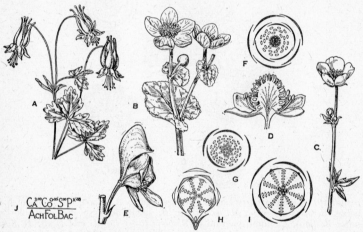

Fig. 102.—The buttercup family, *Ranunculaceae*. *A*, columbine, *Aquilegia* (after Mathews); *B*, marsh marigold, *Caltha palustris* (after Le M. and Dec.); *C*, buttercup, *Ranunculus* (after Le M. and Dec.); *D*, vertical section of a flower of *Ranunculus* showing the floral axis (after Baillon); *E*, single flower of monkshood, *Aconitum* (after Baillon); *F*, floral diagram of *Ranunculus* (after Le M. and Dec.); *G*, floral diagram of marsh marigold, *Caltha* (after Le M. and Dec.); *H*, floral diagram of monkshood, *Aconitum* (after Baillon); *I*, floral diagram of columbine, *Aquilegia* (after Le M. and Dec.); *J*, floral formula for the family.

species, and a few low shrubs and woody climbers, with a very wide distribution in the northern hemisphere. They are found in the Arctic region and at high altitudes in the mountains, but they are not so common in the tropics and in the southern hemisphere. Many highly prized ornamental species and varieties are included in the family.

The leaves are alternate, the acaulescent species frequently with a broad group of radical leaves, but a few of the frutescent types (*Clematis*) with opposite leaves; flowers hypogynous, most commonly perfect and complete, but diclinous in a few forms, commonly actinomorphic, but zygomorphic in certain types such as larkspur (*Delphinium*) and monkshood (*Aconitum*); in *Delphinium* the petals are extended into conspicuous spurs, and in *Aconitum* an upper sepal is hooded and this covers a pair of narrow, elongated sepals; axis often cone-shaped or dome-shaped; sepals 3 to many, separate, often brightly colored in apetalous forms; petals few to many, separate, often with nectaries, absent in numerous species; stamens many, free; carpels few to many, free or slightly united, one-celled, one-many-ovuled; fruit a cluster of achenes or follicles, sometimes berry-like, achenes often with persistent plumose style; seeds with very small embryo and abundant endosperm.

There are many useful plants in this family. Among popular ornamentals may be mentioned the following: peony, *Paeonia*, columbine, *Aquilegia* (Fig. 102, *A*), larkspur, *Delphinium*, Virgin's bower, *Clematis*, marsh marigold, *Caltha* (Fig. 102, *B*), globe flower, *Trollius* and windflowers, *Anemone*. The state flower of Colorado is the blue columbine, *Aquilegia coerulea*, and the South Dakota state flower is the Pasque flower, *Pulsatilla hirsutissima*, both of them members of this family. Medicinal plants in the group include aconite, *Aconitum* sp. (Fig. 102, *E*), snake root, *Cimicifuga* sp., and golden seal, *Hydrastis*. Certain species of *Delphinium* are poisonous to stock and they constitute a menace in certain western grazing grounds.

The buttercup family has come to be regarded as a primitive group of herbaceous Dicotyledons and as closely related to the *Magnoliaceae*, and other low, woody Dicotyledons. The Monocotyledons are thought to have been derived from the dicotyledonous series from near these groups. The lowest Monocotyledons (*Alismales*) have much in common with buttercups and magnolias.

THE WATERLILY FAMILY

The waterlilies, *Nymphaeaceae*, are typically aquatic, perennial herbs with conspicuous floating leaves and large showy flowers of great ornamental value, mostly in the tropics and north temperate zone (Fig. 103).

Leaves mostly floating, large and simple, on long petioles, arising from large horizontal rootstocks rooted in the mud at the bottom of shallow lakes and ponds, or in some cases from floating stems, submerged leaves sometimes dissected (*Cabomba*); flowers usually solitary, large, showy, hypogynous, actinomorphic, perfect; sepals 3 to 4 to 6, or more; petals 3 or numerous, often showing gradual transitions between true petals and true stamens; stamens 3 to many; carpels 2 to 8 or more, commonly numerous, free or united into a many-celled ovary, as in *Nuphar*, or imbedded in the enlarged axis, as in *Nelumbium;* ovules one to many; fruit indehiscent, in *Nelumbium* the axis becomes greatly enlarged and contains many large, dry cavities in the upper surface, in each of which is one of the dry fruits.

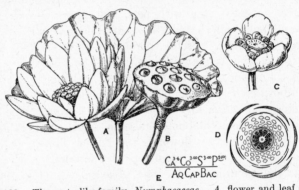

$$Ca^{3-6} Co^{3-\infty} S^{3-\infty} P^{2^{(\infty)}}$$
$$Aq \, Ca_p \, Ba_c$$

Fig. 103.—The waterlily family, *Nymphaeaceae*. *A*, flower and leaf of lotus, *Nelumbium* (*after Le M. and Dec.*); *B*, fruiting receptacle of lotus, *Nelumbium* (*after Le M. and Dec.*); *C*, flower of waterlily, *Nuphar* (*after Le M. and Dec.*); *D*, floral diagram of *Nuphar* (*after Le M. and Dec.*); *E*, floral formula for the family.

The family described above includes the common fishmoss, *Cabomba*, which is sometimes separated from this family and placed in a special family, *Cabombaceae*. This plant is in reality much more like the buttercups in flower structure than the commonly known waterlilies, but it is included here for convenience. It may be regarded as an intermediate type, at least.

Conspicuous members of the *Nymphaeceae* are the yellow waterlilies, *Nuphar*, the white waterlilies, *Nymphaea*, the American lotus (Fig. 103, *A* and *B*), *Nelumbium luteum*, the Indian lotus, *N. speciosum*, and the watershield, *Brasenia*. Many tropical species have brilliantly colored flowers that are popular elements in aquatic gardening. One of the most interesting of all of the waterlilies is the great *Victoria regia*, a native of tropical South

America, that produces very large flowers, and the broad, floating leaves with upturned edges are so large and firm as to support the weight of a small child. This plant was named for Queen Victoria of England. The name of the family is from *Nymphae*, the waternymphs.

THE PEPPER FAMILY

The pepper family (Fig. 104), *Piperaceae*, is included under the order *Ranales* as representative of a buttercup-like form that has become greatly reduced. They are mostly herbs or shrubs, but there are also a few trees and many woody climbers included

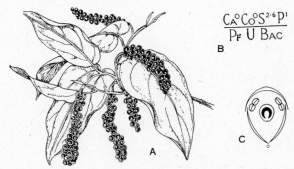

$$\frac{Ca^0 Co^0 S^{2\cdot 6} P^1}{P_F\ U\ B_{AC}}$$

B

C

Fig. 104.—The pepper family, *Piperaceae*. *A*, leaves and clusters of fruits of pepper, *Piper nigrum* (*after Baillon*); *B*, floral formula for the family; *C*, floral diagram of *Piper* (*after Baillon*).

in the family. They are grouped in 10 to 12 genera and about 1,200 species confined to the tropical and subtropical portions of the world.

The leaves are large, alternate, opposite or whorled, and entire; flowers very small, actinomorphic, hypogynous, in dense catkin-like spikes or racemes; perianth 0; perfect or unisexual; stamens 2 to 6 or more, free; ovary superior, one-celled, one-ovuled, stigmas 1 to 5, short; fruit berry-like with a fleshy, thin or dry pericarp; seeds small; endosperm abundant.

The peppers are valuable mostly for the familiar black pepper, which is made from the dry fruits or ground dry fruits of *Piper nigrum* (Fig. 104), a woody vine of the East Indies. The inner stony portions of the dry fruits are powdered as "white pepper." The cubeb is another pepper, *P. cubeba*, and "betel" leaves, a favorite chewing material of the natives of India, are the leaves of

P. betle. There are probably about 700 species of *Piper* that have been described. The family also contains the ornamental genus *Peperomia*, of which there are more than 500 different species, some of which are grown for their foliage.

These plants should not be confused with the "red peppers" and chili peppers, "Jerusalem cherries," etc., of our gardens, which are mostly species of *Capsicum*, belonging to the potato family, *Solanaceae*.

CHAPTER XIII

THE MALLOWS AND GERANIUMS

ORDER MALVALES, THE MALLOW ORDER

The mallows, or *Malvales*, are regarded as among the early modifications of the buttercup type as included in the *Ranales*. This relationship is clearly shown by their position on the chart. The close affiliation appears to be indicated by the many floral features which the two groups have in common.

The mallow flower is typically actinomorphic, hypogynous, and polypetalous as in the buttercups, and often there are also many stamens and pistils, the latter varying from two to many, and being separate or more or less united. The stamens are indefinite in number, with their filaments united to form a continuous or broken sheath about the pistils. A tendency toward syncarpy and gamopetaly clearly indicates the more advanced nature of *Malvales* as compared with *Ranales*. The order is here expanded to include a number of apetalous forms that are distributed among different groups in other systems of classification.

THE MALLOW FAMILY

The *Malvaceae*, or mallow family, represent one of our most clearly marked families (Fig. 105) of herbs, shrubs, and trees of 40 to 50 genera and nearly 1,000 species found practically throughout the world except in the colder regions. Members of the group may usually be identified by the five-merous flowers in which the numerous stamens are coherent by their filaments to form a sheathing tube enveloping the pistils.

Leaves alternate, entire or variously lobed, often palmately veined or palmately lobed; flowers actinomorphic, hypogynous, usually perfect; sepals most commonly 5, sometimes more or less united and subtended by a group of calyx-like bracts (an involucel); petals 5, free, but often joined to the stamen sheath or column at the base; stamens many, monadelphous, with free anthers clustered beneath the stigmas; carpels 5 to many, more or less united; ovules one to several in each carpel; styles

179

commonly as many as carpels; fruit typically dry, capsular or rarely berry-like, breaking into subdivisions as it ripens; seed with little or no endosperm.

The mallow family includes many very valuable economic plants. Among these may be mentioned cotton (Fig. 105, *F*), *Gossypium arboreum, G. brasiliense, G. herbaceum, G. hirsutum*, and other species that are grown for the hairy covering of the seeds which constitutes the "cotton-wool" or "cotton" of commerce. This cotton is used extensively for the manufacture of thread and cloth. Cotton treated with a strong alkali is made stronger and more or less silky and is known as "mercer-

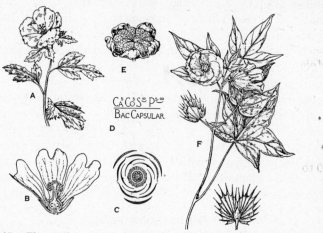

Fig. 105.—The mallow family, *Malvaceae*. *A*, leaves and flowers of rose mallow, *Hibiscus (after Baillon)*; *B*, vertical section of a flower of mallow, *Malva (after Baillon)*; *C*, floral diagram of *Malva (after Le M. and Dec.)*; *D*, floral formula for the family; *E*, fruit of *Malva (after Baillon)*; *F*, leaves and flowers of cotton, *Gossypium (after Robbins)*.

ized" cotton, after Mercer, the discoverer of the method. Besides cotton in one or another of the usual senses, the plant furnishes many other products such as cottonseed oil, meal, etc. Guncotton, a powerful explosive, is made by treating the cotton lint with nitric and sulphuric acids and by various subsequent transformations.

There are also many ornamental species in the family especially in the genera *Hibiscus, Althaea, Callirrhoe*, etc. There are about 200 species of *Hibiscus*, many of which are highly prized on account of their large, showy flowers. One of the species, *H. esculentus*, furnishes the sections of gelatinous, green capsules known as "okra" or "gumbo" used in soups. The common hollyhock is *Althaea rosea*, which is a familiar garden plant, with its large flowers of many colors and its double-flowered varieties.

THE LINDEN FAMILY

The *Tiliaceae*, or linden family (Fig. 106) comprise 35 genera and about 375 species of trees and shrubs that are very widely distributed in the tropics and warmer portions of the world with a number of species also characteristic of temperate climates. Lindens are also known as basswoods and lime trees in certain countries.

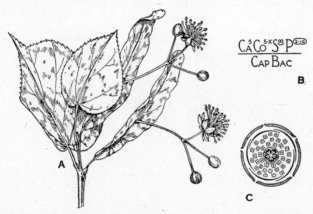

Fig. 106.—The linden family, *Tiliaceae*. *A*, leaves and flowers of linden, *Tilia (after Le M. and Dec.)*; *B*, floral formula for the family; *C*, floral diagram of *Tilia (after Le M. and Dec.)*.

Inner bark very fibrous; leaves alternate, simple, entire, dentate or lobed, often oblique at the base (*Tilia*); flowers actinomorphic, hypogynous, usually perfect; sepals usually 5, separate or slightly united; petals 5 or more, often glandular at the base; stamens numerous, free or slightly united at the base into a number of bundles; ovary superior, two- to ten-celled, with one to many ovules in each cell; fruit two- to ten-celled or one-celled by abortion of the other cells, capsule, berry-like or drupaceous, dehiscent or indehiscent; seed one to many in each cell; endosperm abundant or none.

The lindens are commonly regarded with great favor as ornamental trees. The American linden or basswood, *Tilia americana*, and the European linden, *T. europaea*, are included among the highly prized ornamental trees in the climates to which they are adapted. There are many forms and cultivated varieties of both of these species. The American linden also produces a light, soft, even-grained, tough wood which is much used for veneer backing, cooperage, excelsior, apiarist's supplies, and general woodenware. This is one of the most important commercial woods of the United States.

THE CACAO FAMILY

This is the *Sterculiaceae*, a family of trees and shrubs (Fig. 107) with soft wood (few herbs) of some 50 genera and 750 species, largely confined to the tropics and subtropics.

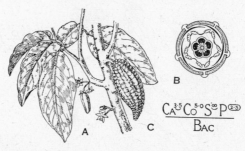

$$\dfrac{C_A^{3.5} C_O^{5.0} S^{\infty} P^{2.5}}{B_{AC}}$$

Fig. 107.—The cacao family, *Sterculiaceae*. *A*, leaves, flowers, and fruit of chocolate, *Theobroma cacao* (*after Baillon*); *B*, floral diagram of *Theobroma* (*after Baillon*); *C*, floral formula for the family.

The leaves are alternate, simple, or digitately compound; flowers resembling those in *Malvaceae*, perfect or diclinous, hypogynous, actinomorphic; sepals 3 to 5, somewhat united; petals 5 or none; stamens numerous, more or less connate into a tube; ovary superior, of 2 to 5 or 10 more or less united carpels; style simple, or divided into lobes or free from the base; fruit dry or rarely berry-like, usually dehiscent; seeds with or without endosperm.

One of the most interesting and commercially important members of this family is the chocolate plant (Fig. 107), *Theobroma cacao*, a small tree native to Central and South America, and now grown as a cultivated plant in the tropical portions of both hemispheres. The fruits in this species are large woody drupes or dry pods containing numerous large oily seeds imbedded in the pulp of the interior. Chocolate and cocoa of commerce are prepared by grinding the roasted seeds of this plant and then adding sugar, vanilla, and other substances to give them their characteristic properties. A very oily product known as "cacao butter" is also prepared from the seeds. This is quite different from the important fats secured from the coconut seed. The cola nuts of commerce are produced by the cola tree, *Cola acuminata*, and from these certain alkaloidal drugs are prepared. The inner bark of certain other species furnish tough fibers that are used for heavy mats and cordage and even for paper.

THE ELM FAMILY

The *Ulmaceae*, commonly known as the elm family (Fig. 108), are comprised of 12 to 13 genera and about 140 species of deciduous trees and shrubs, widely distributed in the north temperate

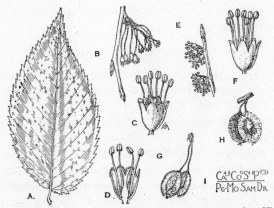

Fig. 108.—The elm family, *Ulmaceae*. *A*, leaf of American elm, *Ulmus americana; B*, flower cluster of same; *C*, and *D*, flowers of same; *E*, flower cluster of red elm, *Ulmus fulva; F*, flower of same; *G*, fruits of *Ulmus americana; H*, fruits of *Ulmus fulva; I*, floral formula for the family (*after Mathews*).

zone, with a few species reaching into the tropics. There are several important ornamental and timber-producing species in the family.

Leaves alternate, simple, pinnately veined, often very unsymmetrical at the base, and coarsely toothed; flowers small, in fascicles from buds on one-year-old twigs, perfect, polygamous or monœcious, the pistillate sometimes solitary; apetalous; sepals 4 to 8, united to form a more or less campanulate calyx; stamens same number as calyx lobes or more, inserted at the base of the calyx; ovary superior, composed of 2 carpels, but usually one-celled, one-ovuled; styles 2; fruit a flat, membranous samara, a nut, or drupe; seed without endosperm.   The flowers are produced long before the leaves appear in many species of elm.

The two best-known members of this family are the American elm, *Ulmus americana*, and the English elm, *U. campestris*, both of which are planted for shade and landscape purposes in many parts of the world.   The former is also a very important timber tree in the United States, the wood being very tough and strong and used for the cheaper grades of furniture.   The slippery elm, *U. fulva*, is noted for the gelatinous inner bark which possesses medicinal properties.   A noteworthy old world elm is the camperdown elm, *U. scabra*, which has pendulous branches that form a rounded or very widely spreading crown. The hackberry, *Celtis*, is a tree that resembles the elm somewhat but the fruit is a drupe rather than a samara.   It is a valuable tree for ornamental purposes in arid and semiarid localities where the elms do not thrive.

THE MULBERRY FAMILY

The *Moraceae*, or mulberry family (Fig. 109), comprise about 55 genera and nearly 1,000 species of trees, shrubs, herbs, and vines with milky juice, that are largely tropical in distribution, but there are also numerous species in the temperate portions of the world.

Leaves alternate, usually simple, often deeply lobed; flowers small and much reduced, often produced in dense heads or hollow receptacles, monœcious or diœcious, actinomorphic; sepals commonly 4, more or less united, sometimes lacking; petals 0; stamens equal in number to calyx lobes; ovary usually superior, one- to two-celled, one- to two-ovuled, stigmas 1 to 2, filiform; fruit an achene, drupe, or nut, sometimes the true fruits are enveloped by or imbedded in a thickened, fleshy perianth as in the mulberry, or in a greatly enlarged axis as in the fig.

The mulberry is some species of *Morus*, the two common species being the white mulberry, *M. alba*, and the black mulberry, *M. nigra*.   The Russian mulberry is a variety of the white mulberry, and there are numerous other varieties of that species that are useful as ornamentals and for silkworm feeding.   The fruit in the mulberry is a ripened pistillate inflorescence in which the individual fleshy segments are formed largely from the enlarged sepals which come to cover the ripened ovary.   The breadfruit of the South Seas and Asiatic Tropics is *Artocarpus communis*, in which the fruit is much the same as a mulberry morphologically, but it may be 4 to 8 inches long, and is usually eaten cooked rather than as a fresh fruit. The so-called paper mulberry, *Broussonetia papyrifera*, of the Far East, is used in paper manufacture.

Other interesting members of the mulberry family are the Osage orange, *Toxylon pomiferum*, of the United States, noted for its extremely hard wood, and its large orange-like fruits, and figs, *Ficus*, which are largely tropical in their distribution. Nearly 800 different species of figs have been described and they vary from

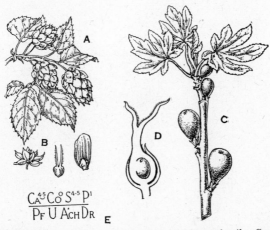

Fig. 109.—The mulberry family, *Moraceae*, and hemp family, *Cannabinaceae*. *A*, flowering stem of hop, *Humulus lupulus (after Bentham)*; *B*, details of flower and fruit of same; *C*, leaves and flower clusters (figs) of fig, *Ficus (after Baillon)*; *D*, single female flower from the interior of one of the inflorescences or figs *(after Baillon)*; *E*, floral formula for the *Urticaceae*.

giant trees to erect shrubs and climbing vines, some of which are grown for fruit and others for ornamental purposes. The edible figs are mostly produced by varieties of *F. carica*. The fig fruit is in reality the hollow and greatly enlarged fleshy receptacle bearing the hundreds of flowers that are thickly clustered on the inner surface. Figs have been grown successfully and on an increasingly important commercial scale in California for about 25 years. The common "rubber plant" of our conservatories is a fig, *F. elastica*, as is the banyan tree of India, *F. benghalensis*. Hemp, *Cannabis*, and hops, *Humulus*, of the *Cannabinaceae* are closely related to the mulberry.

THE NETTLE FAMILY

The *Urticaceae* include herbs or undershrubs and sometimes vines grouped into about 40 genera and 500 species with a very wide distribution, but more abundantly represented in the tropics. The stems and leaves are often armed with stinging epidermal hairs (Fig. 110).

Leaves alternate or opposite, simple; flowers very small and inconspicuous, usually unisexual, variously borne in cymes; calyx mostly four-parted or four- to five-lobed; petals 0; stamens of the

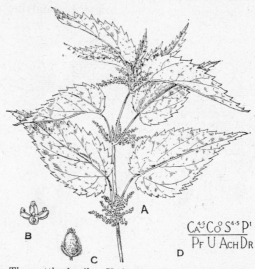

$$\frac{Ca^{4\cdot5}\,C_0^0\,S^{4\cdot5}\,P^1}{P_F\,U\,A_{CH}\,D_R}$$

Fig. 110.—The nettle family, *Urticaceae. A*, flowering branch of nettle, *Urtica dioica; B*, single staminate flower; *C*, single pistillate flower; *D*, floral formula for the family (*after Mathews*).

same number as sepals; ovary solitary, one-celled, one-seeded, free or more or less attached to the calyx; style simple; fruit an achene, or becoming drupaceous on account of the enlarged and succulent calyx which invests the ripened ovary in certain forms; seed with endosperm.

The most of the species of nettles are noxious weeds. A few have a limited value as ornamentals. The ramie or Chinese silk plant, *Boehmeria nivea*, is an important fiber plant in China and Japan, and the plant has some ornamental value.

ORDER GERANIALES, THE GERANIUM ORDER

The Geraniums and their kin, the *Geraniales*, constitute a large order of diversified families of shrubs and herbs which reveal certain features that are more or less similar to those that characterize the mallows. The order is regarded as another early modification of the buttercup type that has developed more or less parallel with the *Malvales*. The greater degree of syncarpy, together with the reduction in the number of carpels and stamens and a decided tendency toward a standardization in the number of these structures mark the *Geraniales* as a group to be considered somewhat more advanced than the *Malvales*.

The geranium flower is typically hypogynous, perfect and actinomorphic, but with a tendency toward zygomorphy; sepals and petals 5; stamens 5 to 10; carpels 5, united. The order as here treated also includes certain apetalous families of more or less uncertain affiliations.

THE GERANIUM FAMILY

The *Geraniaceae*, include the true geraniums (Fig. 111) and their more immediate kin. They are largely annual or perennial

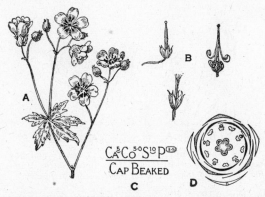

$$\frac{Ca^5 Co^{5-0} S^{10} P^{\textcircled{3\cdot5}}}{Cap\ Beaked}$$

Fig. 111.—The geranium family, *Geraniaceae*. *A*, flowering habit of wild geranium, *Geranium maculatum; B*, three stages in the ripening of the fruit of geranium; *C*, floral formula for the family; *D*, floral diagram for the family, or for geranium *(after Mathews)*.

herbs or undershrubs, or rarely arborescent, with a wide distribution in the north temperate zone and in the subtropics, with a peculiar concentration in South Africa. The family includes 11 genera and about 650 species.

Leaves alternate or opposite, lobed, simple, dissected, or compound; flowers commonly conspicuous, perfect, and usually regular or somewhat zygomorphic; sepals 5, separate or united somewhat in certain species, the dorsal sepals sometimes spurred; petals 5 or 0; stamens 2 to 3 times the number of petals, but usually 10 or 5, some of them sterile, more or less connate at base; pistil three-to five-lobed, commonly of 5 carpels, each prolonged into a style; ovules 1 in each carpel; fruit lobed, dry, one-seeded in each carpel, carpels commonly separating in fruit; seed with little endosperm.

The geraniums are of value principally on account of their beautiful fragrant flowers and the aromatic nature of their leaves. Scores of species are grown in cultivation as house plants and for flower-bed decoration out of doors. The commonest so-called "geranium" in cultivation is not a *Geranium* but a species of *Pelargonium*, a closely related genus of 250 or more species, native of South Africa.

THE OXALIS FAMILY

The *Oxalidaceae*, include the "sorrels" or oxalises; they are herbaceous or somewhat woody plants closely related to the

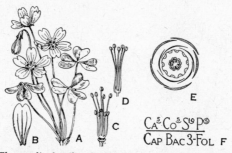

Fig. 112.—The oxalis family, *Oxalidaceae*. *A*, leaves and flowers of sorrel, *Oxalis montana; B*, single petal; *C*, and *D*, stamens (*after .Mathews); E*, floral diagram (*after Le M. and Dec.); F*, floral formula for the family.

geraniums (Fig. 112). There are 10 or more genera and several hundred species in the tropics and subtropics, and they, like the geraniums, are particularly abundant in South Africa. An abundance of oxalic acid in the juice of many species has given rise to the popular name "sheep sour," etc. The presence of this material is also reflected in the technical name, *Oxalis*, which is Greek for *sour*.

Leaves alternate, digitately or palmately compound, often trifoliate; flowers perfect, hypogynous, and regular; sepals and petals 5, more or less united at the base in certain species; stamens 10, more or less connate at base, sometimes 5 of them lack anthers; ovary five-celled, superior, two- to many-ovuled, styles 5; fruit typically a capsule with many seeds, sometimes berry-like; seeds with elastic coat that serves to propel them from the fruit; endosperm abundant. The fruit is one of the most striking differences between the *Oxalidaceae* and the *Geraniaceae*.

Various species and varieties of *Oxalis* are prized as house plants and potted herbs because of their large, brilliant, yellow or purple flowers, and curious sensitive leaves. The carambola, *Averrhoa carambola*, is an evergreen tree of tropical India and China that produces a juicy, fragrant, acid or sweet fruit used as a vegetable and as a dessert.

THE FLAX FAMILY

The flax family, *Linaceae*, is another natural group (Fig. 113) with strong resemblances to the *Geraniaceae*. The family

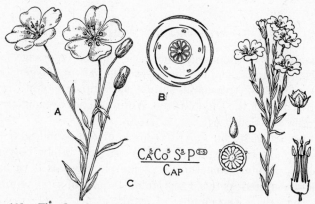

Fig. 113.—The flax family, *Linaceae*. *A*, flowering habit of flax, *Linum* (*after Le M. and Dec.*); *B*, floral diagram of *Linum* (*after Le M. and Dec.*); *C*, floral formula for the family; *D*, flowering stem and flower details of commercial flax, *Linum usitatissimum* (*after Bentham*).

includes 12 to 14 genera and about 150 species of herbs or shrubs of wide distribution in temperate regions.

Leaves simple, alternate or opposite; flowers perfect, actinomorphic, hypogynous; sepals usually 5, free or united at the base, persistent; petals usually 5, free, fugacious, often clawed; stamens 5, sometimes with other small filaments without anthers (staminodes), filaments connate at base; ovary superior, carpels 2 to 5, or sometimes apparently 4 to 10 by the formation of false radial partitions through the carpels; styles same number as carpels; fruit usually a several-seeded capsule; seeds flat, shining; endosperm abundant or 0.

.This is a very important family from the standpoint of the utilitarian values of its products. Flax has been cultivated for its fiber since prehistoric ages. The ancient Egyptians and Hebrews used linen cloth made from flax 3,000 years B. C. Several species of wild flax are known in North America, among them are the forms with yellow flowers of our prairies and the forms with blue flowers of the roadsides and fields. Many species and varieties are grown for fibers and seeds in different parts of the world. A species with blue flowers, *Linum perenne*, and another with red flowers, *L. grandiflorum*, are sometimes grown for ornamental purposes. Various useful products such as linseed oil, are manufactured from the seeds of the flax plants. United States grows flax largely for the seed, Russia grows it mostly for the fiber.

THE ORANGE FAMILY

The *Rutaceae*, commonly known as the rue or orange family (Fig. 114), comprise an important group of about 100 genera and 1,000 species of trees and shrubs of temperate and tropical climates in both the Old and New World. They are numerous in Australia and South Africa.

Leaves alternate or opposite, simple or compound, glandular, aromatic, often evergreen; flowers perfect, rarely polygamo-dioecious, regular, sometimes zygomorphic; sepals 3 to 5, free or slightly united; petals 3 to 5, free; stamens of same number or more than twice the number of petals, attached to a disk, free or rarely united; carpels 2 to 5, usually united to form a superior, four- to five-celled ovary, sometimes free; styles connate; ovules one to many in each carpel; fruit berry-like, drupaceous, or leathery and dry, aromatic, large and heavy in *Citrus;* seeds many, often with more than one embryo; endosperm fleshy or 0.

The most important member of the rue family from the economic viewpoint is the genus *Citrus* which furnishes the various types of "citrus fruits," including oranges, lemons, limes, tangerines, and grapefruits. The genus is mainly confined naturally to the Old World where the species grow in abundance in Asia and Malaysia, but they are also cultivated extensively in many other parts of the world as in Africa, Spain, Florida, Texas, and California, for their edible fruits and for ornament as well. Some of the more important economic species are as follows:

sweet orange, *C. sinensis,* sour orange, *C. aurantium,* king orange, *C. nobilis,* with its variety *deliciosa,* the tangerine, citron, *C. medica,* grapefruit, *C. grandis,* lemon, *C. limonia,* and lime, *C. aurantifolia.* The trifoliate orange, *C. trifoliata,* is grown for ornamental purposes and as budding stock for edible forms

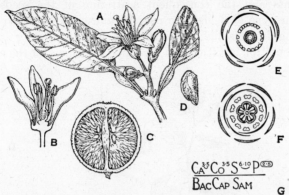

Fig. 114.—The orange family, *Rutaceae.* *A,* flowering twig of sour orange, *Citrus; B,* vertical section of a flower of the same; *C,* section of the fruit of same; *D,* a seed (*all after Robbins*); *E,* floral diagram for *Citrus* (*after Le M. and Dec.*); *F,* floral diagram of rue, *Ruta* (*after Le M. and Dec.*); *G,* floral formula for the family.

Bergamot oil is prepared chiefly from *C. bergamia,* a small tree cultivated in southern Europe. The navel orange or "seedless orange" is a mutant found many years ago in Brazil, and since has been improved and grown successfully on a large scale in California. A certain variety of grapefruit is also known which is ordinarily seedless.

THE BALSAM FAMILY

The *Balsaminaceae* are known commonly as the touch-me-not family (Fig. 115) as well as the balsam family. They are largely succulent herbs of wide distribution but are more prominent in tropical Asia and Africa. There are two or more genera and about 500 species in the family.

Leaves alternate or opposite, simple; flowers perfect, hypogynous, zygomorphic, brightly colored, solitary or somewhat umbellately clustered; sepals 3, rarely 5, unequal, the 2 lateral ones small and greenish, the posterior one prolonged backward into a nectariferous, tubular spur; petals 5, or 3 by the union of two pairs, unequal; stamens 5, filaments short and broad, anthers connate around the ovary; ovary superior, five-celled, with few to many ovules in each cell; fruit a succulent capsule or berry, with several seeds; endosperm 0.

These plants are called "touch-me-nots" because of the sudden elastic and vigorous splitting of the succulent capsule into twisted segments and the consequent scattering of the seeds. This peculiar type of dehiscence may be unusually impressive if the ripening fruit is lightly pinched at just the proper moment. This condition is reflected in the name *Impatiens* for the common balsam.

$$\frac{C_{AZ}^{3-5}\,C_{OZ}^{3-5}\,S^{5}\,P^{5}}{C_{AP}\,B_{AC}}$$

Fig. 115.—The balsam family, *Balsaminaceae.* *A*, flowering twig of jewel-weed, *Impatiens fulva; B*, section of a flower; *C*, ripening fruits (*after Mathews*); *D*, floral formula for the family; *E*, floral diagram of touch-me-not, *Impatiens noli-me-tangere (after Le M. and Dec.).*

There are several species and varieties of *Impatiens*, the common genus, grown in cultivation, among which is the garden balsam, *I. balsamina*, and the Sultan's balsam, *I. sultani*, named after the Sultan of Zanzibar, in whose country the plant is indigenous.

THE SPURGE FAMILY

The *Euphorbiaceae* are a family (Fig. 116) composed of about 250 genera and more than 4,000 species of herbs, shrubs, and trees with milky juice, very widely distributed throughout the world, being very common in the tropics and temperate zones of both hemispheres. Some of them are succulent and thorny and more or less cactus-like.

Leaves alternate, rarely opposite, simple, deeply lobed or compound, sometimes much reduced; monœcious or diœcious, flowers actinomorphic, hypogynous; sepals various, sometimes 0; petals commonly 0; stamens one to many (sometimes 1,000), free or united; ovary superior, usually three-celled, with 1 or 2 ovules in each cell; fruit a capsule or drupe; seeds often with a conspicuous caruncle; endosperm abundant. Sometimes the naked pistillate flowers are surrounded by numerous staminate flowers and sterile stamens and the whole group then surrounded by a corolla-like involucre, the structure as a whole being known as a "cyathium." The uppermost leaves, surrounding the

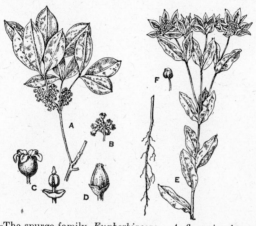

Fig. 116.—The spurge family, *Euphorbiaceae*. *A*, flowering branch of rubber plant, *Hevea guyanensis; B*, cluster of flowers; *C*, a single male flower; *D*, a female flower with calyx removed; *E*, flowering stem of snow-on-the-mountains, *Euphorbia marginata; F*, fruit (*all from Sargent*).

flowers, in a number of species are brightly colored and these structures are popularly known as flowers.

The spurge family includes many plants of great interest and economic value. Many of them are highly prized as pot herbs and ornamentals, among which are the magnificent Christmas Poinsettia, *Poinsettia pulcherrima*, scarlet plume, *Euphorbia jacquinaeflora*, crown-of-thorns, *E. splendens*, a very spiny plant, and the Mexican fire plant, *P. heterophylla*. Certain species and numerous varieties of *Codiaeum*, known as "crotons," are popular as foliage plants. The leaves of *Codiaeum* are slender, as a rule, and are marked with yellow, red, and white mottling or variegation.

The castor-oil plant is also grown for ornamental purposes. This is *Ricinus communis*, the seeds of which furnish the castor oil of commerce.   Hundreds of different forms of this plant are recognized.   The oil is used in medicine, as a lubricant for machinery, and it has been used also as an illuminating oil.

Crude rubber or caoutchouc is secured from several different species in this family.   The more important rubber plants of the family are *Hevea brasiliensis* and *H. guyanensis* of South America. Certain species of *Manihot*, of Brazil, also yield crude rubber, and one of these, *M. utilissima*, is the cassava or tapioca plant from the roots of which tapioca and farina are prepared.

CHAPTER XIV

THE TEAS, POPPIES, AND PINKS

ORDER THEALES, THE TEA ORDER

This group may be known as the tea order, since the teas in the common commercial sense are included as one of the families of the order. They are mostly trees and shrubs or woody climbers but the order also includes a number of herbaceous species. The treatment of the order here is somewhat broader than that in certain other systems, and so one will find some of the following families treated under separate orders by other authors. The teas include another prominent group of families that became differentiated from the *Ranales* at a rather early time.

The flowers are typically hypogynous but with a tendency toward perigyny, mostly perfect and regular, but with a strong tendency toward zygomorphy in certain families; sepals and petals present, free; stamens few or many, free or somewhat connate; ovary superior, compound, of two to more carpels, two to several ovuled, with axile or parietal placentation.

THE TEA FAMILY

The *Theaceae*, commonly known as the tea family (Fig. 117), include 16 genera and about 175 species of trees and shrubs of the tropics and warmer temperate portions of East Asia.

Leaves alternate, simple, usually evergreen; flowers commonly solitary or occasionally racemose or paniculate, often large and showy, hypogynous, regular, perfect, rarely diclinous; sepals 5, free or slightly united, imbricated; petals 5, free or slightly united; stamens numerous, in several series, the outer more or less united into a tube, free or adnate to the base of the petals; ovary superior, three- to five-celled, styles 3 to 5, free or connate below; ovules 2 or more in each cell; fruit a woody capsule or drupaceous; endosperm scanty.

The tea of commerce is the dried leaves of some species of *Thea*, especially *T. sinensis* (or *Camellia thea*), or some of its many cultivated varieties. The camellias are noteworthy on account of their large, showy, white or purplish flowers and beautiful foliage. They are commonly grown for ornamental purposes in warm climates, as in southern United States.

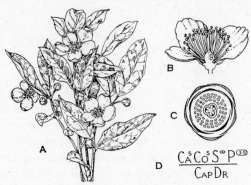

Fig. 117.—The tea family, *Theaceae.* *A,* flowering twigs of tea, *Thea (after Baillon); B,* single flower of *Thea (after Baillon); C,* floral diagram of *Thea (after Baillon); D,* floral formula for the family.

THE GARCINIA FAMILY

This family, *Guttiferaceae,* is also known as the St. John's wort family. They are trees, shrubs and a few herbs to the number of about 45 genera and 700 species that are largely tropical in distribution. The juice is often yellowish or green and resinous.

Leaves opposite, pinnately veined, simple, entire; flowers hypogynous, actinomorphic, perfect or mostly polygamo-diœcious, solitary or cymose; sepals and petals 2 to 6; stamens numerous, free or connate below into several bundles; dwarf ovary commonly present in male flowers, and staminodes usually present in female flowers; ovary superior, two- to many-celled, ovules one to many in each cell; stigmatic lobes often heavy and radiate; fruit fleshy or coriaceous, berry-like or drupaceous; seeds without endosperm; embryo large.

The mangosteen, *Garcinia mangostana,* a small tree of the Malay region, producing orange-like fruits, belongs to this family. Garcinia is from Garcin, a French botanist of the fore part of the eighteenth century. The St. John's wort, or the genus *Hypericum,* of about 200 species, is commonly represented in the flora of temperate climates. Some of these are cultivated for their large and beautiful, waxy, yellow flowers.

THE VIOLET FAMILY

The violet family, *Violaceae*, is probably one of the best known and most popular of all dicotyledonous groups (Fig. 118).   These are largely herbs, but there are also a number of shrubs and even a few trees included in the family along with the modest violet. About 400 species in 15 genera have been described and these have a very wide distribution in temperate and tropical regions.

Leaves all basal or alternate, rarely opposite, simple, sometimes deeply lobed; flowers hypogynous, irregular or regular, usually perfect, sometimes cleistogamous; sepals 5, free or somewhat connate to form a ring about the ovary; petals 5, unequal, the

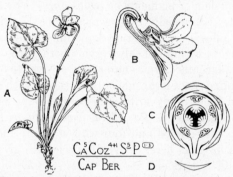

Fig. 118.—The violet family, *Violaceae*. *A*, a species of violet, *Viola* (*after Baillon*); *B*, internal structure of flower in *Viola* (*after Baillon*); *C*, floral diagram of *Viola* (*after Baillon*); *D*, floral formula for the family.

lowest one often larger and saccate or spurred; stamens 5, joined in a ring around the ovary, some of them irregular in form; ovary free, one-celled, but often with 3(or 4 to 5) parietal placentae, style simple, rarely divided, ovules numerous; fruit an elastically opening capsule, or berry-like; endosperm abundant.

The violets and pansies, which are also violets, are among the most popular garden flowers, and some of them are grown by the florists in greenhouses to supply the winter trade of northern countries.   The common cultivated violet is *Viola odorata*, and the pansy is *V. tricolor*, both of which have given rise to many varieties in cultivation.

The *cleistogamous* flowers of violets are of peculiar interest because they are borne on short pedicels or runners more or less underneath the rest of the plant and they have no petals, but they bear an abundance of seeds in species in which the normal flowers are sterile.

THE PASSION FLOWER FAMILY

The passion flowers, *Passifloraceae*, are usually tendril-climbing herbs or woody plants of about 18 genera and 350 species of the tropics and subtropics; abundant in South America. They are called "passion flowers" because of a fancied resemblance of the flower parts to the implements of the crucifixion.

Leaves alternate, simple, entire or lobed; tendrils axillary, simple; flowers perfect or rarely diclinous, actinomorphic, perigynous; sepals 3 to 5, imbricated, free, persistent, often colored; petals 3 to 5, sometimes wanting, inserted on the rim of the calyx, free, sometimes fringed; a corona, made up of one or more rows of slender filaments or scales, formed by a radial outgrowth of the axis usually is present; stamens 5 or more, free or united in bundles; ovary superior, sometimes borne on an elongation of the stalk within the calyx (gynophore), one-celled, with 3 to 5 parietal placentae; ovules numerous; styles 1 to 5, free or stigmas often united; fruit a capsule or berry; seeds with a pitted coat and inclosed by a pulpy aril; endosperm fleshy; embryo large.

The giant granadilla, *Passiflora quadrangularis*, a tropical climber with four-angled and four-winged stems and very large edible fruits, belongs here. Several species are grown for their large and odd flowers.

THE PAPAYA FAMILY

The *Caricaceae*, the papayas, also commonly known as papaws, includes a few species that are mostly succulent-stemmed, tropical trees with soft wood and milky juice. The 30 or more species are mostly confined to the tropics and subtropics of the western hemisphere, but the common papaya, *Carica papaya*, is widely grown for its edible fruits.

The stems are straight, unbranched, and palm-like and they bear a terminal crown of large palmately lobed leaves; flowers hypogynous, commonly dioecious, sometimes perfect, in few-flowered racemes; calyx very inconspicuous, five-lobed; petals 5 in the male flowers, united to form a slender tube, nearly separate in female flowers; stamens 10, inserted in two sets on the corolla; filaments short; ovary superior, sessile, one-celled, with many ovules on five parietal placentae; style short, or stigma sessile; fruit a large, pulpy berry with many seeds; endosperm fleshy.

The fruit of the papaya is oblong or nearly spherical, yellow or orange and varies from 3 to 20 inches long, with a thick wall of fleshy tissue inclosing an angled cavity with many dark seeds scattered over the wall. It is often eaten as a vegetable and the milky juice from the fruit when dried and powdered becomes the papain of commerce. This papaw must not be confused with the North American papaw, *Asimina triloba*, which belongs to the *Anonaceae*, as indicated in an earlier chapter.

ORDER PAPAVERALES, THE POPPY ORDER

This group is known as the poppies and their kin. They are largely herbaceous, but numerous shrubs and a few trees are also included in some of the families that are represented in the tropics. The order as here treated is represented by a number of families that are sometimes broken up into a number of orders, as in the new system proposed by Hutchinson. The broader, more general treatment will serve our purpose much better. The families commonly included in this series show unmistakable relationships with the *Ranales*. They evidently represent another line of development more or less parallel with the *Theales*, *Malvales*, and *Geraniales*, all of which have arisen from the *Ranales*.

The flowers are hypogynous or somewhat perigynous, actinomorphic, with a tendency toward zygomorphy, perfect; sepals and petals present; stamens many to few, free or more or less united into bundles; carpels many to few, syncarpous; ovules many to few; placentation mostly parietal.

THE POPPY FAMILY

The poppies, *Papaveraceae* (Fig. 119), are mostly annual or perennial, milky-juiced herbs included in 25 genera and about 150 species of wide distribution, but more abundant in the north temperate portions of both hemispheres. The milky juice (latex) is sometimes brightly colored.

Leaves alternate or the upper ones sometimes whorled, simple, entire, lobed or deeply divided; flowers usually solitary, hypogynous, often large and showy, actinomorphic, perfect; sepals typically 2, sometimes 3, caducous; petals 4 to 6 or many, free, falling early, often crumpled; stamens many, free, in whorls, filaments slender; ovary superior, of two to many united carpels, usually one-celled, with parietal placentae, or many-celled, carpels separating in fruit in some species, style short or 0, stigma often broad; fruit a many-seeded capsule opening by pores or valves; seeds numerous; embryo very small; endosperm abundant.

There are many very popular garden flowers in this family, among them being several species and varieties of the genus *Papaver*, the bleeding heart, *Dicentra spectabilis*, and the California poppy, *Eschscholtzia californica*. The bloodroot, *Sanguinaria canadensis*, a medicinal plant also belongs here. The opium poppy, *Papaver somniferum*, has been grown as a cultivated plant since ancient times. Opium is prepared from the white latex of the fruit, and this constitutes the source of a series of alkaloidal drugs, the chief of which is morphine.

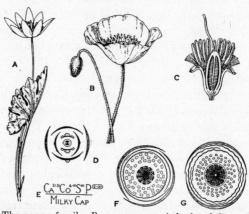

FIG. 119.—The poppy family, *Papaveraceae*. *A*, leaf and flower of bloodroot, *Sanguinaria* (*after Baillon*); *B*, bud and flower of poppy, *Papaver* (*after Le M. and Dec.*); *C*, vertical section of a flower of California poppy, *Eschscholtzia* (*after Le M. and Dec.*); *D*, floral diagram of golden corydalis, *Corydalis* (*after Le. M. and Dec.*); *E*, floral formula for the family; *F*, floral diagram of *Papaver* (*after Baillon*); *G*, floral diagram of *Papaver* (*after Le M. and Dec.*).

THE CAPER FAMILY

The capers or *Capparidaceae* are herbs, shrubs, and trees, largely confined to the tropics (Fig. 120). The family includes about 35 genera and 450 species of plants with watery sap.

Leaves mostly alternate, rarely opposite, simple or digitately compound, leaflets entire; flowers mostly perfect, actinomorphic, sometimes zygomorphic, hypogynous, solitary and axillary or in terminal racemes; sepals 4 to 8, commonly 4, free or slightly united; petals 4 to 8, commonly 4, sometimes 0; stamens six to many, often long exserted; ovary usually seated on a short or an elongated stipe (gynophore) or sessile, one-celled, with two to many parietal placentae, ovules many to few;

fruit a capsule or berry, often borne on an elongated stalk above the corolla; endosperm scanty or 0.

The "capers" of commerce are the pickled flower buds of *Capparis spinosa*, a plant of the Mediterranean region. Certain species of *Cleome*, especially *C. spinosa*, are known for their showy and peculiar flowers. This plant is known as the giant spider plant. Our western spider plant, *Cleome serrulata*, is a very conspicuous species of the plains.

THE MUSTARD FAMILY

This large family, the *Cruciferae*, is commonly known as the mustard family (Fig. 121) because of the genus *Brassica*, of many widely distributed species known as mustards or coles. The long-established technical name, *Cruciferae*, is in recognition of the cross-like figure formed by the two sets of opposite petals radiating from the center of the flower. They are annual

FIG. 120.—The caper family, *Capparidaceae. A*, flowering stem of caper, *Capparis (after Le M. and Dec.); B*, floral formula for the family.

or perennial herbs, rarely shrubby, with watery juice, which is often acrid. There are about 200 genera and 1,800 species included in the group, and they are very widely distributed, but are much more abundant in the temperate and cold parts of the world than in the tropics, many of them being arctic-alpine.

Leaves alternate (rarely opposite), simple, but often deeply lobed or pinnatifid; flowers perfect, regular, small, but often showy because of being grouped in close racemes; sepals 4, free, in two series, falling early; petals 4, usually with a long claw and spreading limb; axis often glandular; stamens 6, in two sets, *i.e.* tetradynamous (4 long, 2 short); pistil sessile, of 2 united carpels, one-celled with 1 to 2 parietal placentae; stigmas often 2 or completely connate; ovules many to few; fruit a globular or oval, flat, or greatly elongated capsule-like pod known as a "silicle" when about as broad as long, and as a "silique" when longer than broad, usually opening by two valves; seeds small; endosperm 0.

The mustard family contributes many products of much value to mankind and there are also numerous ornamental species included in the family. The cabbage is *Brassica oleracea*, of which there are a great many varieties in the usual sense that are cultivated, as well as other varieties that are known by some other name than cabbage. Among the latter are Brussels sprouts, *B. oleracea gemmifera*, cauliflower, *B. oleracea botrytis*, kohlrabi, *B. oleracea caulorapa*, and asparagus broccoli, *B. oleracea italica*. Closely related forms are rutabaga, *Brassica*

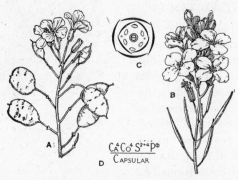

Fig. 121.—The mustard family, *Cruciferae. A*, flowering and fruiting stem of moonwort, *Lunaria* (*after Le M. and Dec.*); *B*, flowering and fruiting stem of cabbage, *Brassica oleracea* (*after Baillon*); *C*, floral diagram of wintercress, *Barbarea* (*after Le M. and Dec.*); *D*, floral formula for the family.

napobrassica, turnip, *B. rapa*, and black mustard, *B. nigra*. Watercress, *Roripa nasturtium-aquaticum*, and garden cress, *Lepidium sativum*, are prized for their fresh, peppery leaves, and the radish, *Raphanus sativus*, for its fleshy, peppery root. Ornamental species of mustards include sweet alyssum, *Alyssum* spp., candytuft, *Iberis amara*, and wallflower, *Cheiranthus cheiri*. There are also numerous persistent and noxious weeds in the family such as peppergrass, *Lepidium* spp., hedge mustard, *Sisymbrium* spp., pennycress, *Thlaspi arvense*, and western mustard, *Sisymbrium altissimum*. The moonwort or "honesty" is *Lunaria annua*, known for the purple flowers, but mainly for the thin, papery and shiny, translucent septum of the pod, sometimes nearly circular and 1 inch in diameter, that remains on the pedicel after the valves fall.

THE MIGNONETTE FAMILY

The members of the mignonette family, *Resedaceae* (Fig. 122), are annual or perennial herbs, with a few woody plants, with watery juice. They are grouped in 6 genera and 65 species that are largely indigenous to the Mediterranean basin. The popular plant of the florist and flower gardens by this name is *Reseda odorata*, grown for its very fragrant, yellowish flowers.

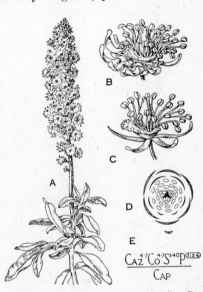

Leaves alternate, simple, entire or often pinnately divided, stipules glandular; flowers usually irregular, perfect, hypogynous, racemose or spicate; calyx four- to seven-lobed, zygomorphic; petals 4 to 7, entire or cleft, small and inconspicuous or 0; stamens 3 to 40, inserted on an irregular fleshy disk, usually exserted beyond the petals even in the bud, filaments free or united below; ovary of 3 to 6 separate or united carpels, often united into a one-celled ovary which is open at the top; stigma sessile; fruit a gaping capsule with many curved seeds; endosperm 0.

FIG. 122.—The mignonette family, *Resedaceae*. *A*, flowering stem of mignonette, *Reseda* (*after Baillon*); *B* and *C*, single flowers of *Reseda* (*after Baillon*); *D*, floral diagram of *Reseda* (*after Le M. and Dec.*) *E*, floral formula for the family.

ORDER CARYOPHYLLALES, THE PINK ORDER

This order includes a rather long list of cosmopolitan families from the true pinks or carnations, the *Caryophyllaceae*, to a number of apetalous families such as the *Amaranthaceae* and *Chenopodiaceae*, and the amentiferous, diclinous *Salicaceae*. The series represents another more or less variable group that has diverged from the *Ranales* somewhat later than have any of the preceding orders.

The flowers are typically perfect and complete, but many are diclinous and apetalous; there are usually 4 to 5 sepals that are free, and 4 to 5 petals in the typical hypogynous, regular flower; stamens as many or twice as many as the sepals; the pistil is superior and composed of 1 to 5 carpels, commonly 3, mostly one-celled, with many (rarely 1) ovules borne on a central or basal placenta; seeds usually with perisperm.

THE PINK FAMILY

This is the *Caryophyllaceae*, a family of herbs including about 70 genera and 1,200 species of annuals and perennials that are largely confined to the north temperate and colder regions of the earth (Fig. 123).

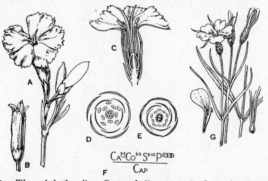

$$\frac{C_A{}^{3\text{-}5} Co^{3\text{-}5} S^{8\text{-}10} P{\text{--}}}{C_{AP}}$$

Fig. 123.—The pink family, *Caryophyllaceae*. *A*, flowering branch of pink *Dianthus; B*, fruit of same; *C*, vertical section of the flower of the same; *D*, floral diagram of starwort, *Stellaria; E*, floral diagram of *Dianthus (all after Le M. and Dec.); F*, floral formula for the family; *G*, flowering habit of corncockle, *Agrostemma githago (after Bentham)*.

Leaves usually opposite or verticillate, simple, entire, often united at the base and attached to swollen nodes; flowers actinomorphic, perfect, hypogynous (or perigynous), axillary, solitary or cymose; sepals 3 to 5, persistent, free or slightly united; petals 3 to 5 or rarely wanting; stamens 8 to 10 (or fewer), free; ovary superior, three- to five-carpelled but one-celled, with central placentation; fruit a capsule, opening by valves or terminal teeth; seeds many; perisperm present.

Many of our most beautiful garden flowers are included in this family among which are various species of catchfly, *Silene, Lychnis*, pinks, *Dianthus*, and babysbreath, *Gypsophila*. The most popular and widely grown of all pinks is probably the carnation or clove pink, *Dianthus caryophyllus*, of which there are scores of varieties grown under glass by the commercial florist.

Many of the cultivated forms produce double flowers that are very variable in size, color, form, etc. The old-fashioned soapwort or bouncing bet is *Saponaria officinalis.*

THE PURSLANE FAMILY

The purslanes or pusleys are included in the family *Portulacaceae*, and they are mostly fleshy or succulent, often prostrate herbs or undershrubs, native largely to the western hemisphere although certain ones are also widely distributed in the Old World. There are about 20 genera and 200 species.

Leaves alternate or opposite, simple, sometimes united at the base, entire, often very fleshy or succulent; flowers hypogynous, actinomorphic, perfect, solitary or clustered; sepals usually 2, free or connate below; petals 4 to 5, or more, free or connate below, falling early; stamens same number as petals and opposite them, or many, free; ovary superior or partly inferior, one-celled, placenta basal, style two- to three-parted, ovules one to many; fruit a many-seeded capsule opening by 3 valves or by the formation of an annular ring that separates a more or less conical cap from the upper part of the capsule (circumscissile); perisperm abundant, mealy.

There are several popular flower-garden plants in this family including rosemoss, *Portulaca grandiflora*, with its cylindrical succulent leaves and showy flowers in bright colors of great variety, usually opening only in sunshine. One of the most beautiful wild flowers of the family is the bitterroot, *Lewisia rediviva*, the state flower of Montana. Lewisia is named for Meriwether Lewis, the famous explorer of the northwest.

THE GOOSEFOOT FAMILY

The members of the *Chenopodiaceae* are mostly succulent, annual or perennial herbs, but there are numerous species that are distinctly shrubby, and they are widely distributed throughout the world especially along seashores and in saline areas in the interior of the continents. Many of them are known as "saltbushes," because of their evident association with saline and alkaline sites (Fig. 124).

Leaves and stems often mealy or scurfy (hence *goosefoots*); the leaves are usually alternate and simple; flowers commonly very small and inconspicuous, greenish, diclinous or perfect, hypogynous, actinomorphic, apetalous; plants sometimes diœcious;

sepals 2 to 5, more or less united; stamens of same number as calyx lobes and opposite them, sometimes fewer; pistil of 2 to 3 carpels, one-celled, superior or imbedded in the calyx; style 1 to 3, terminal, ovule 1; fruit nut-like or an achene, more or less inclosed by the accrescent calyx; seed single; perisperm 0, or present and inclosed by the embryo.

Some species of the family are grown for ornamental purposes, such as summer cypress, *Kochia scoparia*, but the more commonly used species are for food. The beets, including ordinary garden beets (beet root of the British), mangels, and sugar beets, *Beta vulgaris*, are the most useful plants of the group. Leaf beets

$$C\overset{2\cdot5}{A}C\overset{0}{o}S\overset{2\cdot5}{}P^1$$
$$P_F M_o D_i N_{UT} A_{CH}$$

Fig. 124.—The goosefoot family, *Chenopodiaceae*. *A*, flowering stem of goosefoot, *Chenopodium* (*after Le M. and Dec.*); *B*, single flower of the same; *C*, floral diagram for the family; *D*, flowering stems and flower details of *Chenopodium hybridum* (*after Bentham*).

and Swiss chard are other varieties of this species. Spinach, *Spinacia oleracea*, a valuable pot herb, *i.e.* grown for greens, also belongs here.

THE AMARANTH FAMILY

This is the *Amaranthaceae*, another large and widely dispersed family, the members of which are particularly abundant in warm climates. They are mostly annual and perennial herbs but there are a few woody species known, and about 40 genera and 500 species have been described.

Leaves alternate or opposite, simple, sometimes more or less fleshy; flowers small, dry, hypogynous, regular, usually perfect or diclinous, often massed in dense clusters mingled with colored scarious bracts or scales; sepals 3 to 5, free or slightly united; petals 0; stamens usually 5, opposite the sepals, free or united at base into a tube, staminodes sometimes present; ovary superior, one-celled; style 1 or 0, stigma two- to three-lobed or capitate; ovules one to many; fruit capsule-like, (utricle) opening by a lid (*i.e.*, circumscissile), sometimes more nearly an achene, or even berry-like.

Besides the numerous weeds, pigweeds, etc. (*Amaranthus, Acnida*, etc.) that the family includes, the most noteworthy plant of the group is probably the cockscomb, *Celosia cristata*, with its many cultivated varieties and races.

THE BUCKWHEAT FAMILY

The *Polygonaceae*, commonly known as the buckwheats or knotweeds (Fig. 125), include another large series of apetalous

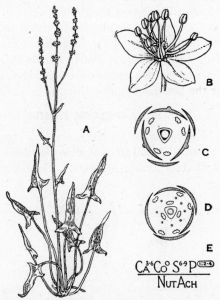

$$\overset{3\text{-}6}{C}\overset{0}{Co} \overset{6\text{-}9}{S} \overset{(1\text{-}2\text{-}4)}{P}$$
$$\text{NutAch}$$

Fig. 125.—The buckwheat family, *Polygonaceae*. *A*, habit sketch of sour dock, *Rumex acetosella* (*Mathews*); *B*, flower of buckwheat, *Fagopyron* (*after Le M. and Dec.*); *C*, floral diagram of *Fagopyron* (*after Le M. and Dec.*); *D*, same for *Rumex*; *E*, floral formula for the family.

forms allied to the *Caryophyllaceae*. They include herbs, shrubs, and trees, some of which are climbers, arranged in 40 genera and 800 species of very wide distribution in both warm and cold regions. The stems are conspicuously jointed and often swollen at the nodes, as in the pinks.

Leaves alternate, rarely opposite or whorled, simple, stipules often forming a membranous sheath, the *ocrea*, about the stem;

flowers small, perfect or diclinous, regular, often in spikes or racemes; sepals 3 to 6, separate or slightly united, often becoming greatly enlarged, winged, spiny, and brightly colored in fruit; petals 0; stamens 6 to 9, rarely more, filaments free or united; ovary superior, sessile, with 2 to 4 carpels, but one-celled, styles 2 to 4, free; fruit an indehiscent, three-angled or lenticular nut or achene, sometimes inclosed by the enlarged calyx; seeds with abundant, mealy endosperm.

The common buckwheat, *Fagopyron esculentum*, is the most useful plant in the family as a cultivated plant of several varieties, from the fruits of which the familiar buckwheat flour is prepared. The plant is not strictly a *wheat* at all, since the wheats in the botanical sense are all *grasses* of the genus *Triticum*. The term is probably a modification of "beechwheat," from the resemblance of the fruits to beechnuts, and the fact that a flour is prepared from the seeds. The common rhubarb, *Rheum rhaponticum*, also belongs here, as do various species of *Polygonum*, some of which are valued for the beautiful spikes of white or purple flowers.

THE FOUR-O'CLOCK FAMILY

The family *Nyctaginaceae* includes about 25 genera and 350 species of herbs, shrubs, and trees of wide distribution but mainly in tropical and temperate America. They are called four

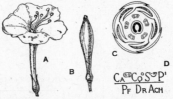

Fig. 126.—The four-o'clock family, *Nyctaginaceae*. *A*, single flower of four-o'clock, *Mirabilis*; *B*, fruit of the same; *C*, floral diagram of *Mirabilis* (all after Baillon); *D*, floral formula for the family.

o'clocks because of the fact that the flowers in certain members of the group (*Mirabilis*) open in greatest numbers in late afternoon (Fig. 126).

Leaves alternate or opposite, simple; flowers perfect or diclinous, hypogynous, regular, usually subtended by an involucre of separate or united, brightly colored bracts that are often mistaken for a perianth; calyx tubular, with 4 to 5 wide-spreading lobes, often petaloid; petals 0; stamens one to many, free or united at the base; ovary superior, one-celled, one-ovuled, sessile or stalked; fruit dry, indehiscent, often ribbed or grooved, sometimes inclosed in the persistent calyx, often glandular; perisperm abundant or scanty. The brightly colored bracts often persist about the fruits long after the flowers have withered.

A few species of four o'clocks are cultivated for ornamental purposes, among which are the bushy, herbaceous four o'clock of the garden, *Mirabilis jalapa*, and the gorgeous *Bougainvillea* (or *Buginvillaea*), a popular ornamental vine of warm countries, with its great masses of purple or magenta bracts. The common species, *B. glabra*, is a native of Brazil.

THE WILLOW FAMILY

The willow family, *Salicaceae*, includes the cottonwoods, aspens, and poplars, *Populus*, as well as the willows, *Salix* (Fig. 127). They are trees or shrubs, but several of the willows of

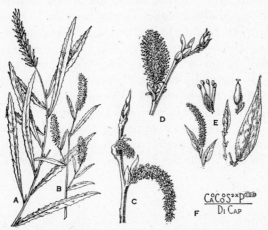

Fig. 127.—The willow family, *Salicaceae*. *A*, leaves and pistillate catkin of sandbar willow, *Salix longifolia*; *B*, twig of same species with staminate catkins (*after Mathews*); *C*, staminate catkins of cottonwood, *Populus* (*after Le M. and Dec.*); *D*, staminate catkin of willow, *Salix* (*after Le M. and Dec.*); *E*, leaves, staminate catkin, staminate and pistillate flowers of peach-leaved willow, *Salix amygdaloides* (*after Mathews*); *F*, floral formula for the family.

Arctic-alpine situations are dwarfed, carpet-like plants, like many herbaceous, more or less woody perennials. These plants are grouped into two genera and about 200 species with a very wide distribution, but they are most abundant in the temperate and cold portions of the northern hemisphere. They are absent from Australasia and the Malay Archipelago. Many of the tree species of both genera grow rapidly. The wood of most of the species is usually light and soft.

Leaves alternate, simple, deciduous, petioles often glandular; stipules sometimes foliaceous and persistent; the species are diœcious; flowers densely clustered in erect or pendulous catkins appearing before or with the leaves; each flower in the axil of a more or less hairy, membranous, fugacious or persistent bract; calyx 0 or reduced to a small disk or to a few glandular scales; petals 0; stamens 1, 2, or more, filaments slender, free or more or less united; ovary sessile or short-stalked, one-celled, with 2 to 4 parietal placentae, stigma two- to four-lobed, ovules numerous; fruit a two- to four-valved, one-celled capsule with many hairy seeds; endosperm none.

Numerous willows are used for ornamental purposes, especially the weeping willow, *Salix babylonica*, of which there are several varieties and hybrid forms, the yellow willow, *S. vitellina*, and white willow, *S. alba*. Other species, such as *S. viminalis*, and *S. purpurea*, are used in basket making. The poplars or cotton-woods, *i.e.*, species of *Populus*, are also used for ornamental planting as well as for windbreaks and woodlots. Popular ornamentals are the white poplar, *Populus alba* (often called silver *maple*), and the closely related bolleana poplar, *P. bolleana*, with its narrow, erect crown, and the Lombardy poplar, *P. nigra*, var. *italica*. The proper name for the common cottonwood, widely planted in the prairie and plains area of North America, appears to be *P. deltoides* Marshall, of which there are several varieties.

CHAPTER XV

THE PRIMROSES, HEATHERS, AND EBONIES

The members of these orders are herbs, shrubs, or trees and are largely characterized by regular flowers in which the petals are united to form a more or less tubular or campanulate corolla, a strong tendency toward epipetalous stamens, and with a superior or inferior ovary composed of several or a few united carpels. Sympetaly is clearly established on a broad scale, and epigyny is also definitely introduced in the families of these orders.

ORDER PRIMULALES, THE PRIMROSE ORDER

The families included in the *Primulales*, or primrose order, are mostly herbs, with regular, perfect, 4- to 5-parted flowers, epipetalous stamens, and a one-celled ovary composed of several carpels, or the axial or basal placentae showing little evidence of more than one carpel in the mature ovary.

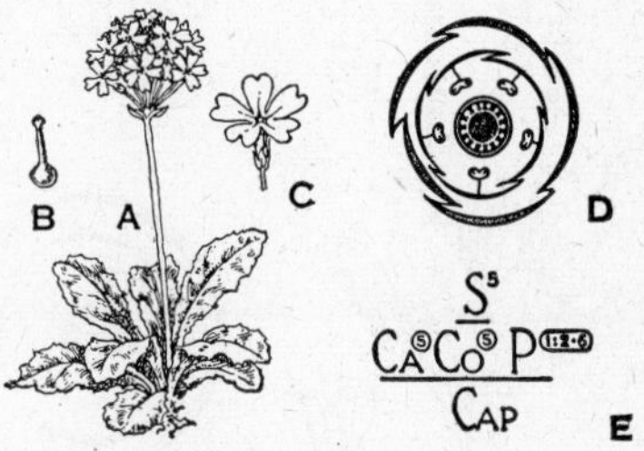

THE PRIMROSE FAMILY

The members of the *Primulaceae* or the primrose family (Fig. 128), are annual or perennial herbs, including about 30 genera and 700 species distributed in abundance mostly in the temperate portions of the northern hemisphere. They are

FIG. 128.—The primrose family, *Primulaceae*. *A*, habit of primrose, *Primula farinosa; B*, pistil of same; *C*, flower of same (*after Bentham*); *D*, floral diagram of *Primula* (*after Le M. and Dec.*); *E*, floral formula for the family.

common in the mountain areas of the north but are rare in the tropics and southern hemisphere.

Leaves alternate, opposite, or whorled, sometimes all basal, simple, regular or lobed, frequently glandular; flowers perfect, actinomorphic, solitary or in various types of bracteate clusters; calyx four- to five-parted, persistent, often becoming foliaceous; corolla tubular, sympetalous, the tube short or long, the 4 to 5

211

lobes commonly spreading; stamens 4- to 5, inserted on the corolla tube opposite the petals; ovary superior (rarely somewhat inferior), one-celled, with 2 to 6 carpels or basal placentae, ovules many; fruit a capsule; seeds with abundant endosperm.

This family includes many very showy wild flowers and cultivated plants of gardens and conservatories. Several species of *Primula*, notably *P. sinensis*, the Chinese primrose, with its many varieties and cultivated forms, are very popular members of the florist's lists of indoor flowers. The cyclamens are also widely cultured for decorative purposes. The rock jasmines, *Androsace* spp. shooting stars, *Dodecatheon* spp., and wild primroses, *Primula* spp., are familiar plants to one who tramps and climbs among the mountains.

THE PLANTAIN FAMILY

This is the *Plantaginaceae*, a group that should not be confused with the *Musaceae*, the banana family, and the *Bromeliaceae*,

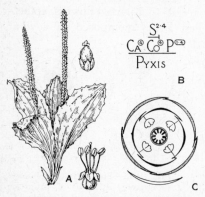

$$\frac{\overset{2\cdot4}{S}}{\underset{Ca}{Ca}\ \overset{\oplus}{Co}\ \overset{\text{4-8}}{P}}$$

Pyxis

the pineapple family, which are also known as "plantains" in certain parts of the world (Fig. 129). There are 3 genera and about 230 widely dispersed herbaceous, annual or perennial species in the family.

Leaves alternate or opposite, or all basal, simple; flowers small, perfect or diclinous, actinomorphic, in dense terminal, bracteate spikes or heads on elongated scapes; calyx four-parted, inferior, persistent; corolla sympetalous, usually four-

Fig. 129.—The plantain family, *Plantaginaceae. A*, habit sketch and details of the flowers of plantain, *Plantago major* (*after Bentham); B*, floral formula for the family; *C*, floral diagram of *Plantago* (*after Le M. and Dec.*).

lobed, scarious; stamens 2 or 4, on the tube or throat of the corolla and alternate with the lobes; ovary superior, one- to four-celled, commonly two-celled, style simple, slender, ovules 1 or more in each cell; fruit a circumscissile capsule (pyxis), or a nutlet, with one seed in each cavity; seeds with fleshy endosperm.

The species in this family possess little or no commercial value, but some of them are of economic significance on account of their persistent weedy nature. Common weeds in the group are *Plantago major*, *P. lanceolata*, a common adulterant of alfalfa seed, and *P. purshii*. A mucilaginous beverage is made from spagel seeds obtained from the Indian *P. ovata*, or ispaghul.

THE LEADWORT FAMILY

This, the *Plumbaginaceae*, is a family of herbs, shrubs, and vines with 10 genera and about 300 species found widely on maritime shores and in other saline situations, particularly in the Mediterranean basin. They are commonly known as sea lavenders, sea pinks and leadworts (Fig. 130).

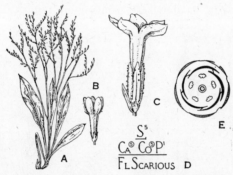

Fig. 130.—The leadwort family, *Plumbaginaceae*. *A*, seapink, *Statice armeria*; *B*, single flower of same (*after Mathews*); *C*, single flower of *Plumbago* (*after Le M. and Dec.*); *D*, floral formula for the family; *E*, floral diagram of *Statice*.

Leaves alternate or grouped in a basal rosette; flowers perfect, actinomorphic, in dry bracted spikes, heads or panicles that are often unilateral; calyx tubular or funnel form, five-lobed or five-toothed, bracted at base, often ribbed, plaited, scarious and colored; corolla tubular, five-lobed, often dry and persistent; stamens 5, epipetalous, opposite the corolla lobes; ovary superior one-celled, ovule 1, styles 5, separate or united; fruit indehiscent, or opening late, usually inclosed by the calyx; seed with or without endosperm.

Several species, especially of *Limonium* and *Statice*, are widely grown in gardens and hothouses for ornamental purposes. Various species are very popular for "dry bouquets" and for the preparation of wreaths and sprays for memorial purposes. The leadwort, *Plumbago capensis*, is frequently seen as a sprawling vine in conservatories where it is prized for its bright blue flowers that resemble the flowers of wild sweet william, *Phlox divaricata.*

ORDER ERICALES, THE HEATHER ORDER

This order includes the heaths, heathers, and wintergreens. They have regular, perfect, actinomorphic, pentamerous, sympetalous flowers, in which the stamens are usually hypogynous and the ovary is usually superior and composed of two to many, united carpels, with numerous minute seeds.

THE HEATHER FAMILY

The *Ericaceae,* commonly known as the heather or heath family, are a large group of shrubs or small trees with mostly evergreen leaves, of about 70 genera and 1,400 species of very

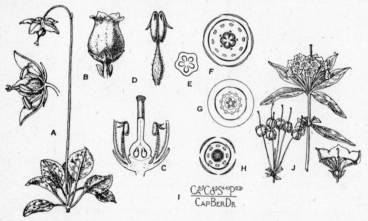

Fig. 131.—The heather family, *Ericaceae. A,* one-flowered wintergreen, *Moneses uniflora; B,* single flower of bearberry, *Arctostaphylos; C,* sectional view of flower of *Arctostaphylos; D,* stamen; *E,* section of ovary; *F,* floral diagram of wintergreen, *Pyrola; G,* floral diagram of blueberry, *Vaccinium; H,* floral diagram of heather, *Erica; I,* floral formula for *Erica* sp.; *J,* flowering twig, section of a flower, and cluster of fruits of mountain laurel, *Kalmia latifolia* (*after Sargent*). *B, C, D, E,* redrawn from Warming-Potter, *Systematic Botany,* published by The Macmillan Company.

wide geographical distribution, especially in relatively cool climates (Fig. 131). Many species are found in South Africa and Western China.

Leaves alternate or whorled, simple, often more or less leathery, and commonly evergreen; flowers perfect, usually actinomorphic, solitary or in terminal or axillary racemes or panicles; calyx four- to five-cleft or parted, persistent; corolla sympetalous, four- to five-lobed, inserted below a fleshy disk; stamens commonly twice as many as corolla lobes, inserted on the outer edge of the disk or on the corolla, filaments free, anthers opening by terminal pores; ovary superior or inferior, two- to five-celled, ovules one to many in each cell, style and stigma 1; fruit a capsule, berry, or drupe; endosperm fleshy.

This family contributes many plants of great value as ornamentals as well as several that are prized in cultivation and in the wild state for their edible fruits. The rhododendrons and the azaleas are among the most beautiful of ornamental plants that are widely grown in parks and conservatories. The state flower of Washington is *Rhododendron californicum*. Several heaths, *Erica* spp. and heathers, *Calluna*, and the laurel, *Kalmia*, are also highly prized for their beauty of flower and foliage. The blueberries, huckleberries and cranberries, species of *Vaccinium*, trailing arbutus, *Epigaea*, and wintergreen, *Gaultheria*, also belong to this family as here treated, although some authors distribute these among two or three other families.

ORDER EBENALES, THE EBONY ORDER

These are trees and shrubs which closely resemble the *Ericales* in flower structure. The stamens are usually epipetalous in this group but in the heathers they are more commonly hypogynous. Both these orders are doubtless more primitive than the *Primulales*.

THE EBONY FAMILY

The plants of the *Ebenaceae* are trees and shrubs with very hard, dark wood, classified into 6 genera and about 275 species distributed mostly in tropical and subtropical countries (Fig. 132). The persimmon, *Diospyros virginiana*, of North America is often seen in temperate climates.

Leaves alternate, entire, often leathery; flowers regular, usually diclinous, often polygamo-dioecious, sometimes perfect, solitary or cymose in the axils of the leaves; calyx three- to seven-lobed, persistent, often enlarging in fruit; corolla three- to seven-lobed, sympetalous; stamens two to four times the number of corolla lobes, hypogynous or epipetalous, filaments free or united at base in pairs; ovary superior, three- to many-celled, ovules 1 to 2 in each cell, styles few to many, free or united; fruit a berry which is sometimes more or less leathery; seeds with endosperm.

The ebony family furnishes many useful products.   The ebony wood of the Orient is secured from *Diospyros ebenum*, a close relative of our American persimmon.   Hard and heavy woods are produced by other genera and species also.   The persimmons

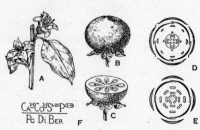

Fig. 132.—The ebony family, *Ebenaceae*.   *A*, flowers and leaves of persimmon, *Diospyros virginiana*; *B*, ripe fruit of same; *C*, section of same (*after Gager*); *D*, floral diagram of pistillate flower of persimmon; *E*, floral diagram of staminate flower of persimmon (*after Le M. and Dec.*); *F*, floral formula for the family.

are important also for the fruits that they produce, especially those of the Kaki plum, or Japanese persimmon, *Diospyros kaki*.

The sapodilla family, *Sapotaceae*, and the storax family, *Styracaceae*, are also included in this order under the Besseyan system.

CHAPTER XVI

THE GENTIANS, PHLOXES, SNAPDRAGONS, AND MINTS

This group of orders is characterized by many families that are largely herbaceous, and by the presence of perfect (rarely diclinous), sympetalous flowers, in which the superior ovary is typically bicarpellary, and the stamens are epipetalous and alternate with the corolla lobes. A high degree of zygomorphy is also developed, especially in the snapdragons, *Scrophulariales*, and in the mints, *Lamiales*.

ORDER GENTIANALES, THE GENTIAN ORDER

The gentian order includes families in which the flowers are perfect, actinomorphic, mostly five-lobed or five-parted, the stamens are of the same number as the corolla lobes and alternate with them, and the bicarpellary ovary is superior. The leaves are usually opposite. The order also embraces the *Oleaceae* or olive family in which the petals are often lacking and the flowers are sometimes diclinous.

THE GENTIAN FAMILY

The *Gentianaceae* are a large group of annual or perennial herbs (a few are woody) arranged in about 65 genera and 750 species with wide distribution, but more abundant in temperate and subtropical regions (Fig. 133).

Leaves opposite (rarely alternate), often more or less connate at base; flowers perfect, regular, in axillary or terminal cymes, often brightly colored and showy; calyx tubular (rarely of separate sepals), usually five-lobed (4 to 12); corolla sympetalous, tube short or long, usually five-lobed (four- to twelve-lobed); stamens same number as corolla lobes and alternate with them, epipetalous; ovary superior, one-celled or with two, parietal placentae (bicarpellary), style simple, ovules numerous; fruit a capsule; seeds with abundant endosperm.

The family contains many species with very beautiful flowers that are cultivated, particularly in the rock gardens of Europe. Many of them have blue flowers and some of these have beautifully fringed corolla lobes, as in the fringed blue gentians, *Gentiana crinita* and *Anthopogon elegans*. The gentians are often conspicuous in montane floras.

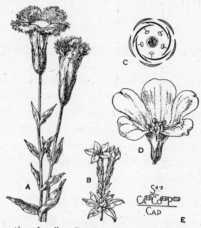

FIG. 133.—The gentian family, *Gentianaceae*. *A*, flowering habit of fringed gentian, *Gentiana crinita* (*Mathews*); *B*, a dwarf alpine species of *Gentiana; C*, floral diagram of gentian (*after Le M. and Dec.*); *D*, single flower of *Eustoma* (*after Baillon*); *E*, floral diagram for the family.

THE OLIVE FAMILY

The *Oleaceae* or olive family, is doubtless the most important family of the *Gentianales*. These are trees and shrubs in about

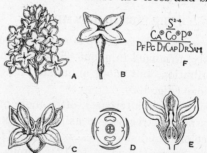

FIG. 134.—The olive family, *Oleaceae*. *A*, flower cluster of lilac, *Syringa vulgaris* (*after Baillon*); *B*, single flower of *Syringa* (*after Baillon*); *C*, flower of olive, *Olea europea* (*after Baillon*); *D*, floral diagram of lilac, *Syringa* (*after Le M. and Dec.*); *E*, vertical section of a flower of olive, *Olea* (*after Baillon*); *F*, floral formula for the family.

20 genera and 500 species that are widely dispersed in temperate and tropical regions of both the Old and New World (Fig. 134).

Leaves opposite (rarely alternate), simple or commonly pinnately compound, often evergreen; flowers regular, perfect, polygamous, or dioecious; calyx four-lobed or four-toothed, rarely 0; corolla sympetalous or petals free or none (red ash); stamens usually 2, (3 to 5 rarely) commonly epipetalous; ovary superior, two-celled, with two or more ovules in each cell, style simple with bifid or capitate stigma; fruit a capsule, drupe, berry, or samara; endosperm usually present.

There are many highly prized and popular ornamental plants in this family, including several species of privet, *Ligustrum,* for hedges, the jasmines, *Jasminum,* lilacs, *Syringa,* of many species and varieties, and the ashes, *Fraxinus,* among which are important forest trees as well as those that are valuable ornamentals. The white ash, *Fraxinus americana,* and the European ash, *F.*

excelsior, are well known. The olive, *Olea europea,* of Southeastern Europe and Asia Minor is widely cultivated in warm climates, as in California and Italy for its edible fruits, the olives of commerce.

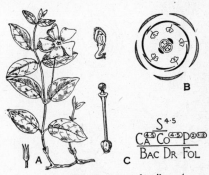

FIG. 135.—The dogbane family, *Apocynaceae. A,* plant of periwinkle, *Vinca minor,* with leaves and flower; *B,* floral diagram of same (*after Le M. and Dec.*); *C,* floral formula for the family.

THE DOGBANE FAMILY

There are about 130 genera and 1,100 species of milky-juiced shrubs and trees included in the *Apocynaceae,* or dogbane family. Some of them are climbers and a few are perennial herbs (Fig. 135). They are most abundant in the tropics and subtropics.

Leaves opposite, whorled or alternate, simple, entire; flowers perfect, actinomorphic; calyx four- to five-lobed, often with glands; corolla tubular, four- to five-lobed; stamens 4 to 5, epipetalous, free or filaments rarely united; anthers sometimes connivent about the stigma; ovary superior, two-celled, syncarpous or one-celled with two parietal placentae or carpels 2, free or united only at base, style 1, ovules 2 or more in each carpel; fruit indehiscent or more commonly of two separate carpels, berry-like, drupaceous, or follicular; seeds often hairy or winged; endosperm present.

A number of species in this family produce fruits of value such as the karaunda, *Carissa carandas,* of India, arrow poisons are prepared from *Acokanthera schimperi* in east tropical Africa, and certain ones are valuable ornamentals, among which are the oleanders, *Nerium*, and the periwinkles, *Vinca*.

THE MILKWEED FAMILY

The milkweeds, *Asclepiadaceae*, are milky-juiced herbs, vines, or shrubs of wide geographical distribution, most numerous in the warmer regions of the earth, and very common in South Africa, but comparatively rare in cold climates (Fig. 136).

Leaves opposite or whorled, rarely alternate, simple, usually entire; flowers perfect, regular, in terminal or axillary umbels or

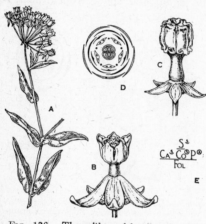

cymes; calyx of 5 separate or connate sepals; corolla sympetalous, five-lobed or five-parted; an additional structure of the nature of a five-lobed crown (corona) arising from the corolla and stamens present inside the corolla; stamens 5, on the base of the corolla alternate with the lobes, filaments united into a column, anthers adherent to or connivent about the stigma, the pollen coherent in waxy or granular masses (pollinia) attached in 2's or 4's to the stigma directly or by arched corpuscula; ovaries 2, or ovary of 2 more or less united carpels, superior, with ventral placentae, short styles united to form a short, thick, discoid stigma; fruit 2 follicles, often widely divergent, each with many seeds crowned with a tuft of silky hairs, endosperm scanty; embryo large.

FIG. 136.—The milkweed family, *Asclepiadaceae. A*, flowering habit of butterfly weed, *Asclepias tuberosa (after Mathews); B*, single flower of milkweed, *Asclepias (after Baillon); C*, flower with petals removed; *D*, floral diagram of *Asclepias (after Le M. and Dec.); E*, floral formula for the family.

A few species of milkweeds are planted for their ornamental values in wild gardens such as butterfly weed, *Asclepias tuberosa*, and swamp milkweed, *Asclepias incarnata*, and certain climbers, *Araujia* and *Stephanotus*, are grown under glass or out of doors in warm countries as in Brazil and Madagascar. Certain ones, such as *Asclepias syriaca*, are sometimes troublesome weeds, as the boy on the farm may testify. The flowers of many species of milkweed are very fragrant, but certain ones, as *Stapelia variegata*, emit a carrion-like odor.

ORDER POLEMONIALES, THE PHLOX ORDER

The phloxes and their kin, the order *Polemoniales*, consist of a group of families that are closely related and that have been so regarded for a great many years. Their relationship to the orders that are placed lower in this series, *i.e.* the *Primulales* and *Caryophyllales*, appears to be quite clear. The order is much more restricted in this treatment than in the Engler system.

The flowers are typically actinomorphic, but with a decided tendency toward the development of zygomorphy in certain families, sympetalous, pentamerous; stamens epipetalous, same number as corolla lobes and alternate with them; ovary tripcarpellary, or bicarpellary, superior; leaves usually alternate; largely herbs or climbers.

THE PHLOX FAMILY

The phloxes, *Polemoniaceae*, are mostly annual or perennial herbs, with few woody plants of the nature of low trees or climbing shrubs, mostly of the western hemisphere, rare in Europe and Asia (Fig. 137). The family includes 10 to 12 genera and about 270 species of wide distribution in the Americas.

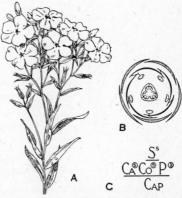

Fig. 137.—The phlox family, *Polemoniaceae*. *A*, flowering habit of a wild phlox or sweet william, *Phlox pilosa; B*, floral diagram for phlox; *C*, floral formula for the family (*after Mathews*).

Leaves alternate or opposite below, simple, usually entire, sometimes pinnate or palmate; flowers perfect, regular or nearly so, often crowded in heads or corymbs; calyx five-lobed; corolla of 5 united petals, tubular, with spreading lobes; stamens 5, epipetalous, alternate with corolla lobes; ovary superior, inserted on a disk, sessile, composed of 3 (or rarely 2) united carpels; ovules one to more in each cell, placentae axile, style 1, stigmas commonly 3 (rarely 2); fruit usually a dehiscent capsule; seeds few or many, with abundant endosperm.

Many members of this family are grown for horticultural purposes, and numerous wild species are highly ornamental. The premier group is doubtless *Phlox*, of which several species are cultivated. The North American *P. divaricata*, of the eastern woodlands, *P. pilosa* of the prairies, and *P. stansburyi* of the Great Basin are worthy of note.

THE MORNING-GLORY FAMILY

Morning-glories, in the botanical sense, are members of the natural family *Convolvulaceae*. They are mostly annual or perennial herbs, many of which are climbers, and a few are woody.

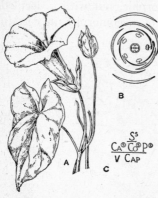

There are 50 genera and about 1,000 very widely distributed species included in the family; particularly abundant in the tropics (Fig. 138).

Leaves alternate, simple or rarely compound (juice sometimes milky) reduced to inconspicuous scales in the Dodders (*Cuscuta*); flowers perfect, actinomorphic, sometimes subtended by a bracteose involucre; sepals 5, free or united; petals 5, united, forming a funnel-shaped corolla with flaring rim, usually twisted in bud; stamens 5, epipetalous, alternate with corolla lobes; ovary superior or surrounded by a disk, one- to three-celled, usually two-celled, ovules solitary or

FIG. 138.—The morning-glory family, *Convolvulaceae*. *A*, leaf and flower of bindweed, *Convolvulus (after Le M. and Dec.)*; *B*, floral diagram of bindweed, *Convolvulus (after Le M. and Dec.)*; *C*, floral formula for the family.

paired in each cell; fruit a capsule, opening by valves; seed with meager endosperm.

This family includes an interesting series of parasitic morning-glories known as the dodders, included in the genus *Cuscuta*. About 55 species of *Cuscuta* have been described, among which are species that attack such plants as alfalfa, flax, mint, willow, and many common weeds. Many bothersome weeds are also included in the family, such as the common field morning-glory, *Convolvulus sepium*, and the little bindweed, *C. arvensis*. Ornamental species are *Ipomoea purpurea*, the common purple morning-glory, and the so-called cypress vine, *Quamoclit pennata*. The most valuable plant of the family is the sweet potato, *Ipomoea batatas*, a true morning-glory, grown extensively for its large, edible, fleshy-fibrous roots.

THE WATERLEAF FAMILY

The *Hydrophyllaceae* include 18 genera and about 225 species of annual and perennial herbs of wide distribution, but evidently more abundant in North America than elsewhere. The group is commonly known as the waterleaf family because certain members of the family, *Hydrophyllum*, were supposed to have cavities in the leaves for holding water.

Leaves alternate or radical, rarely opposite, entire or variously lobed; the whole plant often rough-hairy; flowers perfect, regular, often in rough scorpioid cymes; calyx deeply five-parted; corolla sympetalous, five-lobed, lobes erect or spreading; stamens 5, inserted on the corolla tube and alternate with the lobes, free; ovary with 2 parietal placentae or two-celled, styles 2, separate or united and two-cleft; fruit a two-valved capsule; seeds with fleshy endosperm.

Numerous forms of the family are grown for ornamental purposes such as blue eyes, *Nemophila insignis*, California blue-bell, *Phacelia whitlavia*, and golden bells, *Emmenanthe penduliflora*. One species, *Hydrophyllum canadense*, is listed as a drug plant.

THE NIGHTSHADE FAMILY

The *Solanaceae* are a family of herbs, climbing vines, and a few small trees of about 75 genera and 2,000 species of wide geographical distribution in temperate regions and very abundant in tropical countries (Fig. 139).

Leaves alternate, entire or variously lobed, or pinnately compound; flowers perfect, actinomorphic, sympetalous; calyx five-lobed persistent; corolla five-lobed, often rotate, but much variation in form and structure, sometimes zygomorphic; stamens as many as the lobes of the corolla and alternate with them; ovary superior, two-celled, with axile placentae, ovules many, style 1, stigma simple, or lobed; fruit a capsule or berry; seeds with abundant endosperm.

This family includes many plants that furnish foods and drugs, and species that are highly decorative as well as numerous poisonous plants. Among these is the genus *Solanum* including *S. tuberosum* and *S. melongena*, the Irish potato and the eggplant respectively, also *Lycopersicon esculentum*, the tomato, among the world's most valuable food plants; the drug plants belladonna, *Atropa belladonna*, the henbane, *Hyoscyamus niger*, and the jimson weed, *Datura stramonium*, as well as tobacco, *Nicotiana tabacum*, and *Capsicum frutescens*, the numerous varieties of which are known as peppers; and the highly ornamental petunias, *Petunia violacea*, salpiglossis, *Salpiglossis sinuata*, and matrimony vine, *Lycium halimifolium*.

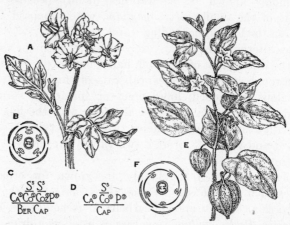

Fig. 139.—The nightshade family, *Solanaceae*. *A*, flowers and leaves of potato, *Solanum tuberosum* (*after Le M. and Dec.*); *B*, floral diagram of same (*after Le M. and Dec.*); *C*, floral formula of the family combining actinomorphic and zygomorphic forms in one formula; *D*, floral formula for the family including actinomorphic forms only; *E*, flowering and fruiting branch of ground cherry, *Physalis alkakengi* (*after Baillon*); *F*, floral diagram of tobacco, *Nicotiana* (*after Le M. and Dec.*).

THE FORGET-ME-NOT FAMILY

The members of the *Boraginaceae* are commonly known as the forget-me-nots, puccoons, and borages (Fig. 140). They are mostly herbs, but the group also includes a few shrubs and trees, grouped in 86 genera and about 1,500 species, that are widely dispersed through temperate and tropical regions, and are abundant in the Mediterranean Basin.

Leaves alternate, simple, mostly entire, rarely opposite; whole plant often rough-hairy; flowers often blue or white, in scorpioid racemes or cymes, perfect, actinomorphic or rarely somewhat oblique; calyx five-cleft, persistent; corolla five-cleft, often appendaged in the throat; stamens 5, inserted on the tube or throat, alternate with the corolla lobes; ovary of 2, united and deeply two-lobed carpels or entire, ovules one in each lobe; fruit usually 4, more or less bony nutlets, each with 1 seed, or sometimes 2 nutlets each with 2 seeds, rarely drupaceous or berry-like; nutlets attached to fruiting axis by base or at the side; endosperm present or 0.

The forget-me-not of popular acclaim is quite different in different areas. A common plant by this name is *Myosotis arvensis*, but the common forget-me-not in the Rocky Mountains is *Mertensia alpina* or *Eritrichium argenteum*, all of which have the bright, blue flowers necessary to qualify as forget-me-nots in

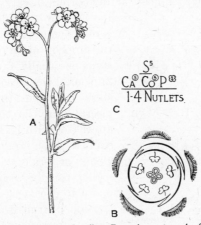

Fig. 140.—The forget-me-not family, *Boraginaceae*. *A*, flowering stem of forget-me-not, *Myosotis* (*after Le M. and Dec.*); *B*, floral diagram of a borage (*after Le M. and Dec.*); *C*, floral formula for the family.

the popular sense. The common heliotrope, *Heliotropium peruvianum*, also belongs here, as do many other beautiful species and varieties.

ORDER SCROPHULARIALES, THE SNAPDRAGON ORDER

This order has much in common with the *Polemoniales*, but is readily separated from the latter by the almost universal zygomorphy and the fact that the number of stamens is usually less (4 or 2) than the number of corolla lobes. The ovary is usually two-carpelled, and the fruit a capsule with many seeds. The group also includes the curious, leafless parasites known as broomrapes, *Orobanchaceae*, as well as the interesting, carnivorous bladderworts, *Lentibulariaceae*.

THE SNAPDRAGON FAMILY

The family *Scrophulariaceae,* is known as the snapdragon, figwort or foxglove family (Fig. 141). The scientific term is from the genus, *Scrophularia,* named in recognition of the belief that a certain species, *S. nodosa,* was a remedy for scrofula. They are mostly herbs of temperate regions, but many shrubs and trees of the tropics belong in this family, and they are very widely distributed. There have been about 75 genera and 3,000 species described that are assigned to this family.

Leaves alternate, opposite, or whorled; flowers perfect, zygomorphic (rarely almost actinomorphic), calyx four- to five-

Fig. 141.—The snapdragon family, *Scrophulariaceae.* A, flowering stem of snapdragon, *Antirrhinum majus (after Mathews);* B, floral diagram of snapdragon *(after Le M. and Dec.);* C, floral formula for the family.

toothed or - divided, persistent; corolla sympetalous, often strongly two-lipped, rotate or campanulate; stamens usually 4, didynamous, or 2, sometimes accompanied by a sterile stamen (in *Pentstemon*), inserted on the corolla tube and alternate with its lobes, sterile stamen sometimes reduced to a gland or scale; ovary superior, sessile, usually bicarpellary, ovules many in each cell, style entire or two-lobed; fruit usually a capsule; seeds numerous, with fleshy endosperm.

There are numerous species in this family with showy flowers and combinations of color pattern and form that are very attractive. The foxglove, *Digitalis purpurea,* is an old-fashioned ornamental and drug plant, and snapdragons, *Antirrhinum majus,* with its numerous varieties, the beardtongues, *Pentstemon* spp., monkey flowers, *Mimulus* spp., and slipperworts, *Calceolaria* spp., are other prized plants of gardens and plant houses.

THE BIGNONIA FAMILY

The *Bignoniaceae* include about 100 genera and 600 species of trees, shrubs and woody vines (and a very few species of herbs) with a wide distribution in tropical and subtropical regions and few in temperate climates (Fig. 142).

Leaves opposite, rarely alternate, or whorled, simple or commonly compound, palmate or pinnate; flowers perfect, zygomorphic, often very showy, in terminal or axillary racemes or panicles; calyx campanulate or tubular, five-lobed or not lobed; corolla usually more or less irregular, sometimes two-lipped, the upper lip of 2, and the lower of 3 lobes; stamens 4, or 2 that are perfect, epipetalous, a fifth stamen (staminode) sterile; ovary superior, two-celled or one-celled with 2 parietal placentae, ovules numerous, stigma two-lobed; fruit usually a capsule, sometimes fleshy and indehiscent; seeds flattened, often winged; endosperm 0.

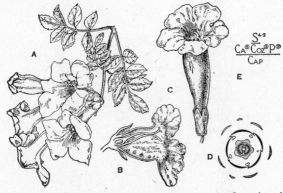

Fig. 142.—The bignonia family, *Bignoniaceae. A*, flowering branch of trumpet vine, *Tecoma radicans (after Le M. and Dec.); B*, sectional view of single flower in catalpa, *Catalpa (after Baillon); C*, a single flower of *Tecoma (after Baillon); D*, floral diagram of *Tecoma (after Le M. and Dec.); E*, floral formula for the family.

This family includes many plants of value as ornamentals such as the trumpetvine, *Tecoma radicans*, a deciduous, woody vine, with pinnate leaves, and large scarlet or orange flowers, and the Jacaranda or Jack tree, *Jacaranda ovalifolia*, with its wonderful masses of blue flowers, often seen in Southern California and other subtropical and tropical areas. The catalpas are trees that are also highly ornamental and some of them, *C. speciosa*, produce valuable wood. These trees grow in fairly cool climates.

THE BROOMRAPE FAMILY

The *Orobanchaceae* are also known as the cancer-root family (Fig. 143) because the group includes plants that are mostly parasitic on the roots of other plants. There are 11 genera and more than 200 species of erect, simple or branched, yellowish, red, or almost colorless parasites in this family, with wide distribution in the northern hemisphere. The family has much in common with the *Scrophulariaceae* except the parasitism.

Leaves often reduced to alternate, chlorophyll-less scales, plants often nearly leafless or with stems scaly only at the base; flowers usually perfect, zygomorphic, often crowded in terminal, bracted spikes, sometimes solitary; calyx four- to five-toothed or lobed or deeply cleft; corolla irregular, sympetalous, five-lobed, two-lipped; stamens 4, in 2 sets, (didynamous), on the tube of the corolla and alternate with the corolla lobes, staminode

Fig. 143.—The broomrape family, *Orobanchaceae*. *A*, flowering habit of *Orobanche americana*, American broomrape; *B*, single flower with the corolla removed; *C*, single flower complete; *D*, floral formula for the family (*after Mathews*).

sometimes present; ovary superior, one-celled, with 4 parietal placentae, ovules numerous, stigma two-lobed or discoid; fruit a two-valved capsule, seeds numerous, small, endosperm fleshy.

There are no particularly valuable species in this family, but some of them are of slight economic interest because of the fact that they parasitize certain cultivated plants. The whole group is of great scientific interest on account of the intense parasitism associated with their flowering-plant life history.

THE ACANTHUS FAMILY

This family, the *Acanthaceae*, include 175 or more genera and about 2,000 species of herbs and climbers (a few are shrubby) of wide distribution in the tropical and subtropical regions of the world. The group is usually difficult for the beginning student of flowering plants because of the technical details that are utilized in the classification of the species.

Leaves opposite, simple; flowers perfect, usually zygomorphic, often in conspicuously bracted spikes or glomerules; calyx four- to five-lobed or rarely reduced to a low ring; corolla sympetalous, four- to five-lobed, two-lipped, sometimes nearly regular; stamens 4, in 2 sets (didynamous), or 2, inserted on the corolla tube and alternate with its lobes; ovary superior, sessile, on a disk, two-celled, style simple or stigmas 2, ovules 1 to many in each cell; fruit a capsule, usually elastically dehiscent; seeds borne on curved projections or hooks, often covered with mucilage and spiral threads when wet; endosperm mostly lacking.

Numerous species and varieties of this family are grown under glass for ornamental purposes. Certain thistle-like species of *Acanthus*, especially *A. mollis*, and the beautiful foliage plant, *Strobilanthus degerianus*, are among the cultivated members of the group.

THE BLADDERWORT FAMILY

The members of the *Lentibulariaceae* are aquatic or marsh herbs, often submerged, or merely on moist soil, sometimes epiphytic. There are 4 or 5 genera and about 190 species of wide distribution.

Leaves in basal rosettes, alternate on branching stems or reduced to scales, often dissected; flowers perfect, zygomorphic, on slender scapes which push the flowers above the water in aquatic forms; calyx two- to five-parted; corolla sympetalous, five-lobed, two-lipped, spurred at the back; stamens 2, inserted at the base of the corolla tube, 2 reduced stamens sometimes present; ovary superior, one-celled, ovules numerous, stigma sessile or style short; fruit a capsule opening by 2 to 4 valves; seeds rough or bristly; endosperm 0.

The submerged stems in *Utricularia* are commonly finely branched, the leaves are dissected into filiform segments and the plants thickly supplied with tiny, flattish bladders that are contracted at the mouth. The plants are sometimes included in aquatic cultures in gardens and conservatories.

ORDER LAMIALES, THE MINT ORDER

We may refer to this order as the mints and their immediate kin, but the order includes the verbena family, *Verbenaceae*, as well as the mint family, *Labiatae*. They are mostly herbs with opposite or whorled leaves and zygomorphic, often two-lipped flowers, stamens 2 to 4, the two-celled ovary is often deeply four-lobed and it commonly develops into 4 separate, bony nutlets.

This order is higher than the *Scrophulariales*, and it represents the terminus of this series of Dicotyledons. Both of these orders reflect many of the features that are regarded as indicative of a relatively high degree of development and hence they are accorded high positions in our arrangment. These features include an extreme reduction in the number of carpels, seeds, and stamens, the almost universal adoption of sympetaly, and a strikingly bizarre zygomorphy.

THE VERBENA FAMILY

The verbenas or the *Verbenaceae* are mostly herbs, but the family also includes numerous shrubs and trees grouped in 70 genera and about 1,000 species of south temperate and tropical countries, with many genera and species in cultivation, some of them being highly prized ornamentals.

Leaves opposite or whorled, simple or compound; flowers perfect, zygomorphic or rarely almost regular, often two-lipped; calyx four- to five-lobed or toothed, persistent; corolla sympetalous, tubular, four- to five-lobed; stamens 4, or rarely 2, on the corolla; ovary superior, of 2 carpels or rarely four- to eight-celled, each cell with 1 ovule, style terminal, simple; fruit a drupe or berry, or dry and containing two to four nutlets; endosperm scanty or none.

This family is separated from the closely related *Labiatae* by the fact that the ovary here is seldom lobed, whereas in the latter the ovary is commonly deeply four-lobed around the style, and it is distinguished from the *Boraginaceae* by its zygomorphic flowers.

There are many fine ornamentals among the verbenas, notably in the genus *Verbena*, with its many species and varieties of brightly flowered bedding plants, and the shrubby or climbing *Lantana*, particularly *L. camara*, and *L. sellowiana*. Teakwood comes from *Tectona grandis*, a member of this family.

THE MINT FAMILY

The mints and their closest kin are included in the family *Labiatae*, or *Lamiaceae* as it is sometimes written (Fig. 144). The former name reflects the bilabiate flower structure so common here, and the latter family name is from *Lamium*, one of the genera of the group, which also is from a word that calls attention to the shape of the corolla. These plants are mostly aromatic herbs and shrubs (few trees) with a distribution through the world under a great variety of climatic and soil conditions, being especially abundant in the Mediterranean Basin, in the Oriental countries, and in mountain regions. There are about 160 genera and 3,000 species now recognized. Many of them are cultivated for ornamental purposes and for their ethereal oils that are used in medicines, confections, and cosmetics.

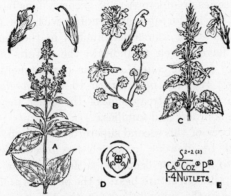

Fig. 144.—The mint family, *Labiatae. A*, flowering stem and details of the flower of peppermint, *Mentha piperita (after Bentham); B*, habit and flowers of a mint, *Lamium amplexicaule (after Bentham); C*, flowering stem and a single flower of mint, *Stachys (after Bentham); D*, floral diagram of *Lamium (after Le M. and Dec.); E*, floral formula for the family.

Leaves opposite or whorled, simple, stems commonly quadrangular; whole plant often very aromatic; flowers perfect, zygomorphic, rarely nearly regular, axillary or whorled, or in terminal spikes; calyx of 5 united sepals, five-toothed, five-cleft, regular or two-lipped; corolla sympetalous, five-lobed, typically two-lipped (bilabiate); stamens 4, in 2 sets (didynamous) or only 2, on the corolla tube; ovary superior, two-celled, each carpel deeply two-lobed, 1 ovule in each lobe, style arising from the center of the four-lobed ovary, stigma two-lobed; fruit of 4 more or less free, one-seeded bony nutlets; endosperm none.

Among the popular, cultivated, ornamental, oil-producing, and drug mints are rosemary, *Rosmarinus officinalis*, sage, *Salvia splendens*, *S. officinalis* and *S. azurea*, lavender, *Lavandula spica*, thyme, *Thymus vulgaris*, peppermint, *Mentha piperita* (Fig. 144 *A*), spearmint, *M. spicata*, horsemint, *Monarda didyma*, *M. fistulosa*, etc.

CHAPTER XVII

BUTTERCUPS TO ASTERS

We have now completed a general survey of one of the two great major series or superorders of Dicotyledons beginning with the *Ranales*, or buttercups, and ending with the *Lamiales*, or mints. Diagnoses of numerous families in the various orders of this line have served to indicate the nature of the plants involved, the general course of their development, and their relationships. We will now return to the *Ranales* and their kin to begin a similar treatment of the other major series of dicotyledonous orders and families.

The members of this second superorder or group of orders are characterized by flowers in which the receptacle or axis is expanded into a disk, or deepened to form a more or less urn-shaped or cup-like structure bearing the perianth and stamens on its margin, or in the sympetalous families the stamens are commonly epipetalous. There are two principal subdivisions of this series as in the other line. The first or lower group includes orders and families in which polypetaly, polycarpy, and actinomorphy are the rule, and the flower ranges from hypogyny to epigyny. The second or higher group includes those in which sympetaly, oligocarpy, epigyny, and epipetalous stamens prevail, and in which a considerable degree of zygomorphy has also developed. The rose order, *Rosales*, is the first order of this great series to become differentiated from the primitive Ranalian plexus.

ORDER ROSALES, THE ROSE ORDER

This is one of the largest orders of flowering plants, there being at least 15,000 species included in the various families of which it is composed. Among these are many plants of great value for agricultural and horticultural purposes. The flowers are cyclic, and usually perfect, actinomorphic to zygomorphic, and polypetalous, usually the perianth is pentamerous, the stamens indefinite in number and free, and the carpels few to many, separate or united, or sometimes inclosed within or becoming grown to (adnate) the inner surface of a discoid or deep, cup-like axis. The flowers often superficially resemble the flowers of the *Ranales*, especially those of the buttercup family, *Ranunculaceae*, from which they may be separated by means of the disklike or cup-like axis or portion of axis which prevails in the *Rosales*. The two orders are evidently closely related.

THE ROSE FAMILY

The *Rosaceae* or rose family (Fig. 145) are a large group of trees, shrubs, and herbs, or climbers of very diverse habit and wide distribution in temperate regions. The family as here treated

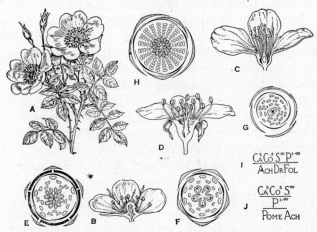

FIG. 145.—The rose family, *Rosaceae*. *A*, flowering spray of rose, *Rosa* (*after Baillon*); *B*, sectional view of a flower of strawberry, *Fragaria* (*after Baillon*); *C*, sectional view of a flower of cherry, *Prunus* (*after Baillon*); *D*, sectional view of a flower of pear, *Pyrus* (*after Baillon*); *E*, floral diagram of strawberry, *Fragaria* (*after Baillon*); *F*, floral diagram of pear, *Pyrus* (*after Baillon*); *G*, floral diagram of peach, *Amygdalus* (*after Le M. and Dec.*); *H*, floral diagram of rose, *Rosa* (*after Le M. and Dec.*); *I*, floral formula for the perigynous *Rosaceae*; *J*, floral formula for the epigynous *Rosaceae*.

includes three subdivisions that are sometimes separated into different families, *i.e.* the roses proper or, in a restricted sense *Rosaceae*, the apples, *Malaceae*, and the plums, *Drupaceae* or *Prunaceae*. The bases for the recognition of these groups are found in certain differences which the axis, ovary, and fruits exhibit in the three subdivisions. We will include all of these in a single more or less heterogenous family which, when so constituted, embraces about 100 genera and 2,500 species.

Leaves usually alternate, simple or compound; flowers perfect, mostly actinomorphic, axis typically cup-shaped or urn-shaped, or sometimes a combination of a conical or dome-shaped central portion, surrounded at the base by a disk-like flange (as in strawberry, *Fragaria*); sepals 5; petals 5, separate, borne on the rim of the cup or urn or on the edge of the disk (*Fragaria*); stamens numerous, free, commonly borne in several cycles of 5 on the rim of the axis, *i.e.* they are *perigynous;* carpels few to many to one, free or variously united, often united with the surrounding axis disk or tubular cup, styles free or connate, commonly as many as the carpels, ovules 2 or more in each carpel; fruit an achene, pome, drupe, or follicle, or an enlarged, hollow, fleshy tórus or axis (hip), often mistakenly called "berries" (see chapter on fruits); seeds with little or no endosperm.

This cosmopolitan family is very rich in its contributions to the pleasure and welfare of mankind. It includes apples, pears and quinces, *Malus, Pyrus, Cydonia,* of hundreds of species and varieties in cultivation, plums, cherries, and prunes, *Prunus,* also in great number, apricots, peaches, almonds and other "stone fruits," *Prunus, Amygdalus,* etc., strawberries, *Fragaria,* blackberries, raspberries, dewberries, loganberries, *Rubus,* and hosts of ornamental garden favorites and conservatory plants. Among the latter may be mentioned the vast and varied group of roses, *Rosa,* of which thousands have been described, the spiraeas and bridal wreaths, *Spiraea,* mountain ash, *Sorbus,* hawthorns, *Crataegus,* and scores of other herbs, shrubs, trees, and vines that are cultivated for their beauty of form, foliage, or flower.

THE SENNA FAMILY

The sennas as here understood are included in the family *Caesalpiniaceae,* a group of about 90 genera and 1,000 species of trees, shrubs, and a few herbs, mainly found in tropical regions.

Leaves mostly compound, pinnate or bipinnate, rarely simple or one-foliate; flowers perfect or rarely diclinous in more or less clustered, showy, racemose inflorescences, zygomorphic or nearly actinomorphic in some forms; sepals 5, free or the upper pair united; petals 5 or fewer, the upper one inclosed by the lateral petals; stamens 10 or less, filaments distinct or variously connate; ovary superior or in base of shallow cup, one-celled, ovules numerous; fruit a legume, dehiscent into 2 valves; seeds with or without endosperm.

The sennas have certain features in common with the beans, *Leguminosae*, but the flowers are only slightly zygomorphic. Many important timber trees of the Tropics belong here such as the purple heartwood, *Copaifera pubiflora*, of British Guiana, West Indian Locust, *Hymenaea courbaril*, and the tamarind, *Tamarindus indica*. The honeylocust, *Gleditsia triacanthos*, is an important tree of temperate North America. There are also many ornamental trees and shrubs in the family including the redbud, *Cercis canadensis*, various species of senna, *Cassia*, and the poinciana, especially *Poinciana pulcherrima*. The curious Algaroba or St. John's bread, *Ceratonia siliqua*, also belongs in this family. This is a large tree of the Eastern Mediterranean countries that produces large, red pods that are edible.

THE MIMOSA FAMILY

This is the *Mimosaceae*, sometimes known also as the acacia family. They are almost exclusively trees or shrubs of about 30 genera and 1,400 species widely distributed in tropical and subtropical regions.

Leaves alternate, usually bipinnate, rarely simply pinnate; flowers perfect, small, in heads, racemes, or spikes, actinomorphic; sepals 3 to 6; corolla 3 to 6, petals separate or united into a short tube; stamens equal in number to sepals or more numerous, free or monadelphous; ovary superior, one-celled, ovules numerous; fruit a legume; seeds with scanty or 0 endosperm.

One of the more striking genera of this family is *Acacia*, of which about 450 species have been described, many of which are cultured out of doors in tropical and subtropical countries. Gum Arabic comes from *Acacia senegal*, of tropical Africa. The so-called sensitive plants of the genera *Mimosa* and *Morongia* are also included in this family. There are about 300 species of *Mimosa* in tropical America, among which the best known one is *Mimosa pudica*, so often used to demonstrate the sensitive nature of the leaves and leaflets. The sensitive brier, *Morongia uncinata*, is almost as sensitive as *Mimosa*, and this plant is found well north in the American prairies.

THE BEAN FAMILY

The technical designation for this family is rather varied, but either *Leguminosae* or *Papilionaceae* is commonly used as the family name for the group. The former term is in recognition of the common fruit of the family, and the latter is from a fancied resemblance of the flower to a butterfly, *i. e.* the flower is papilionaceous or "butterfly-like." This is an enormous, cosmopolitan family including about 400 genera and more than 5,000 species of herbs, shrubs, trees, and many climbing plants, found under extremely varied soil and climatic conditions, but most abundant in temperate and warm climates (Fig. 146).

Leaves alternate, mostly compound, pinnate or digitate, or rarely simple; flowers mostly perfect, zygomorphic, in spikes, heads, racemes, or panicles; axis more or less tubular; sepals 5;

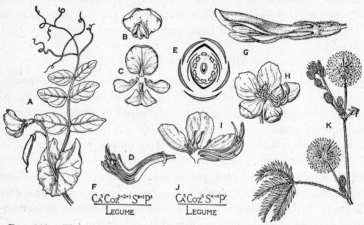

FIG. 146.—The bean family, *Leguminosae. A*, pea, *Pisum (after Baillon); B*, front view of the papilionaceous flower of *Pisum (after Baillon); C*, corolla of *Pisum* dissected; *D*, diadelphous stamens of *Pisum (after Baillon); E*, floral diagram of sweet pea, *Lathyrus (after Le M. and Dec.); F*, floral formula for the generalized family; *G*, flower of clover, *Trifolium (after Baillon); H*, flower of *Cassia (after Baillon); I*, sectional view of flower of *Cassia (after Baillon); J* floral formula for the *Caesalpiniaceae; K, Mimosa*, flower heads and leaves *(after Le M. and Dec.)*.

petals 5, (2 plus 2 plus 1) free or somewhat united, the upper one exterior, commonly larger or broader than the rest and forming the "standard" or "banner," the 2 lateral petals, *i.e.* "wings," smaller and alike and more or less parallel with each other, the other 2 petals are interior, or lower, or in front and more or less united by their lower edges to form the "keel"; stamens usually 10, (9 and 1) inserted on the rim of the axis with the petals, free or commonly monadelphous or diadelphous; ovary superior, one-celled or 2-celled by intrusion of sutures, ovules 1 to many; fruit a legume; seeds usually without endosperm.

This family includes a great many species and varieties that are of major economic importance to man. They contribute products of great variety from foods and flowers to drugs and dyes. Peas, *Pisum sativum*, and beans, *Phaseolus vulgaris*, of numerous kinds are among the most important foods of the world. Peanuts, *Arachis hypogaea*, and lentils, *Lens esculenta*, are additional bean or pea-like plants, the seeds of which are valuable as food. Forage plants like lucerne or alfalfa, *Medicago sativa*, and clover, *Trifolium pratense* and *T. arvense*, have almost inestimable value as food for animals and as means of maintaining proper soil fertility for a varied agriculture. Scores of very excellent ornamentals are also found here, such as sweet peas, *Lathyrus odoratus*, Chinese wisteria, *Wisteria sinensis*, locust, *Robinia hispida*, and Japanese pagodatree, *Sophora japonica*. The logwood of Central America, *Haematoxylon campechianum*, is the source of the dye, haematoxylon, so useful in microscopic technique. Numerous drug plants, including liquorice, *Glycyrrhiza glabra*, and many stock-poisoning plants such as loco weed, *Aragallus lambertii*, are also members of this great natural alliance.

THE SAXIFRAGE FAMILY

The *Saxifragaceae*, or saxifrage family are given this name from the genus *Saxifraga* which means "rock-breaking" with the supposition that because certain species of the family are regularly found growing on rocks the group is composed of "rock-breakers." They are mostly herbs with alternate leaves, often more or less succulent and they are arranged in 75 to 100 genera and 1,000 to 1,100 species of wide distribution in temperate and cold regions (Fig. 147).

Leaves alternate, rarely opposite; flowers perfect or diclinous, actinomorphic, commonly perigynous or rarely more or less epigynous; sepals 4 to 5; petals 4 to 5 or 0; stamens 4 to 5 or 8 to 10, inserted with the petals on the rim of the axis, *i.e.*, perigynous; carpels 1 to 3, usually 2, free or united and imbedded in the more or less tubular axis or definitely inferior, styles usually free, ovules numerous; fruit a capsule or berry; seeds with abundant endosperm.

This family is evidently closely related to the *Rosaceae* although it is placed elsewhere by some authors. The number of stamens and pistils has been reduced and definitized as perhaps the most prominent advance as compared with the *Rosaceae*.

The relationship to the following family, *Hydrangeaceae*, is also close, as it is to the gooseberry family, *Grossulariaceae*.

Several species of *Saxifraga* are cultivated for ornamental purposes, but species of *Astilbe*, especially *A. japonica*, are perhaps better known to flower lovers for their panicles of small white or pink flowers.

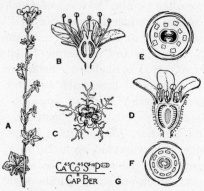

FIG. 147.—The saxifrage family, *Saxifragaceae*. *A*, saxifrage, *Saxifraga cernua* (*after Kerner*); *B*, section of single flower of *Saxifraga* (*after Baillon*); *C*, front view of a flower of miterwort, *Mitella* (*after Baillon*); *D*, sectional view of another species of *Saxifraga* (*after Le M. and Dec.*); *E*, floral diagram of *Saxifraga* (*after Baillon*); *F*, another floral diagram of *Saxifraga* (*after Le M. and Dec.*); *G*, floral formula for the family.

THE HYDRANGEA FAMILY

This family, the *Hydrangeaceae*, is much like the preceding family, but the hydrangeas are mostly *shrubs* and *trees* with opposite leaves. There are 15 or more genera and about 85 species included in the family and these are found in north temperate and tropical regions (Fig. 148).

Leaves opposite, simple; flowers usually perfect, small, or the exterior ones in the cluster may be sterile and showy, in corymbose clusters; the marginal flowers sometimes apetalous, but then with enlarged and conspicuous calyx with spreading lobes; calyx of 4 to 10, usually 4 to 5 sepals, inserted on the rim of the cup-like or tubular axis; petals 4 to 10, usually 4 or 5, on the rim of axis; stamens five to many, on the rim of the axis, free or slightly connate at the base; carpels 2 to 5 (2 to 10), united or tips more or less free, more or less overgrown by the cup-like axis, *i.e.*, partly or wholly inferior; ovules few or numerous; fruit a capsule, often strongly ribbed; seeds numerous, small; endosperm abundant.

There are many beautiful flowering ornamentals included in this family, among which are the numerous species of *Hydrangea* and *Deutzia*, of which there are several that are cultivated mainly for their beautiful clusters of showy flowers. The mock orange, *i.e.* various species of *Philadelphus*, is also included here.

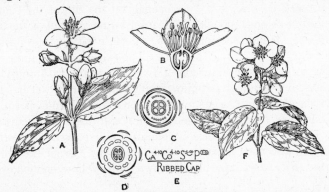

Fig. 148.—The hydrangea family, *Hydrangeaceae*. *A*, flowering twig of *Philadelphus (after Le M. and Dec.)*; *B*, sectional view of a flower in *Philadelphus (after Baillon)*; *C*, floral diagram of *Philadelphus (after Baillon)*; *D*, floral diagram of *Hydrangea (after Le M. and Dec.)*; *E*, floral formula for the family; *F*, flowering branch of another species of *Philadelphus (after Baillon)*.

THE GOOSEBERRY FAMILY

This group, the *Grossulariaceae*, is sometimes included, along with the *Hydrangeaceae*, in the *Saxifragaceae*. It is represented

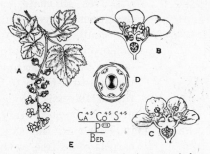

Fig. 149.—The gooseberry family, *Grossulariaceae*. *A*, leaves and flowers of black currant, *Ribes nigrum (after Baillon)*; *B*, section of a single flower of the same *(after Baillon)*; *C*, section of a single flower of *Ribes rubrum (after Kerner)*; *D*, floral diagram of *Ribes (after Baillon)*; *E*, floral formula for the family.

by the single genus *Ribes* which includes the gooseberries and currants (Fig. 149). Some authors split the species into two genera, *Ribes*, the currants, and *Grossularia*, the gooseberries. The latter, *i.e.*, the gooseberries, are spiny shrubs with few-flowered racemes. The former, *i.e.* the currants, are smooth shrubs with many-flowered racemes. There are about 60 species of shrubs in the one or two genera and they are mainly found in the north temperate hemisphere, and in South Africa and the Andes.

Leaves fasciculate, simple, usually lobed; flowers perfect or often unisexual; calyx of 4 to 5 sepals on the rim of the tubular axis, often colored; petals 4 to 5, inserted on the rim of the axis, small or scale-like; stamens 4 to 5, alternate with petals on rim of axis; ovary one-celled, with 2 parietal placentae, wholly imbedded in the axis, *i.e.* inferior, styles 2, free or connate, with undivided stigmas, ovules numerous or few; fruit a pulpy berry with persistent calyx on its summit, seeds numerous or few, with endosperm.

There are many cultivated species and varieties of currants and gooseberries that furnish delightful edible berries. Certain ones are also used as ornamentals, as is the case of the golden currant, *Ribes aureum*, which is grown for its yellow, spicy flowers.

THE WITCHHAZEL FAMILY

The *Hamamelidaceae*, commonly known as the witchhazels, include about 20 genera and 50 species of shrubs and trees that

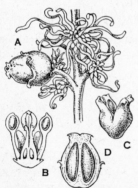

are widely distributed in subtropical and the warmer parts of temperate regions in North America, South Africa and Asia (Fig. 150).

Leaves alternate, rarely opposite, deciduous or evergreen, simple; flowers small, perfect or diclinous, actinomorphic or zygomorphic; axis more or less tubular, bearing 4 to 5 sepals; petals 4 to 5, rarely 0, inserted on the rim of the axis, along with four to many stamens; ovary inferior, *i.e.* imbedded in the axis, bicarpellary, carpels often free at tips, styles free, ovules 1 or several in each carpel; fruit a more or less woody capsule; seeds forcibly discharged when ripe in *Hamamelis;* endosperm thin.

Fig. 150.—The witchhazel family, *Hamamelidaceae. A*, portion of the inflorescence of witchhazel, *Hamamelis*, showing flowers and a young fruit; *B*, vertical section of a flower; *C*, mature fruit; *D*, vertical section of unripe fruit (*all after Sargent*).

The American witchhazel is *Hamamelis virginiana*, a shrub or low tree of eastern United States. This plant is interesting because its flowers do not open until the leaves have fallen in the autumn. It is sometimes planted as an ornamental. This species furnishes the witchhazel extract of the pharmacist. The sweetgum, *Liquidambar styraciflua*, is an important timbertree of southeastern United States, and is the source of styrax.

THE SYCAMORE FAMILY

The sycamores or plane trees belong to the family *Platanaceae*, (Fig. 151) a small group of five or six species of trees included in one genus widely scattered in the north temperate and tropical zones from Europe to India, and from North America south into Central America.

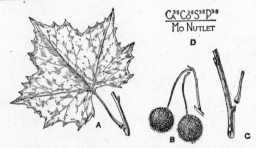

FIG. 151.—The sycamore family, *Platanaceae*. *A*, twig and leaf of American sycamore, *Platanus occidentalis; B*, heads of fruits of same; *C*, twig, buds and base of petiole of same (*after Mathews*); *D*, floral formula for the family.

Leaves alternate, simple, palmately veined and lobed, the expanded petiole base covering the young bud, young leaves rusty tomentose; bark of the branches often exfoliating in thin, irregular plates; flowers monœcious, arranged in dense, globular, pedunculate heads; perianth inconspicuous but represented by 3 to 8 more or less uncertain parts; stamens 3 to 8; pistils 3 to 8, each one-celled; the pistillate head enlarges in fruit, but the carpels remain free and each becomes a narrowly obconical, one-seeded nutlet with a tuft of long hairs at the base; endosperm thin.

The common American sycamore is *Platanus occidentalis*, and the European and Asiatic sycamore is *P. orientalis*. The London plane, *P. acerifolia*, is planted very commonly in eastern United States on streets and in parks. Several varieties are known in cultivation. The nature of the fruiting heads of the sycamores has given rise to the common name, button-ball tree, which one occasionally hears. The name sycamore is also used for a certain fig, *Ficus sycomorus*.   The quarter-sawed wood of the sycamore is very beautiful.

THE STONECROP FAMILY

The stonecrops, constituting the family *Crassulaceae*, are mostly fleshy or succulent herbs or undershrubs arranged in about 20 genera and 900 species widely distributed in the warm, dry regions of both hemispheres (Fig. 152).

Leaves opposite or alternate, simple or pinnate, often extremely succulent; flowers perfect, actinomorphic, usually small and borne in cymes; sepals 4 to 5, free, borne on a tubular receptacle;

Fig. 152.—The stonecrop family, *Crassulaceae*.   *A*, flowering branch of live-for-ever, *Sedum* (*after Le M. and Dec.*); *B*, single flower of *Sedum* (*after Baillon*); *C*, floral diagram of *Sedum* (*after Baillon*); *D*, floral diagram of *Sedum* (*after Le M. and Dec.*); *E*, floral formula for the family; *F*, flowering stem and flower details of *Sedum telephium* (*after Bentham*).

petals 4 to 5 or 0, free or somewhat united; stamens as many as or twice as many as the petals, free; carpels superior or in the bottom of the receptacle, same number as petals, free or united at the base, each one-celled, ovules usually numerous; fruit a one-celled, dehiscent follicle; seeds minute, with fleshy endosperm.

This family includes many species and varieties that are widely used for borders in landscape decoration and in rock gradens and also grown as potted plants in conservatories for their bright yellow flowers.   The genus *Sedum* includes many species known as "live-for-evers" and among these *S. spectabile*, prized for its fine clusters of pink flowers.   The "houseleek" or "hen and chickens," *Sempervivum tectorum*, or *Echeveria secunda*, are popular as border plants.   Very beautiful flower-bed effects are worked out by using these plants with foliage plants to construct various designs.

CHAPTER XVIII

THE MYRTLES, STARFLOWERS, AND CACTUSES

This group of orders is regarded as a lateral development from the general plexus represented by the *Rosales*. The *Myrtales* constitutes the main axis of this lateral phyletic line and this order is regarded as having given rise to two branches including the *Loasales* and the *Cactales*.

The series includes trees, shrubs, and herbs mostly with opposite, simple, often glandular leaves, and actinomorphic, epigynous flowers. The modification of the perigynous and epigynous types of flowers of the *Rosales* in this group of orders is such as to give them a characteristically inferior ovary. A high degree of succulence, leaf reduction, and spininess is reached in the *Cactales*.

ORDER MYRTALES, THE MYRTLE ORDER

This, the myrtle order, includes families of woody and herbaceous plants in which the flowers are usually regular and perfect; the pistil is typically inferior and syncarpous, placentae axile or apical, style one to many, stamens commonly numerous; leaves commonly opposite and simple.

THE MYRTLE FAMILY

The *Myrtaceae*, or myrtle family, include trees and shrubs with opposite (rarely alternate) leaves that are often glandular and aromatic (Fig. 153). There are about 72 genera and 3,000 species in the family, and these are largely confined to the tropics and Australia.

The leaves are usually evergreen, thick, and glandular dotted; flowers actinomorphic, perfect or rarely polygamous, epigynous; sepals 4 to 5, on the rim of the axis, often persistent on the fruit; petals 4 to 5 or 0, also on the axis, imbricated; stamens numerous, rarely few, inserted on the margin of the axis in fascicles opposite the petals, free or connate below; ovary inferior, one- to many-celled, with one to many ovules in each

243

cell, placentae axile, rarely parietal, style simple; fruit a berry capsule, or nut; seeds few to many; endosperm 0 or scanty.

This family includes numerous plants of high economic value on account of the edible fruits and aromatic oils that they produce, in addition to many species that are of value as ornamentals. The fruit of guava, produced by certain species of *Psidium*, especially *P. cattleianum* and *P. guajava*, is a pulpy berry with many seeds and acid juice, used in jelly manufacture. The "cloves" of commerce are the dried, unopened flower buds of *Eugenia aromatica*, a low tree native to the Moluccas, but also widely cultivated in tropical lands. Allspice is the dried, unripe

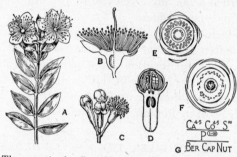

$$\frac{C_A^{4\cdot5} \; C_O^{4\cdot5} \; S^\infty}{P_{(1-\infty)}}$$

G ᴮᴱᴿ ᶜᴬᴾ ᴺᵁᵀ

Fig. 153.—The myrtle family, *Myrtaceae*. *A*, flowering twig of myrtle, *Myrtus* (after Le M. and Dec.); *B*, vertical section of a flower of *Myrtus* (after Baillon); *C*, flowers of clove, *Eugenia* (after Warming); *D*, vertical section of a flower of clove (after Warming); *E*, floral diagram of myrtle, *Myrtus* (after Baillon); *F*, floral diagram of myrtle, *Myrtus* (after Le M. and Dec.); *G*, floral formula for the family.

berry of the closely related *Pimenta officinalis* of the West Indies and Central America.

The genus *Eucalyptus* is a noteworthy member of this family. Certain species of these Australian and Malayan trees reach heights of 400 to 500 feet, and the leaves contribute a series of valuable, volatile oils, gums, and resins. The blue gum, *E. globulus*, and the red gum, *E. rostrata*, are grown in California.

The classic myrtle is *Myrtus communis*, an evergreen shrub with aromatic shining leaves, native to the Mediterranean Basin and Western Asia.

THE POMEGRANATE FAMILY

This interesting family, *Punicaceae*, includes one genus only and two species of low trees or shrubs native from the Balkan countries to the Himalayas, but the pomegranate has been widely cultivated in tropical and subtropical regions from very early times (Fig. 154).

Leaves opposite or whorled, simple, not glandular; branches often spiny tipped; flowers perfect, one to few on the tips of axillary shoots; receptacle (ovary) and calyx colored, more or less leathery, sepals thick, 5 to 7, on the margin of the receptacle; petals 5 to 7, imbricate, crumpled, alternate with the sepals on the edge of the axis; stamens numerous, in a fringe on the inner surface of the axis opposite the petals; ovary inferior, often

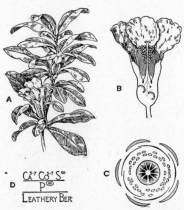

Fig. 154.—The pomegranate family, *Punicaceae*. *A*, flowers and leaves of pomegranate, *Punica granatum* (*after Baillon*); *B*, vertical section of a flower of *Punica* (*after Baillon*); *C*, floral diagram of *Punica* (*after Le M. and Dec.*); *D*, floral formula for the family.

colored, of 4 to 15 united carpels, cells superposed, the lower with axile and the upper with parietal placentae, style simple; fruit a thick-skinned or leathery berry crowned by the sepals, containing numerous seeds surrounded by bright red, juicy pulp; endosperm none.

The pomegranate of commerce is the fruit of *Punica granatum*, a low tree widely cultivated in warm countries. In ancient times the best pomegranates were produced in Carthage, and so they came to be known as "Punic apples" and later as *Punica*. Many cultivated varieties of pomegranates are recognized, among which is a dwarf, double-flowered form sometimes seen in greenhouses and florist's shops.

THE MANGROVE FAMILY

The mangrove family, *Rhizophoraceae*, includes mostly tropical and subtropical trees and shrubs of wide distribution along maritime shores. The family includes 15 genera and about 5 species (Fig. 155).

Leaves opposite, evergreen, commonly leathery; flower perfect, actinomorphic, epigynous, in axillary clusters; sepal 4 to 5 or more, valvate, persistent, on the edge of the axis; petal 4 to 5, small, notched or fringed, on edge of the axis; stamens equal in number to, or more numerous than the petals, opposite the petals on the edge of the axis; ovary inferior, two- to six-celled or rarely one-celled, style simple, ovules 2 or more; fruit a berry or a dry or somewhat fleshy capsule; seeds 1 or more in each cell endosperm fleshy when present.

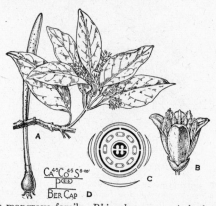

Fig. 155.—The mangrove family, *Rhizophoraceae*. *A*, leafy twig and young fruit of mangrove, *Rhizophora (after Baillon); B*, single flower of *Rhizophora (after Baillon); C*, floral diagram of *Rhizophora (after Baillon); D*, floral formula for the family.

The mangroves commonly form a fringe of tangled shrubs along the shoreline of the sea, especially on muddy coasts and estuaries. The seed germinates within the ovary on the tree and the seedling sometimes reaches a length of a foot or more before it falls away from the tree into the mud or shallow water. This is an illustration of *vivipary*, a phenomenon not at all common among plants. The young plant may become anchored at once or it may float away only to become established at some distance. They may serve to build up or extend the shoreline in such places.

THE EVENING PRIMROSE FAMILY

The *Onagraceae*, or evening primrose family, are a conspicuous group of annuals and perennials that are mostly herbaceous or rarely woody (Fig. 156). They are largely native to the temperate and warm portions of the western hemisphere, but with certain interesting species in Europe and Africa. The family includes about 36 genera and 470 species.

Leaves opposite or alternate, usually simple; flowers perfect, actinomorphic or rarely zygomorphic, epigynous, axillary, spicate or racemose; calyx "adnate to the ovary" or the ovary imbedded in the axis, *i.e.* inferior; sepals 2, 4, or 5, commonly 4, attached to the rim of the axis which is often prolonged beyond the ovary to form a slender tube; petals 2, 4, or 5, commonly 4, free, alternate with the sepals on the rim of the receptacle; stamens as many or twice as many as the petals, free, inserted on

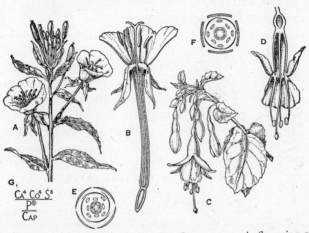

FIG. 156.—The evening primrose family, *Onagraceae. A*, flowering stem of *Oenothera (after Baillon); B*, vertical section of a single flower of *Oenothera (after Baillon); C*, flowering stem of *Fuchsia (after Le M. and Dec.); D*, vertical section of a flower of *Fuchsia (after Baillon); E*, floral diagram of willowherb, *Epilobium (after Le M. and Dec.); F*, floral diagram of *Oenothera (after Baillon); G*, floral formula for the family.

the summit of the axis; ovary two- to six-celled, commonly four-celled, ovules one to many, on axile placentae, style 1, stigma simple, or two- to four-lobed or divided; fruit a capsule or nut with one to many seeds; endosperm scanty or 0. The members of the family are often easily recognized on account of the tetramerous flowers with inferior ovary. Students should bear in mind that this family is very different from the true primroses, which belong to the *Primulaceae.*

Many of these plants are grown for ornamental purposes and numerous wild species are noteworthy for the remarkable beauty of their flowers. The species of *Fuchsia*, often called "fuchsia" are among the most commonly cultivated members of the group. These herbs, shrubs, or low trees are known for the beautiful purple, red or white, usually drooping flowers. The fireweed, *Epilobium angustifolium*, is often a conspicuous invader soon after forest fires. The water-chestnut, *Trapa natans*, a curious aquatic, also belongs here.

THE LOOSESTRIFE FAMILY

The *Lythraceae* is a family of 23 genera and about 450 species of herbs, shrubs, and trees of very wide distribution, but they appear to be most abundant in tropical America (Fig. 157). Annual and perennial species of the group are more numerous in temperate regions, but the woody forms are more often seen in warm climates.

Leaves opposite or verticillate, simple, entire; branches often four-angled; flowers perfect, usually actinomorphic, perigynous, solitary or in panicles or cymes; sepals 4 to 5 or more, inserted on the rim of the axis in which the pistil is inclosed; petals 4 to 6, free or 0, inserted on the rim or somewhat below the rim of the tubular receptacle; stamens 4 to 8 or more, free, inserted on the axis, below the petals, filaments variable in length; pistil superior or more or less surrounded by the tubular receptacle bearing the perianth, two- to six-celled, ovules many in each cell, on axile placentae, style simple; fruit a capsule; seeds numerous; endosperm 0.

Fig. 157.—The loosestrife family, *Lythraceae*. *A*, flowering and fruiting branch of loosestrife, *Lythrum alatum* (*after Mathews*); *B*, floral diagram of *Lythrum* (*after Le M. and Dec.*); *C*, floral formula for the family.

$$\frac{C A^{4.5} C o^{4.6} S^{4.8} P^{2.6}}{C_{AP}}$$

Certain members of this family produce important supplies of timber, as in *Lagerstroemia flos-reginae*, of India, and rose wood, *Physocalymma scaberrimum*, of Brazil. The red dye, henna, is prepared from *Lawsonia inermis*, of tropical Asia. The cigar-flower, *Cuphea platycentra*, is a low shrub that is cultivated in greenhouses and as a bedding plant for its odd flowers.

ORDER LOASALES, THE STARFLOWER ORDER

The plants included in this order usually produce actino-morphic, perfect, or diclinous, mostly epigynous flowers in which the pistil is commonly tricarpellary but one-celled, the placentae are parietal and the stamens are indefinite in number. The leaves are alternate, simple, but often much lobed or divided.

THE LOASA FAMILY

The *Loasaceae* are sometimes known as the starflower family. They are mostly herbs, sometimes climbing, with a few woody species to be found in the Tropics and they are grouped into 13 genera and about 250 species. They are native mostly in the tropical and temperate portions of the Americas. The chief center of distribution of the family appears to be Chile.

Leaves alternate or opposite, entire, or variously lobed or cut, often bearing hooked, barbed, or stinging hairs; flowers perfect, actinomorphic, epigynous; receptacle, more or less tubular, bearing the 5 (or 4 to 7) free sepals and the 5 (or 4 to 7) free petals on the rim; stamens 5 to 10 or more or indefinite, free or collected in groups on the receptacle opposite the petals; ovary inferior, carpels 3 to 7, each with many ovules on parietal placentae, usually one-celled, style entire or two- to three-parted; fruit a many-seeded capsule; seeds with or without endosperm.

There are a few showy ornamentals included in this family, such as *Loasa vulcania*, of South America, and certain species of *Mentzelia* in western North America.

THE BEGONIA FAMILY

The *Begoniaceae*, commonly known as the begonia family (Fig. 158) include 5 genera and about 400 species of widely distributed tropical, mostly succulent herbs or undershrubs. All but a very few of the species are included in the large genus *Begonia*, many of which are climbers, and many others are creeping or acaulescent.

Leaves alternate, simple, often oblique or asymmetrical, stalked and succulent, margin entire, lobed or divided, often large and beautifully variegated; flowers mostly actinomorphic, but often zygomorphic, monœcious, showy, mostly in axillary clusters; the male flowers have 2 opposite sepals, and 2 to 5 or 0 petals inserted on the rim of the axis at the top of the ovary; stamens numerous, free or connate; the female flowers have a perianth about the same as male flowers; ovary inferior, two- to four-celled, commonly tricarpellary, and often three-angled or three-winged, styles 2 to 5, commonly 3, with oddly bent or twisted fleshy stigmas; ovules numerous, on axile placentae; fruit a winged or angular capsule or berry with many fine seeds, with little or no endosperm.

Scores of species and varieties of *Begonia* are grown as glasshouse ornamentals and houseplants, and many are cultivated out of doors in warm countries. They are found in greatest number and luxuriance in the damp shady forests of Brazil and

$$\frac{Ca^2 \; C\overset{2\cdot 5}{o} \; S^{\infty}}{P^{\textcircled{3}}}$$

$$\overline{Suc \; Cap}$$

Fig. 158.—The begonia family, *Begoniaceae.* *A*, leaves and flowers of begonia, *Begonia (after Le M. and Dec.); B*, floral formula for the family.

the Andes. They are also numerous in the Himalayan rain forests and in the Malay Archipelago. The Rex type, *Begonia rex*, is unusually rich in foliage forms, and the floriferous type, represented by the *B. semperflorens* group, is rich in flower forms. Sometimes certain varieties of *B. rex* are known as "beefsteak *geraniums.*"

THE PUMPKIN FAMILY

This large family, the *Cucurbitaceae*, includes a great variety of useful plants such as watermelons, pumpkins, squashes, cucumbers, cantaloupes, gourds, etc. (Fig. 159). They are mostly annual or perennial, weak-stemmed, tendril-climbing herbs, or more rarely somewhat woody, with watery juice. There are about 100 genera and 800 species in the family and these are mainly tropical and subtropical in distribution, with a few species extending into temperate climates.

Leaves alternate, broad, usually simple, but often deeply lobed or divided, sometimes compound, tendrils lateral, spirally coiled; flowers monœcious or diœcious, rarely perfect, actinomorphic; male flower with 1 to 5, mostly 3 stamens, inserted on the rim of the cup-shaped or tubular axis with 3 to 5 narrow sepals and a similar number of free or united petals; ovary in female flower inferior, mostly tricarpellary, with three parietal placentae,

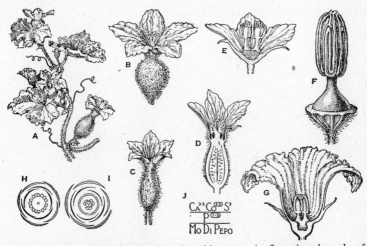

Fig. 159.—The pumpkin family, *Cucurbitaceae*. *A*, flowering branch of muskmelon, *Cucumis melo* (*after Baillon*); *B*, single flower of watermelon, *Citrullus vulgaris* (*after Baillon*); *C*, flower of cucumber, *Cucumis sativus* (*after Baillon*); *D*, vertical section of a female flower of cucumber (*after Le M. and Dec.*); *E*, vertical section of a male flower of *Citrullus* (*after Baillon*); *F*, female flower (with perianth removed) of pumpkin, *Cucurbita pepo* (*after Baillon*); *G*, vertical section of male flower of pumpkin (*after Baillon*); *H*, floral diagram of male flower (*after Le M. and Dec.*); *I*, floral diagram of female flower (*after Le M. and Dec.*); *J*, floral formula for the family.

receptacle often prolonged beyond the ovary, ovules numerous, style simple or with 3, free style branches; fruit a bladdery pod or a fleshy berry-like structure with a hard rind and pulpy, seedy interior, a *pepo*.

Numerous species and varieties of cucurbits are grown for their edible fruits and a few are cultivated for their ornamental values. The common pumpkin is *Cucurbita pepo*, with many varieties, including vegetable marrow and crookneck squashes. Muskmelons, cantaloupes, etc., are forms of *Cucumis melo*, citron and watermelons are from *Citrullus vulgaris*, and the cucumber is *Cucumis sativus*. The balsam apple, *Momordica balsamina*, is grown for its yellow fruit and crimson seeds. The dried, fibrous, bag-like interior of the fruit of the vegetable sponge, *Luffa cylindrica*, is used as a sponge or dishcloth.

ORDER CACTALES, THE CACTUS ORDER

These are succulent, or woody, often very spiny plants of desert and arid regions, with numerous sepals, petals, and stamens. The flowers are mostly actinomorphic, epigynous, and they are often very showy.

THE CACTUS FAMILY

The Cactuses, included in the natural family *Cactaceae*, are perennial herbs, shrubs, or trees of diverse habit (Fig. 160).

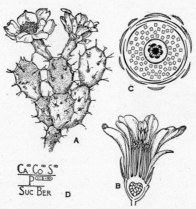

Fig. 160.—The cactus family, *Cactaceae*. *A*, flowering branch of prickly pear, *Opuntia* (*after Mathews*); *B*, vertical section of cactus flower (*after Baillon*); *C*, floral diagram of *Opuntia* (*after Le M. and Dec.*); *D*, floral formula for the family.

They are often quite leafless and very spiny (numerous spineless ones are known) and are mostly native to the warmer regions of America. More than 1,200 species in about 120 genera have been described.

The fleshy, leafless stems are often flat, jointed, and green and so are mistaken for leaves; when true leaves are present they are usually small and succulent and they soon fall; in many erect species the stems are cylindrical, fluted, and much branched; flowers perfect, usually actinomorphic, epigynous, usually solitary, often large and showy; calyx often petaloid, of many sepals on the margin of the receptacle, along with many brightly colored petals in several series; stamens numerous, indefinite, mostly free and inserted at the base of the petals; ovary inferior, one-celled, with 3 or more many-ovuled, parietal placentae; style 1, stigma two- to many-lobed; fruit a berry, juicy, often spiny and edible, many-seeded; endosperm 0.

The Cactuses are peculiarly subtropical American in their modern distribution, but they have been naturalized in many other warm countries. They are of little economic value but are of great scientific interest, and many of them are grown in desert gardens and greenhouses. The "nightblooming Cereus" is a cactus, *Cereus triangularis*. The Christmas cactus is *Zygocactus truncatus*. The tree cactus or giant Sahuaro of southwestern United States and Mexico is *Carnegiea gigantea*. Many of the species of *Opuntia* are known as "prickly pears." Cochineal is a scarlet dye prepared from cochineal insects that feed upon the cochineal cactus, *Nopalea cochinellifera*, a species widely grown in semitropical countries.

CHAPTER XIX

THE BITTERSWEETS, MAPLES, AND PARSLEYS

We now return to the main series in this line of Dicotyledons after having considered the nature of the *Myrtales, Loasales,* and *Cactales,* which together are regarded as a lateral development from the *Rosales.* The *Celastrales* lead upward from the *Rosales* and thus continue the main line established by the latter group. The *Sapindales* are here treated as a lateral branch of the *Celastrales,* but the position of the order is still very uncertain. Growing information seems to support the conclusion that the *Sapindales* are to be regarded as a side development from somewhere among the *Celastrales* and that the line terminates with the diclinous oaks and birches and their kin.

The first two orders include families in which the flowers range from the typically hypogynous form to the typically epigynous form. There are also noteworthy instances of zygomorphy and diclinism to be seen in these groups. The development of a conspicuous glandular, annular, or turgid disk connected with the receptacle is a prominent feature of the floral structure in many plants of this series.

Epigyny becomes the fixed rule in *Umbellales,* and a high degree of flower aggregation is also developed in this group. This order continues the central series of Dicotyledons upward from the *Celastrales.*

ORDER CELASTRALES, THE BITTERSWEET ORDER

This group may be designated as the bittersweet or holly order. They are largely trees, shrubs, or woody climbers, with alternate or opposite, simple leaves and actinomorphic flowers in which a glandular floral disk is often a very prominent feature. Cases of diclinism are seen in the families of the order, but the species are more often monoclinic.

THE BITTERSWEET FAMILY

This is the *Celastraceae,* the type family of the order (Fig. 161). The members of the group are mostly erect trees, shrubs, or woody climbers and these are arranged in about 45 genera and 450 species of wide general distribution except in the colder portions of the earth.

Leaves alternate or opposite, simple, membranous or leathery; flowers small, greenish or white, commonly perfect, but sometimes diclinous, actinomorphic, in axillary or terminal racemes or cymes, or solitary; calyx of 4 to 5 sepals, persistent; petals 4 to 5, usually free, inserted upon or below a conspicuous glandular disk of various form; stamens 4 to 5, free, alternate with the petals, inserted on or below the edge of the disk; pistil two- to five-celled, free or more or less imbedded in the disk, *i.e.* more or less

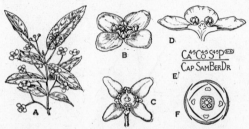

Fig. 161.—The bittersweet family, *Celastraceae*. *A*, flowering twig of wahoo, *Euonymus verrucosus*; *B* and *C*, single flowers of *Euonymus verrucosus* (*after Baillon*) and *E. europæus* (*after Kerner*); *D*, vertical section of a flower of *Euonymus verrucosus* (*after Baillon*); *E*, floral formula for the family; *F*, floral diagram of *Euonymus* (*after Le M. and Dec.*).

inferior; style short, stigma entire, capitate, or three- to five-lobed, ovules 2 in each cell; fruit a capsule, berry, samara, or drupe; seeds with fleshy endosperm.

A number of interesting and popular ornamental species are included in this family. These include the bittersweet or waxwort, *Celastrus scandens*, a climbing vine with beautiful orange capsules that expose crimson seeds as the fruits open in the autumn. Other species of *Celastrus* are abundant in the mountains of India and China. The spindletree, wahoo, or burning bush are species of *Euonymus*, such as *E. atropurpureus* or *E. japonicus*, low trees or shrubs with fruits resembling those of the bittersweet, and sometimes with variegated leaves.

THE GRAPE FAMILY

This family, the *Vitaceae*, includes 11 or 12 genera and 500 species of wide distribution, but mainly developed in tropical and subtropical climates (Fig. 162). Certain wild species of *Vitis*, "grapes," and numerous cultivated varieties are grown in abundance in temperate regions. They are largely tendril-climbing vines or small trees.

Leaves alternate or opposite, simple, deeply lobed or compound; flowers small, greenish, perfect or diclinic, in spikes, racemes, panicles, or cymes, the peduncle often tendril-like or coiled; sepals 4 to 5; petals 4 to 5, free or united, inserted at base of the disk, falling early; stamens 4 to 5, free, opposite the petals, inserted at the base of the disk or in marginal lobes of the disk; pistil superior two-celled (2 to 6), ovules 1 to 2 in each cell, style 1, stigma capitate or discoid; fruit a juicy berry, with one to more seeds; endosperm abundant, often ruminate.

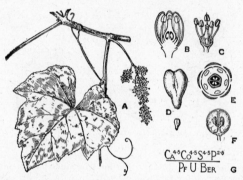

Fig. 162.—The grape family, *Vitaceae*. *A*, leaf, tendrils, and inflorescence of grape, *Vitis labrusca*; *B*, section of single flower of same; *C*, flower after perianth has fallen; *D*, seeds (*after Mathews*); *E*, floral diagram of *Vitis* (*after Le M. and Dec.*); *F*, section of young fruit (*Mathews*); *G*, floral formula for the family.

The most useful plants in this group are the grapes, *i.e.* species and varieties of *Vitis*, but the most abundant native plants in the group are the so-called "ivies" or species of *Cissus*, of which there are said to be more than 300 in tropical and subtropical lands. The "vine" or "grape vine" is *Vitis vinifera* or *V. labrusca*, which includes many varieties such as muscatels, raisins, Concords, sultanas, currants, wine grapes, etc. Important ornamental high-climbing vines of this family are Boston ivy, and Virginia creeper, species of *Parthenocissus*, used widely for covering trellises and walls.

THE BUCKTHORN FAMILY

The *Rhamnaceae*, or Buckthorn family, include trees, shrubs, and some woody vines of very wide distribution in tropical and temperate climates, but absent from cold regions (Fig. 163).

About 45 genera and 500 species have been described in the family.

Leaves alternate or opposite, simple; flowers small, mostly cymose, actinomorphic, perfect or rarely polygamo-diœcious; sepals 4 to 5 on a more or less tubular axis lined with the disk; petals 4 to 5 or 0, free; stamens 4 to 5, free, opposite the petals and inserted with them on the axis at or below the margin or rim of the fleshy disk; ovary superior or inferior, *i.e.* the degree of hypogyny, perigyny or epigyny developed varies greatly in different species, carpels 2 to 4, ovules 1 in each cell, stigma two- to four-lobed; fruit a drupe or capsule; seeds with copious endosperm.

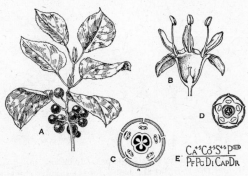

Fig. 163.—The buckthorn family, *Rhamnaceae*. *A*, leaves and fruits of buckthorn, *Rhamnus*; *B*, vertical section of a flower of *Rhamnus*; *C* and *D*, floral diagrams of *Rhamnus* (*all after Baillon*); *E*, floral formula for the family.

The important drug plant, buckthorn or cascara, *Rhamnus purshiana*, of northwestern United States, that produces cascara sagrada, belongs here, as do a number of other medicinal plants. The Indian jujube or Chinese date is *Zizyphus jujuba*. Many species of *Ceanothus* are represented in the bushy vegetation or chaparral of southwestern United States. A few species of this genus are grown as ornamentals.

THE HOLLY FAMILY

The *Aquifoliaceae* are a family of mostly evergreen trees and shrubs grouped in 3 genera and about 300 species (Fig. 164). They are widely distributed from their Central and South American center, but are comparatively rare in Africa and Australia. One species is common from southern Norway to central Turkey and westward to England. Certain other species are found in southeastern United States.

Leaves alternate, simple, usually evergreen, often with spiny teeth on the margin; flowers actinomorphic, perfect or rarely unisexual, small, axillary or in terminal fascicles; calyx of 4 to 5, often 4 (3 to 6) free or united sepals; petals 4 to 5, often 4, free or connate at the base; stamens as many as the petals and alternate with them; disk absent; ovary superior, four-celled (3 to 6), each cell with 1 to 2 ovules; style terminal or stigma sessile; fruit drupaceous, with 2 to 4 stones; endosperm abundant, fleshy.

The hollies are valuable as ornamental plants on account of their glossy evergreen leaves and bright red fruits. The English holly is *Ilex aquifolium*, and the common American holly is *I.*

Fig. 164.—The holly family, *Aquifoliaceae. A*, leaves and flowers of holly, *Ilex (after Le M. and Dec.); B*, floral formula for the family; *C*, habit and details of the flowers of English holly, *Ilex aquifolium (after Bentham).*

opaca, both of which are popular at Christmas time. Forms of holly with variegated leaves are also known. The South American *Ilex paraguayensis* is the source of maté or Paraguay tea.

THE OLEASTER FAMILY

The *Elaeagnaceae* are a small family including 3 genera and 30 to 40 species of erect shrubs or low trees found mostly in the north temperate and subtropical portions of both the Eastern and Western hemispheres (Fig. 165). They are xerophytic inhabitants of seacoasts, dry, sandy barrens, and steppes.

Leaves and young twigs often thickly covered with golden-brown or silvery, peltate or stellate scales; leaves alternate or rarely opposite, entire; flowers perfect or unisexual, often dioecious, solitary or in axillary clusters on 1-year-old twigs; receptacle more or less tubular in the perfect and female flowers in which the ovary is imbedded, hence more or less epigynous; in the male flowers the receptacle is cup-shaped or flattish with the stamens inserted on the throat or on the rim; sepals 2 to 4; petals 0; stamens as many as the sepals and alternate with them or twice as many, filaments free; ovary, one-celled, one-ovuled, more or less closely invested by the axis, style terminal, slender;

fruit an achene or nut inclosed by the fleshy or mealy receptacle, hence more or less drupaceous or baccate; endosperm scanty or 0.

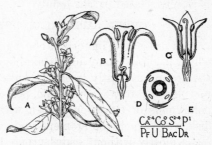

A few species and varieties of *Elaeagnus* are grown for ornament. The fruits of *E. angustifolia* are known as Trebizond dates. The sea buckthorn, *Hippophaë rhamnoides*, has been planted along seacoasts to prevent the blow-

Fig. 165.—The Russian olive family, *Elæagnaceae. A*, a flowering branch of Russian olive, *Elæagnus (after Baillon); B and C*, vertical sections of flowers *(after Le M. and Dec.); D*, floral diagram of *Elæagnus (after Le M. and Dec.); E*, floral formula for the family.

ing of the sand. The buffalo berry, *Shepherdia argentea*, of the American prairie region is planted for hedges and other ornamental purposes.

THE MISTLETOE FAMILY

The *Loranthaceae*, or mistletoe group, are a family of mostly parasitic evergreen shrubs growing upon trees, or rarely they are terrestrial trees and shrubs. There are 21 genera and about 500 species of mistletoes, widely dispersed, mainly in the tropics of the Old and New Worlds. Such trees as chestnuts, oaks, poplars (*Populus*), and pines serve as hosts for these parasites. The "wooden flowers," sometimes gathered by travelers in the tropics, are formed by the attachment of certain of these plants to the woody host.

Leaves opposite or whorled, simple, entire, often leathery, often reduced to mere scales; flowers actinomorphic or slightly irregular, perfect or diclinous, often brightly colored; axis cup-like or disk-like; sepals 2 to 3, free or united, or poorly developed; petals 2 to 3, free or united into a tube; stamens 2 to 3, inserted on the petals; disk present or 0; ovary inferior, one-celled, style simple, terminal or 0; fruit baccate or drupaceous; seed solitary; endosperm abundant.

The pine mistletoe of western United States, *Razoumowskia*, often does considerable damage to the trees. The popular Christmas mistletoe of Europe is *Viscum album*, of America, *Phoradendron flavescens*. The sandalwood family, *Santalaceae*, is closely related to this family.

ORDER SAPINDALES, THE MAPLE ORDER

This order is an important continuation of the *Celastrales*, with which it shows many unmistakable affinities. The members of the group are mostly trees or shrubs, and the flowers are actinomorphic or rarely zygomorphic, perfect or diclinous, hypogynous, perigynous or epigynous, often with a more or less glandular disk with which the stamens and perianth are closely related; seeds mostly without endosperm. Epigyny becomes dominant in the higher families of the order.

THE SOAPBERRY FAMILY

The *Sapindaceae* include about 125 genera and 1,000 species of trees and shrubs, with many climbers, rarely herbs of wide distribution in tropical and subtropical countries. Some of the lianas in the group show a very unusual type of stem structure on account of a peculiar method of secondary growth involving the formation of cortical vascular bundles in addition to the regular central stele.

Leaves alternate, rarely opposite, simple or commonly pinnately, or palmately compound; flowers often much reduced, perfect or polygamo-dioecious, zygomorphic or actinomorphic; sepals 4 to 5; petals 4 to 5 or 0; disk ring-like and well developed between stamens and petals, sometimes unequal; stamens 5 to 10, often 8, inserted within the disk, filaments free or united at the base; ovary superior, one- to four-celled, often three-celled, ovules one to two to many in each cell, style simple or divided; fruit often large, dry, capsular or nut-like, or fleshy and drupaceous or baccate, frequently winged; seeds without endosperm.

The family as here treated includes the buckeyes and horsechestnuts (the genus *Aesculus*) which are sometimes set aside as a special family, the *Hippocastanaceae*. These are trees or shrubs with opposite, palmately three- to nine-foliate leaves and irregular flowers in terminal panicles. The common horse-chestnut is *Aesculus hippocastanum*, a popular ornamental tree, native to southeastern Europe, but with many varieties that are cultivated very widely. The American buckeye is *Aesculus glabra*.

Other cultivated plants of the family are: soapberry, *Sapindus saponaria*, the Chinese litchi or leechee, *Litchi chinensis*, and the balloon vine, *Cardiospermum halicacabum*. Certain other species furnish valuable timber.

THE MAPLE FAMILY

The *Aceraceae* include the genus *Acer*, or the maples (Fig. 166), of which there are more than 100 species known of very wide

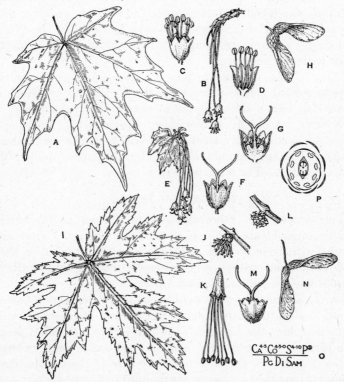

FIG. 166.—The maple family, *Aceraceae*. *A*, leaf of sugar maple, *Acer saccharum;* *B*, cluster of staminate flowers of same; *C*, single such flower; *D*, same flower sectioned; *E*, cluster of pistillate flowers of same; *F*, single flower of same; *G*, same flower sectioned; *H*, fruit of same species; *I*, leaf of silver maple, *Acer saccharinum;* *J*, cluster of staminate flowers of same; *K*, single flower from the cluster; *L*, cluster of pistillate flowers of same species; *M*, single pistillate flower; *N*, fruit of the same species; *O*, floral formula for the family; *P*, floral diagram for the family (*P after Le M. and Dec., all the rest after Mathews*).

distribution, and the genus *Dipteronia* with a single species in central China. The maples are mostly mountain or upland trees and shrubs, with saccharine juice, of the northern hemi-sphere, the greatest number of species being in the eastern Himalaya Mountains to central China.

Leaves opposite, simple or palmately lobed or pinnately com-pound; flowers in axillary or terminal cymes or racemes, actino-morphic, polygamous or diœcious; sepals 4 to 5 (4–10); petals 4 to 5, rarely 0; disk fleshy, annular or lobed, or reduced to mere points; stamens 4 to 10, often 8, inserted on the disk or inside the disk, hypogynous or perigynous, filaments elongated; ovary superior, two-lobed and compressed, two-celled, ovules 1 to 2 in each cell, styles 2, inserted between the lobes of the ovary; fruit a dry samara, two-winged, often splitting into two parts; seeds without endosperm.

Many of the maples are popular ornamentals, such as the American hard maple or sugar maple, *Acer saccharum*, Norway maple, *A. platanoides*, sycamore maple, *A. pseudoplatanus*, and silver maple, *A. saccharinum*. Maple syrup and maple sugar are made mostly from the sap of *A. saccharum*, or hard maple. This species and others also furnish hard, durable wood of great value. The boxelder is *A. negundo*.

THE CASHEW FAMILY

This group, the *Anacardiaceae*, also known as the sumac family, includes about 65 genera and 500 species of trees and shrubs with resinous bark. They are chiefly tropical in their distribution but with several species extending into southern Europe and temperate Asia and America.

Leaves alternate, rarely opposite, simple or compound; flowers small, perfect or with a tendency toward diclinism, usually actinomorphic; axis tubular, with 3 to 7 points (sepals); petals 3 to 7, rarely 0, free or rarely connate; stamens as many or twice as many as the petals, inserted at the base of the annular disk, filaments free; ovary superior, surrounded by the fleshy cup, one-celled, or two- to five-celled, ovule 1 in each cell; styles 1 to 3, often widely separated; fruit usually a drupe; endosperm thin or 0.

Numerous sumacs, species of *Rhus*, are grown for landscape decoration, as is the mastic tree or California pepper tree, *Schinus molle*, a native of the American tropics. The so-called poison ivy, poison oak and poison sumac are also species of *Rhus*. The cashew, *Anacardium occidentale*, of tropical America, produces a delicious, popular, curved nut, on a greatly enlarged receptacle. The pistachio nut comes from *Pistacia vera*, a small native tree of the Mediterranean Basin and the Orient.

THE WALNUT FAMILY

This important family, *Juglandaceae*, includes 5 or 6 genera and about 35 species of deciduous trees often with resinous, aromatic, glandular leaves, native to the north temperate hemisphere, with extensions into the mountains of the northern tropics, as in the Andes to Bolivia (Fig. 167). Many of the species are rich in tannin.

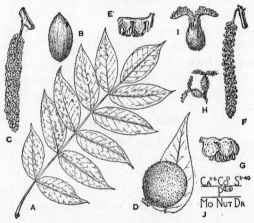

Fig. 167.—The walnut family, *Juglandaceae*. *A.* leaf of butternut, *Juglans cinerea; B*, nut of same; *C*, staminate catkin of same; *D*, single leaflet and nut of black walnut, *Juglans nigra; E*, single staminate flower of butternut; *F*, staminate catkin of black walnut; *G*, single staminate flower of black walnut; *H*, cluster of pistillate flowers of butternut; *I*, single pistillate flower of black walnut; *J*, floral formula for the family (*all after Mathews*).

Leaves alternate, pinnately compound; flowers monœcious, the male in pendulous, spike-like, many-flowered clusters or catkins, the female spikes few-flowered and erect; axis of male flowers three- to six-lobed, adnate to the bract; stamens many (3 to 40) inserted on the axis in two or more series, filaments short; female flowers sessile, axis cup-like, calyx three- to six-toothed or three- to six-lobed or 0; ovary inferior, two- to four-celled, but one-ovuled and finally one-celled, style short, with two plumose branches. ovule 1; fruit a drupe or nut, with dehiscent or indehiscent, fibrous husk, and stony endocarp, dividing in fruit into

2 to 4 (usually 2) compartments; seed solitary, without endosperm; cotyledons very oily, often much lobed and contorted.

The most valuable members of this family are the walnuts, *i.e.* species of *Juglans*, and the hickories, *i.e.* species of *Hicoria*. The American black walnut is *Juglans nigra*, the butternut or white walnut is *J. cinerea*, and the Persian walnut or the so-called English walnut is *J. regia*. The fine dark-colored wood of the black walnut and the lighter, mottled wood of Caucasus walnut (*J. regia*), known as "Circassian walnut," are among the most valuable economic woods in the world.

The hickories are also important timber-producing trees, their light-colored, heavy, and tough wood being very useful for special purposes. Hickory nuts of value are produced by *Hicoria ovata*, *H. laciniosa*, and especially by *H. pecan*, the pecan of commerce of which there are now many varieties including the famous "paper-shell" forms cultivated in the South. Large quantities of these nuts as well as of English walnuts are now produced by planted orchards in the South and on the Pacific Coast.

THE OAK FAMILY

The oaks, chestnuts, and the beeches are conspicuous members of the family *Fagaceae* (Fig. 168). They are trees or shrubs of temperate and tropical regions mostly of the northern hemisphere. Five or more genera and 600 species have been described, the oaks comprising about half the number of species included in the family.

Leaves alternate, evergreen or deciduous, simple, entire, lobed, or cleft; flowers unisexual, plants monœcious; the male flowers in erect capitate clusters or in catkins; sepals 4 to 6, rarely 7; stamens few to many, filaments free; female flower solitary or in few-flowered clusters, surrounded by or inclosed by an involucre, axis cup- or urn-shaped; sepals 4 to 6; ovary inferior, three- to six-celled, ovules 1 to 2 in each cell, but only 1 ripens; styles 3 to 6; fruit a one-seeded nut, free or more or less inclosed by the hardened cupular, bur-like, spiny, or tuberculate involucre; seed solitary; endosperm 0.

The oaks are among the world's most noble and valuable trees. Between 200 and 300 species of oaks, *Quercus*, have been described, but many of these are unimportant shrubs of waste places. Among the famous oaks are the English oak, *Quercus robur*, American live oak, *Q. virginiana*, white oak, *Q. alba*, red oak, *Q. borealis*, cork oak, *Q. suber*, of southern Europe and northern Africa, and the pin oak, *Q. palustris*.

The two famous beeches of the world are *Fagus sylvatica* of Europe, and *F. grandifolia* of North America.

The American chestnut is *Castanea dentata*, and the European or Eurasian chestnut is *C. sativa*.

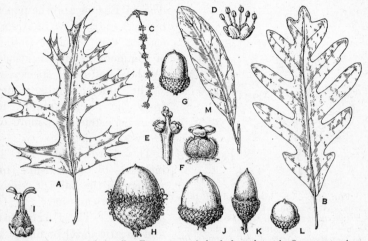

Fig. 168.—The oak family, *Fagaceae*. *A*, leaf of scarlet oak, *Quercus coccinea; B*, leaf of white oak, *Quercus alba; C*, staminate catkin of white oak; *D*, single flower of same; *E*, cluster of pistillate flowers of white oak; *F*, single flower of same; *G*, mature acorn of same species; *H*, acorn of bur oak, *Q. macrocarpa; I*, single pistillate flower of red oak, *Q. borealis; J*, acorn of red oak; *K*, acorn of southern live oak, *Q. virginiana; L*, acorn of willow oak, *Q. phellos; M*, leaf of live oak (*all after Mathews*).

THE BIRCH FAMILY

The birch family, *Betulaceae*, includes about 6 genera and 100 species of deciduous trees and shrubs that occur mainly in the cooler portions of the northern hemisphere (Fig. 169). A few species occur as far south as Bengal in Asia and from Mexico along the Andes to Argentine. They vary from low bushy shrubs to giant trees.

Leaves alternate, simple, penninerved, mostly serrate; flowers monœcious; male flowers small, numerous, borne in long, pendulous terminal or lateral catkins, often developing very early as in the preceding autumn; sepals 2 to 4 or 0; stamens 2, 4 or 10, free, filaments very short; female flowers in short, cylindric, cone-like spikes with imbricate, three-lobed bracts, sepals four-parted or 0; ovary inferior, compressed, two-celled, each cell with 1 ovule; style two-parted; fruiting spikes cylindric or ovoid, the

bracts usually falling away in birch but persistent in other genera
fruit a small, indehiscent one-celled, one-seeded nut, sometimes
included in a foliaceous involucre, or a samara, often membra-
nous-winged and crowned by the persistent styles; endosperm 0

There are many useful plants in this family. Several species
of birch are popular ornamentals, such as the white birch, *Betula
alba*, in Europe and the paper
birch *B. papyrifera* in America. A very valuable timber
of commerce is also furnished
by these and other species.

The alders, *Alnus*, differ
from the birches mainly in
their persistent and more or
less woody cones.

The hard-shelled nut is
inclosed by a leaf-like involucre in the hazel, *Corylus*
The American hazel is *C.
americana*. The European
and Asiatic hazel or filbert is
C. avellana, which is commonly cultivated for the nuts

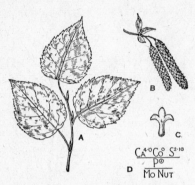

Fig. 169.—The birch family, *Betulaceae*. *A*, twig and leaves of paper birch,
Betula papyrifera; B, fruiting catkins of
same; *C*, single bract from the cones
(*after Mathews*); *D*, floral formula for
the family.

ORDER UMBELLALES, THE PARSLEY ORDER

This large group of woody to herbaceous plants with world-wide
distribution is characterized by the presence of small, actinomorphic usually perfect flowers arranged in umbels or heads. The
flowers are typically 4- to 5-lobed or parted, the stamens are
definite in number, and the ovary is inferior. The leaves are
often compound and they are frequently more or less finely dissected and provided with resin canals. The fruits are often very
resinous, and the seeds are supplied with abundant endosperm

THE GINSENG FAMILY

This family, the *Araliaceae*, includes about 60 genera and 700
species of trees, shrubs, and herbs of wide distribution in temperate and tropical lands, but they are much more abundant in
the tropics, the two chief centers being in tropical America and
the Indo-Malayan region (Fig. 170).

Leaves alternate, rarely opposite, simple or compound, pinnate
or digitate; flowers small, greenish or whitish, regular, perfect

polygamous or diœcious, racemose, capitate, or umbellate,
epigynous, bearing a greatly reduced calyx of 4 to 5 points or
teeth or none on the rim of the axis; petals usually 5, inserted
on the rim of the axis, free or united, or cohering and falling as a
group; stamens usually 5 or the same number as the petals, and
alternate with them and inserted on the rim of the axis; disk at
the top of the ovary; ovary inferior, one- to many-celled, ovules
1 in each cell; styles free or connate, as many as cells in the ovary;

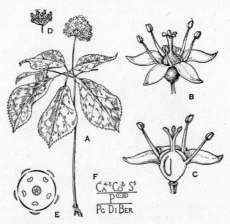

Fig. 170.—The ginseng family, *Araliaceae*. *A*, leaves and flower cluster of
ginseng, *Aralia* (*Mathews*); *B* and *C*, flowers of *Aralia* (*after Baillon*); *D*, cluster of
fruits of *Aralia; E*, floral diagram of *Aralia* (*after Le M. and Dec.*); *F*, floral
formula for the family.

fruit a berry or drupe, or sometimes dry; seeds with copious
endosperm.

This family includes a number of drug plants among which are
wild sarsaparilla, *Aralia nudicaulis*, American spikenard, *A.
racemosa*, and the ginseng, *Panax quinquefolium*.

The English ivy, *Hedera helix*, is an important ornamental that
belongs here. This plant is a wall climber with beautiful evergreen, lobed, shiny leaves, and it is very highly prized in moist
temperate climates. Other ornamentals of the family are the
showy Chinese Angelica, *Aralia chinensis*, and the spiny American Hercules club, *A. spinosa*.

THE DOGWOOD FAMILY

The cornels or dogwoods belong to the *Cornaceae*, a family of
trees and shrubs, or rarely perennial herbs, including 10 genera
and about 100 species with widely scattered distribution, but

most abundant in the temperate portions of the northern hemisphere (Fig. 171).

Leaves usually opposite, or rarely alternate, simple; flowers small, greenish or whitish, in terminal, capitate, or umbellate clusters, sometimes surrounded by a showy involucre, perfect or diœcious, epigynous, actinomorphic; calyx represented by 4 to 5 points or lobes on the rim of the receptacle or 0; corolla of 4 to 5 separate petals or 0, inserted on the rim of the axis along with the 4 to 5 alternate stamens, all attached at the base of a cushion-like disk at the top of the ovary; ovary inferior, one- to four-celled,

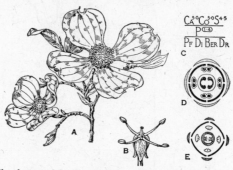

FIG. 171.—The dogwood family, *Cornaceae*. *A*, branch of flowering dogwood, *Cornus florida* with two clusters of flowers, each surrounded by the involucre of white bracts (*after Baillon*); *B*, single flower of *C. sanguinea* (*after Le M. and Dec.*); *C*, floral formula for the family; *D*, floral diagram for *Cornus* (*after Baillon*); *E*, another floral diagram for *Cornus* (*after Le M. and Dec.*)

often two-celled, ovules solitary, style simple or lobed; fruit a one- to four-celled berry or drupe; seeds with copious endosperm.

Several species of dogwood are planted for ornamental purposes, especially the American flowering dogwood, *Cornus florida*, famous on account of its flower clusters with four large white or pinkish bracts. Other species are popular because of the color of the twigs or leaves. The dwarf bunchberry of the northern woods is *C. canadensis*, and the red osier is *C. stolonifera*.

THE PARSLEY FAMILY

The parsley or carrot family, the *Umbelliferae*, is a clearly defined group of herbaceous or rarely somewhat woody plants of very wide distribution mainly throughout north temperate and subtropical regions, but largely absent from the tropics except in the mountains. The family includes about 250 genera and between 2,000 and 2,500 species, many of which are more or less oily and aromatic (Fig. 172).

Leaves alternate, mostly compound, sheathing at the base; flowers small, usually perfect, actinomorphic, epigynous, in simple or compound umbels, the latter often very showy; calyx of 5 sepals or teeth on the rim of the receptacle, or wanting; petals 5, on the rim of the receptacle, separate, falling early; stamens 5, alternate with the petals; ovary inferior, two-celled, ovules 1 in each cell, styles 2, thickened at the base; fruit dry, two-celled, dividing into 2 indehiscent mericarps, each one-seeded, and often winged or ridged, containing longitudinal oil canals to which the characteristic odor and flavor are due; seeds with abundant endosperm.

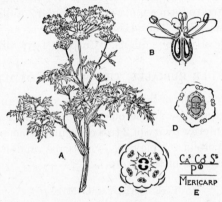

Fig. 172.—The parsley family, *Umbelliferae*. *A, Angelica (After Baillon); B*, sectional view of a flower of *Aethusa (after Le M. and Dec.); C*, floral diagram of carrot, *Daucus (after Baillon); D*, floral diagram of fennel, *Fœniculum (after Le M. and Dec.); E*, floral formula for the family.

Many economic plants of great value are included in this family. Garden celery is *Apium graveolens*, parsley is *Petroselinum hortense*, parsnip, *Pastinaca sativa*, carrot, *Daucus carota*, anise is *Pimpinella anisum*, and caraway, *Carum carvi*. The myrrh of the ancients was probably *Myrrhis odorata*. Certain species are poisonous, as is poison hemlock, *Conium maculatum*.

The members of this family can usually be recognized by the numerous small flowers closely grouped in conspicuous, simple or compound umbels. The flowers on the border of the umbels are sometimes larger than others, and these are sometimes sterile and more or less zygomorphic, a condition somewhat similar to that seen in many of the *Compositae*.

CHAPTER XX

THE MADDERS, BLUEBELLS, AND ASTERS

In this group of orders the axis of the flower is normally expanded to form a cup- or urn-shaped sheath which completely envelops and is united with the syncarpous ovary, which bears the perianth on its margin, *i.e.* the flower is epigynous. The petals are united to form a more or less tubular corolla, inserted at the top of the axis. The stamens are as many as the corolla lobes and mostly epipetalous. Carpels few, united; ovary inferior.

ORDER RUBIALES, THE MADDER ORDER

The families of this order include trees, shrubs, and herbs with opposite leaves and 4- to 5-merous, actinomorphic or zygomorphic flowers, with inferior ovary of 2 to 8 cells, inconspicuous calyx and sympetalous corolla. Epigyny, sympetaly, and epipetaly are noteworthy features of the group.

THE MADDER FAMILY

The madders are included in the large and distinctive family *Rubiaceae* (Fig. 173). They are mostly trees and shrubs, or rarely herbs and climbers of wide distribution in the tropics, but also with numerous extensions into the temperate and frigid zones. There are about 350 genera and 4,500 species described for the family.

Leaves opposite or verticillate, simple, entire or rarely more or less toothed, stipules sometimes leaf-like and scarcely distinguished from the true leaves; flowers mostly perfect, actinomorphic, rarely zygomorphic, solitary or in capitate clusters; ovary inferior, bearing on the rim of the receptacle 2 to 6 sepals, or sepals 0; corolla tubular, 4- to 5-lobed, on the axis inside the rim; stamens as many as the corolla lobes and alternate with them, inserted on the corolla tube; carpels one to eight, mostly 2, united, inferior, ovules one to many in each cell, style 1, slender, often lobed; fruit a capsule, berry, or drupe; endosperm abundant or 0.

270

The family includes many economic plants of first rank, among which are the following: coffee, *Coffea arabica*, an evergreen shrub or low tree of tropical Africa and Asia, and widely cultivated; the quinine plant, *Cinchona officinalis*, of the Andes, and widely grown in India, Java, Jamaica, Australia, etc.; Ipecacuanha, *Psychotria ipecacuanha*, of tropical South America; and many others that are grown for ornamental purposes. The cape jasmine is *Gardenia jasminoides*.

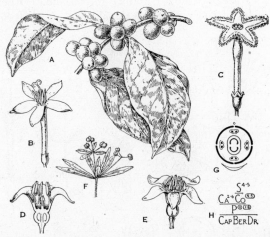

Fig. 173.—The coffee family, *Rubiaceae*. *A*, leaves and fruits of coffee, *Coffea arabica*; *B*, single flower of *Coffea*; *C*, flower of cinchona, *Cinchona*; *D*, vertical section of flower of madder, *Rubia*; *E*, flower of *Rubia*; *F*. leaves and fruits of *Galium*; *G*, floral diagram of *Rubia* (*all after Baillon*); *H*, floral formula for the family.

THE HONEYSUCKLE FAMILY

The honeysuckles constitute the natural family *Caprifoliaceae*, a group of shrubs and vines with rather soft wood, many of them evergreen, with wide distribution mainly in the north temperate zone and in the mountains of the tropics (Fig. 174). The family includes 11 genera and about 350 species.

Leaves opposite, simple or pinnately divided; flowers perfect, actinomorphic, but commonly zygomorphic; calyx of 4 to 5 teeth or lobes on the rim of the receptacle; corolla sympetalous; four- to five-lobed, tubular, or rotate, sometimes bilabiate; stamens as many as the lobes of the corolla and inserted on the tube alternate with the lobes; ovary inferior, two- to five-celled, with 1 or more ovules in each cell, style 1, terminal, slender or

0, stigmas 2 to 5; fruit a berry or rarely a capsule; seeds with bony testa; endosperm abundant, fleshy.

The honeysuckles are mostly familiar in the many bushy shrubs or low trees and vines that are popular ornamentals. The genus *Lonicera* includes 175 species of the northern hemisphere, many of which are widely cultivated outside their natural range.   The more common climbing ones are *L. sempervirens*, *L. japonica*, and *L. periclymenum*.   Among the popular bush-honeysuckles are *L. tatarica* and *L. involucrata*.   Other prominent members of the family are the elders, species of *Sambucus*,

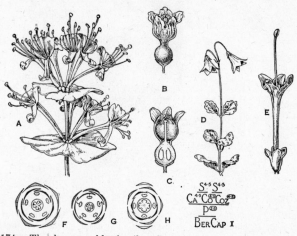

Fig. 174.—The honeysuckle family, *Caprifoliaceae*. *A*, flowering twig of honeysuckle, *Lonicera (after Le M. and Dec.)*; *B* and *C*, flowers of buckbrush, *Symphoricarpos (after Baillon)*; *D*, leaves and flowers of twin flower, *Linnœa (after Baillon)*; *E*, flower of buttonbush, *Cephalanthus (Rubiaceae)*; *F* and *G*, floral diagrams of honeysuckle, *Lonicera (after Le M. and Dec.)*; *H*, floral diagram of buckbrush, *Symphoricarpos (after Baillon)*; *I*, floral formula for the family showing both actinomorphic and zygomorphic types.

the black haw, and the highbush cranberry and their kin, *Viburnum* spp. the snowberry, *Symphoricarpos*, and twin flower, *Linnaea borealis*, named after the great Linnaeus.

THE VALERIAN FAMILY

The members of the *Valerianaceae* are perennial or annual herbs (rarely shrubs) of the northern hemisphere, often with unpleasantly odorous underground parts.   There have been 10 genera and about 350 species included in the group.

Leaves opposite or all basal, often divided; flowers small, perfect or polygamo-diœcious, in conspicuous cymose or capitate clusters, actinomorphic, but often somewhat zygomorphic, epigynous; calyx reduced to a ring at the top of the inferior ovary, becoming enlarged and its parts or lobes more or less plumose in fruit; corolla sympetalous, tubular, the tube often five-lobed or cleft, somewhat irregular, often saccate or spurred at the base; stamens 1 to 3 or 4, inserted on the corolla tube and alternate with its lobes; ovary inferior, one- to three-celled, 2 of the cells abortive, ovule 1, style slender, simple; fruit dry and indehiscent, an achene, sometimes crowned by the beautifully radiate calyx (pappus) with its many plumose segments or by a crown of bristles or hooks; seeds with scanty or 0 endosperm.

Spikenard, a famous drug of the Ancients was secured from the young shoots of *Nardostachyos jatamansi*, a Himalayan plant. The rhizomes of certain species of *Valeriana*, especially *V. officinalis*, furnish a penetrating oil of value in medicine. Certain others, as *Valerianella olitoria*, are grown in the vegetable garden and are used as salad plants.

THE TEASEL FAMILY

The teasels, *Dipsacaceae*, are perennial or annual herbs of the Old World, but with almost world-wide introduction. Their natural home appears to be in the eastern Mediterranean region. The family includes 9 genera and 150 species.

Leaves opposite or verticillate, entire, toothed or deeply cleft, often very rough; flowers small, perfect, zygomorphic, epigynous, in dense, bracted, involucrate heads; calyx poorly developed, cup-like or divided into bristly segments (pappus) on the rim of the receptacle, each flower more or less enveloped by an "epicalyx" formed by the surrounding bracts; corolla tubular or funnel-form, four- to five-lobed, inserted near the center of the axis; stamens usually 4 or 2 to 3, alternate with the corolla lobes, at the base of the tube, filaments free or united in pairs; ovary inferior, one-celled, ovule 1, style filiform, stigma simple or bifid; fruit an achene, one-seeded, inclosed by the epicalyx and often crowned by the persistent, bristly or spiny calyx or pappus.

Teasels are grown for commercial or ornamental purposes. The fruiting heads of Fuller's teasel, *Dipsacus fullonum*, are used in raising the nap on woolen cloth. The pincushion flower or mourning bride is some species of *Scabiosa*, sweet scabious being *S. atropurpurea*, a popular, coarse ornamental of southern Europe.

This group is of peculiar interest, along with the *Valerianaceae*, on account of the many resemblances to the *Compositae* which they exhibit.

ORDER CAMPANULALES, THE BLUEBELL ORDER

These plants are herbaceous to somewhat woody, and the flowers are usually perfect, actinomorphic or zygomorphic, epigynous, sympetalous. The stamens are free or connate by their anthers and often forming a tube in which the pollen collects, later to be swept out as the brush-like style pushes up through the tube. Ovary one- to several-celled, commonly three-celled, ovules numerous. Inflorescence racemose, or more or less capitate.

THE BELLFLOWER FAMILY

This family, the *Campanulaceae*, is also sometimes known as the bluebell family (Fig. 175). It includes about 50 genera and

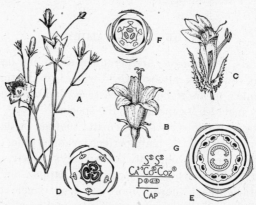

Fig. 175.—The bluebell family, *Campanulaceae*. *A*, flowering stems of bluebell, *Campanula rotundifolia (after Le M. and Dec.)*; *B*, single flower of *Campanula (after Baillon)*; *C*, single flower of *Lobelia (after Baillon)*; *D*, floral diagram of *Campanula (after Le M. and Dec.)*; *E*, floral diagram of lobelia, *Lobelia (after Baillon)*; *F*, floral diagram of *Campanula (after Baillon)*; *G*, floral formula for the family showing both the actinomorphic type (*Campanula*) and the zygomorphic type (*Lobelia*).

1,000 to 1,500 species of annual or perennial herbs (rarely woody) often with milky juice. They are cosmopolitan in range and are very common in temperate and subtropical regions, often extending into cold climates in the north and in high mountains.

Leaves usually alternate, rarely opposite, simple, rarely lobed or divided; flowers perfect, actinomorphic or zygomorphic, often large and very showy, solitary, spicate, racemose or paniculate, epigynous; calyx of 3 to 10, commonly 5, sepals inserted on the rim of the axis, usually persistent on the fruit; corolla sympetalous, tubular or campanulate, five-lobed or five-divided, often blue; stamens 5, inserted near the base of the corolla tube or on the axis, filaments dilated, free or united, anthers sometimes more or less connate, forming a pollen chamber (in *Lobelia*); ovary two to five-celled, often three-celled, rarely one-celled, ovules numerous, style simple, stigmas 2 to 5, often 3, with pollen-sweeping brushes; fruit a capsule, seeds numerous; endosperm fleshy.

This family includes many beautiful wild flowers and choice cultivated ornamentals. The bluebell or harebell is *Campanula rotundifolia*, and Canterbury bells is *C. media*. Another choice plant of the garden is the balloon flower, *Platycodon grandiflorum*, prized for its very large blue or white bell-shaped flowers. The lobelias are also sometimes included in this family. The cardinal flower, *Lobelia cardinalis*, is a well-known member of this group.

ORDER ASTERALES, THE ASTER ORDER

This group, commonly known as the Composites, is the largest order of the vegetable kingdom (Figs. 176 to 180). Various

Fig. 176.—The composite family, *Compositae*. Flowering habit and heads of typical composite, an aster, *Aster novi-belgii* (*after Mathews*).

authors estimate the number of genera included from 800 to 1,000, and the number of species from 15,000 to 23,000. They are very widely distributed in all parts of the world and under very diverse habitat conditions.

The Composites may usually be recognized by the presence of few to many small flowers arranged in dense involucrate heads (Figs. 176, 178 and 179). The individual flower (Fig. 177) is actinomorphic or zygomorphic, epigynous, perfect, unisexual or sterile; calyx reduced to a pappus (Fig. 177) on the rim of the receptacle or 0; corolla sympetalous, tubular, inserted on the receptacle inside the calyx ring; stamens epipetalous, usually with connate anthers; carpels 2, united, ovary inferior, one-celled; fruit an achene.

The Composites are regarded as the highest flowering plants on account of their noteworthy and obvious success in nature as indicated by their great preponderance and cosmopolitan range. This success is probably largely explained on the basis of the perfection reached in the development of the densely aggregated inflorescence containing numerous small flowers so closely grouped as to serve almost as a single flower in the matter of pollination. Dozens of flowers may thus be pollinated by a single visit of the proper insect, whereas a similar visit to the flowers of many other plants would result in the pollination of a single flower. Pollen mechanisms, pollen protection, and nectar placements, etc. are so perfectly worked out that cross-pollination by highly specialized insects becomes an unusually prominent feature of the group.

This group has been included as a family of the order *Campanulales*, but it is generally so readily distinguished from those plants that we prefer to give it somewhat more distinctive treatment. The common classification divides the family thus set apart into 12 to 14 subfamilies or tribes. In his last treatment Bessey divided this order, which he called *Asterales*, into fourteen families, these being the approximate equivalents of the usual tribes or subfamilies. We shall include a somewhat more detailed description under the following family and will then point out some of the more striking and distinctive features of a few of the tribes.

THE COMPOSITE FAMILY

This vast cosmopolitan family, the *Compositae*, includes about 1,000 genera and 15,000 to 23,000 species mostly of annual and perennial herbs, with a few shrubs or low trees (Figs. 176 to 180). It is reported that the single genus *Senecio* includes more than 2,000 species. Nearly every conceivable habit and form of body known for plants is seen among the species of this family in some portion of its world-wide range. They abound under desert conditions and a few of them are true aquatics, and every habitat gradation between these extremes is likely to reveal the presence of species of Composites. They are found in abundance in tropical lands and in cold Arctic-alpine areas.

Leaves generally alternate, but often opposite or whorled, extremely varied, frequently crowded in basal rosettes; flowers (florets) small, in few- to many-flowered heads, closely grouped on a common disk-like, dome-shaped, conical or cylindrical axis which is surrounded by an involucre composed of few to many, more or less leafy or scaly, bracts (Figs. 176 to 180), thus producing a flower cluster resembling a single flower in which the involucre is the calyx and the massed flowers the corolla, a structure which, popularly, commonly passes as a single flower; each flower (Fig. 177) on this disk may be accompanied by a scale-like

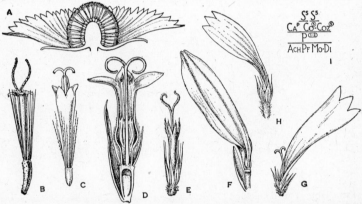

Fig. 177.—*A*, vertical section through the inflorescence (head) in the *Compositae*, as in *Helenium* showing receptacle, involucre, ray flowers, and disk flowers (*after Baillon*); *B*, single, perfect flower of *Eupatorium* (*after Le M. and Dec.*); *C*, same of groundsel, *Senecio* (*after Le M. and Dec.*); *D*, sectional view of a disk flower of sunflower, *Helianthus* (*after Baillon*); *E*, disk flower of *Gaillardia* (*after Baillon*); *F*, ray flower of sunflower, *Helianthus* (*after Baillon*); *G*, ray flower of *Helenium* (*after Baillon*); *H*, ray flower of *Gaillardia* (*after Baillon*); *I*, floral formula for the family, including actionmorphic and zygomorphic forms.

or bristly structure which probably is to be regarded as the floral bract, in which case the receptacle is said to be "scaly," "chaffy," "bristly," etc., or such structure may be lacking, and then the receptacle is "naked." The head thus constituted is represented in the family by three different types: in one form there is a fringe of several to many radiating, zygomorphic (ligulate) flowers (Fig. 177, *A*, *F*, and *G*) on the margin of the common receptacle just inside the involucral bracts, and the rest of the flowers covering the axis (disk flowers) are actinomorphic

(Fig. 177, *B, C, D,* and *E*), the outer flowers being called "ray flowers" and the inner flowers the "disk flowers"; in another type of head, all of the flowers are zygomorphic (ligulate) and there is no true distinction, therefore, between ray flowers and disk flowers; in the third type of head all of the flowers are actino-morphic; the ray flowers are either female or sterile; the disk flowers are usually perfect, sometimes unisexual, rarely diœcious; calyx reduced to a low ring, or crown, or a fringe of scaly, bris-tly, or hairy appendages on the rim of the floral axis which often persist on the ripe fruit; corolla sympetalous, five-lobed or five-divided, actinomorphic (in disk flowers) or zygomorphic, bilabiate or ligulate (in ray flowers); stamens 5, inserted on the corolla tube (Fig. 177, *D)* filaments separate, anthers usually united

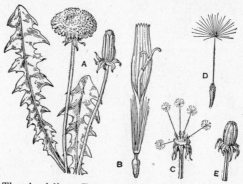

Fig. 178.—The dandelion, *Taraxacum taraxacum. A,* leaves, old, closed head, and open head; *B,* single flower; *C,* receptacle with a few fruits; *D,* single fruit with pappus; *E,* young head (*after Le M. and Dec.*).

to form a tube; ovary inferior (Fig. 177), of 2 carpels, but one-celled, style slender, mostly two-lobed or two-parted in the perfect flowers, style branches provided with various types of pollen-collecting hairs or brushes; fruit a one-seeded achene of great variety of form, bearing the persistent calyx as a crown or tuft of pappus scales, bristles, or hairs of extreme diversity of form and development (Figs. 177, 178, 179) which often aid greatly in the dissemination of the species; endosperm 0.

The family includes many useful species and varieties that are of value as ornamentals, and others contribute foods. To men-tion the *Chrysanthemum, Dahlia, Zinnia, Aster, Calendula, Cen-taurea,* is to indicate their value as cultivated ornamentals. There are also many troublesome and pernicious weeds in this family; among which are dandelion, *Taraxacum taraxacum* (Fig. 178),

Canada thistle, *Cirsium arvense;* burdock, *Arctium lappa;* sunflowers, *Helianthus* spp.; and the hay-fever weeds, such as *Ambrosia* spp. (Fig. 180).

The *Compositae* are usually divided into a number (12 to 14) of subfamilies or tribes. The following artificial key will serve to indicate some of the more common differences and similarities that are useful in the classification of the members of the group and in the differentiation of the various tribes. An English name is suggested for each tribe.

KEY TO THE TRIBES OF COMPOSITES

A. Pappus generally of two or more scales or rigid awns, not hairy or capillary; coarse herbs or shrubs, rarely trees
  1. Receptacle with chaffy scales or bracts
    a. Heads with many complete flowers, including marginal ray flowers.........................*Heliantheae*, the sunflowers
    b. Heads with few reduced flowers, sometimes diclinous...........
                            Ambrosieae, the ragweeds
  2. Receptacle naked, *i.e.* without scales or chaff, or rarely with them
    a. Anthers without appendages
      (1) Involucral bracts usually in two series, slightly imbricated....
                        Helenieae, the heleniums
      (2) Involucral bracts usually in several series, well imbricated...
                        Arctotideae, the gazanias
    b. Anthers with basal appendages or mucronate at the tip........
                        Calenduleae, the marigolds
B. Pappus mostly capillary; plants usually coarse
  1. Involucral bracts in more than one series, more or less imbricated
    a. Involucral bracts in several series, imbricated; receptacle usually bristly; flowers all tubular.................*Cynareae*, the thistles
    b. Involucral bracts slightly imbricated; receptacle usually naked
      (1) Flowers all bilabiate; juice watery..*Mutisieae*, the mutisias
      (2) Flowers all ligulate; juice milky.....*Cichorieae*, the chicories
  2. Involucral bracts usually in a single series, valvate, or with an additional short, outer series; with or without rays..............
                        Senecioneae, the ragworts
C. Pappus from short bracteose to capillary or none; receptacle usually naked; plants typically low to medium sized
  1. Heads usually with ray flowers; pappus capillary..*Astereae*, the asters
  2. Heads usually without ray flowers
    a. Involucral bracts green, imbricated in two to many series
      (1) Pappus plumose, or heads spicate..*Eupatorieae*, the bonesets
      (2) Pappus never plumose nor heads spicate...................
                        Vernonieae, the ironweeds
    b. Involucral bracts scarious, little, or not at all imbricated; pappus capillary.............................*Inuleae*, the everlastings
D. Pappus a short crown, or none; involucral bracts dry, imbricated; heads often with white ray flowers.........*Anthemideae*, the chrysanthemums

The *Heliantheae* or sunflower tribe, include the common sun-flowers which belong to the genus *Helianthus*, as well as many other genera and species some of which are prized ornamentals and others are worthless weeds.   Coneflowers, *Rudbeckia;* zinnias, *Zinnia;* cosmos, *Cosmos;* dahlias, *Dahlia;* tickseeds, *Coreopsis,* are additional prominent members of this tribe.   The group is largely American in its natural distribution.

The *Ambrosieae* or ragweed tribe, are sometimes regarded as a subdivision of the *Heliantheae* and as a separate family (Fig. 180).

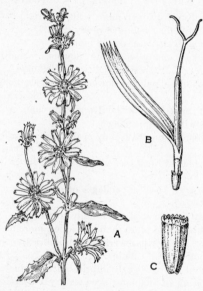

Fig. 179.—The chicory, *Cichorium intybus*. *A*, upper part of plant with open heads below, and young, unopened heads above; *B*, single flower; *C*, ripe achene (*after Mathews*).

The tribe as here treated includes the ragweeds or the species of *Ambrosia*, especially *A. artemisiaefolia*, *A. trifida*, etc., well-known hay-fever plants.   The troublesome cockleburs, species of *Xanthium*, also occur here, as do white weeds, *Gaertneria*.

The *Helenieae* or the heleniums often look like sunflowers. They are mostly plants of Mexico and western United States.   The gaillardias, species of *Gaillardia*, are often seen in cultivation.

The *Arctotideae*, the arctotis or gazania tribe, are a small group, largely confined to Africa.

The members of the *Calenduleae*, or marigold tribe, are also mostly African in their natural distribution, but the common African marigold, *Calendula officinalis* (Fig. 18) is widely cultivated as a very popular potplant. The large, bright yellow or orange heads of this plant are often used for table decoration during the winter months in the northern hemisphere.

Most plants called "thistles" are included in the *Cynareae*. The main center of distribution of these plants is the Mediterranean region. An old-fashioned garden flower within this tribe is the bluebottle or cornflower, *Centaurea cyanus*. About 500 species of *Centaurea* have been recognized. The globe artichoke is the unopened heads of *Cynara scolymus*, with its thick, imbricated involucral bracts. Many worthless weeds such as burdock, *Arctium lappa*, and Canada thistle, *Cirsium arvense*, also belong here.

The *Mutisieae* include a small number of African and Asiatic species of herbs and South American woody climbers that are interesting because of their *bilabiate* flowers.

The *Cichorieae*, often called the lettuce or chicory tribe, are sometimes regarded as a separate family. The heads composed solely of strap-shaped or ligulate flowers (Fig. 179) and the frequently present milky juice make these plants readily recognized. They are very widely distributed, but they are especially numerous in the Old World. Chicory is *Cichorium intybus*, and endive is *C. endivia*, the former cultivated for its root from which a coffee substitute or adulterant is prepared, the latter grown as a salad plant. Vegetable oyster, or salsify is *Tragopogon porrifolius*, and the cultivated varieties of lettuce, of which there are more than 100, have been derived from some species of *Lactuca*. The dandelions (Fig. 178) also belong in this tribe. These are species of *Taraxacum*, of which there are five or six common ones and nearly 100 have been described.

The *Senecioneae*, the ragworts or groundsels, are recognized by the fact that the involucre is usually made up of a single row of valvate bracts which are often more or less united below into a cup. They are widely distributed. There are more than 2,300 species of *Senecio* known, among them being *S. cruentus*, a native of the Canary Islands, from which the *Cinerarias* of the florists have been derived. There are many types of this plant in cultivation, and they are generally marked by the bright, purplish-red ray flowers, as well as various shades of pink and blue.

The *Astereae* or aster tribe, are also a large tribe of wide distribution but they are more numerous in the New World. This group includes the English daisy *Bellis perennis*, as well as the large genus *Aster*, of which there are more than 200 species of wide distribution especially in North America. There are many cultivated species and varieties of *Aster* including New England aster *A. novae-angliae*, New York aster, *A. novi-belgii* (Fig. 176) etc. The large heads of flowers develop a great many colors and shades to which their popularity is due. The goldenrods, species of *Solidago*, also belong to this tribe.

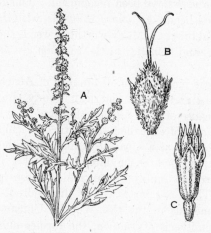

Fig. 180.—The ragweed, *Ambrosia* sp. *A*, leaves and flowering shoots; *B*, single pistillate flower; *C*, single staminate flower (*after Baillon*).

The members of the *Eupatorieae* or boneset tribe, are rayless composites of general distribution in the Western Hemisphere. Certain species are cultivated under glass and out of doors as border plants, especially species of *Ageratum*, such as *A. houstonianum*. The Joe Pye weed is *Eupatorium purpureum*, and the white snakeroot is *E. urticaefolium*, both being ornamental species of the United States.

The ironweeds, Tribe *Vernonieae*, are common to America, Africa, Asia, and Australia. Many species of *Vernonia* are known from various centers. Stokes' aster, *Stokesia laevis*, is sometimes seen in cultivation, but the most of the species of the tribe are worthless weeds.

The *Inuleae* or the everlastings, are often woolly, or dry and more or less scaly plants, or plants with papery flowers and bracts. The edelweiss of Switzerland is *Leontopodium alpinum*, a plant covered with white wool, and with large heads in which the bracts are petal-like and pure white. Certain species of *Gnaphalium* are of the same general nature. Strawflowers are usually species of *Helichrysum*, especially *H. bracteatum*, in which the dry, involucral bracts are developed in many series and are of many shades of red, yellow, orange, or white. This plant is a native of Australia. The Rose of Jericho, *Odontospermum pygmaeum*, also belongs here, as does the "vegetable sheep," *Raoulia*, which forms cushion-like growths in the mountains of New Zealand.

The *Anthemideae*, or chrysanthemum, tribe include many species with highly scented or aromatic leaves and flowers. The numerous species and varieties of *Chrysanthemum* are perhaps the best known types of the tribe. Many of the species are known under quite different names; for instance, the common pyrethrum is *Chrysanthemum coccineum*, the marguerite is *C. frutescens*, and Sweet Mary is *C. balsamita*. The sources of many of the cultivated varieties of *Chrysanthemum* are *C. indicum* and *C. sinense*, native to China and Japan. The common tansy is *Tanacetum vulgare*, and yarrow or milfoil is *Achillea ptarmica*, or *A. millefolium*. The sagebrush is one of several species of *Artemisia*, certain species of which, such as *A. tridentata* and *A. frigida*, have very wide distribution in North America.

CHAPTER XXI

SELECTED ORDERS AND FAMILIES
OF MONOCOTYLEDONS

The Monocotyledons are now regarded as having been derived from ancestors resembling the primitive Dicotyledons at a comparatively early period during the evolution of the flowering plants. It seems probable that their point of divergence from the more primitive dicotyledonous stock was from ancestors that were more or less similar to the Ranalian types of today, possibly from the same general group of primitive flowering plants which gave rise to the Ranalian plexus from which the modern Dicotyledons have also developed.

The Monocotyledon Series.—It will be recalled that our treatment of the Dicotyledons reflects the opinion that the group includes two principal series. Both of these two series have their origin in the Ranalian complex (Fig. 96), and the one terminates in the mints, *Lamiales*, and snapdragons, *Scrophulariales*, and the other ends in the Composites, *Asterales*. The Monocotyledons constitute a third main line of development that originated from about the same ancestral forms and this series terminates in the orchids, *Orchidales* (Fig. 96). Each of these three main branches of the modern flowering-plant stock has given rise to several lateral branches, as has already been indicated for the Dicotyledons.

Vegetative Nature of Monocotyledons.—The stems of Monocotyledons are typically characterized by the presence of fibro-vascular bundles scattered throughout (Fig. 181) the more or less cylindrical mass of ground tissue so completely that there is usually no clear or striking distinction into pith, vascular cylinder, and cortex, as in Dicotyledons. Monocotyledons also lack the annual layers of growth (annual rings), and sharp demarcation of pith, wood, and bark that are so characteristic of most woody Dicotyledons. These features are especially contrasted as one examines transverse sections of the stems of the two types.

Growth and Length of Life.—Monocotyledons are annual or perennial, but the stems of the perennials reach their diameter maximum rather early, after which the growth is mostly terminal. This type of growth of the stem is described as "endogenous," in contrast to that of Dicotyledons which is described as "exogenous." The erect stems of perennial, woody Monocotyledons (palms) are not so freely branched as are such stems in Dicotyledons.   Many perennial Monocotyledons die back to the surface of the ground each fall, and the new growth of erect stem in each succeeding year is produced from the crown or from underground stems or rhizomes, bulbs, corms, or tubers which are very commonly produced by these plants. The species of this group are largely herbaceous in nature, but conspicuously woody and tree-like forms are developed among the palms, bamboos, and others.

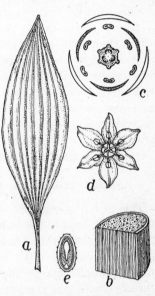

The Embryo and Seed.—The embryo of the Monocotyledon produces but a single primary leaf or cotyledon and this is often so greatly modified as to lose all resemblance to the cotyledons of the Dicotyledons. The cotyledon in many cases is an organ of digestion and assimilation and it is often permanently retained by the seed during germination. The

Fig. 181.—The general morphology and anatomy of Monocotyledons. *A*, leaf; *B*, section of the stem; *C*, floral diagram; *D*, front view of the flower; *E*, section of seed (*after Gager, General Botany*, published by P. Blakiston's Son & Co.).

secondary and mature leaves are commonly alternate, simple, parallel veined, and are often attached to the stem by a sheathing base, and without clear distinction of petiole and blade (Fig. 181).

The Flowers of Monocotyledons.—The flower parts of Monocotyledons are typically in groups of three (*trimerous*) or multiples of three, *i.e.* there are often three sepals, three petals, three or six stamens, and three pistils or carpels (Fig. 181). The flowers in certain groups are variously incomplete or imperfect.

The orders of Monocotyledons may be arranged in two main groups or subclasses, the *Hypogynae* and the *Epigynae*. The former includes the lower orders and families in which the flowers are commonly hypogynous, the latter includes the higher orders and families in which the flowers are epigynous.

HYPOGYNOUS MONOCOTYLEDONS

This subclass includes the more primitive orders and families of Monocotyledons, as is clearly indicated by the similarities which they show to the *Ranales*. The axis of the flower is more or less cone-shaped, spheroidal, or flattened, and this bears the hypogynous perianth and stamens, and the many or few, separate or united, superior carpels. A certain degree of sympetaly is seen in some forms, and the stamens are inserted on the perianth in certain species. The flowers in this series are usually actinomorphic, but there is a slight tendency towards zygomorphy also seen in some families.

ORDER ALISMALES, THE WATER PLANTAIN ORDER

This group is regarded as the one that stands closest of all Monocotyledons to the point from which they diverged from the Dicotyledons, in other words these are the *lowest* Monocotyledons. The floral pattern often bears a striking resemblance to that in the *Ranales* except for the number of perianth segments. Carpels one to many, separate, superior; perianth conspicuous, or lacking. Plants largely aquatic, or paludose herbs.

THE WATER PLANTAIN FAMILY

The *Alismaceae*, the water plantains (Fig. 182) or arrowheads, include perennial aquatic or marsh herbs with scapose stems and long-petioled, basal leaves and more or less showy flowers. The family includes about 14 genera and 60 species of very wide distribution in fresh-water habitats in temperate and warm climates.

Leaves simple, mostly basal, sheathing, often more or less sagittate; petioles long, very variable in outline; flowers actinomorphic, perfect, monœcious or diœcious, in racemose or paniculate clusters; receptacle flat, convex or more or less cone-shaped; sepals 3, free, commonly persistent; petals 3, separate, often white, deciduous; stamens six to many, more or less spirally arranged, free, hypogynous; carpels six to many, separate, usually with a single ovule in each carpel; fruit commonly a head of many achenes; seeds without endosperm.

Conspicuous plants of this family are the Old World water plantain, *Alisma plantago-aquatica* and the American, *Alisma subcordatum*, often seen in shallow water and marshy places. The arrowheads belong to the genus *Sagittaria*, of which there are many species of wide distribution and diverse form.

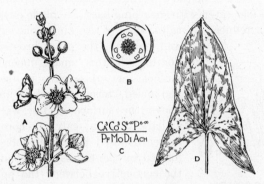

Fig. 182.—The water plantain family, *Alismaceae*. *A*, flowering stem of arrowhead, *Sagittaria* (*after Le M. and Dec.*); *B*, floral diagram of water plantain, *Alisma* (*after Le M. and Dec.*); *C*, floral formula for the family; *D*, a leaf of arrowhead, *Sagittaria*.

THE ARROWGRASS FAMILY

This is the *Scheuchzeriaceae*, named after two brothers by the name of Scheuchzer, Swiss botanists of the latter part of the seventeenth century. These are marsh herbs with rush-like leaves, often growing in standing saline water or fresh-water bogs. There are 4 genera and about 12 species in the family, of wide distribution in temperate and subarctic regions.

Leaves mostly basal, rush-like, broadly sheathing at the base; flowers small, perfect, actinomorphic, hypogynous, in naked terminal spikes or in few-flowered, loose racemes; petals 3; sepals 3, colored alike but distinct in position; stamens 3 to 6, free, commonly 6 in 2 whorls, filaments commonly very short; carpels 3 to 6, separate or more or less united, separating when mature, ovules 1 to 2 in each carpel; fruit follicle-like, one- to two-seeded, dehiscent, the separate carpels more or less coriaceous and cylindrical; seeds without endosperm.

THE PONDWEED FAMILY

The *Zannichelliaceae* or pondweeds, include perennial, aquatic herbs of saline or fresh water, many species of which are submerged (Fig. 183). The family includes 5 to 9 genera and about 75 species of very wide distribution, in fresh-water rivers, ponds, lakes and in brackish water along the seacoast and in the interior. The main stem is usually a branching rhizome that spreads through the mud, rooting at the nodes.

Leaves alternate or the uppermost sometimes opposite, sessile or with petiole, often with sheathing base, the blade expanded or capillary or reduced to scales, often of two kinds, one submerged

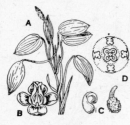

$$Ca^0 Co^0 S^{1\cdot4} P^{1\cdot4}$$
E   Aq Nut Dr

Fig. 183.—The pondweed family, *Zannichelliaceae. A*, habit sketch of pondweed, *Potamogeton natans; B*, a single flower; *C*, fruit at the right, embryo at left; *D*, floral diagram (*all after Rendle*); *E*, floral formula for the family.

and reduced, the other broadened and floating; flowers small, inconspicuous, perfect or unisexual, in sessile or peduncled, terminal spikes, projecting above the surface of the water or in axillary clusters; calyx 0, corolla 0, or flower inclosed by a four-lobed sheath formed by the excessive development of the connective between the pollen sacs of the anthers; stamens 1 to 4; carpels 1 to 4, separate, each with 1 ovule; fruit mostly nut-like or drupe-like; seeds 1 in each carpel; endosperm 0.

These curious and varied plants are often very conspicuous in the submerged gardens of shallow water. Some of them frequently develop massive beds of tangled stems and leaves under such conditions. The principal genus of the family is *Potamogeton*, of which more than fifty species have been described.

THE BUR REED FAMILY

The members of the *Sparganiaceae* are reed-like plants with globular clusters of dry, more or less spiny and bur-like fruits (Fig. 184). They are aquatic or marsh herbs with perennial rhizomes and fibrous roots. The family is represented by a single genus and 30 to 40 species mostly of the temperate and cold regions of the Northern Hemisphere.

Leaves alternate, linear, flat, more or less grass-like, sheathing at the base; flowers unisexual, crowded in globose heads at the nodes of the upper zigzag parts of the stem and branches, the lower heads being pistillate and the upper heads staminate; perianth 0 or composed of a few chaffy scales; stamens several, usually 5, free or connate at the base; female flowers with membranous bracts, ovary sessile or pedicellate, one- or two-celled, ovule 1, style filiform, simple or forked; fruit one-celled, one-seeded, nut-like or drupaceous.

These plants are usually recognized among other marsh plants by the conspicuous bur-like globular heads of fruits arranged in a more or less zigzag series.

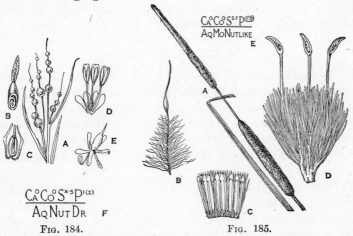

FIG. 184.   FIG. 185.

FIG. 184.—The bur reed family, *Sparganiaceae.* *A*, habit sketch of bur reed, *Sparganium; B*, a single carpel cut open; *C*, fruit and seed; *D*, male flower of *Sparganium; E*, female flower (*all after Rendle*); *F*, floral formula for the family.

FIG. 185.—The cattail family, *Typhaceae.* *A*, leaf and clusters of female flowers (below) and male flowers (above) of cattail, *Typha*, greatly reduced; *B*, fruit; *C*, male flowers; *D*, cluster of female flowers greatly enlarged (*all after Baillon*); *E*, floral formula for the family.

THE CATTAIL FAMILY

This is the *Typhaceae*, a family with a single genus of 10 or more species of aquatic or paludose, perennial herbs with creeping rhizomes, fibrous roots, and smooth, erect, cylindrical stems (Fig. 185). They are widely distributed in temperate and tropical regions. They often grow in very dense communities.

Leaves long, linear, flat, sword-like, distichous, sheathing at the base; flowers small, unisexual, densely crowded in long terminal spikes, the flowering shoot being a stiffly erect, cylindrical shoot from the rhizome; staminate flowers subtended by fugacious bracts covering the upper portion of the spike; pistillate flowers densely grouped in the lower portion of the spike, also subtended by a leafy bract that falls early; perianth composed of numerous bristles; stamens usually 3 (or more, 1 to 7), united at the base to a common filament; ovary stipitate, hairy, one- to two-celled, styles 1 or 2; both types of flowers accompanied by numerous bristly hairs which aid in dissemination; the pistillate flowers mingled with numerous sterile flowers with clavate tips; fruit dry, nut-like; seed 1; endosperm abundant. The cylindrical cluster of brown, closely packed structures in the fruiting terminal spike of the cattail is usually conspicuous in fall and winter. This is sometimes used for decoration.

THE SCREW-PINE FAMILY

The *Pandanaceae* are a group of tropical shrubs or trees with peculiar spiral clusters of pineapple-like leaves at the tips of the main stem and branches. They are sometimes climbers and they then produce prop roots or stilt-like aerial roots. They are grouped in 3 genera and 400 species. They are widely distributed in the tropics of the Old World, especially in Malaya and in the Indian and Pacific islands.

Leaves long and sword-like, stiff, in tufts at the ends of branches, arranged in three, spirally twisted series, edges and back of midrib with rows of spines; flowers in terminal panicles or spike-like clusters, unisexual, species sometimes diœcious, calyx 0; corolla 0; stamens few to many, free or connate; ovary one- to many-celled, indefinite, carpels more or less united, ovules several or single; stamens and pistils sometimes scattered over the axis without definite arrangement; fruit a syncarp or a cluster of drupaceous fruits and more or less berry-like, often large.

Several species of *Pandanus* are grown for ornamental purposes, and the leaves of *P. utilis*, a native of Madagascar, and other species yield fibers that are used for making baskets, fiber hats, and other useful articles.

CHAPTER XXII

THE LILIES, PALMS, AND AROIDS

The members of this group of orders show many marks of advancement over the *Alismales*. They have become more widely and completely adapted to the land habit and their vegetative anatomy is much more varied than that of the earlier group from which the *Liliales* have probably developed. The perianth is typically present (reduced in *Arales* and *Palmales*) and the ovary is tricarpellary and superior.

ORDER LILIALES, THE LILY ORDER

Flowers usually perfect and complete; calyx and corolla of 3, usually separate parts, commonly colored alike; stamens 6; ovary superior, tricarpellary; endosperm abundant.

THE LILY FAMILY

The *Liliaceae* or lily family (Fig. 186) are a very large and important family of herbs, shrubs, and a few trees and climbers of world-wide distribution, but with greatest abundance in temperate and subtropical regions. The family is here treated in the broad sense and as such it includes more than 200 genera and 2,500 species. The group is sometimes subdivided into several families or subfamilies in more extensive systematic works. The most of the species are perennial herbs which develop from bulbs, or bulb-like structures, or fleshy rhizomes; only a few (*Dracaena*, *Yucca*) become woody and tree-like.

Leaves exceedingly various, basal, in rosettes or alternate on a well-developed stem, usually simple, fleshy or dry and leathery, rigid and sharp pointed, ephemeral or evergreen; flowers often showy, or small and inconspicuous, single or in spikes, racemes, or panicles; the perianth of 6, more or less similar, petal-like parts or different (3 sepals, 3 petals), separate or united and six-lobed; stamens usually 6, sometimes 3, inserted on the axis opposite the segments of the perianth or attached to the tubular perianth; ovary tricarpellary, superior; ovules usually numerous,

291

fruit a capsule or berry, usually with many seeds; endosperm copious.

The lily family is extremely rich in valuable plants that man uses for many purposes. Hundreds of species and varieties are in use as ornamentals including such well-known forms as tulips, *Tulipa*, Star of Bethlehem, *Ornithogalum*, mariposa, *Calochortus*, lily-of-the-valley, *Convallaria*, lilies, *Lilium*, such as Easter lily, *L. longiflorum*, tiger lily, *L. tigrinum*, Madonna lily, *L. candidum*, squills, *Scilla*, day lily, *Hemerocallis*, aloe, *Aloë*, hyacinth, *Hyacinthus*, etc.

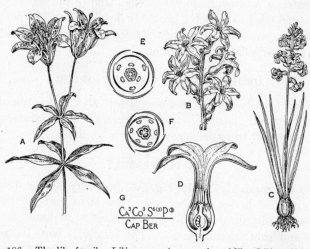

Fig. 186.—The lily family, *Liliaceae*. *A*, a species of lily, *Lilium* (*Mathews*); *B*, flowers of *Hyacinthus* (*after Baillon*); *C*, a plant of squill, *Scilla* (*after Baillon*); *D*, vertical section of a flower of hyacinth, *Hyacinthus* (*after Baillon*); *E*, floral diagram of fritillary, *Fritillaria* (*after Le M. and Dec.*); *F*, floral diagram of asparagus, *Asparagus* (*after Le M. and Dec.*); *G*, floral formula for the family.

Useful vegetables included in the family are the onions and their immediate kin, *Allium*, and asparagus, *Asparagus*. The so-called "asparagus fern" is a true asparagus, *A. plumosus*, and not a *fern* at all. *A. asparagoides* is the common "smilax" of florists.

THE SPIDERWORT FAMILY

This family, the *Commelinaceae* (Fig. 187), includes about 26 genera and 350 species of more or less succulent, annual and perennial herbs that are widely distributed and most abundant in the warmer parts of the earth, but are also seen in temperate climates, except temperate Europe and Asia. The stems are often nodular or knotty and leafy.

Leaves alternate, entire, broad or narrow, sheathing at the base; flowers in axillary clusters, perfect, actinomorphic or somewhat zygomorphic, hypogynous; sepals 3, generally free, green; petals 3, free or united into a tube, commonly blue, withering; stamens usually 6, in 2 sets, or 3, staminodia often present, filaments free, often hairy; ovary two- to three-celled, superior, ovules many or few, style terminal, stigma capitate or slightly two- to three-lobed; fruit a capsule; endosperm copious.

FIG. 187.—The spiderwort family, *Commelinaceae. A*, leaves and flowers of spiderwort, *Tradescantia (after Le M. and Dec.); B*, floral diagram of *Tradescantia (after Le M. and Dec.); C*, floral formula for the family.

The spiderworts produce brightly colored blue flowers and so are popular potted or outdoor plants. The dayflower, *Commelina coelestis*, and *C. tuberosa* are beautiful Mexican species. The familiar Wandering Jew is *Zebrina pendula*, of which there are numerous cultivated varieties. The spiderwort in a more restricted sense includes certain species of *Tradescantia*. A common spiderwort in America is *T. virginiana* or *T. reflexa*

THE PICKEREL WEED FAMILY

The *Pontederiaceae* are a family of erect or floating, aquatic herbs that inhabit marshes and more or less quiet waters in warm regions and with a few species in temperate climates. Absent from Europe. The family includes 6 genera and about 20 species.

Leaves alternate, long petioled, blades floating, emersed or sometimes submerged, petiole sometimes dilated to form a bladder, submerged leaves sometimes without blade; flowers perfect, hypogynous, actinomorphic or sometimes zygomorphic, usually spicate; perianth of 6 parts, petaloid, in 2 series (calyx and corolla), free or united to form a long or short tube; stamens 3 or 6, on the tube or at the base of the perianth; ovary superior, three-celled, or one-celled with 3 parietal placentae; ovules numerous, style 1, stigma entire or three-parted; fruit a many-seeded capsule or an achene; endosperm mealy.

The pickerel weed of the north is *Pontederia cordata*, a common, coarse herb with spikes of purplish flowers, seen in swampy areas. The water hyacinth, *Eichornia crassipes*, is a troublesome aquatic or paludose weed with inflated petioles, common in tropical and subtropical America where it sometimes obstructs navigation in streams and small rivers.

THE RUSH FAMILY

Rushes in the botanical sense belong to the *Juncaceae*, but the term "rush" is often applied to many other plants in daily life (Fig. 188). These are annual or mostly perennial herbs with creeping, underground stems and grass-like nature and habits, commonly found in moist places, marshes, etc., and often referred to as "grass." The family includes 8 genera and about 300 species of wide distribution throughout the temperate and cold portions of the earth.

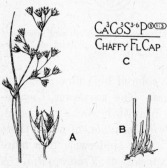

$$Ca^3Co^3S^{3-6}P\textcircled{3}\textcircled{1-3}$$
CHAFFY FL CAP
C

FIG. 188.—The rush family, *Juncaceae*. *A*, flowering habit and single flower of a common rush, *Juncus balticus*; *B*, basal portion of stems of the same; *C*, floral formula for the family.

Leaves grass-like, often stiff and terete or sword-like, or channeled, leaf sheath with free margins, sometimes reduced to membranous sheaths; flowers small, perfect, actinomorphic, hypogynous, often borne in dense spikes or heads, sometimes loosely aggregated or single; sepals 3, petals 3, chaff-like, greenish or brownish; stamens 3 or 6; ovary superior, three-celled, or one-celled with 3 parietal placentae, ovules many to 3, stigmas 3, fruit a capsule with many to few, often tailed, seeds. opening by 3 valves; endosperm starchy.

It is readily seen that the rushes are really grass-like lilies with small inconspicuous and chaffy flowers. They are of very little value.

THE PIPEWORT FAMILY

The family name for this curious and interesting group of Monocotyledons is *Eriocaulonaceae* (Fig. 189). They might be called the "monocotyledonous composites" on account of the flower clusters which resemble the heads of the true *Compositae* (Figs. 176 to 180). They are to be regarded as rather highly specialized lilies. The group includes 9 genera and 360 species of very wide distribution in the warmer and tropical parts of the earth and into temperate regions, the chief center being tropical South America.

The pipeworts are aquatic and bog-inhabiting perennials with alternate, tufted, densely grass-like, basal leaves; flowers minute, unisexual (monœcious), in small, densely crowded, terminal heads, on long, slender scapes, the head subtended by a scaly, bracted involucre as in the *Compositae*, each flower in the axil of a scarious bract; sepals 2 or 3; petals 2 or 3, distinct or connate to form a tube; stamens 4; ovary two- to three celled, ovules 2 to 3, stigmas 2 to 3, filiform; fruit a capsule, two- to three-celled; seeds 2 to 3; endo-

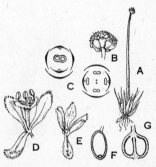

Fig. 189.—The pipewort family, *Eriocaulonaceae. A*, habit sketch of pipewort, *Eriocaulon septangulare; B*, head of flowers; *C*, floral diagrams, male flower at right, female flower at left; *D*, male flower with its bract; *E*, female flower; *F*, seed with minute embryo; *G*, ovary showing pedulous ovules (*all after Rendle*).

sperm abundant, mealy. The staminate flowers are on the outer portion and the pistillate flowers are on the inner portion of the head or *vice versa*.

The conspicuous genus of the family is *Eriocaulon*, meaning "woolly stem," as noted in certain species. A species common to America and Europe is *E. septangulare.*

ORDER ARALES, THE ARUM ORDER

The plants of this group, commonly known as the Aroids, typically produce small and inconspicuous flowers in dense clusters on a simple fleshy spike, *spadix*, which is subtended by and frequently inclosed by a more or less showy bract, *spathe*, which constitutes the "flower" of gardeners. The flowers are perfect or unisexual; the perianth is reduced to scales or entirely lacking, never showy; the ovary is usually tricarpellary and superior.

THE ARUM FAMILY

The *Araceae* (Fig. 190) include perennial herbs, or they are sometimes more or less woody and tree-like, arising from a tuberous rootstock or corm; erect, prostrate or extensively climbing, sometimes epiphytic, of shady, damp or wet places; juice mostly acrid, sometimes milky. The family includes

FIG. 190.—The arum family, *Araceae*. *A*, arum, *Arum italicum (after Baillon)*; *B*, inflorescence of Jack-in-the-pulpit, *Arisæma triphyllum (after Le M. and Dec.)*; *C*, inflorescence of *Arum (after Baillon)*; *D*, floral formula for the family.

about 100 genera and 1,500 species of cosmopolitan plants but developed in greatest number and most varied form in the tropics.

Leaves extremely varied, mostly basal, long petioled, simple or compound, sword-shaped to hastate, entire or lobed, certain species (as of *Monstera*) with large, regular holes in the blade; the flowers are densely aggregated on a fleshy *spadix* (spike), more or less surrounded by a showy bract the *spathe*, which is often conspicuously colored, and so constitutes the "flower" in a popular sense; flowers perfect or unisexual, some species diœcious, spadix very densely flowered, staminate flowers usually above, pistillate flowers below; sepals and petals lacking or of 4 to 6 scaly parts, never showy; stamens many or reduced to 4 to 10, or even to 1, filaments very short, often united; ovary superior, 1- to 3-celled (one to several), ovules one or more in each cell, style short or wanting; fruit a berry, the cluster becoming enlarged and densely grouped on the fruiting spadix; seeds few to many; endosperm present or 0.

There are numerous Aroids of value as ornamentals and a few produce important foods. The best known ornamental is probably the calla lily, *Richardia aethiopica*, a native of South Africa, and grown throughout the world. Others are the elephant ear, *Colocasia esculenta*, and the ceriman or "delicious monster," *Monstera deliciosa*, with its large, perforated leaves. The dasheen, a variety of *Colocasia esculenta*, produces an abundance of large, globular or oblong tubers which are edible and for which the plant is sometimes cultivated. The common Jack-in-the-pulpit of North America, *Arisaema triphyllum*, is also a member of this family.

The duckweeds, *Lemnaceae*, are usually included in the *Arales*. These are minute, floating aquatics without leaves. The plants are small, globular, or flattish bodies bearing one to several or no roots, and extremely simple flowers consisting of 1 tiny stamen and 1 pistil borne on the edge or upper surface of the thallus-like body. The duckweeds sometimes develop very thickly on the surface of shallow, quiet water.

ORDER PALMALES, THE PALM ORDER

The palms are mostly tropical trees or shrubs with variable form, but generally with stout, woody, and unbranched stem which terminates in a crown of large, evergreen, palmate or pinnate leaves. The flowers are very numerous and are borne in a large, compound inflorescence. The individual flowers are small, unisexual, and with inconspicuous perianth; ovary mostly tricarpellary.

THE PALM FAMILY

The *Palmaceae* (Fig. 191) include trees or shrubs of characteristic habit, but more variable than is commonly supposed, some of them being long, trailing, woody vines. They are usually erect, but some are climbing. The stems are slender and usually unbranched. The family includes about 140 genera and more than 1,200 species of general distribution throughout the tropics and extending somewhat into the warmer parts of the temperate zone.

Leaves evergreen, stiff, often very large, usually palmate or pinnate, clustered in a dense, terminal crown; flowers small, mostly greenish, unisexual or perfect, usually in a huge, conspicuous, much branched spadix among the leaves; the spathe covers the bud and it may become woody, but it does not inclose the mature inflorescence; sepals 3; petals 3, leathery or woody; stamens 6 (or more), rarely 3; ovary superior, three-celled, or sometimes the 3 carpels separate; fruit a one-seeded berry, drupe, or nut of various size and nature; seed usually 1, endosperm abundant, oily, or sometimes bony.

The palms are very useful plants. Many of them are widely planted in parks, lawns, and along drives in the tropics. Some of the ornamental species are: Chinese fanpalm, *Livistona chinensis*,

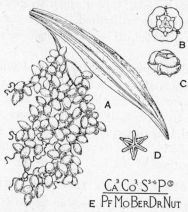

Fig. 191.—The palm family, *Palmaceae*. The datepalm, *Phoenix dactylifera*. *A*, cluster of fruits; *B*, pistillate flower, front view; *C*, same, side view; *D*, staminate flower, front view (*after F. Sargent*); *E*, floral formula for the family.

European fanpalm, *Chamaerops humilis*, royal palm, *Roystonea regia*, cabbage palm, *Inodes palmetto*, and various species and varieties of the datepalms, *Phoenix*. The palm which furnishes the dates of commerce is *P. dactylifera*, of Africa and Asia, where it has been cultivated for 5,000 years. The coconutpalm, *Cocos nucifera*, is used for a great many purposes, the most important involving the use of the oily endosperm for food; the fibers of the husk for ropes, mats, and brushes; the shells for utensils, and the leaves for thatching roofs. The rattan palms are species of creeping or climbing palms of the genera *Calamus* and *Daemonorops*, the slender stems of these plants sometimes reaching lengths of 600 feet. Raffia is a strong wrapping cord or tape made from the epidermis of *Raphia ruffia*, of Madagascar.

The *Palmales* and *Arales* are regarded as highly specialized and modified lateral developments from the general type represented by the *Liliales*.

CHAPTER XXIII

THE GRASSES AND SEDGES

ORDER GRAMINALES, THE GRASSES AND SEDGES

This order includes the grasses and the sedges, plants with herbaceous or woody shoots that are annual or perennial. The flat, linear leaves and tiny, reduced flowers produced in chaffy spikelets are characteristic of the group. The perianth is absent or represented by two or more very inconspicuous scales, the stamens are mostly 3 or 6, and the pistil is two- to three-carpelled but one-celled and with a single ovule; the fruit in the grasses is a *grain* or *caryopsis*, or rarely an achene.

The grasses are frequently regarded as having developed from some lily-like ancestral stock. Whatever may have been their origin, it is plain that they have become extremely modified and differentiated to such a degree that they have been considered as the highest of all Monocotyledons by some students of the group, especially by Clements.

THE SEDGE FAMILY

The sedges, *Cyperaceae*, are grass- or rush-like herbs with solid, triangular, quadrangular, cylindrical or flattened stems and fibrous roots often arising from perennial rootstocks (Fig. 192). They are world wide in their distribution, being found under a great variety of natural conditions. The family includes about 75 genera and 3,500 species, mostly of little economic worth.

Leaves often in three ranks or longitudinal rows, sheaths usually closed around the stem, blade narrow; flowers perfect or unisexual, arranged in spikelets and the latter solitary or grouped in spike-like, or panicled clusters; each flower in the axil of a scale or glume, the latter in two ranks or imbricated, persistent, or deciduous; perianth of scales, or bristles or hairs, or wanting, rarely calyx-like; stamens generally 3, sometimes 2 or 1; filaments slender; ovary superior, two- to three-carpelled, one-celled, one-ovuled, style single, stigmas 2 or 3, more or less feathery; fruit an achene, often trigonous; endosperm abundant, mealy.

Several genera of sedges are widely represented throughout the world. More than 600 species of *Cyperus*, and 1,000 species of *Carex* have been described. The paper plant of the Egyptians, the papyrus, is *Cyperus papyrus*, a native of Southern Europe, Africa, and Syria, and it is widely grown as an aquarium plant, as is its close relative, *C. alternifolius*, the umbrella plant. The bulrushes are species of *Scirpus*, of which there are many species recognized.

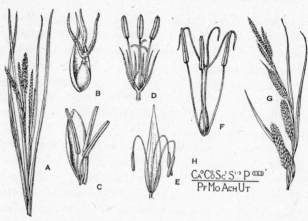

Fig. 192.—The sedge family, *Cyperaceae*. *A* and *G*, two species of *Carex* (*after Baillon and Le M. and Dec.*); *B*, pistillate flower of *Carex* (*after Baillon*); *C*, staminate flower of *Carex* (*after Baillon*); *D*, perfect flower of *Scirpus* (*after Le M. and Dec.*); *E*, staminate flower of another species of *Carex* (*after Le M. and Dec.*); *F*, perfect flower of *Cyperus* (*after Baillon*); *H*, floral formula for the family.

THE GRASS FAMILY

The commonest technical name for the grass family (Figs. 193 to 199) is *Gramineae*, but the group is also described under such names as *Graminaceae*, and *Poaceae*. The grasses are mostly erect, annual, or perennial herbs with fibrous roots, but some of them, as the bamboos, are distinctly woody and shrub-like or even tree-like. They usually develop conspicuously jointed, hollow stems. They exhibit a great variety of form and size, and some species or another is likely to be seen in almost every condition of soil and climate from the equator to far within the Arctic and Antarctic regions and from sea level to the tops of high mountains. Some of them are aquatic and others are characteristic of extremely arid and desert places. Grasses dominate vast expanses of territory in the prairies and plains of North

America, the pampas and llanos of Central and South America and the steppes of Russia and the Balkan states. They are among the most cosmopolitan of all flowering plants. The species are most numerous in the tropics but the abundance is greatest in temperate regions. The family includes about 400 genera and 5,000 species. There are about 1,500 species of grasses in the United States, of which 140 are important native, wild, forage plants. About 60 species of grasses are cultivated in the United States.

Leaves alternate, usually in two ranks, parallel veined, blade often greatly elongated, attached to the node by means of a

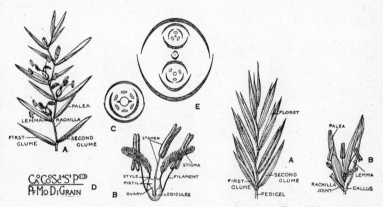

FIG. 193.

FIG. 194.

FIG. 193.—The grass family, *Gramineae*. *A*, diagrammatic representation of the structure of a grass spikelet with the two empty glumes and several flowering glumes and florets (*after Chase*); *B*, a grass flower, with stamens, pistil, and vestigial perianth (*after Chase*); *C*, floral diagram of rice, *Oryza* (*after Le M. and Dec.*); *D*, floral formula for the family; *E*, floral diagram of the oat, *Avena* (*after Le M. and Dec.*).

FIG. 194.—*A*, generalized spikelet of the grasses with two empty glumes and several florets (*after Chase*); *B*, a grass floret at flowering time, or when it is open (*after Chase*).

sheathing base, the *sheath* usually open on the side opposite the blade and furnished with a membranous or hairy projection, the *ligule*, which is pressed against the stem at the point where the blade gives way to the sheath; blade and sheath smooth or more or less hairy; flowers (Figs. 193 to 199) tiny, chaffy, usually perfect, rarely unisexual (plants rarely dioecious) grouped in spikelets (Figs. 193, 194, 195, 196, 197 and 198) each of which consists of a shortened, jointed and more or less zigzag axis, the *rachilla* (Figs. 193 and 194), bearing 2 to many two-ranked scales or bracts (Figs. 193 and 194), the lowest two (or rarely one) being empty, and, therefore called the "empty glumes" or merely the "glumes," and the one or many succeeding scales, the *flowering glumes* or "lemmas," each bearing a flower in its axil, with another scale or bract (usually two-nerved), the *palet* or *palea* standing between the flower and the rachilla (Figs. 193 and 194); this unit, composed of lemma, flower, and palea is called a "floret" (Figs. 193 and 194); each lemma may be sharp pointed or blunt, or in many cases the midrib is prolonged into a slender *awn* or *beard*, which is straight, twisted, or bent (Figs. 195 and 196); the spikelet may be composed of one or many such

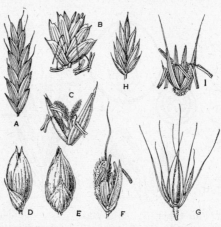

Fig. 195.—Different types of spikelets and flowers in grasses. *A*, spikelet of brome grass, *Bromus secalinus* (*after Chase*); *B*, spikelet of wheat, *Triticum* (*after Le M. and Dec.*); *C*, single floret from the latter; *D*, side view of the spikelet of Proso, *Panicum miliaceum*; *E*, dorsal view of same (*after Chase*); *F*, one-flowered spikelet of rice, *Oryza sativa* (*after Baillon*); *G*, joint of spike of wild barley, *Hordeum nodosum*, with a cluster of spikelets (*after Chase*); *H*, spikelet of bluegrass, *Poa pratensis* (*after Chase*); *I*, spikelet of rye, *Secale* (*after Baillon*).

florets arranged at the joints of the rachilla above the empty glumes, the uppermost ones sometimes being sterile; spikelets such as these are arranged in spikes, racemes, or panicles (Figs. 197 to 199), the position of a single flower in other plants being occupied by a spikelet which may contain many flowers; they usually become dry and chaffy; the perianth is often lacking or is represented by two or three very delicate and usually incon-spicuous scales, *lodicules* (Fig. 193), at the base of the ovary inside the lemma and palea; stamens usually 3, sometimes 6, 2, or 1, free filaments very slender and hygroscopic; ovary superior, three-carpelled but usually one-celled and one-ovuled, styles 1 to 3, usually 2, with plumose stigmas; fruit a *caryopsis*, *i.e.* a single-seeded dry fruit with thin pericarp which adheres closely to the seed (seed rarely free, as in *Sporobolus*), often enveloped by the lemma and palea as in certain varieties of oats, barley, etc. the whole structure usually passing as a "seed," and indeed serving as such for practical purposes; endosperm starchy.

The grass family is usually divided into two or more sub-families and these in turn into tribes, the most of which are quite distinctively marked. The following key will serve to illustrate the possibilities with reference to the separation of the different tribes as an aid in their classification.

Key to the Tribes of Grasses

A. Plants woody, aerial stems perennial; leaves with a joint between blade and sheath; spikelets with several florets............Tribe *Bambuseae*, the bamboo grasses

B. Plants herbaceous, aerial stems annual; leaves without a joint between blade and sheath; spikelets with several florets, or the latter reduced to one

   .I. Spikelets more or less flattened laterally, jointed above the empty glumes, which are persistent after the rest of spikelet falls

      1. Spikelets with one to several florets, usually more than 1; inflorescence usually a spike

         a. Spikelets in two rows on opposite sides of the rachis, thus forming a symmetrical spike...............Tribe *Hordeae*, the barley grasses

         b. Spikelets in two rows on the same side of the rachis, thus forming a one-sided spike......Tribe *Chlorideae*, the grama grasses

      2. Spikelets with two to several florets, inflorescence usually an open or contracted panicle

         a. Empty glumes usually shorter than the lemmas, and shorter than the spikelet as a whole; lemmas awnless, or with a straight terminal awn..Tribe *Festuceae*, the fescue grasses

         b. Empty glumes longer than the lemmas, usually inclosing the whole spikelet; lemmas awnless, or with a bent dorsal awn......................Tribe *Aveneae*, the oat grasses

      3. Spikelets with one floret, or with 1 or more sterile lemmas below the fertile floret; inflorescence a panicle, or a raceme

         a. Spikelets with 2 sterile lemmas below the fertile floret, *i.e.* spikelet with 5 scales...Tribe *Phalarideae*, the canary grasses

         b. Spikelets without sterile lemmas below perfect floret, *i.e.* spikelet with 3 scales..Tribe *Agrostideae*, the timothy grasses

   II. Spikelets strongly flattened laterally, jointed below the empty glumes, the spikelet falling in its entirety, or empty glumes commonly lacking....................Tribe *Oryzeae*, the rice grasses

III. Spikelets round, or more or less flattened dorsally, usually jointed below the empty glumes, so that the spikelet falls as a whole

    1. Empty glumes membranous, lemma and palea hardened; spikelets solitary................Tribe *Paniceae*, the millet grasses

    2. Empty glumes hardened, at least firmer than the lemma and palea; spikelets in pairs

        a. Both spikelets of the pair with perfect florets, or 1 sessile and perfect, the other pedicellate and perfect, staminate or sterile............Tribe *Andropogoneae*, the sorghum grasses

        b. Spikelets unisexual, in separate inflorescences, *i.e.* plants monoecious...............Tribe *Maydeae*, the maize grasses

The grasses constitute the most important economic group of Monocotyledons, if indeed they are not the most valuable of all of the groups of flowering plants from this point of view.   They

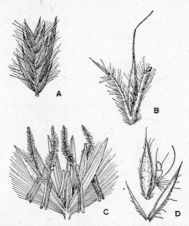

Fig. 196.—Spikelets that are more or less hairy. *A*, reedgrass, *Phragmites communis (after Chase); B*, little bluestem, *Andropogon scoparius (after Chase); C*, sugar cane, *Saccharum officinarum (after Baillon); D*, blue grama, *Bouteloua gracilis*, empty glumes below, fertile lemma, and sterile lemmas above (*after Chase*).

include the cultivated cereals with hundreds of varieties that furnish invaluable foods for man and beast, as well as many species that furnish varied materials for construction, and certain of them are used for ornamental purposes.   The great grassland areas of the world constitute one of the most prominent features of the native vegetation of the earth.

The bamboos, Tribe *Bambuseae*, are noteworthy on account of the perennial nature of their aerial stems which become tree-like in many species.   The great bamboo of Malay, *Dendrocalamus giganteus*, reaches a height of more than 100 feet and a trunk diameter of 6 to 10 inches. Extensive bamboo forests occur in Burma. The stems, leaves, and seeds of the bamboos are used for a great many purposes including food, in the daily life of the primitive and modern people of the regions where they grow.

The barley grasses, Tribe *Hordeae*, include many species and varieties of wheat, *Triticum*, rye, *Secale*, barley, *Hordeum*, and many worthless weeds. Most of our cultivated varieties of wheat have been developed from a few original species. Thus *Triticum sativum*, has given rise to a long series of common wheat, club wheat, durum wheat, etc. Polish wheat is *T. polonicum*, and Poulard wheat is *T. turgidum*, the latter having been cultivated

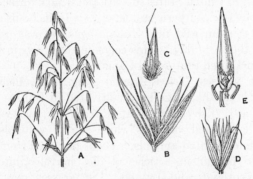

Fig. 197.—Oat grasses. *A*, the panicle of spikelets of *Avena* (*after Le M. and Dec.*); *B*, spikelet of wild oats, *Avena fatua*, entire spikelet; *C*, floret of same (*after Chase*); *D*, spikelet of another wild oat, *Trisetum spicatum* (*after Chase*); *E*, floret of cultivated oat, *Avena sativa*, with palea (*after Le M. and Dec.*).

in Europe for 2,000 years. There are now several hundred named varieties and races of wheat known. Barley has been used as a cultivated plant since prehistoric times.

The grama grasses, Tribe *Chlorideae*, are usually recognized by the one-sided spikes, or spike-like racemes in which the spikelets are borne. Prominent members of the tribe are Bermuda grass, *Capriola dactylon*, an Old World species, but introduced as a valuable lawn and pasture grass in southern United States; the grama grasses, about 30 species of *Bouteloua*, native to America and abundant in the southwestern states and Mexico; and the buffalo grass, *Bulbilis dactyloides*, another distinctive American species. Buffalo grass and several species of *Bouteloua* are among the world's most valued forage grasses.

The fescue grasses, Tribe *Festuceae*, include many valuable plants such as bluegrasses, species of *Poa*, orchard grass, *Dactylis glomerata*, besides many species of fescue, *Festuca*, and brome grasses, *Bromus*. Meadow fescue, *F. elatior*, and awnless brome, *B. inermis*, are grown as pasture and meadow grasses. Worthless and troublesome weeds also abound in this tribe, as *F. octoflora* and *B. tectorum*.

The rice grasses, Tribe *Oryzeae*, are of immense value to mankind mainly because of a single species, *Oryza sativa*, with its several cultivated varieties. Rice is native to the East Indies, but is now widely grown in many countries, especially in China where it forms about one-half of the food of the people. Rice culture in China is known since 3,000 B. C. The plant was introduced into the United States in 1694 and it now forms an important crop in the southern states, especially in Louisiana. The grain of American wild rice, *Zizania aquatica*, was used by the Indians in the early day. This coarse plant grows in wet places in northern United States and Canada.

The oat grasses, Tribe *Aveneae* (Fig. 197), include other economic plants that have been cultivated in Europe since prehistoric times. The common oat is *Avena sativa*, of which there are many cultivated varieties which supply valuable food for man and domesticated animals. Foods prepared from the grain of oats are prominent articles of diet in the United States, England, Scotland, and Ireland. Oat grasses may often be recognized by the bent, dorsal awn on the lemmas.

The canary grasses, Tribe *Phalarideae*, are usually recognized by the two sterile, or staminate florets between the empty glumes and the one perfect floret in the spikelet. The grass that is grown in Europe for birdseed is *Phalaris canariensis*. American canary grass, *P. arundinacea*, is a fine hay plant for the southern states. Ribbon grass is a variety of the latter species, *P. arundinacea*, var. *picta*, which produces leaves that are striped with white and yellow. Sweet vernal grass, *Anthoxanthum odoratum*, produces fragrant herbage. Vanilla grass, *Savastana odorata*, is a native of northern Europe and America, the leaves of which are very fragrant, and are often woven into mats and baskets and used in trimming boxes, baskets, and other articles in which the sweet, lasting odor is desired.

The timothy grasses, Tribe *Agrostideae* (Figs. 198 and 199), include some of our most valuable forage and pasture grasses, with many wild species in cool climates. The inflorescence in these grasses is sometimes a densely flowered spike, or spike-like panicle. Timothy or cattail grass, *Phleum pratense* (Fig. 198), is the most important hay plant of cultivated meadows in the north where it is extensively naturalized. Mountain timothy, *P. alpinum*, is found in the mountains of North America. Redtop grass, *Agrostis alba*, is an important hay grass. Beach grass or marram grass, *Ammophila breviligulata*, is a prominent plant of coastal dune areas of eastern North America and Europe, and it has often been used for planting as a sand binder. Species of *Stipa* are included in the flora of prairies and plains of America and Europe. The needlegrass (Fig. 199, *E*, *F*) of America is *S. spartea*, or *S. comata*.

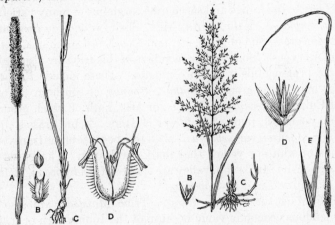

FIG. 198.   FIG. 199.

FIG. 198.—Timothy. *A*, the spike of *Phleum pratense; B*, empty glumes and floret of same; *C*, basal part of plant (*after Hitchcock*); *D*, a single spikelet of timothy (*after Baillon*).

FIG. 199.—Redtop. *A*, the inflorescence of *Agrostis alba; B*, spikelet; *C*, basal part of stem and rhizomes (*after Hitchcock*); *D*, spikelet of *Calamagrostis canadensis*, floret raised above the glumes (*after Chase*); *E*, needlegrass, *Stipa spartea*, empty glumes at left; *F*, floret with its long, twisted awn at right (*after Chase*).

The millet grasses, Tribe *Paniceae*, are widely distributed and include many important species. The genus *Panicum* includes about 400 species, most of which are of little value. Crab grass, *Digitaria sanguinalis*, is a troublesome lawn pest. The familiar sandbur is *Cenchrus pauciflorus*, and the foxtail grasses are species of *Chaetochloa*. Millet or Hungarian grass is *C. italica*, with several varieties that are valuable cultivated forage plants in America, but in Europe the seed is often used for human food. Pearl millet is *Pennisetum glaucum*, also grown for forage and grain, especially in Africa; feather grass, *P. villosum* and *P. ruppelii*, are grown as ornamentals, particularly as border plants.

The sorghum grasses, Tribe *Andropogoneae*, are a large group in warm climates particularly, but with certain species well represented in temperate regions. The most important plant of the tribe is sugar cane, or simply cane, *Saccharum officinarum*, a coarse, perennial grass with a woolly, plume-like panicle. This plant is one of the principal sources of cane sugar for which it is grown in all tropical countries. The cultivated sorghum is *Holcus sorghum*, of which there are four principal series of varieties, *Sorgo*, the forage and saccharine sorghums of many varieties, *grain sorghums*, Kafir, Dura, Milo, Shallu, etc. *Hay Sorghums*, Johnson grass, Sudan grass, etc. and *broom-corn* sorghums, of two or more types. Some of the members of this tribe are also highly prized ornamentals in warm countries. These include Ravenna grass or pampas grass, *Erianthus ravennae*, of southern Europe, and Eulalia, *Miscanthus sinensis*, of Asia, both of which produce large, beautiful, plume-like flower clusters. Zebra grass is *Miscanthus sinensis*, var. *zebrinus*, called this because of the transverse bands of white or yellow that mark the leaves. The bluestem grasses of the Mississippi valley are species of *Andropogon*, including *A. furcatus* and *A. scoparius*.

The Maize or "corn" grasses, Tribe *Maydeae*, are also of tremendous economic value because of the Indian corn or maize of America, *Zea mays*, which is not now known in the wild state. This plant has been grown from Peru to central North America since prehistoric times and it is today one of the world's most important field crops. It may be noted that this plant is known in Europe as *maize* or *Indian corn*, whereas "corn" there is likely to be what is known in America as wheat or barley. A great many named varieties of maize have been described, and are now in cultivation. Some of the more important or interesting varieties or groups of varieties are dent corn, var. *indenta*, popcorn, var. *everta*, flint corn, var. *indurata*, pod corn, var. *tunicata*, zebra corn, var. *japonica*, sweetcorn, var. *saccharata*. The curious teosinte, *Euchlaena mexicana*, sometimes thought to be the ancestor of maize, and Job's-tears, *Coix lacryma-jobi*, also belong here.

CHAPTER XXIV

THE WATER WEEDS, IRISES, AND ORCHIDS

EPIGYNOUS MONOCOTYLEDONS

This subclass includes the higher orders and families of Mono-cotyledons. They are among Monocotyledons somewhat similar to the *Rosales-Asterales* line among the Dicotyledons. The axis of the flower in this series is normally expanded into a cup, and this cup-shaped receptacle bears the perianth and stamens on the rim, or the stamens are attached to the perianth in certain forms. The carpels are usually united and are more or less deeply imbedded in the receptacle below the insertion of perianth and stamens, *i.e.* the carpels or the ovary are inferior. The flowers here are actinomorphic, or zygomorphic, exhibiting extremely bizarre and varied, irregular forms in the Orchids.

ORDER HYDRALES, THE WATER WEED ORDER

This small group of aquatics is characterized by diclinous, actinomorphic flowers in which the tricarpellary ovary is inferior, and these are more or less inclosed by or surrounded by a bracted involucre or spathe. The latter feature may possibly indicate a relationship with the *Arales*. The order is here regarded as another reduced lateral development from the region of the *Liliales*. A single family as follows:

THE TAPEGRASS FAMILY

This family, the *Vallisneriaceae*, includes 14 to 15 genera and about 50 species of floating or submerged herbs of wide distribution in both fresh and salt water in warm and temperate climates. They develop so luxuriantly sometimes as to choke streams and canals with their more or less stringy forms.

Leaves various, simple, linear, lanceolate, or rounded kidney-shaped, submerged or floating, often crowded at the base of the stems; flowers actinomorphic, usually diœcious or polygamous, rarely perfect, more or less inclosed by a spathe of 1 to 3 bracts, or leaf-like scales; sepals 3; and petals 3, usually present; sepals and petals distinguishable or all petaloid, borne on the margin of the receptacle, sometimes tubular; stamens 3 to 12, separate or more or less united, inserted on rim of axis or on the perianth tube; ovary inferior, three-carpelled, but one-celled, or three-celled, ovules several, style 3, with entire or two-cleft stigmas; fruit leathery or fleshy, ripening under water; seeds numerous; endosperm 0.

These plants are sometimes cultured in aquaria and fish bowls. The water weed or water thyme, *Elodea canadensis*, is frequently seen in such places. The frogsbit, *Hydrocharis morsus-ranae*, a plant with rosettes of long-petioled leaves with rounded and heart-shaped blades is also grown in aquaria.

ORDER IRIDALES, THE IRIS ORDER

This is a rather large group containing about a dozen families of land plants of diverse habit. The flowers are epigynous, *i.e.* the ovary is inferior, the perianth is actinomorphic and composed of free, or united parts, and the seeds are supplied with endosperm. The order is derived from the upper *Liliales* and represents a distinctly higher type than the lilies. The irids are distinguished from the lilies, which they resemble in habit and mode of life, largely by the inferior ovary which is seen in practically all of the *Iridales*.

THE AMARYLLIS FAMILY

This, the *Amaryllidaceae*, is a large family (Fig. 200) mostly of perennial, bulbous herbs, or with stems and leaves arising from rootstocks, of very diverse habit, but often resembling lilies and, in fact, they are frequently confused with the lilies. The family includes about 70 genera and 800 or more species that inhabit the warm and temperate portions of the world, but more largely developed in South America, South Africa, and the Mediterranean region.

Leaves alternate, narrow, entire, radical or cauline; flowers perfect, regular or nearly so, usually one or more borne on a leafless scape subtended by 2 or more bracts; sepals 3; petals 3, separate, inserted on a tubular receptacle, sometimes with 3 additional inner parts that are corolla-like, sometimes with a cup-shaped or tubular "crown" (*Narcissus*) resembling an additional corolla tube, inserted outside the stamens; stamens 6, inserted on the throat or at the base of the axis segments, separate; ovary inferior, three-celled, ovules often numerous, style filiform, entire, lobed or three-divided at the tip; fruit a capsule or sometimes berry-like; seeds black, endosperm fleshy.

This family is rich in highly prized ornamentals grown as pot plants inside or planted in lawns or parks out of doors. Among such plants may be mentioned the belladonna lily, *Amaryllis belladonna*, Knight star, *Hippeastrum reginae*, swamp-lily, *Crinum americanum*, snowflake, *Leucojum vernum*, snowdrop, *Galanthus*

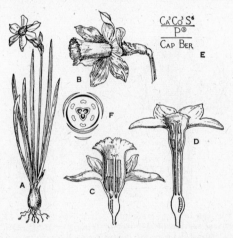

Fig. 200.—The amaryllis family, *Amaryllidaceae. A*, plant of poet's narcissus, *Narcissus poeticus; B*, single flower of *N. pseudonarcissus; C*, section of flower of *Narcissus; D*, section of narcissus flower with long tube; *E*, floral formula for the family; *F*, floral diagram of *Hypoxis (after Le M. and Dec.).*

nivalis, spider-lily, *Hymenocallis americana*, and the narcissuses, the genus *Narcissus*, including poet's narcissus, *N. poeticus*, with a shallow, red-bordered crown, paper-white narcissus, *N. tazetta*, the daffodil or trumpet narcissus, *N. pseudonarcissus*, and the jonquil, *N. jonquilla*.

The family also includes the American aloë or century plant, *Agave americana*, of Mexico and Central America, and widely cultivated in warm countries. About 300 species of *Agave* have been described. Sisal hemp is prepared from *A. sisalana*. The intoxicating liquors known as *mescal* and *pulque* are prepared from the juice of certain agaves.

THE IRIS FAMILY

The irises, or "flags" as they are often called in America (Fig. 201), are included in the family *Iridaceae* along with about 60 other genera and a total of 1,000 or more species of herbs of world-wide distribution in temperate and tropical regions.

Leaves mostly basal, equitant, two-ranked, linear or sword-shaped, arising from rootstocks, tubers or corms; flowers usually showy, terminal or paniculate, perfect, actinomorphic or somewhat zygomorphic, emerging from a spathe of 2 or more bracts; perianth of 6 parts in 2 series, the 3 outer ones (sepals) often petal-like, all 6 parts usually inserted at the top of a more

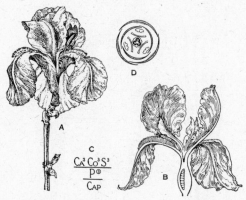

FIG. 201.—The iris family, *Iridaceae*. *A*, a single flower of iris, *Iris* (*after Baillon*); *B*, vertical section of a flower of *Iris* (*after Baillon*); *C*, floral formula for the family; *D*, floral diagram of *Iris* (*after Le M. and Dec.*).

or less tubular receptacle above the ovary; stamens 3, separate or united; ovary three-celled, inferior, style single, the 3 stigmas sometimes expanded and colored to resemble another set of 3 petals; ovules numerous; fruit a dehiscent, three-angled capsule with many seeds; endosperm fleshy or horny.

The iris or fleur-de-lis family includes many of the most popular, cultivated ornamental plants known. This is reflected in the mere mention of the irises, the crocuses, the freesias, and the gladioluses. The genus *Iris* comprises about 700 named species and varieties, many of which produce gorgeous flowers. *Iris florentina* produces the orris root of commerce. There are also hundreds of species and cultivated forms of *Gladiolus*. Species of *Crocus* are also popular plants on account of their large, showy flowers. The saffron crocus is *C. sativus*, a fall-blooming species of southern Europe, whose dried, orange-colored stigmas constitute the saffron of commerce. It is said that it requires more than 4,000 flowers of this plant to produce 1 ounce of saffron. The cloth-of-gold crocus of the Crimea is *C. susianus.*

THE PINEAPPLE FAMILY

The *Bromeliaceae* are a family composed of about 40 genera and 1,000 species of caulescent or acaulescent, more or less scurfy herbs that are often epiphytic, and somewhat shrubby plants mostly native to tropical America. Certain forms are widely introduced into other warm countries for ornamental purposes and for food production.

Leaves commonly in rosettes, elongated, sword-like, with scaly or smooth, entire or spinulose margin and overlapping or sheathing base; flowers perfect, actinomorphic, in dense spikes or heads with colored and showy bracts, or in less showy panicles; sepals 3, petals 3, free or united to form a tubular perianth with erect or spreading lobes; stamens 6, at base of the perianth; ovary inferior (or semisuperior), or superior, three-celled, ovules many, style filiform, three-lobed or three-parted; fruit a berry or capsule, more or less surrounded or crowned by the persistent calyx; seeds small, hairy or winged; endosperm copious, mealy.

The pineapple, *Ananas sativa,* is the most valuable economic plant of this family. The "fruit" of this plant is a fleshy, *multiple fruit* or *syncarpium* formed from the enlarged axis of the spike, densely covered by the spirally arranged ripened ovaries and adherent parts, all enlarged and more or less grown together to form the oval or elongated "pineapple" of the market. The *true* fruit, or one of the aborted ovaries in the surface, is a seedless berry. Florida "moss" or "long moss", *Tillandsia usneoides,* a strikingly different type of plant, is often seen in characteristic streamers and festoons on the trees of southeastern United States. This plant is sometimes used for stuffing upholstered furniture.

THE BANANA FAMILY

The *Musaceae* are the banana family (Fig. 202). The group includes 6 genera and more than 60 species of large perennial herbs, sometimes more or less woody, widely distributed through the tropics of both hemispheres. The so-called banana "tree" (Fig. 202, *A*) is really only an erect stem or branch from a huge rhizome or underground rootstock.   This erect stem is composed mostly of the long, stiff, and overlapping leaf sheaths.   The erect shoots die after they bear the bananas.

Leaves simple, often very large, 6 feet or more long, entire, pinnately veined, with rolled and overlapping sheaths; flowers zygomorphic, perfect, or monœcious, borne in spikes or panicles which are subtended by spathes and the flower clusters often in the axils of large and showy bracts (Fig. 202, *B*); sepals 3, free or united; petals 3 or fewer, free or united, the outer one larger than the others; stamens 6, but 1 of these is sterile, all free; ovary inferior, three-celled, ovules numerous or only one,

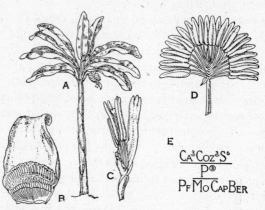

$$\frac{Ca^3 Coz^3 S^6}{P^\circledR}$$
$$Pf \overline{Mo Cap Ber}$$

Fig. 202.—The banana family, *Musaceae.* *A*, greatly reduced sketch of a banana "tree"; *B*, a bract with a cluster of flowers; *C*, single flower; *D*, leaves of traveler's tree, *Ravenala* (*all after Rendle*); *E*, floral formula for the family.

style simple, stigma capitate or three- to six-lobed; fruit a berry or capsule, dehiscent or indehiscent, or separating into the 3 carpels; seeds few to many, hard, often with an aril; endosperm mealy.

The banana which furnishes most of the fruit of commerce is *Musa sapientum*, a form in which the seeds are aborted.   These are produced in large quantities in the plantations of Central America.   Many other species and varieties are known, some of which produce large seeds as in *Musa ensete*, the Abyssinian banana.   Another species, *M. textilis*, is widely cultivated, especially in the Philippine Islands for the fiber, Manila hemp, which is secured from the leaf bases.   The curious traveler's tree (Fig. 202, *D*) of Madagascar is *Ravenala madagascariensis*, a striking ornamental on account of the immense leaves that are arranged in

2 ranks at the top of the stem in such a manner as to give the crown a fan-like appearance. The bird-of-paradise plant of South Africa is *Strelitzia reginae*, also a member of this family.

THE GINGER FAMILY

This is the *Zingiberaceae*, a family of 40 genera and more than 400 species of perennial herbs with creeping or tuberous rootstocks and short, simple stems. They are nearly all tropical, being found in both hemispheres, but most numerous and abundant in tropical Asia.

Leaves simple, petiolate or sessile, sheathing, entire, linear, lanceolate, or broader, radical and cauline, ligule prominent; flowers perfect, zygomorphic, in heads, bracted spikes, or panicles; perianth in 6 parts, calyx tubular, three-toothed; corolla tubular, unequally three-lobed; stamens 6, but only 1 is functional, the others sterile and sometimes broad and petal-like (staminodia); ovary inferior, three-celled or one-celled, with 3 axile placentae, ovules many, style and stigma 1, the slender style held in a groove in the fertile stamen; fruit a capsule; seeds many; endosperm present.

Commercial ginger is prepared from the aromatic, creeping, thick-jointed, branching rootstocks of common ginger, *Zingiber officinale*, of Asia and New Guinea. Some of the gingers are also grown for ornamental purposes as in ginger lily, *Hedychium coronarium*.

Other families that are more or less closely related to those that have been included in this order are the *Cannaceae*, the cannas, *Dioscoreaceae*, the yams, and the *Marantaceae*, the arrowroots.

ORDER ORCHIDALES, THE ORCHID ORDER

This is an enormous group of extremely varied plants with world-wide distribution and the most extreme floral differentiation, commonly regarded as the highest of all Monocotyledons. The order includes two families, the *Burmanniaceae*, with a dozen genera and about 60 species with mostly actinomorphic flowers, and the *Orchidaceae*, a vast family with varied, zygomorphic flowers (Fig. 203) which really stamp the order as an outstanding group. The flowers are usually perfect, corolla extremely zygomorphic, with 3 sepals and 3 petals, stamens 2 or 1, ovary inferior and usually tricarpellary, but one-celled. The most varied flower forms and detail of floral mechanism known are found in this group in which entomophily has apparently played the leading rôle.

THE ORCHID FAMILY

This is the *Orchidaceae*, a family (Fig. 203) of probably more than 500 genera and 15,000 species of low, erect, sprawling or climbing herbs of very wide distribution in temperate and tropical regions throughout the world. Besides the ordinary terrestrial forms there are many epiphytic and even saprophytic species known. They are perennials with bulbous, tuberous, or thickened, fleshy stems and roots and extremely varied stem form.

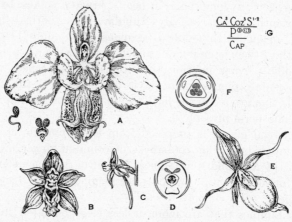

Fig. 203.—The orchid family, *Orchidaceae*. *A*, single flower of orchid, *Phalaenopsis*, front view (*after Kerner*); *B*, front view of single flower of *Epipactis* (*after Kerner*); *C*, single flower of *Orchis*; *D*, floral diagram of *Orchis*; *E*, single flower of lady's slipper, *Cypripedium*; *F*, floral diagram of *Cypripedium* (*after Baillon*); *G*, floral formula for the family.

Leaves usually alternate, simple, entire, thin, or often thick and more or less fleshy, linear, oblong, or orbicular; flowers from the base of the plant or from the axils on leafy stems or terminal, often very showy because of size or color, often grotesquely irregular (Fig. 203) and oddly splotched in the cultivated species, but small, greenish and inconspicuous in many other species; usually perfect, sometimes heteromorphic; sepals 3, usually narrow and not showy; petals 3, the 2 lateral ones similar in form and coloration, the third forming a *lip* of different shape and color which is extremely varied as to form and color, sometimes spatulate or saccate, and often spurred, all of these parts free and attached to the rim of the receptacle above the ovary (Fig. 203); stamens and pistil united to form an unsymmetrical *gynandrium* or *column* composed of 1 (or 2) fertile stamens in which the anther alone with its 2 to 8 masses of pollen is present and this is grown to the style, the pear-shaped, stalked masses of pollen known as "pollinia" (Fig. 203, *A*) and these united by strongly elastic threads, the masses powdery or waxy, and attached at the base to a glandular disk; style often ending in a beak, the *rostellum*, at the base of the anther or between the anther cells; stigma viscid, facing the lip, under the rostellum or in a cavity (clinandrium) between the anther sacs; ovary inferior, three-celled, or one-celled and three-angled, usually long and twisted, ovules numerous, on 3 parietal placentae; fruit a capsule; seeds very small, very numerous, seed coat loose, reticulated; endosperm none.

A great many orchids are grown by florists and others for their large, showy flowers of great variety of color and form. Some of the popular types of ornamental orchids are as follows: *Cattleya labiata*, with a more or less tubular lip of varied color in the different varieties, *Odontoglossum crispum*, with a lobed and toothed lip, *Oncidium varicosum*, and *Epidendrum vitellinum*. The lady's slipper or moccasin flower of the woods is *Cypripedium* (Fig. 203, *E*) of which several species with purple and yellow flowers are known. The fringed orchid of meadows and prairies is *Blephariglottis ciliata*. Extract of vanilla is prepared from the pods of certain orchids, especially *Vanilla planifolia* and *V. pompona*. The former species is a climbing epiphyte with fleshy leaves and it is often cultivated for the crop of fruits from which vanilla is obtained. The flowers of vanilla are commonly hand-pollinated in the plantations in areas outside of Mexico where the pollinating bees do not occur.

CHAPTER XXV

A BIT OF EARLY HISTORY

Men have puzzled over the origin, nature, and classification of plants since ancient times. Very early agricultural and medical demands stimulated an interest in plants and led to attempts to name and classify them.

WORK OF THE ANCIENTS

Numerous writers of ancient times described certain general plant characteristics and cataloged many of the more evident properties of plants. Thus Theophrastus (372–287 B.C.), the

ARISTOTLE (384–322).—(*Photo furnished by Brooklyn Botanic Garden.*)

immortal Athenian, and later Dioscorides, Galen, and Pliny, about the beginning of the Christian era, were among the most important writers on botany of antiquity. Theophrastus was a pupil of Aristotle (384–322 B.C.) who had been a pupil of Plato (426–347 B.C.) and he described about 450 cultivated plants, and classified them as *herbs*, *undershrubs*, *shrubs*, and *trees*. Theophrastus considered trees to be the very highest expression of plant development and he placed them at the top of the plant world. He noted the difference between centripetal and centrifugal inflorescences. Nearly twenty centuries later Linnaeus wrote of Theophrastus as the "father of botany," as indeed he had been known long before that time. Dioscorides prepared a "Materia Medica" but his descriptions are so meager and his classification so crude as to be of little value. Pliny wrote nine books on useful plants in which he presented many details for the cultivation of certain plants for their gums and spices.

The Middle Ages.—The good work that had been done by Theophrastus and his contemporaries was lost and forgotten for many centuries following their time. Little was accomplished in the classification of plants, or in fact with reference to anything else, during the long and chaotic period of the Dark Ages and the Middle Ages until about the beginning of the sixteenth century.

THEOPHRASTUS (372–287).—(*Photo furnished by Brooklyn Botanic Garden.*)

THE TIME OF THE HERBALS

With the sixteenth century came a period known in the history of botany as the time of the *herbals*. This period, which lasted for about 200 years, was characterized by a renewed enthusiasm for the study of plants among German, French, Belgian, and Dutch botanists, along with the general revival of learning. Such 'men as Fuchsius (1501–1566) (or Fuchs, after whom *Fuchsia* or "fushia" is named), Bock (1498–1554), Brunfels (1500–1534) and Clusius (or de l'Eclus, 1526–1609) wrote much about plants at that time. The invention of printing and the introduction of printed books at about the same time made the preservation of their work possible.

The principal object of the plant classifications and descriptions that these men published was to enable interested persons to identify medicinal plants. Many of their drawings and descriptions were little if any better than those left by the ancients, thus reflecting the terrible stagnation that resulted from the long period of intellectual inactivity that had intervened. Fuchs arranged an alphabetical classification. Bock (Hieronymus) contended that natural similarity of form should be considered in the separation of plants into different groups, and he appears to have sensed something of natural affinities, but he fell into the common practice of the period when he made his major groups herbs, shrubs, and trees. Centuries before this Theophrastus had grouped plants into *trees, shrubs, undershrubs,* and *herbs* as clearly defined *classes,* and he also made certain further subdivisions within these classes. It would seem that these earlier herbalists should have contributed much more than they

did toward the development and advancement of more adequate schemes for the nomenclature, classification, and description of plants when they inherited so much of value from Aristotle, Theophrastus, and the other natural philosophers of their time. Certain modern historians tell us that many of the plant descriptions prepared by the herbalists "are almost word for word translations of the ancient paragraphs of Theophrastus" and others.

ANDREA CESALPINO (1519–1603).—(*Photo furnished by Brooklyn Botanic Garden.*)

Workers in Southern Europe.—Cesalpino (or Caesalpinus, 1519–1603), the Italian physician, and one of the herbalists, is sometimes credited with the promulgation of the first real and important classification of plants. He recognized the importance of the seed and the fruit, and his arrangement of plants in fifteen classes is based largely upon these structures. The influence of the Aristotelian school is seen in his two major groups as trees and shrubs, and undershrubs and herbs, but he went further and divided the first group into two classes and the latter into thirteen classes on the basis of fruits and seeds. Little or no hints of phyletic relationships are seen in Cesalpino's classification, however. It would seem strange, with his attention to fruits and seeds, that he did not stumble upon some of the characteristics that have come to be used to separate Dicotyledons and Monocotyledons. Cesalpino was still impressively imbued with the ancient scholasticism and philosophy, which fact probably interfered more or less with his understanding of the true nature of plants.

Dawn of Binomial Nomenclature.—The writings of C. Bauhin (1550–1624), a Swiss, about the same time are noteworthy of the vigorous attempt to pull away from the type of reasoning that had come down from antiquity. He set himself the task of clearing away the confusion that had persisted for so many centuries. The fact that he made considerable advance in this endeavor is mirrored in the frequent use of binomial nomenclature. He utilized this method with such frequency and consistency that he might, indeed, be credited with the introduction of this important tool of systematic botany. He described many plants with a generic and specific name, but this tendency was varied now and then by the introduction of a third or even a fourth name. His great work the "Phytopinax" of 1596 is a noteworthy contribution in which he states that clearness in

Caspar Bauhin (1550–1624).—(*Photo furnished by Brooklyn Botanic Garden.*)

botanical writing is to be secured only by applying one name to each plant. Many of the descriptions of plants in Bauhin's works are much like modern descriptions of species, and his groupings often reflect relationships, but this was probably more accidental than intentional. He still held to the doctrine that shrubs and trees are the most specialized plants irrespective of the floral features in which he apparently did not sense indications of affinities. A belief in a progressive development from simpler to higher is reflected in Bauhin, as in several other men of his time, but their attempts to express this belief in an arrangement or classification of plants usually shows great uncertainty and inconsistency in the distribution of the various forms.

Certain Groups of Plants Recognized.—M. de l'Obel's (or Lobelius, 1538–1616) principal contributions were of considerable merit because he pointed out very clearly that leaves are of great value in a general scheme of plant classification. On the basis of leaf characteristics he differentiated two groups in which we can readily recognize Dicotyledons and Monocotyledons in about their modern forms. He clearly recognized certain natural affinities in plants. A very interesting and valuable fea-

Mathias de Lobel (1538–1616).— (*Photo furnished by Brooklyn Botanic Garden.*)　　John Ray (1628–1705).—(*Photo furnished by Brooklyn Botanic Garden.*)

ture of l'Obel's great work, the "Kruydtboeck" of 1581, is found in the many excellent illustrations which it contains. These old wood engravings were so carefully prepared and the reproductions so well done that the plants illustrated are very readily recognized.

THE FOUNDATION OF MODERN BOTANY

Toward the close of this period, *i.e.*, late in the seventeenth century and the beginning of the eighteenth century, there appeared a number of important workers whose contributions laid the foundations of modern botany. John Ray (1628–1705), an Englishman, shares preeminently in the great advancement of botany that began during these years which in reality mark the close of the herbals and the beginning of modern botany. Ray's most important work was the "Historia plantarum" (1686-1704) in which "the first germ of the natural system" is said to occur. He clearly sensed the importance of the monocotyledonous and dicotyledonous nature of the embryo from the standpoint of relationship and classification. But the shades of antiquity appeared again, at this late date, in "Herbae" and "Arbores" that constituted the main divisions of his classification. He uses the terms *Dicotyledons* and *Monocotyledons* for the first time, and he divides these into many classes some of which show natural affinities as we understand them today, but others are badly jumbled. He used many binomial names especially in descriptions of grasses. The main subdivisions in Ray's classification are as follows:

I. Herbae:
    A. Imperfecti (flowerless)
    B. Perfecti (flowering)
        Dicotyledons (with two cotyledons)
        Monocotyledons (with one cotyledon)

II. Arbores:
    A. Monocotyledons
    B. Dicotyledons

It is worthy of note, in passing, that Ray was also greatly interested in vegetable physiology, as well as in systematic botany. One volume of his "Historia" is devoted to this branch of our subject, and in it he described some of his own experiments on the ascent of sap.

The Demonstration of Sexuality in Flowers.—Camerarius, a German (1665-1721), should be mentioned because of the fact that he was the first to demonstrate sexuality in the flowering plants by experiment. Very little had been learned about this important phenomenon from the time of Theophrastus until Camerarius began his experiments in the last decade of the seventeenth century. He proved by experiment that pollen is absolutely necessary for fertilization and the formation of seeds in the normal life history of plants. His first experiments were performed on herb mercury, *Mercurialis annua, Euphorbiaceae*, but he also worked with the mulberry, *Morus*, nettle, *Urtica romana*, castor bean, *Ricinus*, maize, *Zea*, spinach, *Spinacia*, and hemp, *Cannabis*.

Tournefort and the Genus.—Tournefort (1656–1708) was among the very last to classify plants as herbs, shrubs, and trees. His most valuable contribution is in the careful delimitation of many genera of plants. He is sometimes referred to as the "founder" of genera. His efforts in that direction stand in contrast to those of many of his contemporaries whose main effort was with species. Generic names had been used before him, but Tournefort was the first to provide genera with descriptions and thus to set them definitely apart from species. Tournefort also directed attention to the value of the corolla in classification. He used the expressions *Petalodes* and *Apetali* to distinguish those flowers with and those without petals, respectively. He has been criticised somewhat for his disregard for specific differences within the genera, but certainly his efforts to definitize a larger group, the genus, mark an important epoch in the history of classification.

JOSEPH P. DE TOURNEFORT (1656–1708).—(*Photo furnished by Brooklyn Botanic Garden.*)

LINNAEUS AND HIS WORK

Linnaeus, (or Carl Linné) the great Swede, and the father of modern botany, was born in 1707, the year before Tournefort died. Botanical lore was so rapidly improved and greatly expanded by Linnaeus and his contemporaries that botanical science has continued to advance from that day to this. Botany, indeed all science and culture, will profit forever from the inspiration that flows from the contemplation of the vigorous and varied life and the very extensive work of this great man with whom modern botany began.

Linnaeus did much to revise and reorganize botanical nomenclature and he employed the binary system of naming plants to a degree that is not seen in the writings of any of his predecessors.

He described hundreds of plants from many parts of the world, including many from North America. He revised many of the older genera and gave great stability to species.

The Basis of the System of Linnaeus.—But, master though he was, Linnaeus was not prepared to bring out a classification of plants based on natural relationships. His *sexual system* was a tremendous advance over anything that had been done in systematic botany before his day, but that system is largely artificial, although he seemed to recog-

nize that a natural system of classification was highly desirable. His classification was based upon the number of stamens (24 *classes*) and pistils (67 *orders*) in flowers, and it became at once very popular because it readily enabled men to classify the plants that came to their attention. The sixty-seven orders of Linné were groups of genera that he designated *natural orders*. It was quite impossible for him to define the various orders critically, but it is a noteworthy fact that the beginnings of numerous natural groups are seen that

CARL VON LINNÉ or LINNAEUS
(1707–1778).

have come to have a lasting status in modern systems of classification. The outline of the system was given in his "Systema Naturae" in 1735, and again in "Genera Plantarum" in 1737, along with a systematically diagnosed and arranged collection of all genera known at that time.

The System Proposed by Linnaeus.—The twenty-four classes in the system of Linnaeus were differentiated on the basis of stamen characters. The outline of the system so far as classes are concerned, with examples of the various classes is as follows:

KLASS 1. *Monandria:* stamens one.
        Duckweed, *Lemna,* samphire, *Salicornia,* bulrush, *Scirpus,* chickweed, *Stellaria.*

KLASS 2. *Diandria:* stamens two.

Peppergrass, *Lepidium*, speedwell, *Veronica*, ash, *Fraxinus*, sage, *Salvia*.

KLASS 3. *Triandria:* stamens three.

Iris, *Iris*, cleavers, *Galium*, valerian, *Valeriana*, water chickweed, *Montia*.

KLASS 4. *Tetrandria:* stamens four.

Plantain, *Plantago*, whitlow grass, *Draba*, dogwood, *Cornus*, elm, *Ulmus*, mint, *Mentha*.

KLASS 5. *Pentandria:* stamens five.

Primrose, *Primula*, mullein, *Verbascum*, touch-me-not, *Impatiens*, borage, *Borago*, mousetail, *Myosurus*.

KLASS 6. *Hexandria:* stamens six.

Barberry, *Berberis*, dock, *Rumex*, water-plantain, *Alisma*, calla, *Calla*, starflower, *Trientalis*.

KLASS 7. *Heptandria:* stamens seven.

Horse-chestnut, *Aesculus*, starflower, *Trientalis*.

KLASS 8. *Octandria:* stamens eight.

Certain heaths, *Ericaceae*, evening primroses, *Onagraceae*, and buckwheats, *Polygonaceae*.

KLASS 9. *Enneandria:* stamens nine.

Rhubarb, *Rheum*, buttercup, *Ranunculus*.

KLASS 10. *Decandria:* stamens ten.

Flax, *Linum*, maple, *Acer*, agrimony, *Agrimonia*, certain heaths, *Ericaceae*, and pinks, *Caryophyllaceae*.

KLASS 11. *Dodecandria:* stamens eleven to nineteen.

Mignonette, *Reseda*, calla, *Calla*, buttercup, *Ranunculus*, spurge, *Euphorbia*.

KLASS 12. *Icosandria:* stamens twenty or more, attached to the calyx (axis).

Rose, *Rosa*, bridal wreath, *Spiraea*, blackberry, *Rubus*, dryas, *Dryas*, and other members of the rose family, *Rosaceae*.

KLASS 13. *Polyandria:* stamens twenty or more, attached to the axis.

Linden, *Tilia*, baneberry, *Actaea*, poppy, *Papaver*, larkspur, *Delphinium*, and certain waterlilies, *Nymphaeaceae*.

KLASS 14. *Didynamia:* stamens didynamous.

Verbena, *Verbena*, twin flower, *Linnaea*, certain mints, *Labiatae*, and snapdragons, *Scrophulariaceae*.

KLASS 15. *Tetradynamia:* stamens tetradynamous.

The mustard family, *Cruciferae*.

KLASS 16. *Monodelphia:* stamens in one bundle.

Flax, *Linum*, mallows, *Malvaceae*, goosefoots, *Chenopodiaceae*, geraniums, *Geraniaceae*.

KLASS 17. *Diadelphia:* stamens in two bundles.

Certain poppies, *Papaveraceae*, and many legumes, *Leguminosae*.

KLASS 18. *Polyadelphia:* stamens in several bundles.

Linden, *Tilia*, St. John's-wort, *Hypericum*.

KLASS 19. *Syngenesia:* stamens with united anthers.

Nightshade, *Solanum*, lobelia, *Lobelia*, violet, *Viola*, and most composites, *Compositae*.

KLASS 20. *Gynandria:* stamens grown to the pistil.

Birthwort, *Aristolochia*, and orchids, *Orchidaceae*.

KLASS 21. *Monœcia:* plants monœcious.

Duckweeds, *Lemnaceae*, cattail, *Typha*, arrowhead, *Sagittaria*, pigweeds, *Amaranthaceae*, mulberry, *Morus*, oak, *Quercus*, beech, *Fagus*, birch, *Betula*, hazel, *Corylus*, and arborvitae, *Thuya*.

KLASS 22. *Diœcia:* plants diœcious.

Nettle, *Urtica*, willows, *Salix*, cottonwood, *Populus*, hemp, *Cannabis*, ash, *Fraxinus*, juniper, *Juniperus*.

KLASS 23. *Polygamia:* plants polygamous.

Maple, *Acer*, crowberry, *Empetrum*, many composites, *Compositae*, goosefoots, *Chenopodiaceae*, and umbellifers, *Umbelliferae*.

KLASS 24. *Cryptogamia:* flowers concealed.

Plants without flowers such as ferns, mosses, fungi and algae.

The orders into which the Klasses were divided were named according to the nature of the ovary. We find, for instance,

LINNAEUS in LAPP COSTUME.

under Klass 2, *Diandria* (2 stamens) the following orders: Ordnung 1, *Monogynia;* Ordnung 2, *Digynia;* Ordnung 3, *Trigynia;* Ordnung 4, *Tetragynia;* to include plants with pistils or styles that correspond more or less closely to the condition inferred in the order names. Klass 14, *Didynamia*, included two orders, namely *Gymnospermia* and *Angiospermia*. The gymnosperms according to this classification did not embrace the plants that are now included in that group, but they were made up largely of the mints, *Labiatae*, and snapdragons, *Scrophulariaceae*.

Odd Combinations.—Many odd features are noted as we look over this brief synopsis of the system, and in the light of modern information concerning the phyletic relationships of plants we are able to point out many inconsistencies such as the placement of *Myosurus, Borago, Quercus,* and *Sagittaria* in the same groups. The two classes that stand out most nearly as we know flowering plants today are Klass 15, *Tetradynamia,* or the mustards, *Cruciferae,* and Klass 12, *Icosandria,* which includes many roses, *Rosaceae.* It is interesting to note that Linnaeus was puzzled by the axis or "calyx-cup" problem among the roses and related forms.

Value of the Work of Linnaeus.—Linnaeus taught that "the foundation of botany is two-fold: classification and nomenclature." On the whole the system of classification and nomenclature that Linnaeus gave us is a truly remarkable one when we consider the relatively few plant characteristics that were employed in making it. If he had only hit upon the greater value of a larger number of characters he doubtless would have introduced a system that would be in use to this day. But that is probably expecting too much from even one of the world's greatest men at a time when civilization had only lately emerged from a long period of superstition and almost impenetrable darkness.

For many years after Linnaeus the measure of a botanist was largely determined by the number of species of plants that he knew. The stimulation of his remarkable accomplishments reached into all lands and greatly accelerated the accumulation of enormous stores of reliable information concerning the flora (and fauna as well) of the world.

CHAPTER XXVI

FROM LINNAEUS TO ENGLER AND BESSEY

The invigoration that followed the Linnaean period soon took form in many countries in the rapid expansion and specialization of various branches of science. Advances in chemistry and physics about that time contributed greatly to the development of sane points of view and to the formulation of logical hypotheses in physiology that rapidly laid the foundations of present-day knowledge of plant and animal behavior. Improvements in the microscope and in technique brought a knowledge of the finer details of plant structures that was truly astounding. But most of all there came into men's minds a keen sense of a scientific spirit which more and more cried out for experimentation and careful reasoning. Thousands of new plants had been described from all parts of the world and a knowledge of plant-life histories and details of development were greatly extended. The natural consequence of these advances had greatly extended the interest in systematic botany and botanists were beginning to see more clearly their way toward the development of a natural system of classification which would be helpful for purposes of identification and at the same time would reflect something tangible concerning relationships.

THE NATURAL SYSTEM FOUNDED

Contributions of B. and A. L. de Jussieu.—Two Frenchmen, Bernard de Jussieu (1699–1777) and his nephew, A. L. de Jussieu (1748–1836), near the close of the eighteenth century worked out a scheme of classification that was based upon the sexual system of Linnaeus, but it was a great improvement over the best that the Swedish master had accomplished. B. de Jussieu made many changes and rearrangements in the system of Linnaeus so that he really worked out a plan of classification that was essentially new and his own but he never published it. The nephew, A. L. de Jussieu, modified the plan of his uncle still further and published it along with his own scheme in 1789. A. L. de Jussieu's "Genera

Plantarum" in which he published his classification gives us an arrangement that is in reality a much more nearly natural system than was that of Linnaeus. This man is commonly given the

credit of founding the natural system. He included fifteen classes and these were divided into one hundred orders which were clearly differentiated and described for the first time. So that, with de Jussieu, botanists had rather clearly distinguished species, genera, orders, and classes. These "orders" have become approximately the *families* in modern systems of classification. Many of de Jussieu's orders (families) are to be recognized in the most modern classifications. This is a tribute to the care with which he did his work and the keen insight which marked his

A. L. DE JUSSIEU (1748–1836).—(*Photo furnished by Brooklyn Botanic Garden.*)

contributions. The general plan of his system is indicated by the following extract:

ACOTYLEDONES..Class I

MONOCOTYLEDONES
- Stamina *hypogyna*......................Class II
- Stamina *perigyna*......................Class III
- Stamina *epigyna*.......................Class IV

DICOTYLEDONES

Apetalæ
- Stamina *epigyna*.......................Class V
- Stamina *perigyna*......................Class VI
- Stamina *hypogyna*......................Class VII

Monopetalæ
- Corolla *hypogyna*......................Class VIII
- Corolla *perigyna*......................Class IX
- Corolla *epigyna*
  - Antheris connatus.....Class X
  - Antheris distinctis.....Class XI

Polypetalæ
- Stamina *epigyna*.......................Class XII
- Stamina *hypogyna*......................Class XIII
- Stamina *perigyna*......................Class XIV

Diclines irregulares..Class XV

He included all of what we understand today as thallophytes, bryophytes, and pteridophytes as well as a few puzzling flowering plants (*Naiadales*) in Class I coördinate with the flowering plants.

Certain Families Recognized.—At that late date it was impossible to arrange the forms below the flowering plants into any sort of a natural system because of a lack of information about them. That task is extremely difficult, except in connection with the larger groups, even today after a century of refinement in microscopic technic. Such familiar groups as grasses, *Gramineae*, and sedges, *Cyperoideae*, were included in Class II. Class III contains palms, *Palmae*, asparagus, *Asparagus*, lilies, *Lilia*, pineapples, *Bromeliae*, irises, *Irides*, and narcissuses, *Narcissi*. In Class IV we find bananas, *Musae*, cannas, *Cannae*, and orchids, *Orchides*. Class VIII includes a long list of orders (families) such as nightshades, *Solanaceae*, mints, *Labiatae*, borages, *Boraginaceae*, morning-glories, *Convolvuli*, phloxes, *Polemonia*, and gentians, *Gentianeae*, about as we understand the group today. Many other family names, still familiar entries in our manuals, are noted in the various classes of his system.

Monographs of Families.—These illustrations are sufficient to indicate clearly that de Jussieu's system of classification clearly foreshadows the schemes that were proposed by later workers of the modern school of systematic botanists. The men who came after him improved the classification mainly by drawing somewhat clearer or more definite lines between the groups. His ideas of relationships among the flowering plants were far in advance of any that had been promulgated up to his time. He spent many years on working out more careful characterizations of the orders (families) since he believed that the development of a rational natural system depended upon a careful diagnosis of these groups. For many years after his time the popular line of work was to prepare monographs of families. He published several such monographs himself, notably on the *Ranunculaceae*.

INFLUENCE OF DE CANDOLLE

The Scheme of de Candolle.—de Jussieu did the most of his work in Paris. Another great Frenchman, A. P. de Candolle (1778–1841) contributed a very suggestive system of classification. He spent much time in Paris and Montpellier in his younger years but after 1816 he lived in Geneva, Switzerland, where his brilliance of intellect and his broad interests outside as well as within science contributed much to mark that city as a notable center of natural science and culture. He wrote many monographs of plant families and he was also greatly interested in physiology and plant geography. His "Theorie elementaire de la botanique"

was published in 1813, and in this he developed his theory of classification and laid down the laws of classification in such an improved and definite manner as to establish the natural system for all time. Naturally, he was greatly aided in this work by the quantity of material that had been accumulating for a century dealing with the morphology of flowering plants. He pointed out the value and the necessity of a knowledge of the detailed morphology of plant organs if the most perfect natural classification is to be made.

A. P. DE CANDOLLE (1778–1841).—(*Photo furnished by Brooklyn Botanic Garden.*)

The plan of de Candolle's system as published in 1819 is as follows:

I. VASCULARES: Plants with vascular bundles, or plants with cotyledons.

Class 1. EXOGENAE.—Exogens or Dicotyledoneae; vessels arranged in a "ring" or in concentric layers; the embryo with two cotyledons.

A. DIPLOCHLAMYDEAE: Flowers with a double whorl of perianth parts, *i.e.*, calyx and corolla both present.

a. THALAMIFLORAE: Polypetalous and hypogynous.

Cohort 1. Carpels many or stamens opposite the petals. Orders 1 to 8 *Ranunculaceae, Nymphaeaceae, Berberidaceae*, etc.

Cohort 2. Carpels solitary or joined; placentae parietal. Orders 9 to 20. *Cruciferae, Cistaceae, Violaceae*, etc.

Cohort 3. Ovary solitary, placenta central. Orders 21 to 44. *Caryophyllaceae, Geraniaceae, Malvaceae*, etc.

Cohort 4. Fruit gynobasic. Orders 45, 46, *Simarubeae*, etc.

    b. CALYCIFLORAE: perigynous or epigynous, stamens on the calyx; includes certain gamopetalae.

        Orders 47 to 84.

    c. COROLLIFLORAE: gamopetalous and hypogynous, stamens epipetalous.

        Orders 85 to 108.   The hypogynous gamopetalae.

B.   MONOCHLAMYDEAE: flowers with a single perianth whorl, *i.e.* calyx only present.

        Orders 109 to 128.

Class 2.   ENDOGENAE.—Endogens or Monocotyledoneae; vascular bundles scattered, not arranged in a ring; the embryo with a single cotyledon.

A.   PHANEROGAMAE: Flowers present, *i.e.*, visible and regular.

        Orders 129 to 150.

B.   CRYPTOGAMAE: Flowers absent, hidden or unknown.

        Orders 151 to 155.

    II. CELLULARES: Plants without vascular bundles or without cotyledons.

Class 1.   FOLIACEAE.—Leafy; sexuality known.

        Orders 156 to 157 (mosses, liverworts).

Class 2.   APHYLLAE.—Not leafy; sexuality unknown or uncertain.

        Orders 158 to 161 (algae, fungi, lichens).

The orders in de Candolle's system, like those of de Jussieu, are more nearly the *families* of our modern books on classification. This system contains 161 such orders, de Jussieu's 100, and that of Linnaeus 67. The last edition of de Candolle's "Theorie elementaire," published in 1844 by Alphonse de Candolle (a son), contained 213 orders or families.

Work in England.—An interesting point noted in all these systems of classification, including de Candolle's, is that the pines and their kin (*Coniferae, Cycadae,* etc.) are distributed among well-defined groups of dicotyledonous flowering plants in a more modern sense. Robert Brown, an Englishman, was the first to point out (in 1827) that those plants really have naked ovules and seeds and so should be excluded from flowering plants proper, or at least be given a special group by themselves. Brown's researches indicated that the *Gymnosperms* must be regarded as a separate and independent group.

Lindley (1799–1865), an Englishman, designed a system of classification that is of great interest because of its influence in England and elsewhere. Lindley's work has been severely criticised and belittled in certain quarters, especially in Germany, but his work contributed greatly to the clarification of the principles involved in a natural system of classification in spite of the fact that his proposals are often inconsistently represented in his classification.

On the Continent.—Stephen Endlicher (1804–1849) was another prominent systematist of the first half of the nineteenth century. That was a period rich in suggestions as to classification and many systems were proposed. Endlicher's scheme of classification was published in his "Genera Plantarum secundum Ordines Naturales disposita" in 1836–1840 and it was widely used by the countries of continental Europe. The general nature of the system is shown in the following synopsis:

Regio I.   **Thallophyta.**   Plants without true stems and roots, tracheary vessels, and sex organs.
  Sectio I.   *Protophyta*
    Class   I.   Algae-aquatic
    Class II.   Lichens-aerial
  Sectio II.   *Hysterophyta*
    Class III.   Fungi
Regio II.   **Cormophyta.**   Plants with true stems and roots, vessels; sex organs for the most part present.
  Sectio III.   *Acrobrya.*   Stems with apical growth only.
    Cohors 1.   Anophyta
      Class   IV.   *Hepaticae*
      Class   V.   *Musci*
    Cohors 2.   Protophyta
      Class   VI.   *Equiseta*
      Class   VII.   *Filices*
      Class VIII.   *Hydropterides*
      Class   IX.   *Selagines*
      Class   X.   *Zamiae*
    Cohors 3.   Hysterophyta
      Class   XI.   Rhizanthae
  Sectio IV.   *Amphibrya.*   Stems with cylindrical growing zone.
      (Here are mostly monocotyledons, distributed in Classes XII to XXII, with 34 orders.)
  Sectio V.   *Acramphibrya.*   Stem with both apical and cylindrical growing zones.   Here are conifers and dicotyledons.
    Cohors 1.   *Gymnospermae*
    Class XXIII.   Coniferae, with four orders.
    Cohors 2.   *Apetalae.*   Perianth lacking or simple.
    Class XXIV to XXIX, with 36 orders.
    Cohors 3.   *Gamopetalae.*   Perianth with calyx and corolla, petals united, rarely absent.
    Classes XXX to XXXIX, with 45 orders
    Cohors 4.   *Dialypetalae.*   Perianth with calyx and corolla, petals free, hypogynous, perigynous or epigynous, rarely absent.
    Classes XL to LXII, with 116 orders.

Curious notions regarding stem growth extant at the time are reflected in the terms for the three sections of *Cormophyta* in Endlicher's system. The list of orders (families) that we find under the various classes are much the same as those that appear in de Candolle's works. Many of them are in use today with about the same inclusions that occur in this system. The difficulty of disentangling the Gymnosperms from the Angiosperms is also evident in Endlicher's plan, as it is in several prominent systems that were proposed long after his day.

The Frenchman, Brongniart, published a system of classification in 1843 that is interesting in that he drops out the *Apetalae* as a definite group. He indicates that these are imperfect forms of petaliferous types and so he distributes such species among the orders of *Dialypetalae*. Systematists are not agreed even yet as to what the *Apetalae* really are and so their treatment is still uncertain. It seems, however, that there is a growing tendency to regard them as reduced forms and to distribute them among the orders to which they appear to be related on other grounds, as Brongniart suggested.

JOSEPH DALTON HOOKER (1817–1911). (*Photo furnished by Brooklyn Botanic Garden.*)

The Classic System of Bentham and Hooker.—An important system of classification that appeared during the last half of the nineteenth century was that of Bentham and Hooker. George Bentham (1800–1884) and Sir Joseph Hooker (1817–1911) were two Englishmen whose researches were greatly enhanced by the rapidly growing collections of plants at the great herbarium of the Royal Botanical Garden at Kew. Sir Joseph Hooker was director of the Garden for twenty years, following the death of his illustrious father, Sir W. J. Hooker. Bentham and Hooker's system, containing 202 orders (families), was published in a monumental work, "Genera Plantarum" (1862–1883), the most popular plant classification in European countries except France for many years. It was used in practically all of the early botanical work in the United States where it held undisputed preference until the Engler system came out near the close of the century. This system reflects many of the features of the systems of de Jussieu and de Candolle, but it stands out as a very marked improvement over those and other schemes of classification that had been proposed previously. The arrangement of groups in Bentham and Hooker follows de Candolle rather closely but the English investigators appear to have recognized the possibility of the "reduced nature" of the Apetalae, rather than that the plants of that group are primitive. The general plan of Bentham and Hooker's system, in brief synopsis, is indicated below, with a few illustrative orders (families) under each series.

A. DICOTYLEDONS

I. **Polypetalae.**—Petals separate.

SERIES I. THALAMIFLORAE. Hypogynous, stamens and pistils many, indefinite, mostly free.

Cohort 1. Ranales, Orders: *Ranunculaceae, Magnoliaceae, Anonaceae, Berberideae,* etc.

Cohort 2. Parietales. Orders: *Papaveraceae, Cruciferae, Resedaceae, Violaceae,* etc.

Cohort 3. Polygalineae. Orders: *Polygaleae,* etc.

Cohort 4. Caryophyllineae. Orders: *Caryophylleae, Portulacaceae,* etc.

Cohort 5. Guttiferales. Orders: *Hypericaceae, Guttiferaceae, Dipterocarpeae,* etc.

Cohort 6. Malvales. Orders: *Malvaceae, Tiliaceae,* etc.

SERIES II. DISCIFLORAE. Hypogynous, calyx usually free from ovary, stamens usually definite, receptacle often expanded as a disk, ovary free or imbedded in the disk.

Cohort 7. Geraniales. Orders: *Lineae, Geraniaceae, Rutaceae, Meliaceae,* etc.

Cohort 8. Olacales. Orders: *Olacineae, Ilicineae,* etc.

Cohort 9. Celastrales. Orders: *Celastrineae, Rhamneae, Ampelideae,* etc.

Cohort 10. Sapindales. Orders: *Sapindaceae, Anacardiaceae,* etc.

SERIES III. CALYCIFLORAE. Perigynous, ovary enclosed by the axis, sometimes inferior.

Cohort 11. Rosales. Orders: *Leguminosae, Rosaceae, Saxifrageae, Crassulaceae,* etc.

Cohort 12. Myrtales. Orders: *Myrtaceae, Lythracae, Onagraceae,* etc.

Cohort 13. Passiflorales. Orders: *Loaseae, Passifloreae, Cucurbitaceae, Begoniaceae,* etc.

Cohort 14. Ficoidales. Orders: *Cactaceae, Ficoideae.*

Cohort 15. Umbellales. Orders: *Umbelliferae, Araliaceae, Cornaceae.*

II. Gamopetalae. Petals united.

SERIES I.—INFERAE. Ovary inferior, stamens as many as lobes of the corolla, rarely fewer.

Cohort 1. Rubiales. Orders: *Rubiaceae, Caprifoliaceae.*

Cohort 2. Asterales. Orders: *Valerianae, Dipsaceae, Calycereae, Compositae.*

Cohort 3. Campanales. Orders: *Campanulaceae,* etc.

SERIES II. HETEROMERAE. Ovary usually superior, carpels more than two, stamens as many as or fewer than corolla lobes, epipetalous or free.

Cohort 4. Ericales. Orders: *Ericaceae, Vaccinieae, Monotropeae, Epacrideae,* etc.

Cohort 5. Primulales. Orders: *Primulaceae,* etc.

Cohort 6. Ebenales. Orders: *Ebenaceae, Sapotaceae, Styraceae.*

SERIES III. BICARPELLATAE. Ovary usually superior, carpels usually two, rarely 1 or 3; stamens alternate with the corolla lobes, and equal in number or fewer.

Cohort 7. Gentianales. Orders: *Oleaceae, Apocynaceae,* etc.

Cohort 8. Polemoniales. Orders: *Polemoniaceae, Solanaceae,* etc.

Cohort 9. Personales. Orders: *Scrophularineae, Bignoniaceae, Acanthaceae,* etc.

Cohort 10. Lamiales. Orders: *Verbenaceae, Labiatae,* etc.

III. Monochlamydeae.—Perianth simple, often sepaloid or wanting.

SERIES I. CURVEMBRYEAE. Embryo curved; endosperm mealy; ovule usually single; flowers perfect, commonly apetalous; stamens equal to or fewer than perianth divisions.

Orders: *Nyctagineae, Amarantaceae, Chenopodiaceae,* etc.

SERIES II. MULTIOVULATAE AQUATICAE. Submerged herbs; carpels united. Ovules numerous.

Order: *Podostemaceae.*

SERIES III. MULTIOVULATAE TERRESTRES. Terrestrial herbs and shrubs. Carpels united. Ovules numerous.

Orders: *Nepenthaceae, Aristolochiaceae,* etc.

SERIES IV. MICREMBYEAE. Embryo very small, imbedded in copious endosperm. Carpels separate or united. Ovules usually solitary.

Orders: *Piperaceae, Myristiceae,* etc.

SERIES V. DAPHNALES. Ovary usually of one carpel. Ovules solitary. Perianth sepaloid. Mostly trees and shrubs with perfect flowers.

Orders: *Laurineae, Proteaceae, Elaeagnaceae,* etc.

Series VI. Achlamydosporeae. Pistil one-celled. Ovules one to three.

Orders: *Loranthaceae, Santalaceae*, etc.

Series VII. Unisexuales. Flowers unisexual. Pistil simple or syncarpous. Ovules solitary or in pairs. Perianth sometimes lacking.

Orders: *Euphorbiaceae, Urticaceae, Platanaceae, Juglandeae*, etc.

Series VIII. Ordines anomali. Relationships uncertain, near Series VII, but not closely related to any other.

Orders: *Salicineae, Empetraceae, Ceratophylleae*, etc.

GYMNOSPERMAE

Orders: *Gnetaceae, Coniferae, Cycadaceae.*

B. MONOCOTYLEDONES

Series I. Microspermae. Ovary inferior, tricarpellary. Seeds very small and numerous, exalbuminous. Inner perianth (and also outer sometimes) petaloid.

Orders: *Orchideae, Burmanniaceae*, etc.

Series II. Epigynae. Ovary usually inferior. Albumen copious.

Orders: *Bromeliaceae, Irideae, Amaryllideae, Haemodoraceae*, etc.

Series III. *Coronarieae*. Ovary superior. Albumen copious.

Orders: *Liliaceae, Pontederiaceae*, etc.

Series IV. Calycineae. Perianth inconspicuous, sepaloid, stiff or herbaceous. Ovary superior. Albumen copious.

Orders: *Juncaceae, Palmae.*

Series V. Nudiflorae. Perianth lacking or reduced to scales or bristles. Ovary superior.

Orders: *Pandaneae, Typhaceae, Aroideae, Lemnaceae*, etc.

Series VI. Apocarpae. Perianth in one or two series or wanting. Ovary superior. Carpels single or separate.

Orders: *Alismaceae, Naiadaceae*, etc.

Series VII. Glumaceae. Flowers in spikelets or heads, subtended by imbricated bracts. Perianth scale-like or chaffy. Ovary one-celled, one-ovuled.

Orders: *Gramineae, Cyperaceae*, etc.

Eichler's System.—The system proposed by A. W. Eichler, in 1883, is worthy of passing note because of the fact that it constitutes the basis of the Englerian system which has come to be the most widely used of all modern systems of classification. A condensed summary of Eichler's arrangement follows:

A. CYPTOGAMAE

B. PHANEROGAMAE

I. Gymnospermae
II. Angiospermae
   1. KLASSE: *Monocotyleae*
      Series 1. *Liliiflorae*
      Series 2. *Enantioblastae*
      Series 3. *Spadiciflorae*
      Series 4. *Glumiflorae*
      Series 5. *Scitamineae*
      Series 6. *Gynandrae*
      Series 7. *Helobiae*
   2. KLASSE: *Dicotyleae*
     Subclass: *Choripetalae*
      Series 1. *Amentaceae*
      Series 2. *Urticineae*
      Series 3. *Polygoninae*
      Series 4. *Centrospermae*
      Series 5. *Polycarpicae*
      Series 6. *Rhoeadinae*
      Series 7. *Cistiflorae*
      Series 8. *Columniferae*
      Series 9. *Gruinales*
      Series 10. *Terebinthinae*

Series 11. *Aesculinae*
Series 12. *Frangulinae*
Series 13. *Tricoccae*
Series 14. *Umbelliflorae*
Series 15. *Saxifraginae*
Series 16. *Opuntiinae*
Series 17. *Passiflorinae*
Series 18. *Myrtiflorae*
Series 19. *Thymelaeinae*
Series 20. *Rosiflorae*
Series 21. *Leguminosae*
  Anhang: Hysterophyta
Subclass: *Sympetalae*
Series 1. *Bicornes*
Series 2. *Primulinae*
Series 3. *Diospyrinae*
Series 4. *Contortae*
Series 5. *Tubiflorae*
Series 6. *Labiatiflorae*
Series 7. *Campanulinae*
Series 8. *Rubiinae*
Series 9. *Aggregatae*

Orders and Families.—The "series" (Reihe) in this system is essentially our modern *order*. Each series was divided into a number of "orders" that are approximately the equivalents of our later *families*. The inclusion of the Hysterophyta as an "anhang" of the *Choripetalae* is an indication that these interesting parasitic flowering plants were not clearly understood at that time and that their relationships were very puzzling. The group includes the mistletoes, *Loranthaceae*, the rafflesias, *Rafflesiaceae*, and the balanophoras, *Balanophoraceae*. Eichler also included the Indian pipes, *Aristolochiaceae*, in this group although they are not parasitic.

It should be noted that Eichler's system finally separates the Gymnosperms from their usual position between the Dicotyledons and Monocotyledons and raises the group to coördinate rank with the Angiosperms, and lower than the latter. The prestige of Bentham and Hooker's system had resulted in the retention of the anomalous position of the Gymnosperms far longer than the facts of morphology and development warranted.

A NOTABLE SYSTEM BY ENGLER

The system proposed by Adolph Engler is based largely upon Eichler's system, but he also adopted certain features of the systems of classification proposed by A. Braun (1864) and A. Brongniart (1843). Engler, a German botanist, was born in 1844, and for about thirty years was professor of botany in the University of Berlin, and director of the great botanical garden and museum in that city. His system of classification was first published as a guide to the botanical garden of Breslau in 1892.

The system soon began to appear in a more elaborated form in Engler's "Die Natürlichen Pflanzenfamilien," the publication of which has continued with numerous volumes, various supplements, syllabi, and revisions from 1895 to the present. The work is now represented by more than twenty volumes of copiously illustrated text, contributed by numerous authors, but from the beginning it has been under the master editorial hand of the originator. A second edition is now being prepared, of which several numbers have already appeared. This system has

ADOLF ENGLER (1844–1930).—(*Photo furnished by Brooklyn Botanic Garden.*)

been the dominant scheme of plant classification in most of the world for many years since 1900. Practically all of the flowering plant manuals of all countries are now arranged according to the Englerian system.

Outline of Engler's System.—Numerous and more or less significant changes in details have been made by the author during the years since the system was first proposed. Nevertheless, the latest arrangement and sequence of groups in the Engler system are much the same as in the original. The following synopsis of the system is taken from the ninth and tenth German edition of the "Syllabus der Pflanzenfamilien" by Engler and Gilg, published by Gebrüder Borntraeger, Berlin, in

1924. The synopsis is given for the flowering plants alone since we are concerned primarily with these.

CLASS 1. MONOCOTYLEDONEAE

1. ORDER: PANDANALES.
    Families: *Typhaceae, Sparganiaceae*, etc.
2. ORDER: HELOBIAE.
    1. Suborder: Potamogetonineae.
        Families: *Potamogetonaceae, Naiadaceae*.
    2. Suborder: Alismatineae.
        Family: *Alismataceae*.
    3. Suborder: Butomineae.
        Families: *Butomaceae, Hydrocharitaceae*.
3. ORDER: TRIURIDALES.
        Family: *Triuridaceae*.
4. ORDER: GLUMIFLORAE.
        Families: *Gramineae, Cyperaceae*.
5. ORDER: PRINCIPES. Family: *Palmae*.
6. ORDER: SYNANTHAE. Family: *Cyclanthaceae*.
7. ORDER: SPATHIFLORAE.
        Families: *Araceae, Lemnaceae*.
8. ORDER: FARINOSAE.
    1. Suborder: Flagellariineae.
        Family: *Flagellariaceae*.
    2. Suborder: Enantioblastae.
        Families: *Restionaceae, Mayacaceae, Xyridaceae, Eriocaulaceae*.
    3. Suborder: Bromeliineae.
        Families: *Thurniaceae, Bromeliaceae*.
    4. Suborder: Commelinineae.
        Family: *Commelinaceae*.
    5. Suborder: Pontederiineae.
        Family: *Pontederiaceae*.
    6. Suborder: Philydrineae.
        Family: *Philydraceae*.
9. ORDER: LILIIFLORAE.
    1. Suborder: Juncineae. Family: *Juncaceae*.
    2. Suborder: Liliineae.
        Families: *Liliaceae, Haemodoraceae, Amaryllidaceae*.
    3. Suborder: Iridineae. Family: *Iridaceae*.
10. ORDER: SCITAMINEAE.
        Families: *Musaceae, Zingiberaceae, Cannaceae, Marantaceae*.
11. ORDER: MICROSPERMAE.
    1. Suborder: Burmanniineae.
        Family: *Burmanniaceae*.
    2. Suborder: Gynandrae. Family: *Orchidaceae*.

CLASS 2. DICOTYLEDONEAE

1. *Subclass* ARCHICHLAMYDEAE (*Choripetalae* and *Apetalae*).
    1. ORDER: VERTICILLATAE. Family: *Casuarinaceae*,

342

2. ORDER: PIPERALES.
Families: *Saururaceae, Piperaceae*, etc.
3. ORDER: SALICALES.   Family: *Salicaceae.*
4. ORDER: GARRYALES.   Family: *Garryaceae.*
5. ORDER: MYRICALES.   Family: *Myricaceae.*
6. ORDER: BALANOPSIDALES.   Family: *Balanopsidaceae.*
7. ORDER: LEITNERIALES.   Family: *Leitneriaceae.*
8. ORDER: JUGLANDALES.   Family: *Juglandaceae.*
9. ORDER: BATIDALES.   Family: *Batidaceae.*
10. ORDER: JULIANALES.   Family: *Julianaceae.*
11. ORDER: FAGALES.   Families: *Betulaceae, Fagaceae.*
12. ORDER: URTICALES.
     Families: *Ulmaceae, Moraceae, Urticaceae.*
13. ORDER: PROTEALES.   Family: *Proteaceae.*
14. ORDER: SANTALALES.
   1. Suborder: Santalineae.
     Families: *Santalaceae, Olacaceae*, etc.
   2. Suborder: Loranthineae.
     Family: *Loranthaceae.*
   3. Suborder: Balanophorineae.
     Family: *Balanophoraceae.*
15. ORDER: ARISTOLOCHIALES.
     Families: *Aristolochiaceae, Rafflesiaceae, Hydnoraceae.*
16. ORDER: POLYGONALES.   Family: *Polygonaceae.*
17. ORDER: Centrospermae.
   1. Suborder: Chenopodiineae.
     Families: *Chenopodiaceae, Amarantaceae.*
   2. Suborder: Phytolaccineae.
     Families: *Nyctaginaceae, Phytolaccaceae.*
   3. Suborder: Portulacineae.
     Families: *Portulacaceae, Basellaceae.*
   4. Suborder: Caryophyllineae.
     Family: *Caryophyllaceae.*
18. ORDER: RANALES.
   1. Suborder: Nymphaeineae.
     Families: *Nymphaeaceae, Ceratophyllaceae.*
   2. Suborder: Trochodendrineae.
     Families: *Trochodendraceae, Cercidiphyllaceae.*
   3. Suborder: Ranunculineae.
     Families: *Ranunculaceae, Berberidaceae, Menispermaceae,* etc.
   4. Suborder: Magnoliineae.
     Families: *Magnoliaceae, Anonaceae, Myristicaceae, Lauraceae,* etc.
19. ORDER: RHOEADALES.
   1. Suborder: Rhoeadineae.   Family: *Papaveraceae.*
   2. Suborder: Capparidineae.
     Families: *Capparidaceae, Cruciferae*, etc.
   3. Suborder: Resedineae.   Family: *Resedaceae*

4. Suborder: Moringineae. Family: *Moringaceae.*
5. Suborder: Bretschneiderineae. Family: *Bretschneideraceae.*

20. ORDER: SARRACENIALES.
Families: *Sarraceniaceae, Droseraceae, Nepenthaceae.*

21. ORDER: ROSALES.
1. Suborder: Podostemonineae. Family: *Podostemonaceae*, etc.
2. Suborder: Saxifragineae.
Families: *Crassulaceae, Saxifragaceae, Pittosporaceae, Hamamelidaceae*, etc.
3. Suborder: Rosineae.
Families: *Platanaceae, Rosaceae, Leguminosae.*

22. ORDER: PANDALES. Family: *Pandaceae.*

23. ORDER: GERANIALES.
1. Suborder: Geraniineae.
Families: *Geraniaceae, Oxalidaceae, Tropaeolaceae, Linaceae*, etc.
2. Suborder: Malpighiineae.
Families: *Malpighiaceae, Trigoniaceae*, etc.
3. Suborder: Polygalaceae. Families: *Polygalaceae*, etc.
4. Suborder: Dichapetalineae. Family: *Dichapetalaceae.*
5. Suborder: Tricoccae.
Family: *Euphorbiaceae.*
6. Suborder: Callitrichineae. Family: *Callitrichaceae.*

24. ORDER: SAPINDALES.
1. Suborder: Buxineae. Family: *Buxaceae.*
2. Suborder: Empetrineae. Family: *Empetraceae.*
3. Suborder: Coriariineae. Family: *Coriariaceae.*
4. Suborder: Limnanthineae. Family: *Limnanthaceae.*
5. Suborder: Anacardiineae. Family: *Anacardiaceae.*
6. Suborder: Celastrineae.
Families: *Cyrillaceae, Aquifoliaceae, Celastraceae, Staphyleaceae*, etc.
7. Suborder: Icacinineae. Family: *Icacinaceae.*
8. Suborder: Sapindineae.
Families: *Aceraceae, Hippocastanaceae, Sapindaceae.*
9. Suborder: Sabiineae. Family: *Sabiaceae.*
10. Suborder: Melianthineae. Family: *Melianthaceae.*
11. Suborder: Didiereineae. Family: *Didiereaceae.*
12. Suborder: Balsaminineae. Family: *Balsaminaceae.*

25. ORDER: RHAMNALES.
Families: *Rhamnaceae, Vitaceae.*

26. ORDER: MALVALES.
1. Suborder: Elaeocarpineae. Family: *Elaeocarpaceae.*
2. Suborder: Chalaenineae. Family: *Chalaenaceae.*
3. Suborder: Malvineae.
Families: *Tiliaceae, Malvaceae, Bombacaceae, Sterculiaceae.*
4. Suborder: Scytopetalineae. Family: *Scytopetalaceae.*

27. ORDER: PARIETALES.
1. Suborder: Theineae.
Families: *Dilleniaceae, Ochnaceae, Guttiferae*, etc.

2. Suborder: Tamaricineae.
    Families: *Elatinaceae, Tamaricaceae*, etc.
3. Suborder: Cistineae.   Families: *Cistaceae, Bixaceae*.
4. Suborder: Cochlospermineae.   Family: *Cochlospermaceae*.
5. Suborder: Lacistemineae.   Family: *Lacistemaceae*.
6. Suborder: Flacourtiineae.
    Families: *Violaceae, Turneraceae, Passifloraceae*, etc.
7. Suborder: Papayineae.   Family: *Caricaceae*.
8. Suborder: Loasineae.   Family: *Loasaceae*.
9. Suborder: Datiscineae.   Family: *Datiscaceae*.
10. Suborder: Begoniineae.   Family: *Begoniaceae*.
11. Suborder: Ancistrocladineae.   Family: *Ancistrocladaceae*.

28. ORDER: OPUNTIALES.   Family: *Cactaceae*.
29. ORDER: MYRTIFLORAE.
    1. Suborder: Thymelaeineae.
        Families: *Thymelaeaceae, Elaeagnaceae*, etc.
    2. Suborder: Myrtineae.
        Families: *Lythraceae, Punicaceae, Myrtaceae, Oenotheraceae*,
        etc.
    3. Suborder: Hippuridineae.   Family: *Hippuridaceae*.
    4. Suborder: Cynomorineae.   Family: *Cynomoraceae*.
30. ORDER: UMBELLIFLORAE.
    Families: *Araliaceae, Umbelliferae, Cornaceae*.

2. *Subclass:* METACHLAMYDEAE, or *Sympetalae*.
    1. ORDER: DIAPENSIALES.
        Family: *Diapensiaceae*.
    2. ORDER: ERICALES.
        1. Suborder: Ericineae.
            Families: *Clethraceae, Pirolaceae, Ericaceae*.
        2. Suborder: Epicridineae.   Family: *Epicridaceae*.
    3. ORDER: PRIMULALES.   Family: *Primulaceae*, etc.
    4. ORDER: PLUMBAGINALES.   Family: *Plumbaginaceae*.
    5. ORDER: EBENALES.
        1. Suborder: Sapotineae.   Family: *Sapotaceae*.
        2. Suborder: Diospyrineae.
            Families: *Ebenaceae, Symplocaceae, Styracaceae*.
    6. ORDER: CONTORTAE.
        1. Suborder: Oleineae.   Family: *Oleaceae*.
        2. Suborder: Gentianineae.
            Families: *Loganiaceae,   Gentianaceae,   Apocynaceae,*
            Asclepiadaceae.
    7. ORDER: TUBIFLORAE.
        1. Suborder: Convolvulineae.
            Families: *Convolvulaceae, Polemoniaceae*.
        2. Suborder: Lennoineae.
        3. Suborder: Boraginineae.
            Families: *Boraginaceae, Hydrophyllaceae*.
        4. Suborder: Verbenineae.   Families: *Verbenaceae, Labiatae*.
        5. Suborder: Solanineae,

Families: *Solanaceae, Scrophulariaceae, Bignoniaceae, Orobanchaceae,* etc.

6. Suborder: Acanthineae.   Family: *Acanthaceae.*
7. Suborder: Myoparineae.   Family: *Myoporaceae.*
8. Suborder: Phrymineae.   Family: *Phrymaceae.*

8. ORDER: PLANTAGINALES.   Family: *Plantaginaceae.*
9. ORDER: RUBIALES.

Families: *Rubiaceae, Caprifoliaceae, Adoxaceae, Valerianaceae, Dipsacaceae.*

10. ORDER: CUCURBITALES.   Family: *Cucurbitaceae.*
11. ORDER: CAMPANULATAE.

Families: *Campanulaceae, Brunoniaceae, Calyceraceae, Compositae.*

Numerous Subdivisions.—As one examines the system of Engler for the flowering plants he is impressed by the unnecessary multiplication of "unterreihe" or suborders. There are many of these groups with a single family. In such instances it would seem quite adequate if the families were included directly under the respective orders instead of interpolating another subdivision between the order and family. When we examine the system more closely we also note that this tendency to introduce subdivisions that are frequently unnecessary and more or less confusing is extended so far as to interpolate subfamilies between many families and groups of genera.

Position of Apetalae and Amentiferae.—The apetalous and amentiferous families are still placed at the beginning of the system, as to indicate that these are still regarded as the most primitive flowering plants. Investigations during the past two decades would dictate that this old notion should be abandoned and that the magnolias and the buttercups and their kin are to be regarded as the most primitive groups from which the other flowering plants have developed. There is a growing volume of information that leads to a conviction that apetalous and amentiferous (wind-pollinated) plants, indeed, are the very *highest* rather than the *lowest* types of flowering plants. These notions are certainly more nearly in accord with modern opinions of the evolution of Angiosperms and the relationships should therefore be reflected in our attempts to classify flowering plants according to a natural or phyletic system.

Influence of European Systems.—Systematic botany has been dominated from the beginning by European botanists. The modern period in the history of botany may be considered as beginning with Linnaeus (1707–1778). Since the time of Linnaeus many systems of classification have been proposed by Europeans which have left a lasting impress upon the subject. A few of the more important of these have been briefly considered in the preceding sections of this book as an introduction to the history of the development of the natural system.

Classification in America.—For the most part American botanists have been content to accept the schemes of classification proposed by their old world contemporaries with little or no modification. Asa Gray (1810–1888), the nestor of systematic botany in this country, utilized the essential features of the de Candollean and later the Bentham and Hooker systems in his extensive publications on the flora of North America. The latter system of classification appears with little modification in the sixth edition of Gray's "Manual" published in 1889 and 1890. Gray's work at Harvard doubtless did more than that of any other American botanist to acquaint the world with the flora of our country in the nineteenth century. Gray was more interested in the discovery and determination of the plants of America than in the development of systems of classification. He did not work out a scheme of classification of his own.

THE SYSTEM PROPOSED BY BESSEY

The system of classification proposed by Bessey (1845–1915) is probably the most important contribution of this sort by an American botanist. The Besseyan system has attracted some attention in other parts of the world, but it has never been accepted and adopted to any great degree in any country. Bessey was one of Gray's students. Early (1884) in his botanical career he became professor of botany in the University of Nebraska where he did the most of his work. The latest synopsis of his proposed system of classification was published after his death in 1915.

Earlier Proposals by Bessey.—Bessey's system in the beginning was largely modeled after the de Candollean system as modified by Bentham and Hooker as is shown in his first publication[1] (1894) dealing with his scheme of classification. This is essentially a revised arrangement of the Bentham and Hooker system with new names suggested for the orders. The system with the

[1] "Evolution and Classification," Cont. Bot. Dept. Univ. Nebr., N. S. VII, 1894.

Bentham and Hooker groups in parentheses is presented in outline form below:

Subclass Monocotyledones

ORDER: ALISMALES (Apocarpae). *Alismaceae*, etc.
ORDER: LILIALES (Coronarieae). *Liliaceae*, etc.
ORDER: AROIDALES (Nudiflorae). *Araceae*, etc.
ORDER: PALMALES (Calycinae). *Palmaceae*, etc.
ORDER: GLUMALES (Glumaceae). *Gramineae*, etc.
ORDER: HYDRALES (Hydrales).
ORDER: IRIDALES (Epigynae). *Iridaceae*, etc.
ORDER: ORCHIDALES (Microspermae). *Orchidaceae*.

Subclass Dicotyledones

POLYPETALAE (Choripetalae)

I. THALAMIFLORAE.
ORDER: RANALES. *Ranunculaceae, Magnoliaceae*, etc.
ORDER: PARIETALES. *Cruciferae, Violaceae*, etc.
ORDER: POLYGALALES. *Polygalaceae*, etc.
ORDER: CARYOPHYLLALES. *Caryophyllaceae*, etc.
ORDER: GUTTIFERALES. *Hypericaceae*, etc.
ORDER: MALVALES. *Malvaceae*, etc.

II. DISCIFLORAE.
ORDER: GERANIALES. *Geraniaceae*, etc.
ORDER: CELASTRALES. *Celastraceae*, etc.
ORDER: SAPINDALES. *Sapindaceae*, etc.

III. CALYCIFLORAE.
ORDER: ROSALES. *Rosaceae, Leguminosae*, etc.
ORDER: MYRTALES. *Myrtaceae, Onagraceae*, etc.
ORDER: PASSIFLORALES. *Loasaceae*, etc.
ORDER: CACTALES. *Cactaceae*, etc.
ORDER: UMBELLALES. *Umbelliferae*, etc.

GAMOPETALAE

I. HETEROMERAE.
ORDER: PRIMULALES. *Primulaceae*, etc.
ORDER: ERICALES. *Ericaceae*, etc.
ORDER: EBENALES. *Ebenaceae*, etc.

II. BICARPELLATAE.
ORDER: GENTIANALES. *Gentianaceae*, etc.
ORDER: POLEMONIALES. *Polemoniaceae*, etc.
ORDER: PERSONALES. *Scrophulariaceae*, etc.
ORDER: LAMIALES. *Labiatae*, etc.

III. INFERAE.
ORDER: RUBIALES. *Rubiaceae*, etc.
ORDER: CAMPANALES. *Campanulaceae*, etc.
ORDER: ASTERALES. *Compositae*, etc.

The most evident differences noted in this plan of Bessey's as compared with Bentham and Hooker's, besides changes in the names of a number of the groups, are the rearrangement of the Monocotyledons, the distribution of the *Monochlamydeae* among the other orders, the dropping out of the gymnosperms, and the exchange of position of the *Heteromerae* and the *Inferae*, Bessey placing the latter above the former.

Later Plans by Bessey.—A later plan published by Bessey in 1897 differs from the above system, mainly in relating the *Disciflorae* to the *Calyciflorae* rather than to the *Heteromerae*, and in the inclusions of some of the orders. He also returned to the use of Bentham and Hooker's names for the orders of Monocotyledons. The paper also contains valuable statistical data and the beginnings of Bessey's "dicta" which appear in definite form in his last published synopsis in 1915. His outline of flowering-plant classification was somewhat modified in 1907 and again in 1909, along with the publication of an outline for the whole vegetable kingdom.

The outline of classification suggested by H. Hallier during this period had many features in common with the systems proposed by Bentham and Hooker and by Bessey.

The Besseyan System in Final Form.—Bessey's last arrangement was published in 1915[1] with a discussion of the principles of classification (dicta) which were followed in the development of the system. This scheme subdivides the flowering plants (*Anthophyta*) into 32 orders and 300 families.

An outline of the system of classification of flowering plants proposed by Bessey (1915), with the orders and a few representative families, concludes our brief study of the evolution of the natural system of classification for flowering plants.

Class: Alternifoliae (Monocotyledoneae)

SUBCLASS: STROBILOIDEAE.

ORDER: ALISMATALES: *Alismataceae, Typhaceae, Pandanaceae, Sparganiaceae*, etc.

ORDER: LILIALES: *Liliaceae, Commelinaceae, Juncaceae, Naiadaceae, Xyridaceae.*

ORDER: ARALES: *Araceae, Lemnaceae.*

ORDER: PALMALES: *Palmaceae.*

ORDER: GRAMINALES: *Cyperaceae, Poaceae.*

[1] "The Phylogenetic Taxonomy of Flowering Plants." *Ann. Missouri Botan. Garden,* **2**: 108–164, 1915.

SUBCLASS: COTYLOIDEAE.

  ORDER: HYDRALES: *Vallisneriaceae.*

  ORDER: IRIDALES: *Amaryllidaceae, Iridaceae, Musaceae, Cannaceae, Zingiberaceae, Dioscoreaceae.*

  ORDER: ORCHIDALES: *Orchidaceae, Burmanniaceae.*

Class: Oppositifoliae (Dicotyledoneae)

SUBCLASS: STROBILOIDEAE. "Cone flowers."

 SUPERORDER: APOPETALAE-POLYCARPELLATAE.

  ORDER: RANALES: *Magnoliaceae, Anonaceae, Myristicaceae, Saururaceae, Piperaceae, Ranunculaceae,* etc.

  ORDER: MALVALES: *Malvaceae, Tiliaceae, Ulmaceae, Moraceae, Urticaceae.*

  ORDER: SARRACENIALES: *Sarraceniaceae, Nepenthaceae.*

  ORDER: GERANIALES: *Geraniaceae, Oxalidaceae, Linaceae, Balsaminaceae, Rutaceae, Euphorbiaceae.*

  ORDER: GUTTIFERALES: *Theaceae, Guttiferaceae,* etc.

  ORDER: RHOEADALES: *Papaveraceae, Nymphaeaceae, Capparidaceae, Brassicaceae (Cruciferae).*

  ORDER: CARYOPHYLLALES: *Caryophyllaceae, Portulacaceae, Salicaceae, Phytolaccaceae, Amaranthaceae,* etc.

 SUPERORDER: SYMPETALAE-POLYCARPELLATAE.

  ORDER: EBENALES: *Ebenaceae, Sapotaceae, Styracaceae.*

  ORDER: ERICALES: *Ericaceae, Pyrolaceae, Clethraceae.*

  ORDER: PRIMULALES: *Primulaceae, Plantaginaceae.*

 SUPERORDER: SYMPETALAE-DICARPELLATAE.

  ORDER: GENTIANALES: *Gentianaceae, Oleaceae, Apocynaceae, Asclepiadaceae.*

  ORDER: POLEMONIALES: *Polemoniaceae, Convolvulaceae,* etc.

  ORDER: SCROPHULARIALES: *Scrophulariaceae, Acanthaceae, Martyniaceae, Bignoniaceae.*

  ORDER: LAMIALES: *Phrymaceae, Lamiaceae,* etc.

SUBCLASS: COTYLOIDEAE. "Cup flowers."

 SUPERORDER: APOPETALAE.

  ORDER: ROSALES: *Rosaceae, Malaceae, Mimosaceae, Cassiaceae, Fabaceae, Saxifragaceae,* etc.

  ORDER: MYRTALES: *Lythraceae, Punicaceae, Myrtaceae, Oenotheraceae. Aristolochiaceae, Rafflesiaceae.*

  ORDER: LOASALES: *Loasaceae, Cucurbitaceae, Begoniaceae.*

  ORDER: CACTALES: *Cactaceae.*

  ORDER: CELASTRALES: *Rhamnaceae, Vitaceae, Celastraceae, Aquifoliaceae, Staphyleaceae, Elaeagnaceae, Loranthaceae.*

  ORDER: SAPINDALES: *Sapindaceae, Aceraceae, Anacardiaceae, Juglandaceae, Betulaceae,* etc.

  ORDER: UMBELLALES: *Araliaceae, Apiaceae (Umbelliferae), Cornaceae.*

 SUPERORDER: SYMPETALAE.

  ORDER: RUBIALES: *Rubiaceae, Caprifoliaceae, Valerianaceae, Dipsacaceae.*

  ORDER: CAMPANULALES: *Campanulaceae.*

  ORDER: ASTERALES: 14 families, including *Ambrosiaceae,* that are usually treated as "tribes" by other authors.

The Arrangement in General.—These orders and families are distributed in three main groups diverging from the *Ranales*. One group is the Monocotyledons beginning with the hypogynous arrowheads, *Alismatales*, and then leading successively to lilies, *Liliales*, and epigynous irises, *Iridales*, and ending in the orchids, *Orchidales*. The *Hydrales*, *Arales*, *Palmales*, and *Graminales* are all derived from the *Liliales*. These latter orders are regarded as lateral branches of the *Liliales* which lie in the main series of Monocotyledons.

The Dicotyledons are represented as in two separate series, each originating in the *Ranales*. One of these gives rise to the roses, *Rosales*, bittersweets, *Celastrales*, umbellifers, *Umbellales*, madders, *Rubiales*, and ends in the composites, *Asterales*. The myrtles, *Myrtales*, are regarded as a side line from *Rosales*, with the loasas, *Loasales*, and cactuses, *Cactales*, as branches of this order. The soapberries, *Sapindales*, are a branch of *Celastrales*, and bluebells, *Campanulales*, represent a lateral branch from the lower composites, *Asterales*. The other line of Dicotyledons begins in the *Ranales* and leads to pinks, *Caryophyllales*, and a group of closely related orders including mallows, *Malvales*, geraniums, *Geraniales*, teas, *Guttiferales*, and crucifers, *Rhoeadales*, and then continues to another group including primroses, *Primulales*, heathers, *Ericales*, and ebonies, *Ebenales*, and terminates in a group of four orders including phloxes, *Polemoniales*, gentians, *Gentianales*, mints, *Lamiales*, and snapdragons, *Scrophulariales*. The first series leads from the hypogynous buttercups through the epigynous and sympetalous madders, to the bluebells and asters. The other series leads from the buttercups through the polypetalous, actinomorphic geraniums, pinks, and crucifers, to the sympetalous primroses and their kin, to the phloxes and gentians, and finally to the sympetalous and zygomorphic mints and snapdragons. This line is, with few exceptions, hypogynous. The order of development and the grouping of orders within the several superorders of the system are shown in the accompanying figure.

Bessey proposed the doubtfully useful terms *Alternifoliae* and *Oppositifoliae* for the old terms *Monocotyledoneae* and *Dicotyledoneae* respectively, since he states that the old terms are now somewhat misleading. The new terms are based upon the position of the first leaves (cotyledons) of the embryo in the two groups.

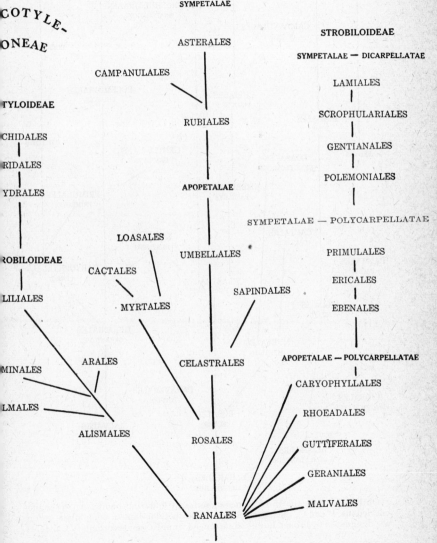

Diagram to show the sub-classes, super-orders, and orders of flowering plants and their relationships according to the last arrangement by Bessey.

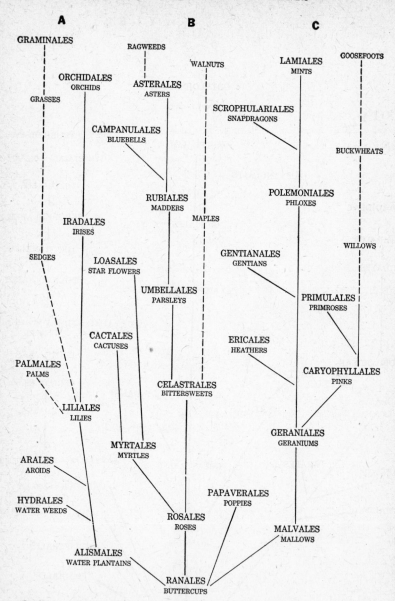

Outline to show the three principal series of flowering plants, A, the monocotyledons, B and C, the dicotyledons. The apetalous and anemophilous groups are designated by broken lines. Rearranged from Bessey according to Clements.

The more conspicuous differences noted in this arrangement as compared with the earlier (1893) proposal of the author are in the subdivision of the Monocotyledons into two subclasses based upon hypogyny and epigyny, the introduction of new names for the subclasses of Dicotyledons, and the separation of the *Gamopetalae* of the Bentham and Hooker system to form the two groups that constitute the upper series and the termini of the two main lines of Dicotyledons in the Besseyan system. The last change also featured the 1897 edition of Bessey's system.

Comparison with Engler's System.—The most striking contrasts between the Engler system and the Bessey system for flowering plants may be noted. The numerous suborders of the Engler system are not featured in the Besseyan system. Engler regards the diclinous Apetalae and Amentiferae as primitive forms and hence he places them at the beginning of his arrangement, but Bessey regards the monoclinous, apopetalous, spiral, buttercup type (*Ranales*) as the primitive form from which all other flowering plants have developed; the latter author regards the diclinous Apetalae and Amentiferae as "reduced" or "simplified" forms of higher types so he distributes these among various other derived groups. Engler gives more weight to apopetaly versus sympetaly than to hypogyny versus epigyny in the establishment of his groups and lines of relationships. Bessey likewise ranks sympetaly high, but he also regards epigyny as a mark of higher types. A more extended illustration of these and other "principles" upon which our modern systems of flowering-plant classification are founded has been outlined in Chapters X and XI.

CHAPTER XXVII.

COLLECTING AND PREPARING SPECIMENS

Precautions for the Collector.—Ideally, flowering plants should be classified in the field at the time they are gathered, but that is often impossible, so it is necessary to collect specimens and prepare them for future study and reference. Accuracy and facility in the determination of flowering plants on the basis of specimens secured in the field are largely dependent upon the care and completeness with which the materials are gathered and prepared. Poorly treated, incomplete, and fragmentary specimens are usually unpleasant to work with and they may often lead to uncertainties and inaccuracies in identification even by the most careful specialists. One should not submit such materials for determination when it is possible to secure more nearly perfect and satisfactory specimens. If one is making his own private collection of plants he should bear the same precautions in mind in order that much time may be saved, his work be more pleasant, his specimens be much more accurately named, and the whole collection be an object of beauty as well as of scientific merit.

Equipment for Collecting.—The equipment necessary for such work is relatively simple and inexpensive. Makeshift apparatus is often useful, especially to the beginner. However, if one intends to continue his collecting indefinitely or if he is planning an extensive collecting expedition, it will be profitable for him to give more thought and care to assembling the equipment that will return the most efficient and pleasurable service.

Notebooks.—A field notebook is an indispensable feature in the kit of a careful collector. The type of notebook used may rest upon the personal demands of the individual, but, in this day of almost unlimited resources of this nature he may easily err in his choice. Of the numerous kinds available, the best for this purpose is probably one of the pocket-size, loose-leaf forms with flexible leather or leatheroid cover. An important advantage possessed by this type of notebook is the ease with which one's invaluable field notes and records dealing with material collected

354

may be removed and filed away for safe keeping and future reference.   A handy numerical scheme should be adopted for keeping the record of the individual collections.   Careful records should also be made of dates, habitat details, abundance, associated species, and other features of interest and value concerning the specimens.   The field notes kept in this way should later furnish all of the details necessary for the temporary and permanent labels for the specimens collected, as well as for an orderly account of the flora and general phytogeographical features of the areas involved.

Containers for Specimens.—A container of some sort must be at hand in which the specimens may be placed as they are gathered in the field.   This may take the form of a collecting can

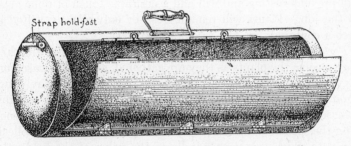

Fig. 204.—A convenient collecting can or *vasculum*.   Description in text.

or *vasculum* (Fig. 204) or a light, portable press (Fig. 208) may be used for the same purpose.   Almost any sort of a bag, pack, or rücksack may be used, but best results are likely to be secured for the largest number of specimens by the use of a vasculum.   This is made of tin and it may be of any desirable size.   A convenient form is oval in section, and about 20 inches long by 8 inches wide and 10 inches high.   Larger cases are likely to be bunglesome and to become too heavy when filled.   This oblong case should have a lid 5 or 6 inches high on one side extending to within 1 inch of each end and hinged to the body along the entire lower edge.   The upper edge of the lid should be provided with a substantial clamp or sliding bolt made of heavy wire in order that the vasculum may be handily and securely closed.   This large opening will enable one to place the specimens in the case with greatest ease and with the least folding and also will permit their removal with the least tearing or other injury.   The vasculum should have a ring or buckle at each end for the attachment of a carrying strap. A comfortable handle with wooden or leather handhold should also be firmly riveted to the top of the vasculum on the center line (Fig. 204).   This combination of carrying strap and handle is often very welcome on long trips with a heavy vasculum. All of the joints should be very firmly soldered and the hinges very substantially constructed if one is to secure uninterrupted and efficient service from such a collecting can for many seasons.

A good tin shop is usually prepared to construct such containers at a nominal price or they may be purchased from the regular dealers in botanical supplies. If the local tinner makes them it is well to have them thoroughly japanned black or preferably painted with a good grade of light green or white paint. This will prevent rusting and will add a desirable touch of refinement to the job. Plants will remain fresh or only slightly wilted in such a container for 2 or 3 days if necessary.

Portable Presses.—A portable field press (Figs. 208 and 209) may receive the plants as they are gathered, and so the vasculum may not be needed, but as a rule such a press cannot entirely supplant the vasculum. The portable press is especially valuable in cases where the flowers close or the leaves wilt badly soon after the specimens are taken even if they are placed in the collecting can. Such experiences indicate the value of the field press to be used either with or without the vasculum. Likewise, if one is doing only a very limited amount of collecting, the portable press may meet all the demands of a temporary container.

Construction of Presses.—The portable press at best can hold relatively few specimens but even then it must be constructed of the lightest materials practicable. Most plant presses, portable or otherwise, are 10 to 12 inches wide and 15 to 18 inches long, and are made of two thin boards, wire netting, or slatted strips of thin wood laid crossways (Figs. 208 and 209), and the two bound together more or less like the cover boards of a book by means of straps, cords, chains, or other sorts of clamps. The desired pressure is secured by tightening the straps or clamps by means of any of the convenient methods available. The two sides of a very serviceable portable press are made by stretching galvanized wire netting with $\frac{1}{4}$- or $\frac{1}{2}$-inch mesh over two oblong frames 12 inches wide by 18 inches long (Fig. 209).   The frames may be made of thin strips of heavy wood rigidly mortised at the corners, or preferably of heavy $\frac{1}{2}$-

inch strap iron firmly welded at the corners. If the iron frame is used the wire netting may be neatly and firmly soldered about the frame. The pressure on such a press may be secured by the use of two broad leather or web straps, or by means of four strong flat-link chains anchored at the edges of one of the sides of the press and caught by corresponding hooks or clamps at the edges of the other side of the press. In this case the total thickness of the press would be determined by the length of the chains used. A convenient handle may be secured for the press by the use of an ordinary shawlstrap or a permanent handle may be attached to the frames or chains of the press. The press is completed by the addition of a few sheets of drying paper, filing sheets, and ventilators, all of which will be described in the following pages.

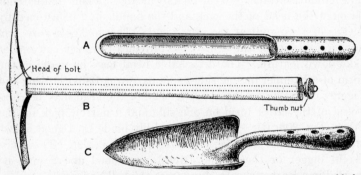

Fig. 205.—Useful collecting tools, diggers, etc. *A*, trowel with narrow blade; *B*, combination pick and adz with detachable handle; *C*, trowel with broad blade. See descriptions in text.

Useful Diggers.—Some sort of a trowel or plant digger (Fig. 205) is usually necessary for obtaining roots, tubers, bulbs, and other subterranean parts. Here again the possible choices are numerous and the mistakes are frequent on the part of the amateur. The ordinary light trowels used by the florist and gardener are usually constructed of too light materials and these are put together poorly to serve the varied needs of the plant collector. The florist and the gardener usually work with light, crumbly, and shallow soils, whereas the collector is required to dig his plants from a great variety of soils that may be extremely hard and firm or even rocky and it may be necessary to go to considerable depth in such soils. The collector's digger must, therefore, be used more roughly and it must be more rigidly constructed (Fig. 205, *A*, *C*). The best kind of trowel for the varied needs of the plant collector is one with a narrow, slightly hollow blade, say about 2 inches wide, made of heavy steel, in which the steel is continuous backward into the shank or "tang" (Fig. 205, *A*). The handle may be made of hardwood driven into and riveted in the steel shank, or better yet, the handle should be formed by the backward prolongation of the steel of the blade and shank thus making a one piece instrument. The trowel with a broad, thin blade and a narrow, rod-like shank and cheap handle is practically worthless for these purposes. The best plant digger that we have used is a small but firmly constructed pick with a broad cutting edge and take-down feature (Fig. 205, *B*). The heavy handle 12 inches long is made of hickory and both ends are supplied with a steel binding ring. The handle is attached to the pick by means of a bolt that extends through the head of the pick and the handle and is fastened by means of a wingnut at the upper end. This makes a very firm connection and at the same time provides the very convenient take-down feature. The detachable head may be made in the form of a hammer on one side and a narrow, adz-like cutting and digging extension on the opposite side, or the head may be composed of the latter form on one side and a narrow pick on the other (Fig. 205, *B*). This tool is readily made by a good blacksmith. Nothing just like it is listed by any dealer. This very useful digger or the special trowel mentioned above may be carried in a leather sheath slung from the belt or may be conveniently stowed away in a shoulder pack or bag.

Selection of Specimens.—The intelligent collector selects the specimens that he will take with considerable care. Promiscuous and careless snatching of material is wholly unscientific and is likely to lead to many disappointments. One should take several specimens of each plant unless it is very rare and likely to be exterminated. The plant collector should be a real conservationist, and as such he is able to minimize his feeling of personal loss when he passes by a fine specimen of a rare orchid, lily, columbine, or some other form that is threatened with obliteration on account of man's thoughtlessness and ignorance. But as a rule it is wise to take more than one specimen, unless the one selected is especially representative and complete. Oftentimes one finds that it is impossible to identify a plant accurately on the basis of a single specimen, and it is also often desirable to secure several specimens in order to illustrate certain variations of the plant in question.

Neat and Complete Specimens.—Each specimen should be as complete as possible; *i.e.,* if possible it should show enough of the roots, rhizomes, tubers, bulbs, corms, or other underground parts, stems, buds, leaves of all forms, flowers, fruits, and seeds to insure unquestionable identification. Naturally it is seldom possible to gather all of these parts for any species at a single visit, so it may be necessary to go to where the plants grow two or more times in order to secure the material to make complete

specimens. Many plants have different forms of leaves at the base and on the stem, and certain species produce unisexual flowers, and there are other differences in the individual or among the individuals of many species that the collector must take in order to have the whole story of the plant.

All specimens should be neatly made. A sharp knife is needed to

Fig. 206.—A very handy and efficient type of dissecting microscope for use in the study of flowers (*after Bausch and Lomb Optical Co.*).

Fig. 207.—Useful and practical pocket magnifiers. These may be secured in various sizes and with different magnifying value (*after Bausch and Lomb Optical Co.*).

remove specimens of woody twigs and to divide the stems of herbaceous plants in order to prepare attractive material. Few plant parts can be broken roughly without leaving more or less lacerated and untidy ends or edges that reduce the attractiveness of the finished and mounted specimens, to say nothing of the appearance of the rest of the plant left in the field. Neatness is, in short, a virtue that should be fastidiously cultivated by the collector.

Specimens should be taken on a clear, dry day whenever possible, since the beauty as well as much of the value of such materials depends to a large degree upon the rapidity of drying. Ordinarily they should be removed from the vasculum or portable press at the end of each day when the collector returns to his home or base station. If they are left too long in the temporary container they may become discolored, moulded, or so badly wilted and shriveled that it is wholly impossible to make satisfactory preparations of them.

Dissecting Microscopes.—A good dissecting microscope (Fig. 206) and a pocket lens (Fig. 207) are indispensable adjuncts to careful field work and the final determination of the species collected.

Transfer to Press.—An important phase of the technique of preparing attractive plant specimens is involved in the transfer of the material from the vasculum and portable press to the final press where they are to be dried. First of all one should see that each specimen is freed from all foreign material, that any adherent soil is shaken or washed from the roots, tubers, etc. that the stems are untangled, that the leaves are untangled and flattened, that the flowers and fruits are made to look as natural as possible, and that the specimens are trimmed to fit the drying sheets. Then they are ready for the press.

A Practical Plant Press.—Many different kinds of plant presses have been made and used with success. If one is to prepare relatively few specimens for a season or two he may do it satisfactorily with very simple equipment, such as two flat boards, a few old newspapers, large blotters, and a big rock or other weight. But these items would prove very inconvenient and unsatisfactory if a more extensive program is in mind and if one is to become a collector of hundreds of specimens. In the latter event more nearly permanent and efficient apparatus would be demanded.

A very substantial plant press is made by using two plywood boards about 12 inches wide by 18 inches long for the sides of the press (Fig. 208). These may be of three-ply material and planed down to about $3/8$ inch in thickness. The corners should be rounded. Three transverse strips of oak or birch 1 inch wide and $3/4$ inch thick are laid across each of the plywood boards and securely fastened by means of screws started on the plywood side. One of the cross strips is fastened about 2 inches from each end of the boards and the third one is placed across the center. The ends of these cross sticks are knobbed and extend about 1 inch beyond the edge of the plywood boards in order to catch the small rope or heavy cord used to hold the press together and apply the pressure. A piece of window cord or clothesline serves very nicely for the latter purpose and it should be securely fastened to one of the ends of a crossbar at one end of the press (Fig. 208). When the specimens have been arranged in the press and the press is ready to be closed the cord is laced over the knobbed ends of the crossbars on one side of the press and then crossed over to the other side where the

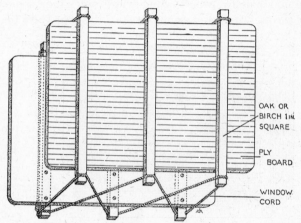

OAK OR
BIRCH 1 IN.
SQUARE

PLY
BOARD

WINDOW
CORD

FIG. 208.—A very useful and practical type of press for the field.

same procedure is followed until the desired pressure is obtained, then the cord is tied securely and the press is ready to be placed in the sun.

With sufficient cord and driers one may fill such a press until it is 2 or 3 feet high when lying flat. One may secure the proper pressure in the press by bearing down upon the upper cover (as the press lies flat) with his foot or knee as he laces it up. The amount of pressure necessary to make the best specimens of varied material can be determined only by practice. The most succulent specimens may be crushed to such a degree as to be spoiled by a pressure that is none too great to make the best specimens that are relatively dry and woody. One is compelled to strike a compromise in such matters, but he soon learns the best possible practice by experience. A press of this type is strong enough and durable enough to last for many years even under heavy and rough usage.

Fillers for the Press.—Too much attention cannot be devoted to the fillers for the press (Fig. 210), *i.e.*, the drying sheets, ventilators, etc. that should be used to secure the most rapid and complete drying of the specimens, and that facilitate the handling of the latter. The fillers consist of three elements that we may designate as *folders, drying sheets*, and *ventilators* (Fig. 210).

The *folders* (Fig. 210) are thin sheets of absorbent paper twice the size of one of the plyboards of the press and these are folded on the long axis to form a symmetrical folder that is about the area of the plyboards and drying sheets, *i.e.*, about 12 by 18 inches.

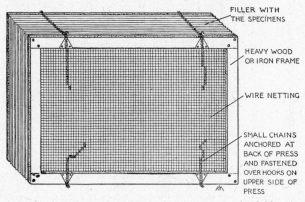

FILLER WITH THE SPECIMENS

HEAVY WOOD OR IRON FRAME

WIRE NETTING

SMALL CHAINS ANCHORED AT BACK OF PRESS AND FASTENED OVER HOOKS ON UPPER SIDE OF PRESS

Fig. 209.—Another satisfactory form of press for use in the field. See details in the text.

Newspaper stock serves very nicely for folders, or even old newspapers may be used for this purpose with almost as much success. The purpose of the folder is to receive the specimens and to serve as their container as they are passing through the press. They also serve very well as temporary files in which the specimens may be kept or stored until they are to be mounted.

The *drying sheets* (Fig. 210) are the most important absorbent element among the fillers. These may be furnished by the dealers in botanical supplies and they should be used as single sheets cut to the appropriate dimensions. They are of the nature of heavy, gray or blue felt paper and are much tougher than ordinary blotting paper. They may be secured in two or three different weights. Blotting paper cut to fit the press may be used for drying sheets, but this is more easily torn in handling and may not prove to be as valuable as the regular driers.

The *ventilators* (Fig. 210) are merely sheets of corrugated cardboard similar to that used in packing boxes and trimmed to the size of the folders and drying sheets. The most efficient type of corrugated board to use is that which is surfaced with paper on one side only. These sheets are cut double the size required and then folded through the middle with the facing in the center and the transverse corrugations on both outer surfaces. But this type of ventilator makes a bulky press for comparatively few specimens, so perhaps is to be rejected in favor of the single sheet of corrugated board. The facing should be made of as thin and as porous a paper as possible.

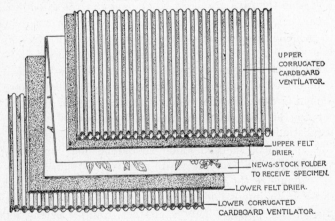

UPPER CORRUGATED CARDBOARD VENTILATOR.

UPPER FELT DRIER.

NEWS-STOCK FOLDER TO RECEIVE SPECIMEN.

LOWER FELT DRIER.

LOWER CORRUGATED CARDBOARD VENTILATOR.

FIG. 210.—Fillers for a more elaborate type of press and method of manipulation. See descriptive details in the text.

Placing Specimens in the Press.—The specimens are placed in the press (Fig. 210) by first spreading them out on the right side of the open folder as it lies in front of the operator. It is well to have a drying sheet or two under the folder or have the latter on a table or box in order that the specimens may be firmly pressed against the thin paper of the folder without tearing it. The plants should be placed and spaced very carefully over the surface of the folder because the form that they are given there will in most cases be their permanent form when removed from the press. Each specimen must be arranged so that it will look best and as natural as possible, keeping in mind that it will have the same appearance on the sheets upon which it will be mounted. The specimens ought not to be crowded or piled upon each other. Unruly twigs should be flattened and the

leaves neatly spread out with the minimum amount of folding
and overlap. One should endeavor to secure the natural lie of
all of the parts. Bulky organs must be reduced as much as
possible by hollowing out the back, or by sectioning them in
such a manner as not to affect the surface appearance. This
can be done very skillfully for bulky roots, bulbs, stems, and
even fruits, after a little practice. Some of the *Compositae*
with large, radiate heads are difficult to press nicely unless one
sections the heads or blocks up the head by disks of drying
paper that fit closely about the involucre and that permit the
rays to lie out more nearly flat. If something of this nature
is not done the rays are likely to dry and shrivel so badly as to
conceal their real nature in the mounted specimen. So, flowers
with bell-shaped or inflated corollas, as in bluebell, *Campanula*,
lady's slipper, *Cypripedium*, slipperwort, *Calceolaria*, etc. may
be kept from being mashed out of all naturalness by placing a
pad of cotton of appropriate size inside the corollas before the
specimen is closed in the press. Other devices of the sort will
occur to the thoughtful worker who wishes to preserve the
naturalistic impressions of the material.

The specimens in each folder should be distributed as uniformly as possible over the entire area of the folder. This will
tend to equalize the pressure throughout the press in a degree
that would be impossible if the materials are gathered near the
center of the folders. This is another example of the refined
technique that the collector should develop rapidly.

Temporary Labels.—When the specimens have been arranged
upon the folder a temporary label should be added for each
species represented and then the folder is closed and placed
in the press with a sheet of drying paper underneath and above
it, and this in turn with a corrugated ventilator underneath and
above the folder inclosed by the two drying sheets. Thus it
will be seen that the layer of specimens has a sheet of absorbent
folder, drying paper, and corrugated cardboard (Fig. 210) both
above and below in every case when the press is made up in this
manner. The ventilators are thus distributed through the press
in such a manner that the drying out of the specimens is very
greatly accelerated. In fact this plan of press management
makes it unnecessary to remove the specimens from the press
and change the driers when one is collecting in rather dry countries. The necessity to conserve space in the press when one is

collecting a great deal of material may require that the ventilators be used less freely. Under such conditions they may be inserted between every other folder or even at greater intervals as may be necessary or desirable.

Care of the Press.—The press should be placed in the open air and in the sun whenever that is possible, even in dry climates. But in humid regions it is best to change the press frequently if the most satisfactory results are to be secured with even this type of press. In very moist, cloudy weather it may be necessary to hang the press over a stove, or camp lamp, or in some other manner to supplement nature in the drying process if good specimens are to be secured. If the ventilators are omitted the press must be changed more frequently under all conditions. Some plants may be dried by this process in a few days, say less than a week, but most species will require a longer time and some may not be removed safely from the press for two weeks or more.

The material in the press should be examined each day in order to remove any specimens that are sufficiently cured, and to replace the moist driers with dry sheets. This may be done at the time new specimens are added when one is doing much collecting. Thus at any one time the press may contain material that is ready to be removed, some specimens that are not yet sufficiently dry to remove, and fresh material just added. The very best result can be secured only by constant attention to the press and the drying process, in order that changes in the drying sheets and ventilators may be made at proper intervals to insure the most perfect and rapid drying

Changing the Press.—The work and time involved in changing the press are reduced to the minimum when the press is made up according to the above plan. To change the press it is only necessary to loosen the cord, strap, clamps, or other binders and then remove the plyboard at the top. If the entire press is to be changed (which would ordinarily be unnecessary) one simply removes the ventilator and drying sheet over the first folder and then the latter is placed over a fresh, dry sheet and ventilator and then covered with the next drying sheet and ventilator as the start of the fresh pile of fillers. This is continued until all of the folders have been removed and placed between fresh driers and ventilators when the new bundle is again inclosed in the press. In practice the open press is placed immediately in front of the operator, with a fresh stack of drying sheets to the right of the press and just to the right of that a stack of fresh ventilators. As the folders with the undried plants are removed from the press they are at once assembled in the usual manner between the driers and ventilators in a new pile at the left of the press. When transfer is completed the specimens that were at the top of the press will be at the bottom of the freshly stacked series, and those that were at the bottom will be at the top. If the press is running very full for many days and if folders of fresh specimens are being added frequently it is well that the fresh material be more or less segregated toward one side of the press and the drier material toward the opposite side rather than having the fresh and the older material promiscuously mixed. This can be easily done without inconvenience if the added specimens are always placed in the press next to the last ones added and if the order is maintained each time the press is changed.

Convenience of the Folders.—The great convenience in having the folders (Fig. 210) that carry the specimens is clearly evident during the changing of the press. If they were not used it would be necessary to pick up each individual specimen and transfer it to the new drying sheet, but with the folder one removes all of the specimens within a given folder at one operation and without necessarily touching a single specimen. The collector should look into the folders when changing the press, especially during the first two or three times that the folders are handled since it will be easily possible to spread out parts, straighten tangled specimens, and make very much better preparations than if no attention is given the individual specimens from the time they are placed in the press until they are removed.

Aids in Drying the Specimens.—If the press is being run at maximum capacity and the supply of driers and ventilators is not sufficient to permit of as frequent and complete changes as necessary, then one may pile the folders with the specimens together for a few minutes while the moist drying sheets and ventilators are being dried in the sun. The drying specimens are also more thoroughly aired by this plan and the folders themselves would be more nearly dried out than would be the case if the press is changed rapidly and the folders quickly made into the new bundle. Herein lie other advantages of the folders.

The moist drying sheets and ventilators (Fig. 210) should always be spread out in the sun and wind as they are taken from the press, or if such a procedure is impossible on account of the weather they may be dried out over a radiator, stove, or other artificial source of heat indoors. The dried fillers may be kept in a convenient place and ready for the press-changing operation. When the specimens are dried they may be removed with the folders from the press and filed away or bundled up for shipment to the office or home to await the next or final process of preparation.

Preparing the Specimens for the Herbarium.—The last phase of preparing the specimens for the herbarium is *mounting*. The plants may be filed in the herbarium in the folders in which they passed through the press (Fig. 210), but this is not satisfactory, the specimens are not readily examined, and they may become broken or lost. It is best to mount the specimens in a more permanent manner upon white cardboard, or firm ledger paper. The best mounting paper is a rather heavy and tough linen ledger paper, cut into sheets about 12 inches wide by 17 inches long, a common size furnished by the regular botanical supply houses being 11.5 by 16.5 inches. Smaller sheets may be used for a small, private collection, but if one is to collect and mount many specimens he will soon appreciate the numerous advantages of the larger mounting sheets.

Attaching Specimens to the Sheets.—Various methods have been used to attach the plant specimens to the mounting paper such as sewing them on with thread, fastening them by means of gummed strips of paper or cloth, or gumming the plant to the paper. The best way is to use a strong, permanent adhesive or gum, such as gum tragacanth, or fishglue such as Lepage's liquid glue. The latter is probably the best adhesive readily available for this purpose. Many of the mild and more pleasant-to-use and popular pastes are utterly worthless for this use. Large or heavy specimens may be reinforced by the addition of a few cross-bands of adhesive paper or linen straps.

Application of Adhesive.—The glue may be spread upon the under surface of the specimen by means of a small brush dipped in the adhesive, but this is a very slow and tedious process if there are hundreds or thousands of specimens to mount. The specimens may be rapidly glued and mounted if one will spread a thin coating of the glue over a glass plate of appropriate size and then drop the specimens, one at a time, upon this surface, after which they are carefully lifted by the fingers or by means of tweezers and then transferred to the mounting paper. This method places the glue on the proper portions of the specimen (*i.e.* the high or slightly projecting areas) where it comes into immediate and lasting contact with the surface of the mounting paper. The specimens must not be crowded upon the mount, unless some personal demand requires such untidy and inartistic procedure. Excess adhesive should always be removed. Fragments of material that may accumulate upon the glue-plate must be removed from time to time. The glue on the plate may be kept at the proper consistency by thinning with water or a weak solution of acetic acid or vinegar. A little practice will indicate the proper thickness of glue to use for each specimen. But even so it may be necessary to keep very delicate flowers from sinking too deeply into the glue or to add more glue to the contact points of heavy specimens by means of a brush.

The mounted specimens, accompanied by their temporary labels, may be stacked upon one another in a loose pile. The pressure secured in this manner will usually be sufficient to hold each specimen against the paper until the glue hardens. When the glue has thoroughly solidified the mounted specimens may be inspected for any needed reinforcement and prepared to receive their final labels.

The Matter of Permanent Labels.—Each sheet bearing specimens must have a neat label, 2 by 3 inches or slightly larger, affixed to it with glue. The preferred position of the label is in the lower right-hand corner, flush with the edges of the mounting sheet. The label should give the name of the plant, *i.e.* the genus and species, including the authority, the place collected, the date of taking the specimen, and the name of the collector, as the minimum requirements. Some collectors add notes concerning the nature of the habitat, abundance, etc. but the label should not be crowded. A statement as to altitude is a worth-while addition to the labels for specimens gathered in the mountains. If many of the species are determined by some specialist other than the collector it is helpful to add that item to the label also. An appropriate heading, such as "Flora of Nebraska," "Yosemite Flora," "Flora of Santa Catalina Island," "Herbarium of John Smith," is a desirable feature of the label. An indication of the complete classification of the species, such as the class, order, family, is not necessary except in an amateur collection, or in a high-school herbarium where it is helpful to have these data in addition to those used in the professional herbarium. The name of the plant should in all cases be the most conspicuous entry on the label. Sometimes it is helpful to add a prominent synonym or two, but this is not often necessary if the author of the name is given. The labels should be printed for large herbaria, but for a small herbarium, or for private collections, the data may be written neatly upon the labels with good ink.

Filing the Specimens.—When the specimens have been mounted and the labels attached to the sheets, they should be filed away in any convenient case according to some definite plan of classification. The large herbarium is arranged by families in accordance with one of the well-known systems of classification. A small collection may also be grouped in this manner in the cupboard, but possibly a simple alphabetical arrangement of the families would be better until the number of specimens has increased to several hundred. Special genus and species portfolios of distinctive colors are sometimes employed in the great collections, but this plan is scarcely necessary until the number of specimens reaches several thousand.

Subsequent Care Necessary.—The specimens will require constant attention even after they are mounted and filed in the herbarium if the owner wishes to keep them in good condition. They must be dry when they are filed and they must be kept dry, otherwise destructive molds will develop to such a degree as to ruin some of the material. Insects will also attack the dried plants in the herbarium and unless held in check will cause a great amount of irreparable damage, especially in the flowers and fruits. If the specimens are dry when filed and if they are kept dry there will be little or no trouble from mold. Mercuric chloride, phenol, or other fungicides may be used against the molds, but the methods of application are so laborious and tedious that one should adopt every possible precaution to render their use unnecessary. Herbarium insects can usually be kept out or controlled by frequent fumigation with carbon disulphide or by keeping naphthalene flakes in the filing cabinets. The former material is usually effective if placed in a few of the upper compartments of the cabinets in shallow containers two or three times each year.

CHAPTER XXVIII

REFERENCE BOOKS, MONOGRAPHS, MANUALS, AND FLORAS

The following lists and notes concerning a few selected monographs, books, floras, and other references dealing with flowering plants may be helpful to students and others interested in the life history and classification of these plants. No attempt has been made to make this list complete or extensive, but it has been the intention to include a number of the more valuable works of reference that are more or less classic, as well as many technical and popular publications that are helpful to American students particularly. The publisher is noted in nearly all cases.

An outline map (Fig. 211) shows the approximate ranges of certain American manuals.

A. Works of Broad Scope, That Are More or Less Monumental in Treatment or Influence upon the Development of Knowledge

BAILLON, H. (Trans., M. M. HARTOG). The natural history of plants. 8 Vols. Reeve & Co., 1871–1888. (5 Additional volumes in French.)

BENTHAM, G. and J. D. HOOKER. Genera Plantarum. 3 Vols. 1862–1883.

BESSEY, C. E. The phylogenetic taxonomy of flowering plants. *Ann. Missouri Botan. Garden,* 1915.

BONNIER, G. and L. DuSABLON. Cours de botanique. 1905.

CLEMENTS, F. E. and F. LONG. Experimental pollination. An outline of the ecology of flowers and insects. Pub. 336 Carneg. Inst. Washington, D. C., 1923.

COULTER, J. M. and C. J. CHAMBERLAIN. Morphology of spermatophytes. D. Appleton & Company, 1901.

COULTER, J. M. and C. J. CHAMBERLAIN. Morphology of angiosperms. D. Appleton & Company, 1909.

DARWIN, C. The contrivances by which orchids are fertilized by insects. 2nd Ed. D. Appleton & Company, 1884.

DARWIN, C. The effects of cross and self fertilization in the vegetable kingdom. D. Appleton & Company, 1885.

DARWIN, C. Insectivorous plants. D. Appleton & Company, 1896.

DeCANDOLLE, A. Prodromus systematis naturalis regni vegetabilis. 17 Vols. and 4 index Vols. Paris, 1824–1873.

EICHLER, A. W. Blüthen-Diagramme. 2 Vols. 1875–1878.

ENGLER, A. and H. PRANTL. Die natürlichen Pflanzenfamilien. 1st Ed. 20 Vols, 1897–1915, 2nd Ed. now in process of publication. Engelmann, 1924.

ENGLER, A. Das Pflanzenreich. Issued in many separate parts, not yet completed. Engelmann, 1900.

ENGLER, A. and S. GILG. Syllabus der Pflanzenfamilien. 9th and 10th Eds. Borntraeger, 1924.

GOEBEL, K. (Trans.) Outlines of classification and special morphology of plants. Clarendon Press, 1887.

HALLIER, H. Provisional scheme of the natural (Phylogenetic) system of flowering plants. *New Phytologist*, 1905.

HUTCHINSON, J. The families of flowering plants. Arranged according to a new system based upon probable phylogeny. I. Dicotyledons. The Macmillan Company, 1926.

KERNER, A. (trans. F. W. OLIVER). The natural history of plants. 4 Vols. in 2. Henry Holt & Company, 1894–1895.

KNUTH, K. (trans. J. R. A. DAVIS). Handbook of flower pollination. 3 Vols. Clarendon Press, 1906–1909.

LEMAOUT, E. and J. DECAISNE (trans. MRS. HOOKER). A general system of botany. Longmans, Green and Company, 1876.

LINDLEY, J. An introduction to the natural system of botany, or a systematic view of the organization, natural affinities, and geographical distribution of the whole vegetable kingdom, together with the uses of the most important species in medicine, the arts, and rural or domestic economy. Longmans, Green and Company, 1830.

LINDLEY, J. The vegetable kingdom, or the structure, classification and uses of plants, illustrated by the natural system. Bradbury & Evans, 1853.

LOVELL, J. H. The flower and the bee. Plant life and pollination. Charles Scribner's Sons, 1918.

MÜLLER, H. (trans. D. W. Thompson). The fertilization of flowers. The Macmillan Company, 1883.

RENDLE, A. B. The classification of flowering plants. Vol. 1, 1904, Vol. 2, Cambridge University Press, 1925.

WARMING, E. (trans. A. F. POTTER). A handbook of systematic botany. The Macmillan Company, 1904.

WETTSTEIN, R. R. Handbuch der systematischen Botanik. Denticke, 1911.

B. GENERAL MANUALS AND CYCLOPEDIAS OF BROAD SCOPE AND WIDE USE

BAILEY, L. H. Manual of cultivated plants. A flora for the identification of the most common or significant species of plants grown in the continental United States and Canada for food, ornament, utility, and general interest, both in the open and under glass. The Macmillan Company, 1924.

BAILEY, L. H. The standard cyclopedia of horticulture. A discussion for the amateur, and the professional and commercial grower, of the kinds, characteristics, and methods of cultivation of the species of plants grown in the regions of the United States and Canada for ornament, for fancy, for fruit and for vegetables; keys to the natural families and genera, descriptions of the horticultural capabilities of the states and provinces and dependent islands, and sketches of eminent horticulturists. Copiously illustrated with thousands of figures, many of them colored. New edition in 3 Vols. The Macmillan Company, 1925.

BRITTON, N. L. and others. North American Flora. A great work projected in 34 Vols. to cover all groups of plants. Only one volume, and many scattered parts published to date. New York Botanical Garden.

GRAY, A. The genera of the plants of the United States. Illustrated by figures and analyses from nature. 2 Vols. G. P. Putnam's Sons, 1849.

GRAY, A. Synoptical flora of North America. 2nd Ed. Ivison, Blakeman, Taylor & Company., 1886.

GRAY, ASA, and JOHN TORREY. Flora of North America. 2 Vols. 1838–1843.

GRAY, A. Field, forest and garden botany. A simple introduction to the common plants of the United States east of the 100th meridian, both wild and cultivated. Revised and extended by L. H. Bailey. American Book Company, 1895.

REHDER, A. Manual of cultivated trees and shrubs hardy in North America except in the subtropical and warmer temperate regions. The Macmillan Company, 1926.

C. REGIONAL MANUALS AND FLORAS (SEE FIG. 211)

ABRAMS, L. An illustrated flora of the Pacific states. Washington, Oregon, California. Every species of ferns, gymnosperms, and flowering plants known to grow wild in the Pacific states is here illustrated and described. 3 Vols., Vol. 1, Stanford Press, 1923.

BRITTON, N. L. Manual of the flora of the northern states and Canada. Includes the ferns, gymnosperms and flowering plants from Newfoundland and Labrador to Manitoba, the southern boundary of Virginia, Kentucky, and Kansas, and the west boundary of Kansas and Nebraska. Has gone through three editions; last edition, Henry Holt & Company, 1910.

BRITTON, N. L. and A. BROWN. An illustrated flora of the northern states and Canada and the British possessions from Newfoundland to the parallel of the south boundary of Virginia and from the Atlantic Ocean westward to the 102nd meridian. 3 Vols. 2nd Ed. Charles Scribner's Sons, 1913.

CHAPMAN, A. W. Flora of the southern United States. An abridged description of the ferns and flowering plants of Tennessee, North and South Carolina, Georgia, Alabama, Mississippi, and Florida, according to the natural system. 3rd Ed. Cambridge Botanical Supply Company, 1897.

COULTER, J. M. Botany of western Texas. A manual of the phanerogams and pteridophytes of western Texas. Contributions from the United States National Herbarium, Vol. II. 1891–1894.

COULTER, J. M. and A. NELSON. A new manual of Rocky Mountain botany. With Colorado as a center this manual includes Wyoming, Yellowstone National Park, Black Hills of South Dakota, most of Montana, southern Idaho, eastern Utah and northern New Mexico and Arizona. American Book Company, 1909.

FRYE, T. C. and G. B. RIGG. Northwest flora. The gymnosperms and flowering plants of Oregon, Idaho, Washington and southwestern British Columbia. University of Washington, 1912.

GRAY, ASA. New manual of botany. See under Robinson and Fernald.

HOWELL, THOS. A flora of northwest America. Brief descriptions of all the known indigenous and naturalized plants, growing without cultivation north of California, west of Utah and south of British Columbia. Author, 1903.

JEPSON, W. L. A manual of the flowering plants of California. Including a complete account of the native ferns, gymnosperms and flowering plants of the state, and 1,023 original drawings. University of California, 1923–1925.

MACOUN, J. Catalog of Canadian plants. 7 Parts. Geological and Natural History Survey of Canada, Montreal, 1883–1902.

PIPER, C. V. and R. K. BEATTIE. Flora of southeastern Washington and adjacent Idaho. New Era Press, 1914.

PIPER, C. V. and R. K. BEATTIE. Flora of the northwest coast. The native ferns, gymnosperms and flowering plants found west of the summit of the Cascade Mountains from the 49th parallel south to the Calapooia Mountains of the southern border of Lane County, Oregon. New Era Press, 1915.

ROBINSON, B. L. and M. L. FERNALD. Gray's new manual of botany. 7th Ed. A handbook of the flowering plants and ferns of the central and northeastern United States and adjacent Canada. American Book Company, 1908.

RYDBERG, P. A. Flora of the Rocky Mountains and adjacent plains. Includes Colorado, Wyoming, Idaho, Montana, Saskatchewan, Alberta, and neighboring parts of Nebraska, North and South Dakota, and British Columbia. Author, 1917. 2nd Ed. 1922.

SMALL, J. K. Flora of the southeastern United States. Describes the ferns, gymnosperms, and flowering plants that grow naturally in North Carolina, South Carolina, Georgia, Florida, Alabama, Tennessee, Arkansas, Mississippi, Louisiana, and Oklahoma and Texas east of the 100th meridian. 2nd Ed. Author, 1913.

D. REGIONAL, STATE, AND LOCAL FLORAS, INCLUDING MORE OR LESS POPULAR TREATISES

ABRAMS, L. Flora of Los Angeles and vicinity. The gymnosperms and flowering plants of the coast slope of Los Angeles and Orange counties, California. New Era Press, 1917.

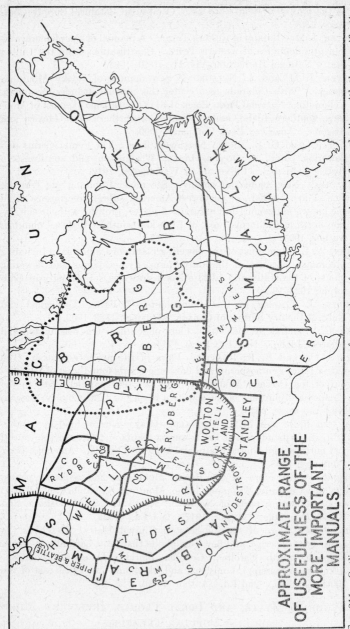

FIG. 211.—Outline map showing the approximate ranges of a number of useful manuals and floras dealing with the classification of flowering plants of North America.

BERGMAN, H. F.   Flora of North Dakota.   In 6th Biennial Report of the Director, North Dakota Soil and Geological Survey, 1912.

BRITTON, N. L.   Catalog of plants found in New Jersey.   1889.

BRITTON, N. L.   Flora of Bermuda.   Includes thallophytes and bryophytes as well as ferns, gymnosperms and flowering plants.   .Illustrated. Charles Scribner's Sons, 1918.

BRITTON, N. L. and C. F. MILLSPAUGH.   The Bahama flora.   A general flora including all major groups of the vegetable kingdom.   Authors, 1920.

BROWN, S.   Alpine flora of the Canadian Rocky Mountains.   A popular guide to the flora of the Canadian Rockies and Selkirk Mountains, or that portion traversed by the Canadian Pacific R. R. between Banff and Glacier.   Many illustrations from photographs and water-color drawings.   G. P. Putnam's Sons, 1907.

CLEMENTS, F. E. and E. S.   Rocky Mountain flowers.   An illustrated guide for plant lovers and plant users.   Twenty-five plates in color and twenty-two plates in black and white.   The range of this flora is about the same as that for Coulter-Nelson flora, but in a general way is useful over a much wider area since many of the species occur from the Canadian Rockies to New Mexico and Arizona.   H. W. Wilson Co., 1920.

COVILLE, F. V.   Botany of the Death Valley expedition.   A report on the botany of the expedition sent out in 1891 by the United States Dep. Agr. to make a biological survey of the region of Death Valley, Calif. Contributions from the United States National Herbarium, Vol. IV. 1893.

DAVIDSON, A. and G. L. MOXLEY.   Flora of southern California.   The ferns, gymnosperms, and flowering plants of southern California as limited by Santa Barbara, San Bernardino, Riverside, Imperial, San Diego, Orange, and Los Angeles counties.   Times-Mirror Press, 1923.

FAWCETT, WM. and A. B. RENDLE.   Flora of Jamaica.   Descriptions of the flowering plants of the island.   4 Parts.   Illustrated.   1910–1912.

FITZPATRICK, T. J.   Manual of the flowering plants of Iowa.   1899.

GARRETT, A. O.   Spring flora of the Wasatch region.   A brief series of keys to the gymnosperms and early summer flowering plants of the eastern edge of the Great Basin in Utah.   3rd Ed.   New Era Press, 1917.

GRAVES, C. B. et al.   Catalog of the flowering plants and ferns of Connecticut.   1910.

HALL, H. M. and C. C.   A Yosemite flora.   Descriptions and simple keys for plants in Yosemite National Park.   Illustrated.   Paul Elder, 1912.

HENRY, J. K.   Flora of southern British Columbia and Vancouver Island, with many references to the plants of Alaska and other northern species. Gage & Company, 1915.

HOUSE, H. D.   Wild flowers of New York.   2 Vols.   1918.

JEPSON, W. L.   A flora of western middle California.   2nd Ed.   Cunningham, Curtis & Welch, 1911.

JEPSON, W. L.   Manual of the flowering plants of California.   Sather Gate Bookshop, Berkeley, 1925.

LOWE, E. N.   Plants of Mississippi.   1921.

MACKENZIE, K. K. and B. F. BUSH.   Manual of the flora of Jackson County, Missouri.   1902.

MACMILLAN, C.   The Metaspermae of the Minnesota valley.   Geological and Natural History Survey of Minnesota.   Botanical Series I.   University of Minnesota, 1892.

MILLSPAUGH, C. F. and L. W. NUTTALL.   Flora of Santa Catalina Island, California.   Illustrated.   Includes all major groups.   Field Museum of Natural History, *Pub.* 212, 1923.

NELSON, A.   Spring flora of the intermountain states.   For Colorado, Wyoming, northern Utah, Montana, Idaho (except the northern part). Ginn & Company, 1912.

MOHR, CHAS.   Plant life of Alabama.   Contributions from the United States National Herbarium.   Vol. VI.   1901.

PEPOON, H. S.   An annotated flora of the Chicago region.   1927.

PETERSEN, N. F.   Flora of Nebraska.   A list of the ferns, conifers, and flowering plants of the state, with keys for their identification.   3rd Ed.   Author, 1923.

PIPER, C. V.   Flora of the State of Washington.   Contributions from the United States National Herbarium.   Vol. XI.   Illustrated.   1906.

RYDBERG, P. A.   Flora of Colorado.   *Bull.* 100, Colo. Agr. Exp. Sta., 1905.

RYDBERG, P. A.   Catalog of the flora of Montana and the Yellowstone National Park.   Memoirs of the New York Botanical Garden.   Vol. I. 1900.

RYDBERG, P. A.   Flora of the Black Hills of South Dakota.   Contributions from the United States National Herbarium.   Vol. III.   No. 8.   1896.

SCHAFFNER, J. H.   Field manual of the flora of Ohio.   R. G. Adams Company, Columbus, O., 1928.

STANDLEY, P. C.   Flora of Glacier National Park.   Contributions from the United States National Herbarium.   Vol. XXII, Part 5.   1921.

STEVENS, G. T.   An illustrated guide to the flowering plants.   For the plants of the middle Atlantic and New England states, the descriptive text written in popular language.   Copiously illustrated.   Dodd, Mead & Company, 1910.

TIDESTROM, I.   Flora of Utah and Nevada.   Contributions from the United States National Herbarium, Vol. 25.   1925.

WIEGAND, K. M. and A. J. EAMES.   The flora of the Cayuga lake basin, New York.   1926.

WOOTON, E. O. and P. C. STANDLEY.   Flora of New Mexico.   Contributions from the United States National Herbarium.   Vol. XIX.   1915.

E. MANUALS FOR TREES, TREE BOOKS

APGAR, A. C.   Trees of the northern United States, their study, description and determination.   American Book Company, 1892.

BAILEY, L. H.   The cultivated evergreens.   A handbook of the conifers and most important broadleaved evergreens planted for ornament in the United States and Canada.   Includes notes on insect pests, diseases, and injuries, adaptation, cultivation.   Illustrated.   The Macmillan Company, 1923.

BAILEY, L. H. Manual of cultivated plants. Contains many trees and shrubs. The Macmillan Company, 1924.

BLAKESLEE, A. F. and C. D. JARVIS. Trees in winter. Their study, planting, care, and identification. Illustrated. The Macmillan Company, 1913.

BRITTON, N. L. North American trees. Henry Holt & Company, 1908.

BROWN, H. P. Trees of New York state, native and naturalized. Illustrated. *Tech. Pub.* 15, The New York State College of Forestry, 1921

BURNS, G. P. and C. H. OTIS. The trees of Vermont. Illustrated. *Bull.* 194, Vt. Agr. Exp. Sta., 1916.

CLEMENTS, F. E., C. O. ROSENDAHL, and F. K. BUTTERS. Minnesota trees and shrubs. An illustrated manual of the native and cultivated woody plants of the state. *Report,* Minnesota Botanical Survey, IX, 1912.

CURTIS, C. C. A guide to the trees. Greenberg, N. Y., 1925.

EMERSON, A. I. and C. M. WEED. Our trees and how to know them. A guide to the recognition of trees at any season and notes on their characteristics, distribution, and cultivation. J. B. Lippincott Company, 1908.

GIBSON, H. H. American forest trees. Descriptions of many American trees, with extensive notes with reference to their properties and values in forestry. Illustrated. Hardwood Record, 1913.

HOUGH, R. B. Handbook of the trees of the northern states and Canada east of the Rocky Mountains. Many halftone illustrations and distribution maps. Author, 1907.

HUNTINGTON, A. O. Studies of trees in winter. A description of the deciduous trees of northeastern America in their winter condition. Knight and Millet, 1905.

ILLICK, J. S. Pennsylvania trees. 4th Ed. Illustrated. *Bull.* 11, Pennsylvania Department of Forestry, 1923.

JEPSON, W. L. The trees of California. A working manual of value to botanists, foresters, horticulturists, lumbermen, teachers, travelers, and nature students. Cunningham, Curtis & Welch, 1909.

JEPSON, W. L. The silva of California. Memoirs, University of California II. 1910.

KEELER, H. L. Our native trees and how to identify them. A popular, illustrated study of the habits and peculiarities of many eastern and northern trees. Charles Scribner's Sons, 1915.

LONGYEAR, B. O. Trees and shrubs of the Rocky Mountain region. With keys and descriptions for their identification. G. P. Putnam's Sons, 1927.

MATHEWS, F. S. Fieldbook of American trees and shrubs. A concise, illustrated description of the character and color of species common throughout the United States, with maps to show their general distribution. G. P. Putnam's Sons, 1915.

OTIS, C. H. Michigan trees. A handbook of the native and most important introduced species. Illustrated. University of Michigan, 1913.

POOL, R. J. Handbook of Nebraska trees. A guide to the native and most important introduced species. The Botanical Survey of Nebraska, N. S. No. 3, 1909. 2nd. Ed. 1929.

Pratt, M. B.   Shade and ornamental trees of California.   California State Board of Forestry.   1921.

Ramaley, F.   Wild flowers and trees of Colorado.   A. A. Greenman, 1909.

Rehder, A.   Manual of cultivated trees and shrubs, hardy in North America except in the subtropical and warmer temperate regions. The Macmillan Company, 1926.

Rock, J. F.   The indigenous trees of the Hawaiian Islands.   Illustrated. Author and patrons, Honolulu, 1913.

Rogers, J. E.   The tree book.   A popular guide to a knowledge of the trees of North America, their uses and cultivation.   Illustrated.   Doubleday Page & Company, 1907.

Sargent, C. S.   The silva of North America.   A description of the trees which grow naturally in North America exclusive of Mexico.   Copiously illustrated by fine engravings.   14 Vols.   Houghton, Mifflin Company, 1891–1902.

Sargent, C. S.   Manual of the trees of North America exclusive of Mexico. Illustrated.   This is really an abridgment of the author's silva.   2nd Ed.   Houghton, Mifflin Company, 1922.

Schaffner, J. H.   Field manual of trees.   R. G. Adams Company, Columbus, O., 1926.

Scott, C. A. and F. C. Gates.   Trees in Kansas.   State Board of Agriculture, 1928.

Small, J. K.   Florida trees.   A handbook of the native and naturalized trees of Florida.   Author, 1913.

Standley, P. C.   Trees and shrubs of Mexico.   Contributions from the United States National Herbarium.   Vol. XXIII.   1920–1926.

Sudworth, G. B.   Forest Trees of the Pacific Slope.   Illustrated.   U. S. Dept. Agr. Forest Service, 1908.

Sudworth, G. B.   Check list of the forest trees of the United States, their names and ranges.   An authoritative work for the forester and tree student.   *Miscellaneous Circ.* 92, U. S. Dept. Agr., 1927.

Trelease, Wm.   Winter botany.   Plant materials of decorative gardening. Author, 1918.

Trelease, Wm.   The American oaks.   Includes the oaks of both North and South America.   *Memoirs*, National Academy of Sciences.   Vol. XX, 1924.

F. Popular Works on Flowers

Armstrong, M. and J. J. Thornber.   Field book of western wild flowers. A guide to the commoner wild flowers west of the Rocky Mountains. G. P. Putnam's Sons, 1915.

Brown, S.   Alpine flora of the Canadian Rocky Mountains.   A popular guide to the flora of the Banff to Glacier area.   Colored illustrations. G. P. Putnam's Sons, 1907.

Clements, F. E. and E. S.   Rocky Mountain flowers.   An illustrated guide, useful throughout the Rocky Mountain region, but particularly helpful in the central Rockies.   H. W. Wilson Company.   1920.

Clements, F. E. and E. S.   Flower families and ancestors.   H. W. Wilson company, 1928.

CLEMENTS, E. S. Wild flowers of the west. The National Geographic Magazine, May, 1927.

CLEMENTS, E. S. Flowers of Coast and Sierra. H. W. Wilson Company, 1928.

CLEMENTS, F. E. and W. J. SHOWALTER. The family tree of the flowers. The National Geographic Magazine, May, 1927.

DANA, W. S. How to know the wildflowers. A guide to the names, haunts, and habits of our native wildflowers. Charles Scribner's Sons.

DURAND, H. My wild flower garden. G. P. Putnam's Sons.

KEELER, H. L. Our early wild flowers. A study of the herbaceous plants blooming in early spring in the northern states. Charles Scribner's Sons, 1916.

KEELER, H. L. The wayside flowers of summer. A study of the conspicuous herbaceous plants blooming upon our northern roadsides during the months of July and August. Charles Scribner's Sons, 1917.

MATHEWS, F. S. Field book of American wild flowers. Character and habits, description of colors, pollination, etc. G. P. Putman's Sons, 1927.

PARSONS, M. E. The wild flowers of California. Their names, haunts, and habits. 4th Ed. Payot, Upham & Company, 1902.

RAMALEY, F. Wild flowers and trees of Colorado. A. A. Greenman, 1909.

SAUNDERS, C. F. Useful wild plants of the United States and Canada. Robert M. McBride & Company, 1920.

SHOWALTER, W. J., M. E. EATON, G. GROSVENOR, and E. J. GESKE. The book of wildflowers. An introduction to the ways of plant life, together with biographies of 250 representative species, and chapters on state flowers and familiar grasses. National Geographic Society, 1924.

TAYLOR, NORMAN. A guide to the wildflowers. Greenberg, N. Y. 1928.

WEED, C. M. Wild flower families. The haunts, characteristics and family relationships of the herbaceous wild flowers, with suggestions for their identification. Illustrated. J. B. Lippincott Company, 1908.

WICKSON, E. J. California garden flowers. Shrubs, trees, and vines, being mainly suggestions for working amateurs. 2nd Ed. Pacific Rural Press. 1923.

WRIGHT, R. The practical book of outdoor flowers. Deals largely with the use of flowering plants in outdoor gardens. Copiously illustrated. J. B. Lippincott Company, 1924.

G. BOOKS ON CULTIVATED PLANTS

BAILEY, L. H. Manual of cultivated plants. A flora for the identification of the most common or significant species of plants grown in the continental United States and Canada for food, ornament, utility, and general interest, both in the open and under glass. The Macmillan Company, 1924.

BAILEY, L. H. The cultivated evergreens. A handbook of the coniferous and most important broadleaved evergreen plants for ornament in the United States and Canada. The Macmillan Company, 1923.

BAILEY, L. H. The standard cyclopedia of horticulture. A discussion for the amateur, the professional and commercial grower of plants for any purpose. New edition in 3 Vols. The Macmillan Company, 1924.

BROWN, H. B. Cotton. History, species, varieties, morphology, breeding, culture, diseases, marketing, and uses. McGraw-Hill Book Company, Inc., 1927.

BURT-DAVY, J. Maize. Its history, cultivation, handling, and uses, for farmers, agriculturists, and teachers of nature study. Longmans, Green and Company. 1914.

CHENEY, R. H. Coffee. An economic monograph. New York University Press, 1925.

COIT, J. E. Citrus Fruits. The Macmillan Company, 1915.

COPELAND, E. B. The Coconut. 2nd Ed. The Macmillan Company, 1921.

DECANDOLLE, A. (English Ed.) Origin of cultivated plants. D. Appleton & Company, 1885.

DYKES, W. R. The Genus Iris. Cambridge University Press, 1913.

EISEN, G. The fig: its history, culture, and curing. Div. Pom. U. S. Dept. Agr., *Bull.* 9, 1901.

GARDNER, V. R., F. C. BRADFORD and H. D. HOOKER. The fundamentals of fruit production. McGraw-Hill Book Company, Inc., 1922.

HUNTER, H. Oats: their varieties and characteristics. A practical handbook for farmers, seedsmen, and students. E. Bern, 1924.

HUTCHESON, T. B. and T. K. WOLFE. The production of field crops. McGraw-Hill Book Company, Inc. 1924.

JEPSON, W. L. A flora of the economic plants of California for agricultural purposes. Crop plants, weeds, honey plants, poisonous plants, medicinal plants, native timber trees, and spring plants. University of California. 1924.

MILLAIS, J. G. Rhododendrons. 2 Vols. Longmans, Green and Company, 1917–1924.

PEMBERTON, J. H. Roses: their history, development and cultivation. 2nd Ed. Longmans, Green and Company. 1920.

POPENOE, W. Manual of tropical and subtropical fruits, excluding the banana, coconut, pineapple, citrus fruits, olive, and fig. The Macmillan Company, 1920.

ROBBINS, W. W. The botany of crop plants. A text and reference book. 2nd Ed. Blakiston's, 1924.

STUART, WM. The potato, its culture, uses, history, and classification. J. B. Lippincott Company, 1923.

THOMPSON, H. C. Vegetable crops. McGraw-Hill Book Company, Inc., 1923.

TRELEASE, WM. Plant materials of decorative gardening. The woody plants. Author, 1917.

H. BOOKS ON GRASSES

BEAL, W. J. Grasses of North America. 2 Vols. Henry Holt & Company. 1896.

CARLETON, M. A. The small grains. The Macmillan Company, 1916.

CHASE, A. First book of grasses. The structure of grasses explained for beginners. The Macmillan Company, 1922.

FRANCIS, M. E. The book of grasses. Doubleday, Page & Company.

HACKEL, E. (trans. SCRIBNER, F. L. and E. A. SOUTHWORTH). The true grasses. Henry Holt & Company. 1890.

HITCHCOCK, A. S. A textbook of grasses. With especial reference to the economic species of the United States. The Macmillan Company, 1914.

HITCHCOCK, A. S. The genera of grasses of the United States. With special reference to the economic species. U. S. Dept. Agr., *Bull.* 772. 1920.

HUNT, T. F. The cereals of America. Orange Judd, 1905.

MACSELF, A. J. Grass. A new and thoroughly practical book on grasses for ornamental lawns and all purposes of sports and games. C. Palmer, London, 1924.

MONTGOMERY, E. G. The corn crops. The Macmillan Company, 1913.

Several states have issued bulletins dealing with the classification of the grasses found within the respective areas.

I. VALUABLE WORKS PUBLISHED SINCE THE FIRST EDITION OF THIS BOOK

ARBER, AGNES. Herbals: their origin and evolution. 2nd Ed. The Macmillan Company, 1938.

BAILEY, L. H. How plants get their names. The Macmillan Company, 1933.

BAILEY, L. H. The garden of larkspurs. The Macmillan Company, 1939.

BAKER, M. F. Florida wild flowers. The Macmillan Company, 1938.

BLOMQUIST, H. L. and H. J. OOSTING. A guide to the spring and early summer flora of Piedmont, N. C. Authors, Durham, 1936.

BORG, J. Cacti. The Macmillan Company, 1937.

CLEMENTS, F. E. and E. S. Flower pageant of the Midwest. *National Geographic Magazine*, August, 1939.

CORREVON, H. Rock garden and alpine plants. The Macmillan Company, 1930.

DEGENER, O. The new illustrated flora of the Hawaiian Islands. Author, 1933.

ELLIOTT, C. Rock garden plants. Edward Arnold & Co., 1936.

FASSETT, N. C. A manual of aquatic plants. The McGraw-Hill Book Company, Inc., 1940.

FREAR, M. D. and O. G. MCLEAN. Flowers of Hawaii. Dodd. Mead & Company, Inc., 1938.

GABRIELSON, I. N. Western American alpines. The Macmillan Company, 1932.

GATES, F. C. Flora of Kansas. *Contrib.* 391, *Dept. Botany, Kansas State Coll.*, Manhattan, 1940.

GILKEY, HELEN M. Handbook of northwest flowering plants. Metropolitan Press, 1936.

GREEN, CHARLOTTE H. Trees of the South. University of North Carolina Press. 1939.

HARLOW, W. M. and E. S. HARRAR. Textbook of dendrology. McGraw-Hill Book Company, Inc., 1937.

HESS, K. P. Textile fibers and their use, J. B. Lippincott Company, 1936.

HILL, A. F. Economic botany. McGraw-Hill Book Company, Inc. 1937.

HITCHCOCK, A. S. Manual of the grasses of the United States. *Miscellaneous Pub.* 200, *U.S. Dept. Agr.*, 1935.

HITCHCOCK, A. S. Manual of the grasses of the West Indies. *Miscellaneous Pub.* 240, *U.S. Dept. Agr.*, 1936.

HOUSE, H. D. Wild flowers. 364 Colored Illustrations. The Macmillan Company, 1934.

JOHNSON, A. M. Taxonomy of the flowering plants. D. Appleton-Century Company, Inc., 1931.

JONES, S. G. Introduction to floral mechanism. Chemical Publishing Company of New York, Inc., 1939.

KIRKWOOD, J. E. Northern Rocky Mountain trees and shrubs. Stanford University Press, 1930.

MACFARLANE, J. M. The evolution and distribution of flowering plants. Noll Printing Company, 1933.

McMINN, H. E. An illustrated manual of California shrubs. J. W. Stacey, Inc., 1939.

MADSGER, O. P. Edible wild plants. The Macmillan Company, 1939.

MUENSCHER, W. C. Poisonous plants of the United States. The Macmillan Company, 1939.

MUENSCHER, W. C. Weeds. The Macmillan Company, 1935.

MUNZ, P. A. A manual of southern California botany. J. W. Stacey, Inc., 1935.

PREECE, W. H. A. North American rock plants. The Macmillan Company, 1937.

PRESTON, R. J. Rocky Mountain trees. Iowa State College Press, 1940.

ROBBINS, W. W. and F. RAMALEY. Plants useful to man. 2nd Ed. P. Blakiston's Son & Company, Inc., 1937.

ROHDE, E. S. Herbs and herb gardening. The Macmillan Company, 1937.

ROUNTREE, L. Flowering shrubs of California. Stanford University Press, 1939.

RYDBERG, P. A. Flora of the prairies and plains of central North America. New York Botanical Garden, 1932.

ST. JOHN, H. Flora of southeastern Washington and adjacent Idaho. Student's Book Corporation, 1937.

SHARPLES, ADA W. Alaska wild flowers. Stanford University Press, 1938.

SILVEUS, W. A. Texas grasses. Author, San Antonio, 1933.

SLATE, G. L. Lilies for American gardens. Charles Scribner's Sons, 1939.

STANFORD, E. E. Economic plants. D. Appleton-Century Company, Inc., 1934.

STEMEN, T. R. and W. S. MYERS. Oklahoma flora. Harlow Publishing Company, 1937.

STEVENS, G. A. Garden flowers in color. The Macmillan Company, 1935.

STEYERMARK, J. A. Spring flora of Missouri. Missouri Botanical Garden, and Field Museum of Natural History, 1940.

THORNBER, J. J. and F. BONKER. The fantastic clan (the Cactus family). The Macmillan Company, 1932.

TIDESTROM, I. and T. KITTELL. The flora of Arizona and New Mexico. *Contrib. U. S. National Herbarium,* Vol. 25, 1940.

U.S. Department of Agriculture, Forest Service. Range plant handbook. U.S. Government Printing Office, 1937.

VAN DERSAL, W. R. Native woody plants of the United States. *Miscellaneous Pub.* 303, *U.S. Dept. Agr.,* 1938.

VAN LAREN, A. J., E. J. LABARRE, and S. E. HASELTON. Succulents other than cacti. Abbey San Encino Press, 1935.

WODEHOUSE, R. P. Pollen grains. McGraw-Hill Book Company, Inc., 1935.

WOODCOCK, H. D. and J. COUTTS. Lilies. Charles Scribner's Sons, 1935.

GLOSSARY

Abaxial. On the side away from the axis.

Acaulescent. Without a stem; or with very short, scarcely evident stem.

Achene. A small, dry, hard, one-chambered, one-seeded fruit.

Actinomorphic. Said of a flower having radial symmetry; regular; more or less star-shaped.

Acuminate. Narrowly tapering to a sharp point.

Acute. Tapering more broadly than acuminate to a sharp point.

Adaxial. Facing the primary axis.

Adnate. United, synonymous with *adherent*, referring to the union of one organ with another, as ovary with receptacle, and stamen with corolla.

Adventitious. Appearing in other than the usual place, as roots springing from cuttings of the stem or from leaves.

Aggregate fruit. Fruit formed by the coherence of the pistils that were distinct in the flower, as in raspberry.

Albuminous. Provided with albumen or endosperm or perisperm, or both.

Allogamy. Cross-pollination.

Alternate. Arranged in a zigzag manner, as when leaves are on opposite sides of the stem but at different levels.

Ament. A catkin, a type of pendulous, scaly spike, as in willows and birches.

Amentiferous. Bearing aments or catkins.

Analytical key. An orderly arrangement of contrasting or comparable statements about plants or plant structures, leading to identification.

Anatropous. Bent over or inverted; said of an ovule with the hilum and micropyle near together at one end, and opposite the chalaza.

Andrœcium. Collective term for the stamens.

Androgynous. Bearing staminate and carpellate flowers in the same inflorescence.

Anemophilous. Wind-pollinated; literally, "wind-loving."

Annual. Of one year's growth; a plant that dies after one year's activity.

Anther. The pollen-bearing organ of a flower; compare with filament.

Anthesis. The period of opening of the flower; the period of pollination.

Apetalous flower. Lacking petals.

Apocarpous. Composed of distinct or separate carpels; compare with syncarpous.

Arachnoid. Having the appearance of a cobweb; composed of entangled hairs.

Aril. A small appendage from or around the hilum of a seed.

Aristate. Awned; bearing a stiff, bristly appendage

Articulate. Jointed; easily separating at nodes or joints, as in spikelets of grasses.

Artificial classification (key). A classification or key that does not consider natural relationships.

385

Ascending.   Growing obliquely upward, or curving upward during growth. Applied to branches, hairs of stems, and ovules.

Attenuate.   Drawn out into a long, slender point.

Auricle.   An ear-shaped appendage, as at the top of the leaf sheath in grasses.

Auriculate.   With auricles or "ears," as in hastate and saggitate leaves.

Autogamy.   Self-pollination.

Awn.   A stiff, bristle-like appendage; a beard.

Axial.   Belonging to the axis.

Axil.   The angle formed by a leaf with the stem to which it is attached.

Axillary.   Situated in the axil of a leaf.

Axis.   The line running lengthwise through the center of an organ, as of a flower or a stem; also applied to the stem itself, and the torus or receptacle of a flower.

Baccate.   Having the nature of a berry.

Banner.   The large, broad, upper petal in the flower of a legume (same as standard).

Beaked.   Furnished with a prominent tip, as the persistent base of the style in some spike-rushes.

Beard.   An awn, as in the grasses.

Berry.   A fleshy fruit, with one or more carpels and usually several or many seeds.

Bidentate.   Two-toothed.

Biennial.   A plant that lives through two growing seasons, fruiting the second year, and then dies.

Bifid.   Two-cleft; forked into two slender limbs to near the middle.

Bilabiate.   Two-lipped, referring especially to the corolla.

Bilocular.   Two-celled, as applied to an ovary or an anther.

Bipinnate.   Twice-pinnate, referring to compound leaves.

Bipinnatifid.   Twice-pinnatifid.

Bisexual.   Having both stamens and carpels (a "perfect" flower).

Blade.   The principal part of a leaf, usually broad, flat, thin, green (compare with petiole).

Bract.   A much reduced leaf, as of an inflorescence or rhizome.

Bracteate.   Furnished with bracts.

Bud.   An undeveloped shoot or a shoot in the resting condition.

Bulb.   A short, thick stem, most of the leaves of which are thickened and stored with reserve food.

Bulbil.   Small bulbs borne singly or in clusters.

Bulbous.   Of the character of a bulb.

Bullate.   Blistered or puckered.

Bundle scars.   Scars left in a leaf scar by the severance of vascular bundles at leaf fall.

Caducous.   Falling off very early, as the sepals and petals of certain flowers.

Caespitose.   Tufted; growing in tufts, as in many grasses.

Calyx.   The outer set of perianth segments of a flower.

Calyx tube.   The tube of a gamosepalous calyx.   Sometimes used for the hypanthium or receptacle of perigynous and epigynous flowers.

Campanulate.   Bell-shaped.

Campylotropous. Bent so as to bring the hilum, micropyle, and chalaza close together, said of ovules.

Canescent. Bearing a hoary, grayish pubescence.

Capillary. Hair-like, thread-like, filiform.

Capitate. Head-like; collected into a dense cluster. Like a pinhead, as in gland-tipped hairs; the inflorescence of composites.

Capsular. Belonging to or having the character of a capsule.

Capsule. A dry dehiscent fruit (pod); with two or more carpels, usually with several or many seeds.

Carpel. The ovuliferous organ of the flower; a simple pistil or one of the segments of a compound pistil.

Caryopsis. The grain (fruit) of grasses; one-seeded, indehiscent.

Catkin. An ament; a scaly, spicate inflorescence, as in willows and birches.

Caudate. Bearing a tail-like appendage.

Chaff. Small, more or less dry, membranaceous bract; especially the small bracts at the base of the disk flowers of some composites.

Chalaza. The basal part of an ovule where the stalk or funiculus enters.

Circinate. Said of a leaf that is coiled or rolled from the tip toward the base with the lower surface outermost.

Circumscissile. Dehiscing or separating by a circular zone, as the capsule of *Plantago.*

Cladophyll. A branch modified in the form of a leaf; a leaf-like stem as in certain species of *Asparagus.*

Clasping. Said of a sessile leaf in which the blade partly invests the stem.

Clavate. Club-shaped; gradually thickened upward.

Claw. The narrow stalk of some petals, as in mustard, resembling a petiole.

Cleistogamous. Self-pollinated or self-fertilized in the bud stage, the flowers not opening, as in violets.

Coherent. Fused or united, when the organs are of the same kind.

Coleoptile. The sheath surrounding the young stem (plumule) in grasses.

Coleorhiza. The sheath surrounding the radicle of grasses.

Collateral. Placed side by side, as some carpels and ovules, or as the glumes of some grasses, or as xylem and phloem in certain vascular bundles.

Column. That part of the flower of an orchid which is formed by the union of the style and the filaments and which supports the anthers and the stigma.

Complete flower. A flower with all parts represented, sepals, petals, stamens, pistil.

Compound. Composed of a number of similar united parts, as carpels in a syncarpous gynœcium (compound pistil), or divided into a number of similar parts or divisions, as the leaflets of "compound" leaves.

Conduplicate. Said of a leaf in which the blade is folded lengthwise along the midrib, the two halves face to face, with the lower surfaces outermost.

Connate. Said of leaves in which the bases of two opposite leaves appear to have fused about the stem.

Connivent. Coming together; the converging or bending toward one another of two or more similar organs (anthers).

Convolute. Said of a leaf in which the blade is rolled lengthwise from side to side like a scroll.

Cordate. Heart-shaped, referring to the base of a leaf.

Corm. A short, erect, thick, solid, underground stem, as in *Cyclamen. Crocus,* with stored food.

Corolla. The inner, colored perianth segments of a flower.

Corona. A collar-like or tubular appendage of the corolla, as in *Narcissus.*

Corymb. A flat-topped racemose inflorescence, the main axis of which is elongated, but the pedicels of the older flowers longer than those of younger flowers.

Corymbose. Of the nature or form of a corymb.

Crenate. Scalloped, or with broad rounded teeth.

Crown. The tubular or ring-like appendage of a corolla as in *Narcissus;* or the top or stem part of a fleshy taproot, as in carrot, parsnip.

Culm. The erect stem of grasses.

Cuneate. Wedge-shaped, usually narrow, but broader above the base, with the straight sides tapering toward the base.

Cuspidate. Ending with a sharp rigid point.

Cyathium. The type of inflorescence found in *Euphorbia.*

Cyme. A determinate inflorescence, in which the central or apical flower opens first.

Cymose. Of the form or nature of a cyme.

Deciduous. Falling off, not persistent.

Decumbent. Growing flat along the ground, but with the tip ascending.

Decurrent. The blade appearing to continue down the sides of the stem, as in a leaf.

Deltoid. Triangular or like a delta.

Dentate. With sharp spreading teeth.

Diadelphous. Said of stamens when united into two sets.

Diandrous. Said of flowers having two stamens.

Dicarpellate. Composed of two carpels—said of a gynœcium (same as bi- or dicarpellary).

Dichogamous. Said of flowers in which stamens and pistils mature at different times.

Diclinous. Bearing the andrœcium (stamens) and the gynœcium (pistils) in separate flowers.

Didymous. Twin; occurring in pairs.

Didynamous. Having the stamens in two unequal sets (as in mustards).

Digitate. Veined, lobed, or divided as fingers radiating from the palm.

Diœcious. Bearing the staminate flowers on one individual and the carpellate on another of the same species (as in willows).

Disk. An outgrowth (often glandular) of the receptacle or hypanthium; hypogynous or epigynous according to the position of the ovary. Also used in referring to the common receptacle of the head of composites.

Dissected. Divided into many slender segments.

Distichous. In two rows, on opposite sides of the stem, said of leaves, the two rows lying in the same vertical plane.

Divided. Cut or separated nearly to the base or to the midrib, as in a leaf.

Double flower. A flower in which some or all of the stamens and carpels are transformed into perianth segments.

Drupaceous. Of the nature or texture of a drupe.

Drupe. A simple fleshy fruit, from a single carpel, usually one-seeded, with fleshy mesocarp and stony endocarp.

Elliptical. Like an ellipse, broadest at the middle, tapering broadly and evenly toward each end.

Emarginate. Decidedly notched at the tip.

Endocarp. The inner layer of a fruit.

Endogenous. Growing from the inside; said of the growth of stems in thickness.

Endosperm. The tissue with stored food, or "albumen" of a seed.

Entire. Without marginal serrations or teeth.

Entomophilous. Insect-loving, referring to insect pollination; insect-pollinated.

Epicotyl. That portion of an embryo above the cotyledonary node; the plumule.

Epigynous. Borne upon or on top of the ovary or gynœcium.

Epipetalous. Borne upon the petals or the corolla tube, referring to stamens.

Exocarp. The outer layer of a fruit.

Exserted. Projecting beyond the summit of, as stamens beyond the petals.

Extrorse. Facing outward from the center of the flower, as anthers.

Fertilization. The fusion of gametes, especially heterogametes.

Filament. The stalk supporting the anther of a stamen (see **anther**).

Filiform. Like a filament or thread.

Fimbriate. Fringed along the edge.

Floccose. With tufts of soft silky hair.

Floret. A small flower, as in the spikelets of grasses or the heads of composites.

Foliaceous. Having the character of a leaf.

Follicle. A dry fruit formed from a single carpel and usually dehiscing along the ventral suture, usually several-seeded.

Free. Distinct, not united, as of floral organs.

Fruit. The seed-bearing organ of a plant.

Fruticose. Shrubby; shrub-like.

Fugacious. Falling off early, early deciduous; ephemeral; evanescent.

Funiculus. The stalk of an ovule, by which it is attached to the placenta.

Fusiform. Spindle-shaped.

Galea. A hooded or helmet-shaped sepal or petal, as in *Aconitum*.

Galeate. Shaped like a hood or helmet; furnished with a galea.

Gamopetalous. Having united petals; referring to a sympetalous corolla.

Gamosepalous. Having united sepals, synsepalous.

Geitonogamy. Pollination between flowers of the same individual.

Gibbous. Swollen at the base.

Glabrous. Not hairy.

Glabrate. Somewhat glabrous, or becoming glabrous.

Glandular. Supplied with glands.

Glaucous. Covered with a whitish or bluish "waxy bloom" that rubs off.

Glumaceous. Bearing glumes; of the character of glumes.

Glumes. Rigid, chaff-like or scale-like bracts, referring especially to the two empty bracts at the base of the spikelet in grasses.

Glutinous. Sticky or mucilaginous.

Grain.   The fruit or caryopis of grasses.

Gynœcium.   A carpel or an aggregation of carpels, free or united.

Hastate.   Halberd-shaped or spear-shaped with auricles turned outward.

Head.   The inflorescence or capitulum of composites; a compact inflorescence.

Hermaphrodite.   Bisexual; having the andrœcium and the gynœcium in the same flower.

Hesperidium.   The fruit of the orange and other citrus plants.

Hilum.   The scar on a seed, marking the point where the seed broke from the stalk.

Hirsute.   With stiff hairs.

Hispid.   With bristly hairs.

Hypanthium.   The tube of the receptacle upon which the calyx, corolla, and stamens are borne; "calyx tube"; perianth tube.

Hypocotyl.   The part of an embryo below the cotyledons and including the cotyledonary node; the stem of the embryo.

Hypogynous.   Borne beneath or below the gynœcium or ovary, referring to stamens, petals, sepals, and disk.

Imbricate.   Overlapping like tiles of a roof, referring to sepals and petals in the bud.

Imperfect flower.   A flower lacking stamens or pistils; a unisexual flower.

Incised.   Margin with deeply cut, irregular or jagged teeth.

Incomplete flower.   A flower lacking one or more of the four regular sets of parts.

Indefinite.   Inconstant in number; applied also to the continuous growth in length of a racemose inflorescence.

Indehiscent.   Not splitting open; remaining closed, as a drupe or an achene.

Indeterminate.   Of indefinite growth, as a racemose inflorescence.

Indigenous.   Native to a region.

Inferior.   Below, usually referring to the position of the ovary in an epigynous flower.

Inflexed.   Said of a leaf in which the upper part of the blade is bent over the lower part; same as reclinate.

Inflorescence.   A flower cluster, such as a panicle, spike, or raceme.

Integument.   The jacket of an ovule.

Internode.   Part of a stem lying between two successive nodes.

Interrupted.   Broken or irregular in arrangement, said of inflorescences or leaves.

Introrse.   Facing inward or facing the stigma, referring to anthers.

Involucel.   A small involucre, as the bracts subtending the secondary umbels in the *Umbelliferae*.

Involucral.   Belonging to the involucre.

Involucrate.   Bearing an involucre.

Involucre.   Cluster of bracts subtending an inflorescence, as in the heads of composites or in the umbels of umbellifers.

Involute.   Said of a leaf in which the two sides are rolled lengthwise over the upper surface toward the midrib.

Irregular.   Differing in size and shape; unsymmetrical, referring to flowers.

Keel.   A prominent dorsal rib or ridge, as in some carpels or in glumes of grasses; the lower petals of the flowers of a legume.

Labiate. Lipped, as the corolla of mints.

Lanceolate. Lance-shaped, broadest below the middle and tapering gradually to the apex.

Lamina. The expanded part of a leaf; same as the blade.

Leaf scar. A scar left on a twig at the point from which a leaf falls.

Leaflet. A segment of a compound leaf.

Legume. The pod of members of the pea family, a pod dehiscent along both sutures.

Leguminous. Having the character of a legume or of a leguminous plant.

Lemma. The outer (lower) bract of the floret of grasses.

Lenticel. A porous spot in the periderm of woody plants, usually rich in cork.

Ligulate. Strap-shaped or tongue-shaped, like the corolla of a flower of the dandelion or the ray flowers of a sunflower.

Ligule. The strap-shaped part of the corolla of composites; the annular collar-like process at the junction of the leaf blade and sheath in grasses.

Linear. Long and narrow, with sides nearly parallel.

Lobed. Margin cut rather deeply into curved or angular segments.

Lodicule. A rudimentary organ at the base of the ovary in grasses.

Loment. A leguminous fruit (pod) that is constricted between the seeds.

Mericarp. One of the halves of the fruit of an umbellifer.

Mesocarp. The middle coat or layer of a fruit.

Monadelphous. Having the stamens united by their filaments into one body.

Monocarpous. Having one carpel.

Monoclinous. Having the androecium (stamens) and the gynoecium (pistils) in the same flower. *See bisexual*

Monoecious. Having the androecium (stamens) and the gynoecium (pistils) in separate flowers but on the same plant.

Monogynous. Having one carpel or gynoecium.

Natural classification (key). Classification or key that utilizes natural relationships.

Naturalized. Running wild from cultivation and becoming established.

Nectary. A nectar-secreting gland; often associated with petals.

Node. A joint, as in a stem, the point where buds and leaves occur.

Nomenclature. The naming of plants.

Nut. A dry, hard-shelled, usually one-seeded, indehiscent fruit; diminutive form, often used, is nutlet.

Oblanceolate. Inversely lanceolate.

Oblique. With the two sides of the blade unequal, especially at the base, as in a leaf.

Oblong. Longer than broad, with nearly parallel sides.

Obovate. Inversely ovate.

Obtuse. Tapering abruptly to a point.

Officinal. Sold in apothecaries; medicinal.

Oligomerous. Having fewer than the usual number of parts.

Orbicular. More or less nearly circular.

Orthotropous. Straight, erect, as an ovule.

Ovary. Part of a carpel or gynoecium containing the ovules.

Ovate. Egg-shaped, much broader below the middle.

Ovule. The macrosporangium (megasporangium); forerunner of the seed.

Ovuliferous. Bearing ovules.

Palea. The upper or inner of the two bracts of the floret in grasses, often partly inclosed by the lemma.

Palet. Older term for palea.

Palmate. Palm-like; applied to the venation of a simple leaf when the principal veins radiate from a common point at the base of the blade; same as digitate; also applied to a compound leaf in which the leaflets are arranged in this manner.

Panicle. A compound racemose inflorescence, as in the oat.

Paniculate. Of the character of a panicle; bearing panicles.

Papilionaceous. Butterfly-shaped, referring to the corolla of some leguminous flowers.

Pappus. The modified bristly or scale-like calyx of composites.

Parietal. Borne on the sides or wall of a locule, as ovules in the ovary.

Parted. Margin cut nearly to the midrib, as in a leaf.

Pedicel. The flower stalk.

Peduncle. The stalk of an inflorescence.

Peltate. Shield-shaped.

Pentamerous. Having five members in a whorl, or 5-merous.

Pepo. The fruit of a gourd or pumpkin; a sort of berry with a hard rind.

Perennial. Living through more than two years.

Perfect. Having both androecium (stamens) and gynoecium (pistils) in the same flower; bisexual.

Perfoliate. Having the stem apparently passing through the leaf.

Perianth. The floral envelop; sepals and petals.

Pericarp. The wall of the ovary, referring especially to a fruit.

Perigynium. The inflated sac (bract) enclosing the gynoecium or carpellate flower in *Carex*.

Perigynous. Standing around the gynoecium, borne on the margin of the floral axis.

Perisperm. The remnant of the nucellus; often stored with accessory food (compare with endosperm).

Petal. One of the colored inner perianth (corolla) segments.

Petiole. A leaf stalk (compare with blade).

Phyllotaxy. Leaf arrangement on a stem.

Phylogeny. The racial or genetical relationship or development of organisms.

Pilose. With soft slender hairs.

Pinnate. Feather-like; applied to the venation of a simple leaf or leaflet of a compound leaf when the principal veins extend from the midrib toward the margin and are more or less parallel; also to a compound leaf when the leaflets are so arranged.

Pinnatifid. Cleft or parted in a pinnate manner.

Pistil. The ovuliferous or seed-bearing organ of a flower; carpel; gynoecium; consisting of ovary, style, and stigma.

Pistillate. Bearing the pistil or pistils only; carpellate.

Placenta. The tissue within an ovary to which the ovules are attached.

Placentation. The arrangement or orientation of the placentae.

Plicate. Said of a leaf in which the blade is folded back and forth along the main veins like the pleats in an accordion.

Pollination. The transfer of pollen from the anthers to the stigma.

Pollinium. The mass of cohering pollen grains of orchids and milkweeds.

Polygamous. Bearing unisexual and bisexual flowers on the same plant.

Polypetalous. Having separate petals.

Polysepalous. Having separate sepals.

Pome. A fruit, like an apple or pear, in which most of the edible part is the enlarged axis of the flower, rather than the ovary.

Protandrous flower. A flower in which the stamens mature before the pistil.

Protogynous flower. A flower in which the pistils mature before the stamens.

Pruinose. Dusted with coarse granular material.

Puberulent. With very fine down-like hairs.

Pulverulent. Dusted with fine powder or dust.

Punctate. Dotted, often with resinous glands.

Receptacle. The part of the floral axis (pedicel or peduncle) that bears the floral organs; the hypanthium of perigynous and epigynous flowers; also used for the common axis of the flowers in the inflorescence of the composites.

Regular flower. Having radial symmetry; actinomorphic.

Reniform. Kidney-shaped.

Repand. With a slightly wavy margin.

Retuse. Rounded or slightly notched.

Revolute. Said of a leaf in which the two sides of the blade are rolled lengthwise over the lower surface toward the midrib.

Rhizome. An elongated subterranean stem or branch; usually horizontal.

Rootstock. Same as a rhizome.

Rosette. A cluster of closely crowded radiating leaves arising from a very short stem near the surface of the ground.

Rostellum. A little beak; a projection from the upper edge of the stigma in orchids.

Rotate. Wheel-shaped, referring to a sympetalous corolla as in *Solanum*.

Sagittate. Arrow-shaped, with the basal lobes directed downward.

Samara. An indehiscent, dry, one- or two-seeded, winged fruit as in maples.

Scabrous. Rough; rough-pubescent.

Scape. A stout or slender peduncle rising from the ground and bearing one or more flowers at the summit.

Scapose. Of the character of a scape.

Scarious. Dry, thin, scale-like; membranaceous.

Seculate. Sickle-shaped, more or less like a curved lanceolate form.

Sepal. A segment of the calyx.

Septum. A partition, referring especially to the partitions in a compound ovary.

Sericeous. With silky hairs.

Serrate. With sharp marginal teeth that point forward.

Sessile. Without a stalk, as a leaf without a petiole.

Sheath. The tubular, basal portion of a leaf of a grass or sedge, which encircles the culm.

Sheathing.   Said of a leaf in which the expanded base of the petiole more or less completely invests the stem.

Silicle, silique.   The fruit (pod) of crucifers.

Simple.   Not branched, referring to stems; not compound, referring to gynœcia; or not compound, referring to leaves.

Sinuate.   With more abruptly wavy margin than repand.

Sinus.   The cleft or indentation between the lobes of a leaf blade.

Spadix.   A succulent axis supporting an inflorescence, as in the aroids.

Spathe.   The leaf-like colored bract investing the inflorescence (spadix) of aroids and palms.

Spatulate.   Spoon-shaped, broad and rounded above the middle and tapering gradually to a narrow base.

Spicate.   Having the form of a spike.

Spike.   An elongated inflorescence bearing sessile flowers.

Spikelet.   A small spike; the unit of inflorescence of grasses and sedges.

Spiral.   Arranged in a winding series, as leaves or floral organs.

Squarrose.   With minute scales.

Stamen.   The pollen-bearing organ of a flower, consisting of filament and anther.

Staminate.   Bearing stamens; consisting of stamens, as a flower.

Standard.   The broad upper petal of many leguminous flowers.

Sterile.   Not productive.   Not capable of producing seed, as a neutral flower.

Stigma.   That part of the style which is modified for the reception and germination of the pollen.

Stigmatic.   Belonging to or of the nature of the stigma.

Stipe.   A stalk, as of a gynœcium or a flower.

Stipule.   A leaf-like appendage of the base of the petiole of leaves; often in pairs.

Stolon.   A slender modified stem growing along the surface of the ground and rooting at the nodes.

Stoloniferous.   Bearing stolons.

Strigose.   With rigid hairs or bristles.

Style.   The contracted upper part of a carpel or gynœcium that supports the stigma; often considerably elongated, sometimes lacking.

Superior.   Wholly free from the receptacle, referring to the ovary.

Suture.   The line of dehiscence of dry fruits.   The line of junction or of cleavage of two united organs.

Syconium.   The fleshy fruit of the fig.

Symmetrical.   Regular in shape, size, and number of parts; actinomorphic.

Sympetalous.   Having united petals, or a one-piece corolla; gamopetalous.

Synandrous.   Having the anthers united.

Syncarpous.   Having united carpels.

Synergids.   The two nuclei, which with the egg constitute the "egg apparatus" of a flower.

Synsepalous.   Having united sepals; gamosepalous.

Taproot.   A permanent, more or less thickened, often fleshy. primary root.

Tassel.   The staminate inflorescence of maize.

Taxonomy. Systematic botany, involving the naming and classification of plants.

Tendril. A slender, leafless, spirally coiling, and sensitive organ of climbing plants.

Testa. The outer, usually hard, coat of a seed.

Torus. The receptacle of a flower.

Trifoliate. Three-leaved, sometimes confused with following.

Trifoliolate. Having three leaflets, as in a compound leaf.

Trimorphic. Existing in three forms.

Truncate. Seemingly cut off square or nearly so.

Tuber. A much thickened, usually short, subterranean stem, as in the Irish potato.

Tuberous. Of the nature of a tuber.

Twiner. A plant that climbs by means of spirally coiling stems.

Umbel. An umbrella-shaped inflorescence, in which the pedicels radiate from a common point at the summit of the peduncle.

Umbellate. Of the form of an umbel.

Umbellet. A secondary umbel; one of a set of smaller umbels of a compound umble.

Umbelliferous. Bearing umbels.

Unilocular. Composed of one locule, as in an ovary.

Valvate. Dehiscing by valves or equal sections. In aestivation, when the segments of the perianth are so placed that their edges touch; not overlapping.

Valve. A section of a dry, dehiscent fruit (capsule) separated in dehiscence.

Venation. Nervation. The arrangement of the nerves or veins of a leaf.

Vernation. The arrangement or mode of folding of leaves in the bud.

Verrucose. With minute warts or blunt projections.

Versatile. Attached by the middle so as to swing freely, as an anther on the filament.

Verticillate. A whorled cluster of leaves or flowers.

Villous. With long shaggy hairs.

Whorl. A circle or ring of organs inserted around an axis, as the organs of a flower or leaves on a stem; a cycle. Whorled.

Wing. An outgrowth from the side of an organ; the lateral petals in the flowers of many legumes.

Winter annual. A plant that grows from seed in the late summer or autumn, lives through the winter, matures and dies the following summer, as winter wheat.

Xenogamy. Pollination between flowers of totally separate individual plants.

Zygomorphic. Said of a flower having bilateral symmetry, such as that of a mint or snapdragon.

INDEX

Pages on which illustrations occur are indicated by **bold-faced** type; names of orders, families, genera, and species are in *italics*, as are references to certain historic publications.

A

Abutilon, 32
Abyssinian banana, 314
Acacia, 235
  senegal, 235
Acanthaceae, 228
Acanthus, 228, 229
  mollis, 229
Acanthus family, 229
Accessory fruits, **49**, 51, 52, 54
  organs, 4
Acer, **46**, **64**, 117, 142, 161, **261**, 262
  negundo, **4**, 161, 262
  platanoides, 262
  pseudoplatanus, 262
  saccharinum, **261**, 262
  saccharum, 161, **261**, 262
Aceraceae, **261**, 262
Achene, **43**, 45, 51, 54
Achillea millefolium, 283
  ptarmica, 283
Acnida, 207
Acokanthera schimperi, 220
Aconite, floral diagram of, **89**, 90
Aconitum, **16**, **44**, **89**, 90, 169, **174**, 175
Acorn, 43, 46, **265**
Acorus, inflorescence of, 107
Actinomorphic flowers, 15, 83, 153, 159
Actinomorphy, 15, 83, 153, 159
Adhesives, 367
Adonis, 43
  achenes of, **43**
Adventitious buds, 115, 120
Adventitious roots, 117
Aerial roots, 115, **118**, 121

Aerial stems, 121
Aesculus, inflorescence of, 111, 260
Aesculus glabra, 260
  hippocastanum, 260
Aethusa, **269**
African marigold, 281
Agave, 311
Agave americana, 311
  sisalana, 311
Ageratum, 282
  houstonianum, 282
Age, of roots, 117, 118
  of stems, 120, 121
Ages, dark, 319
  middle, 319
Aggregate fruits, **49**, 51, 52, 54
Agrimonia, inflorescence of, 105
Agrimony, inflorescence of, 105
Agropyron, **68**
  rhizome of, **68**
Agrostemma githago, **204**
Agrostideae, 303, 306, **307**
Agrostis alba, flowers of, **307**
  inflorescence of, **307**
  spikelet of, **307**
Aids, in drying specimens, 366
  to migration, 63, 72
Ailanthus, 7, **46**, **64**
Ajuga, **16**
Albuminous seeds, 60
Alchemilla, 27
Alder, 30, 266
Alfalfa, 222, 237
Algaroba, 235
Alisma, 16, **43**, **287**
  floral diagram of, **89**, 287
  floral formula of, **101**, 287
  plantago aquatica, **287**

P